HAWAI'I
THE BIG ISLAND

Making the Most of Your Family Vacation

by John Penisten

Prima Publishing in affiliation with
Paradise Publications

HAWAI'I: THE BIG ISLAND, Making the Most of Your Family Vacation
Copyright © 1996 Paradise Publications, Portland, Oregon

First Edition: May 1989   Fourth Edition: Nov 1994
Second Edition: March 1991   Fifth Edition: Nov 1996
Third Edition: Oct 1992

Illustrations: Janora Bayot
Layout & Typesetting: Paradise Publications

Prima Publishing and colophon are registered trademarks of Prima Communications, Inc.

Library of Congress Cataloging-in-Publication Data

Penisten, John
        Hawai'i, the Big Island: making the most of your family vacation / by John Penisten - 5th ed.

        p.   cm. (Paradise family guides)
        Includes bibliographical references and index.
        ISBN 0-7615-0656-X
        1. Hawaii Island (Hawai'i)--Guidebooks. 2. Family recreation-Hawaii-Hawaii Island. I. Title. II. Series
    DU628.H28P46   1996
    919.69'1044--dc20   96-24673
                                                                             CIP
96 97 98 99 00 01 02 HH 10 9 8 7 6 5 4 3 2 1
Printed in the United States of America

WARNING-DISCLAIMER
Prima Publishing in affiliation with Paradise Publications has designed this book to provide information in regard to the subject matter covered. It is sold with the understanding that the publishers and authors are not liable for the misconception or misuse of information provided. Every effort has been made to make this book as complete and as accurate as possible. The purpose of this book is to educate. The author, Prima Publishing, and Paradise Publications shall have neither liability nor responsibility to any person or entity with respect to any loss, damage, or injury caused or alleged to be caused directly or indirectly by the information contained in this book. They shall also not be liable for price changes, or for the completeness or accuracy of the contents of this book.

HOW TO ORDER
Quantity discounts are available from the publisher, Prima Publishing, P.O. Box 1260BK, Rocklin, CA 95677; telephone (916) 632-4400. On your letterhead, include information concerning the intended use of the books and the number of books you wish to purchase.

Visit us online at http://www.primapublishing.com

DEDICATION

"Hawai'i Kuauli"
(Hawai'i is a verdant countryside)

This edition is dedicated to my wife, Susan

ME KE ALOHA PUMEHANA

(With warm Aloha)

This fifth edition was produced with the help of many wonderful folks, residents and visitors alike, in Hawai'i and elsewhere.

A special "Mahalo!" to the many readers who have shared their unique insight on Big Island travel discoveries, experiences and perspectives (good and bad!) and added to the accuracy and content of this book. I'd especially like to thank Bob and Doreen Sonday, Patricia Townsend, Sue and Dennis Legan, Dick Huggins, Rob and Becky Coykendall, Aldolfo Lopez and Larry Mowinckel.

I'd also like to thank the following folks for the many ways in which they assisted with this project: Charlene Goo, Bernie Caalim-Polanzi, Katherine Leahy, Deborah Taylor, Elizabeth DeMotte, Donald Dickhens, Aubrey Hawk and Valerie Sakanoi. These fine folks provided me with information, assistance and their own unique insight into experiencing the Big Island.

And, as always, a special thanks once again to my wife, Susan, and my two daughters, Janelle and Joelle, for sharing their ideas, suggestions and the many adventures of traveling around and continuously rediscovering our island home, the Big Island of Hawai'i. We are fortunate to live in such a beautiful place.

HAWAIIAN CHANT

NA KUAHIWI

"THE MOUNTAINS"

Aia i ka 'iu o ka moku la,
Ho'oku'i ka honua laua 'o ka lewa
'Ohu'ohu'ia e ka 'ohu po'ai la
I luna lilo loa me Poliahu laua 'o Lihau
'O na hoa pilikua na mauna la
Molale 'O Mauna Kea laua 'o Mauna Loa
Na kupuna kia'i i ka wa pau'ole la
He 'ike ia o ka wa mua laua 'o ka hope
Ha'upu iho ka pilimau me na kuahiwi la
I na wekiu hano o Mauna Kea laua 'o Mauna Loa
He kau aloha ia no ka 'iu o ka moku la.

There on the heights of the island
The earth and the sky are connected
Adorned by the encircling mist
With Poliahu and Lihau at the top
The mountainous giant companions
Clearly visible are Mauna Kea and Mauna Loa
The ancestral guardians through the ages

A vision of the past, of the future
A strong relationship with the mountains stir within me
The glorious heights, Mauna Kea and Mauna Loa
A song of fond regards for the crest of the island.

An original Hawaiian chant composed by
Pualani Kanahele of Hawai'i Community College,
Hilo, Hawai'i
Reprinted with permission, 1994.

TABLE OF CONTENTS

III. WHERE TO STAY - WHAT TO SEE

IV. RESTAURANTS

V. ACTIVITIES AND TOURS

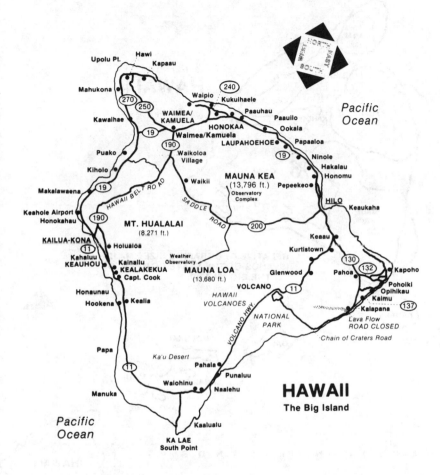

HAWAII
The Big Island

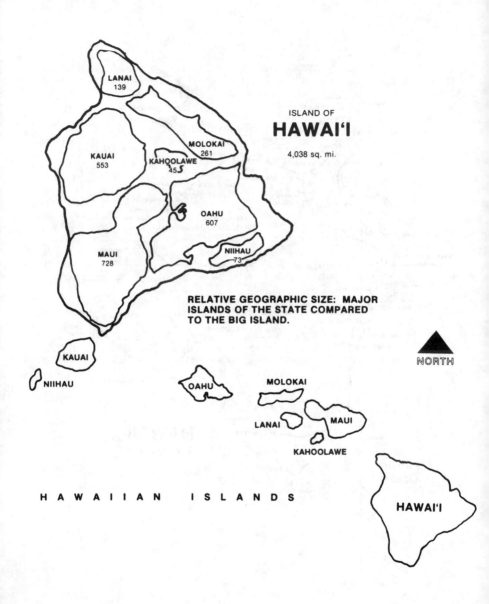

ISLAND OF
HAWAI'I
4,038 sq. mi.

LANAI
139

MOLOKAI
261

KAUAI
553

KAHOOLAWE
45

OAHU
607

MAUI
728

NIIHAU
73

RELATIVE GEOGRAPHIC SIZE: MAJOR ISLANDS OF THE STATE COMPARED TO THE BIG ISLAND.

NORTH

KAUAI

NIIHAU

OAHU

MOLOKAI

LANAI

MAUI

KAHOOLAWE

HAWAI'I

H A W A I I A N   I S L A N D S

PREFACE

Upon publication of this fifth edition of **Hawai'i - The Big Island**, Hawai'i's visitor industry is working hard to recover from a general slowdown in travel to the islands during the past three years or so. The Big Island, like the rest of Hawai'i, has had some difficult times as it adjusts to a new era and changing economy. Part of that change the last couple of years, has been the closing down of the Big Island's once dominant sugar cane industry which has impacted the wider island community in a variety of ways. The loss of the sugar industry has made the visitor industry much more important to the island's economy.

But if recent events are any indication of the future, then perhaps the future is bright indeed. The airlines have been adding new flights and seat capacity direct to Kona to serve growing demand. The visitor industry has been more aggressive in its marketing and promotion of the Big Island and more visitors seem to be finding out about what makes visiting the Big Island so special. This is great time to visit the Big Island of Hawai'i. Because of the recent economic slowdown throughout Hawai'i, there are good bargains to be had in local airfares and ground transportation such as rental cars, hotel/condo and B&B accommodations, restaurants, tours and more. The visitor industry is eagerly promoting special rates and special incentives to get more folks to discover the Big Island's unique charms and attractions.

Over a million visitors arrived on the Big Island in 1995, part of the over six million visitors statewide. Big Island visitors continue to be drawn by the island's friendly multi-cultural population, variety of lodging facilities, its diverse scenic and cultural sites and attractions, numerous sporting events and recreational activities like deep-sea fishing, diving, sailing, related water sports, championship golf and tennis, hiking, volcano watching and much more.

Visitors continue to enjoy discovering and exploring at leisure the special grandeur of Hawai'i Volcanoes National Park, the verdant tropical rain forests of the Puna, Hilo and Hamakua Coast areas, the stark deserts and lava flows of Ka'u and Kohala, and the pastoral beauty of upcountry Waimea and its rolling ranch lands and wide-open spaces.

As a Big Island resident and photojournalist for some twenty years, it has been my pleasure to have written and photographed island subjects for various publications. I can't claim to know everything about the Big Island--it's far too big for one person to know it all--but hopefully this book provides the latest up-to-date information on accommodations, what to see and do, dining and other activities and general information about traveling around and exploring the Island of Hawai'i.

This edition's revised section on accommodations includes an expanded listing of Bed & Breakfast operations around the island. B&B's continue to be one of the island's fastest growing segments of the visitor industry as more visitors seek a non-resort/hotel travel experience that is eco-tourism/cultural-tourism related, closer to nature and to local people who can provide a personal perspective on the Big Island.

That's not to say visitors avoid the Big Island's wonderfully diverse resorts, hotels and vacation condos. It's just the opposite. The island's majority of visitors are attracted by the wide range of budget to first-class hotels and condos around the island including the plush world-class resorts and luxury condos of the Big Island's fabulous Kona and Kohala Coasts.

Whatever it is you're looking for in an island-style vacation, you're sure to find the Big Island big enough to suit your needs. From lodging to dining, to adventure tours and activities, to scenic beauty, historic attractions and cultural events, to shopping or just relaxing in a soothing tropical ambiance, the Island of Hawai'i has it all. The Big Island continues to live up to its reputation of delivering a quality vacation experience.

A sincere effort has been made to ensure the accuracy of this guidebook at the time of publication. However, changes do occur frequently and with little notice, in the transitory travel-visitor industry. Hotels, resorts, B&B's, condominiums, restaurants-menus, car rental agencies, airlines, tour operators, attractions, shops, etc. can and do change frequently along with hours of operation, schedules, prices and services. For the latest update information on the island, Paradise Publications has available **HAWAI'I - THE BIG ISLAND UPDATE,** a quarterly newsletter which chronicles current changes in the Big Island travel industry scene. To order a complimentary issue or a yearly subscription see ORDERING INFORMATION.

Finally, I sincerely hope that this book contributes in some small way to the enjoyment of your Big Island vacation. I also hope that your visit to the Island of Hawai'i is pleasant, safe and totally relaxing. And when it is time to go home, you'll leave refreshed and renewed and your heart filled with Aloha memories of the wonders and wonderful people of the Big Island of Hawai'i.

Aloha!

John Penisten

GENERAL INFORMATION

INTRODUCTION

WHY IT'S CALLED THE BIG ISLAND

There have been various explanations of the name "Hawaii," which is the name of largest island and the group of islands known as Hawaii. Tradition has it that the islands were named by Hawaii Loa, the first discoverer of the islands, after himself. Hawaii, or Hawaiki, the ancestral home of the early Polynesians is also given as the origin. The compound word has different meanings. *Hawa-* is the name of the traditional place of residence, and *-ii*, or *-iki*, means little or small. Together, it's translated to mean smaller or new homeland. But *-ii* can also mean raging or furious, a reference to the volcanic activity of the island. The word is also correctly written with the glottal-stop mark (okina): *Hawai'i*.

For a long time it's been known variously as "The Volcano Island," or "The Orchid Island," and perhaps more commonly as "The Big Island."

To some, it's been something of a long-standing identity problem, at least to those in business and industry and especially the visitor industry. To most others, and to those who live here, it doesn't really seem to matter. To those who perceive it as a problem, the name "Hawai'i," the name of this island, too often is confused with the name of the state, also known as "Hawai'i" or the "Hawaiian Islands."

In an attempt to avoid confusion between the island and the state of the same name, many have coined labels over the years to clarify, once and for all, its name, its singular identity, and to set it apart from the other islands. Whether it's "The Volcano Island," "The Orchid Island," "The Island of Hawai'i," "Hawai'i Island," "Hawai'i-The Island," "Hawai'i, Hawai'i" (a former mayor's favorite, like New York, New York!), "The Big Island of Hawai'i," "Hawai'i-The Big Island," by any name, it is purely and simply, "The Big Island."

A few years ago, the Hawai'i Visitors Bureau-Big Island Chapter went through the same struggle to come up with a slogan to promote its visitor industry. After considering all the possibilities, "The Big Island of Hawai'i: Celebrate Great Moments With Us" was adopted. And thus it is, for all practical purposes, "The Big Island of Hawai'i." For the record, the telephone company's local directory yellow pages lists some 130 businesses and organizations under the name "Big Island" and some 160 under the name "Hawai'i" or "Hawai'i Island."

So how did it come to be the Big Island. Well, one story has it that a group of World War II soldiers who were stationed on the Big Island were on leave in Honolulu. They were asked where they were stationed and one of them replied, "Well, we're on the island of....uh, island of....oh, you know, that "Big Island" over there!" From then on it came to be the "Big Island."

In fact, it is an accurate description of the island, it is a pretty big place, in more ways than one. There's no disputing the fact that the Big Island is biggest in land size of all the Hawaiian Islands. At 4,038 square miles, the Big Island is twice the size of all the other Hawaiian Islands combined. And it's still growing due to the recent eruptions and lava flows of Kilauea Volcano which have added many acres of new shoreline.

The Big Island also has the highest mountain in Hawai'i, 13,796 ft. *Mauna Kea* (White Mountain in Hawaiian), a dormant volcano which last erupted some 10,000 years ago. Mauna Kea along with its twin peak, 13,677 ft. *Mauna Loa* (Long Mountain), an active volcano which erupted as recently as 1984, comprise the bulk of the Big Island. Mauna Kea is, in fact, often called the biggest mountain in the world, Mt. Everest included, when it is measured from its base some 32,000 ft. below the ocean's surface.

And then there is the *Mauna Kea Observatory Complex*, located at the very summit of Mauna Kea, which is the recognized premier site for optical-infrared-submillimeter astronomy in the entire world. The observatory boasts several "largest" categories: collectively, the telescopes of Mauna Kea have more light gathering power than any other location in the world; in addition, it lays claim to the largest infrared telescope in the world, the 150 inch (3.8 m) United Kingdom Infrared Telescope; the largest optical-infrared telescope in the world, the 144 inch (3.6 m) Canada-France-Hawai'i Telescope; and the two largest submillimeter telescopes in the world, the 410 inch (10.4 m) Caltech Submillimeter Observatory and the 590 inch (15 m) James Clerk Maxwell Telescope; and the twin 10-meter W.M. Keck Telescopes multi-mirror instruments are the largest such operational telescopes in the world, period. The 100' high antenna dish of the Very Long Baseline Array is the western-most site of a 5,000-mile wide radio telescope reaching from the Virgin Islands across the U.S. mainland to Mauna Kea. The value of Mauna Kea's numerous high tech astronomical telescopes is as astronomical as the nature of the work they perform. And plans are already underway for more telescopes to be built by the year 2000, ensuring Mauna Kea's place as the premier site in the world for astronomical research. For many folks from colder climes, the following claim may not be too meaningful, but the Big Island has had the biggest recorded snowfalls of any tropical mountain in the Pacific Basin area. Over 12 feet of snow is not uncommon during severe winter storms at Mauna Kea's nearly 14,000 ft. summit. Snow skiing is a unique seasonal activity available only on the Big Island.

Hawai'i's biggest park is none other than *Hawai'i Volcanoes National Park*, 229,177 acres. It features the biggest active volcano in the world, 13, 677 ft. Mauna Loa, and an even more active sister peak, Kilauea at 4,077 ft. Two of Kilauea's many vents, Pu'u O and Kupaianaha, have been in an ongoing eruptive stage since January 3, 1983, one of the longest continuous eruptions ever recorded. Hawai'i Volcanoes National Park also has the biggest lava tube in Hawai'i, Thurston Lava Tube, 1494 ft. long, 22 ft. wide, and 20 ft. high. Waipio Valley near the town of Honoka'a on the Hamakua Coast is the state's biggest. The verdant valley runs a huge gap in the coast six miles long and 2000 ft. deep. This lush and fertile valley still produces taro as it did in the days of old Hawai'i. The Big Island boasts numerous waterfalls along the Hamakua Coast including Hiliawe

Falls in Waipio Valley at about 1000 ft. and the magnificent 422 ft. cascade of Akaka Falls State Park just north of Hilo.

In Kohala is the biggest, oldest, and best preserved Hawaiian heiau (a temple where the ancient religion of old Hawai'i was practiced). The temple of Mookini Luakini is near the birthplace of King Kamehameha the Great. Built entirely of waterworn basalt rocks, it is in the shape of an irregular parallelogram, 267 ft. x 135 ft. x 250 ft. x 112 ft. with 30 ft. high walls all around. The walls vary in width from 13 ft. to 15 ft. It is estimated to be 1500 years old.

The port town of Hilo features the biggest annual hula dance celebration, the Merry Monarch Festival, which is held each spring. This competition draws hula halau (groups) from all over Hawai'i and even the mainland U.S. It is the recognized "Super Bowl" of hula dance competition. It regularly sells out its three night performances well in advance. Meanwhile over in Kona, one can find two of the biggest sporting events in the world. One is the annual Hawaiian International Billfish Tournament held each August and which attracts fishing teams and media from around the world who take part in the chase for record Kona marlin and yellow-fin tuna. In October, Kona takes on a different sporting mood as it plays host to the annual Ironman Triathlon World Championship. This incredible triple endurance event attracts over a thousand triathletes who take part in a 2.4 mile open ocean swim, a 112 mile bike ride, and a 26.2 mile marathon run. The Hawai'i Ironman Triathlon gave birth to the now worldwide sport of triathlon competitions.

The Parker Ranch at Kamuela is the state's largest ranch and one of the largest in the U.S. It has over 50,000 head of Hereford cattle roaming over 220,000 acres of rolling green pasture land.

The Big Island has the world's largest anthurium and orchid flower industries. According to the latest data available, 1993, the island's 66 commercial anthurium farms produced some 882 thousand dozens of the popular blooms valued at $7.5 million. Also in 1993, many growers produced millions of orchids of various types, single flowers, sprays, and potted plants, valued at over $10 million. Combined, the Big Island's floriculture and nursery industry, which also produces bird of paradise, ginger, carnations, heliconia, protea, roses and others, had some $33.7 million in total sales according to 1993 figures, by far more than any other island in the state.

Data for 1993 reveals that Hawai'i's macadamia nut industry had 650 farms with some 20,100 acres of orchards under cultivation which produced 53 million pounds of the popular gourmet nuts worth almost $32.9 million. The bulk of this industry and production is on the Island of Hawai'i even though orchards are being planted on other islands as well. The world's largest processor of macadamia nut products, the Mauna Loa Macadamia Nut Corporation, is located just outside of Hilo. The company's modern factory and visitors center make it the industry leader not only in Hawai'i but the world.

In 1993, there were 211 Big Island papaya farms with 2,425 acres in production, which produced 6 million pounds of papaya with a value of $12.8 million, almost all of the state's entire production of the delectable fruit.

15

In 1993, the Big Island had 110 guava farmers cultivating 415 acres of the tropical guava fruit, producing 7.1 million pounds valued at $1 million, most of it used for juice and juice flavoring products.

In 1993, Hawai'i's gourmet coffee industry, located almost exclusively on the cool-sunny slopes of Mt. Hualalai in Kona (although coffee is now being produced on other islands, notably Kaua'i and Maui), had 574 farms on 1,865 acres which produced 1.5 million pounds of Kona coffee beans valued at over $5.8 million. Hawai'i is the only place in the U. S. where coffee is grown commercially. The Big Island is the only place where genuine *Kona Coffee* is produced.

In 1993, the Big Island had just 21 banana farms cultivating 440 acres which produced 9.1 million pounds valued at $3.1 million, the bulk of the state's total production.

But beyond all of this, the Big Island of Hawai'i is big on friendliness, scenic beauty, diversity and activities and the casual air of a basically rural lifestyle which is unhurried, unharried, and definitely underrated. Oh yes, I think you're going to like it here. Welcome to the Big Island of Hawai'i!

THE BIG ISLAND'S BEST BETS

Here's a personal list of recommended best things to do, see and experience among all the wonderful things available on the Big Island of Hawa'i.

Annual Event: The Merry Monarch Festival, Hilo, each April

Beautiful Beach: Kaunaoa Bay Beach (Mauna Kea Beach)

Beautiful Sunrise: From Mauna Kea overlooking Hilo

Beautiful Sunset: From Mauna Kea overlooking Kona-Kohala

Botanical Garden: Hawai'i Tropical Botanical Garden north of Hilo on old Hamakua Highway scenic route

Most Scenic Drive: Seventeen mile Kohala Mountain Road, Highway 250, from Waimea to Hawi, North Kohala, the Big Island's north end

Second Most Scenic Drive: Four-mile stretch of Old Hamakua Highway just north of Hilo from Papa'ikou to Pepe'ekeo

Scenic View: Waipio Valley Overlook

Easy Hike: Across the floor of steaming Kilauea Iki Crater, Hawai'i Volcanoes National Park

Nature Hike: Akaka Falls State Park, Hamakua Coast

Unusual Tour: Weekly star-gazing astronomy program at the Onizuka Center for International Astronomy at 9,200 ft. level of Mauna Kea

Cultural Tour: Visit to Polynesian Village for hands-on arts and crafts, entertainment and authentic island lunch, Highway 11, Captain Cook.

Dive Tour: An underwater tour on one of the submarine cruises over Kona's reefs

Cruise: Any of the glassbottom snorkel cruises along the Kona Coast to Kealakekua Bay Marine Reserve and Captain Cook monument.

Thrill: Helicopter or small plane ride over Kilauea Volcano eruption and lava flows

Backroad Adventure Tour: The Mana Road around Mauna Kea's upper flanks through forest and ranch country from Saddle Road to Kamuela. There are no commercial tours available but you can rent a four-wheel drive vehicle and do it yourself.

Golf Course: A toss-up - The Mauna Kea Beach Hotel course, ranked among "America's 100 Greatest" and "Hawai'i's Finest" by *Golf Digest*, or the Francis I'i Brown South Course at Mauna Lani Resort, equally acclaimed by the same magazine for its 17th. hole, which it ranks as a "Pearl of the Pacific."

Snorkeling: Anaeho'omalu Beach which fronts the Royal Waikoloa Hotel on the Kohala Coast.

Diverse Shopping: Downtown Hilo is experiencing a renaissance of sorts with many new shops, specialty stores, art galleries and boutiques worth exploring.

Family-style Restaurant: Don's Grill, 485 Hinano Street, Hilo

Meal for the money: Kay's Lunch Center, 684 Kilauea Avenue, Hilo

International Cuisine: Edelweiss, Highway 19, Waimea (885-6800)

Splurge Meal: Dinner at The Canoe House, Mauna Lani Bay Hotel & Bungalows, noted for Pacific-Asian regional cuisine fine dining

Splurge Weekend: An oceanfront room package at the Mauna Lani Bay Hotel & Bungalows with breakfast and dinner included at their award-winning restaurants; better yet, a weekend in one of their plush private bungalows, personal butler included.

Sweet Bread: Punalu'u Brand from Punalu'u, Ka'u District

Shave Ice: Kawate Seed Shop, 1990 Kinoole St., Hilo, (Food Fair Supermarket Complex)

Macadamia Nuts: Mauna Loa Macadamia Nuts brand, Hilo

Macadamia Nut Chocolates: Big Island Candies brand

Potato Chips: Furukawa Kitch'n Cook'd brand, Kona

Taro Chips: Atebara brand, Hilo

Kim Chee: Kohala Kim Chee brand (hot spicy pickled cabbage), Kohala

Baked Goods and Pastries: Suzanne's Bakery, Kailua-Kona

Malasadas: Tex's Drive In, Honoka'a

Fresh Coconut Pie: Holy's Bakery, Kapa'au, Kohala

Cookies: Donna's Cookies, Pa'auilo, Hamakua Coast

Buffet Lunch: The Terrace, Mauna Kea Beach Hotel, Kohala Coast

A HISTORY OF HAWAI'I

It is somewhat ironic that much of the history of today's Hawai'i is inextricably linked to the Big Island, the youngest and still growing member of the archipelago. And the history of early Hawai'i was affected by one man, Kamehameha the Great, a Big Island native son.

The history of Hawai'i is generally recognized as covering four periods. The first is the ancient pre-historic period before the discovery of the islands by the western world. The Polynesian race that populated Hawai'i migrated across the vast Pacific in simple sailing canoes. Their origin is believed to have been in Southeast Asia via Indonesia. They island-hopped across the Pacific in their great migratory journeys although anthropologists disagree on the routes they took and other details. The fact of all this is that these ancient sea-faring peoples crossed

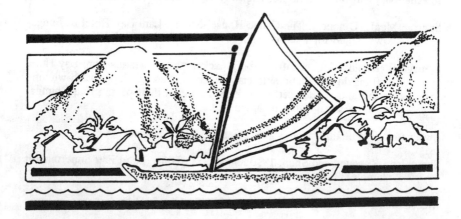

vast stretches of open ocean in simple craft using only their knowledge of the ocean, currents, winds, and stars to navigate. Hawai'i has been settled since about the fourth century A.D., even before Europeans dared to explore beyond their own borders.

The second period spans the discovery of the islands by the great British explorer, *Captain James Cook*, in 1778. This period also covers the rise to power of Kamehameha and his conquest of all the islands of Hawai'i by 1796 and the coming of traders, missionaries, and settlers. The monarchy established by Kamehameha lasted but a century as the Kingdom of Hawai'i under Queen Liliuokalani was overthrown in 1893.

The third period covers the founding of the Republic of Hawai'i in 1894 and the eventual annexation by the United States in 1898, and its organization as the Territory of Hawai'i in 1900. The period covers the rise of Hawai'i's agricultural economy, its pivotal role in World War II, and its admission into the Union as the Fiftieth State in 1959.

The fourth period of Hawai'i's history covers the time from statehood and its rapid assimilation into the American mainstream to the current age of electronics, high tech communications, jet transportation and mass tourism.

DISCOVERY OF THE HAWAIIAN ISLANDS

It was Captain James Cook, the famed British explorer of the Pacific, who was the first westerner to land in Hawai'i in January, 1778. Cook was enroute to the west coast of North America in search of the fabled Strait of Anian, a passage through North America that would shorten the voyage from Europe to Asia. While enroute from Tahiti, Cook stumbled upon Hawai'i, sighting the islands of Kaua'i and O'ahu. He made his first landfall at Kaua'i. Cook named the group the Sandwich Islands in honor of his friend and patron, the Earl of Sandwich, then First Lord of the British Admiralty.

He spent a fortnight there but did not visit any of the other islands of the group. Cook's men traded nails and bits of iron to the Hawaiians for fresh supplies of pork, fish, fowls, sweet potato, taro, yams, and water. With his ships, Resolution and Discovery, Cook sailed on to North America to continue his explorations.

After spending the next eight months exploring North America's west coast, Cook's party returned to Hawai'i with the intention of wintering there to refit and reprovision. They made the north coast of Maui in November, 1778, and Cook made it a point to sail leisurely through the Hawaiian group during the next few weeks learning what he could about the people of Hawai'i. At the various stops along the way, Cook took several of the Hawaiian chiefs aboard his ship to exchange gifts and courtesies. One of Cook's guests was the then obscure chief Kamehameha from the Big Island. Little did these two men know at their casual meeting then that, between them, they would bring about incredible changes upon Hawai'i that have a lingering impact today.

On January 17, 1779, the two ships anchored in Kealakekua Bay on the Kona Coast of the Big Island. When Cook landed, he was taken to a heiau (temple) where he underwent a religious ceremony recognizing him as the incarnation of Lono, the Hawaiian god of the makahiki (harvest) season. The Hawaiians believed that with Cook's arrival at such an auspicious time, the makahiki, that he indeed was the revered god, Lono.

Having refit and resupplied their ships, Cook's party set sail along the Kona Coast on February 4th. Unfortunately, a storm off the Kohala Coast damaged the mast of the Resolution and the group turned back to the safety of Kealakekua Bay. It was a fateful decision.

On February 13th while Cook's group was tending to repairs, various altercations arose between Cook's men and the Hawaiians. The next morning, it was discovered that a small boat from the Discovery had been stolen. Cook intended to get it back and landed with an armed marine guard. He planned to take the chief hostage until the boat was returned, a plan that had worked in previous such incidents with the Polynesians.

With Cook and his armed guards on the shore, and a large restless crowd of Hawaiians armed with daggers, clubs, and spears, the situation became quite tense. The Hawaiians were alarmed at the hostile intent of Lono and his armed guard. Word came that another chief had been killed by a shot from another boat. The Hawaiians now became visibly angered and made threatening advances toward the Cook party. Cook ordered his men to withdraw to the small boats on the shore. In the heated exchange, a Hawaiian threw his dagger at Cook who in turn fired one barrel of his gun which injured no one but angered the crowd more. Cook fired his second barrel and killed a Hawaiian. At that point, Cook's guards opened fire and a general melee broke out. Cook apparently turned to run to the boats but was struck down with a club and stabbed in the back with a dagger. He fell into the water and died on the spot.

And so, the world's foremost explorer of the Pacific met a tragic and untimely death in a place he introduced to the world. Today, a monument stands on the shore of Kealakekua Bay on the Kona Coast marking the exact spot where Captain James Cook met his fate.

HAWAI'I UNITED UNDER ONE RULE

Kamehameha (The Lonely One) was born in Kohala on the Big Island of Hawai'i about 1758. And although his parents were of noble rank, he was not in a direct line of succession to an alii (leading chief) position. Kamehameha grew up to be a fierce warrior noted for his tenaciousness, strength and intelligence.

The Hawai'i of the period was marked by inter-island civil war among the individual island chiefs and kings. And even on the Big Island, there was civil war among the chiefs who vied for dominance. Some chiefs from the Kona district, fearful of losing their lands under a new leading chief, asked Kamehameha to be their leader. Kamehameha had an ambition to conquer the Big Island and all of Hawai'i and unite the islands under one rule.

The 1780's saw the Big Island embroiled in civil war between Kamehameha of Kona-Kohala, Keawemauhili of Puna, Keoua of Ka'u, and Kahekili, king of neighboring Maui Island. In 1790-91, Kamehameha consulted a prophet from Kaua'i, Kapoukahi, who advised him that he would conquer all the islands if he built a large temple to his family war god, Ku-ka-ili-moku.

And so it came to be that Kamehameha did build his temple, Pu'ukohola Heiau (Hill of the Whale), located on a hill above Kawaihae Bay, Kohala, in 1791 and launched his rendezvous with destiny. Kamehameha's plans to conquer Hawai'i were primarily hindered at this time by his cousin, Keoua Ku'ahu'ula, his last major Big Island rival. Kamehameha invited Ku'ahu'ula to his temple dedication to make peace and Ku'ahu'ula willingly accepted. As Ku'ahu'ula and his companions landed on the beach below the heiau, Kamehameha's warriors swept down and killed them all. Ku'ahu'ula's body was carried up to the temple and was offered as the principal sacrifice to Kamehameha's war god.

After Keoua Ku'ahu'ula's death, virtually all opposition on the Big Island to Kamehameha ended and the prophesy began to be fulfilled. By 1794, Kamehameha had conquered Maui, Moloka'i, and Lana'i, and in 1795, the island of O'ahu. It was little wonder that he became known as Kamehameha the Great and established his kingdom over most of the islands of Hawai'i. In 1796, an attempted invasion of Kaua'i was disrupted by a storm. It wasn't until 1810, through an agreement with its king, that Kaua'i came under Kamehameha's control. Thus Kaua'i and nearby Ni'ihau have the distinction of being the only Hawaiian Islands not conquered in battle by Kamehameha.

However, Kamehameha did fulfill the prophesy and united all the Hawaiian Islands under one kingdom. Kamehameha the Great ruled his realm from Kailua on the Kona Coast until his death in 1819. He strictly observed the ancient religion of the Hawaiians and served as the official guardian of the war god which had brought him success in his conquests of Hawai'i. Upon his death, his son, Liholiho, became Kamehameha II.

However, little did Kamehameha the Great know, prior to his death, of the impending changes that were about to take place in his Hawai'i. Since the discovery of Hawai'i by the western world in 1778, the islands were increasingly exposed to an influx of traders, explorers, settlers, and in 1820 just after Kamehameha's death, the arrival of the first of many New England Congregational and Presbyterian missionaries. All of these westerners were to bring about significant changes over the coming generations as Hawai'i was forced into a world of which it knew nothing when it was "discovered" in 1778.

Soon after Kamehameha the Great's death, his son and successor, Liholiho, overthrew the "kapu" system and belief in the old Hawaiian religion. During this period in the early 1820's, the Christian missionaries, traders, and other foreigners who ventured into the islands did so at an opportune time. They easily established footholds and through their various efforts gained power and influence. Contacts with the western world increased and by the early 1840's, the Kingdom of Hawai'i was recognized by the United States, France, and Great Britain.

HAWAI'I IN THE MODERN ERA

Sugar, first grown commercially in Hawai'i in 1835, became the kingdom's principal industry with large tracts of land developed into plantations. In the early years, the cultivation, harvesting, and processing of sugar was labor-intensive and the sugar planters needed laborers. Throughout the nineteenth century the native Hawaiian population declined from about 85,000 in 1850 to some 40,000 in 1890. This was due in part to such things as the introduction of western disease and the loss of many of its youth to the whaling ship industry in the 1840's.

In the last half of the nineteenth century, the Hawaiian government began allowing the importation of foreign laborers to support the increasingly important sugar industry. Thus, the great waves of immigration began with large numbers of Chinese, Portuguese, Japanese, Koreans, and Filipinos being brought in to work the plantations, often under harsh conditions and standards. Labor immigration continued on into the early 1900's and to an extent still continues today. From these mixed ethnic groups came Hawai'i's label as a cosmopolitan melting-pot of diverse peoples.

The monarchy begun by Kamehameha the Great survived for a century until Queen Liliuokalani's reign was overthrown in 1893 by a group of primarily American revolutionists, and replaced by a provisional government headed by Sanford B. Dole. On July 4, 1894, the islands became the Republic of Hawai'i and after repeated efforts, in August, 1898, the islands were annexed as a territory of the United States.

The early 1900's in Hawai'i were years of relative peace and development. Hawai'i burst upon the American consciousness once again on the morning of Sunday, December 7, 1941 when Japan attacked Pearl Harbor. In one quick change of scene, Hawai'i entered the stage to play a pivotal role in the tragic drama that was World War II in the Pacific. Like the rest of post-war America, Hawai'i was on the threshold of even greater social, cultural, and economic development. The post-war years have seen Hawai'i grow tremendously. Hawai'i's admission to the Union as the Fiftieth State in 1959 was recognition of its achievements and future potential as part of the United States.

In 1993 on the centennial observance of Queen Liliuokalani's overthrow by American interests, the U.S. Congress officially offered an apology for the overthrow of the sovereign government of Hawaii and recognized the act as illegal. Various native Hawaiian groups and organizations have long been pushing for such congressional action to recognize the Hawaiian sovereignty movement and as a step toward reestablishing a sovereign Hawaiian nation and reclaiming native Hawaiian land rights. The next few years will no doubt be dramatic as the Hawaiians decide themselves what directions and results are to be expected from the sovereignty movement.

COUNTY OF HAWAI'I

The County of Hawai'i is comprised solely of the geographical boundaries of Hawai'i Island. The County of Hawai'i (most recent 1994 state data pop. 135,500) has its seat of government in Hilo (pop. 45,000-50,000 estimated) the commercial center and main port. The other major population centers are Kailua-Kona (pop. 26,000 estimated), the South Kohala District (pop. 11,000 estimated) and the South Kona District (pop. 9,000 estimated). The rest of the island population is spread among rural villages and small towns. The Big Island has slightly more than one-tenth of the total statewide population of 1,178,564 according to most recent 1994 state government data. The county is governed by a mayor and an elected nine-member county council who set legislative law and policy. The Big Island populace in turn elects its own senators and representatives to the state legislature which convenes annually in Honolulu.

HAWAIIAN LANGUAGE

SPEAKING HAWAIIAN

One of the more positive things the early missionaries did for the Hawaiians was to standardize their Polynesian based language into a written language. Previously, Hawaiian was a spoken language only. Hawaiian is one of the family of languages in the Pacific and shares much similarity to the languages of other Pacific islands.

The missionaries organized the Hawaiian language into an alphabet of twelve letters, five vowels (a, e, i, o, u) and seven consonants (h, k, l, m, n, p and w). Every letter of a word is sounded. Syllables end in vowels and many syllables contain only vowels. All Hawaiian words end in a vowel. There are no double consonants in Hawaiian. A vowel always separates consonants.

The five vowels are pronounced as follows:

a	as in father, above	o	as in note, own
e	as in obey, weigh	u	as in rule, true (oo)
i	as in marine (ee)		

In addition, there are some vowel combinations which resemble diphthongs and are pronounced as follows:

ai and ae (eye) as in mile, line
ao and au (ow) as in cow, how
ei (ay) as in day, say
oe (oy) as in boy, toy

The accent generally falls on the next to last syllable, although some words are unaccented. The inverted comma ('), called an "okina," is used in some words to indicate the "glottal stop", a sign that a k sound found in other Polynesian dialects has disappeared in Hawaiian usage. Where this mark appears, the accent falls on the preceding vowel as in the following: Ka'u (Kah'oo), Kapa'au (Kahpah'ow).

The consonants are pronounced as they are in English, with w being the only exception. When w introduces the last syllable of a word, it sometimes is sounded as a v. Examples are the famous Polynesian ceremonial drink, awa, is actually pronounced "ava" and the area on O'ahu called Ewa is pronounced "Ehva."

Learning and trying to use Hawaiian on your visit will add a new dimension to your travel experience. Learning, listening for, and using some of the local language can also prove useful in interpreting road maps, street signs, and place names. The following is a glossary to give you an introduction to Hawaiian words in common use. You will often hear and see these words and expressions used throughout Hawai'i and it will be useful to be familiar with them.

HAWAIIAN GLOSSARY

a'a - rough, clinky lava
ae - yes
aina - land
akamai - smart, clever, expert
ala - a road or a path
alii - chief, member of chiefly class
aloha - love, affection, farewell, hello
aole - no
auwai - a stream
auwe - alas!, woe is me!
ehu - a red-haired Hawaiian
hala - the pandanus tree from which leaves (lauhala) are used to make baskets
          and woven mats
hale - a house
hana - work
hao - iron
haole - stranger, foreigner, generally means a white person
hapa - part, sometimes means a half
hapai - pregnant, carry
hauoli - to rejoice
heiau - temple, place of worship
holoholo - to run from one place to another, to visit
holoku - gown, often with a train
holomuu - cross between a holoku and a muumuu, less formal dress or gown
          with no train
honi - to kiss, a kiss
hoomalimali - take it easy, patience
huhu - angry, upset
hui - a group, union, club, etc. most often referred to business groups who pool
          their money for investment purposes
hukilau - a communal fishing party in which everyone helps drive the fish into
          a huge net, pulls it in, and divides the catch
hula - the traditional dance of Hawai'i
imu - the underground ovens used in luaus to roast food
imua - forward, in front of
ipo - sweetheart

kahuna - a priest, doctor of old Hawai'i having supernatural or spiritual powers

kai - the sea, salt water

kalo - the taro plant root from which poi is made

kamaaina - native born or old timer, refers to those who have lived in the islands a long time

kanaka - a man, male Hawaiian

kane - man, male, used to identify men's restroom, toilet

kapa - the tapa cloth pounded from mulberry tree bark and usually colorfully decorated

kapakahi - crooked, uneven

kapu - forbidden, prohibited, keep out

kaukau - food, to eat

keiki - a child; keikikane - a boy; keikiwahine - a girl

kiawe - algarroba tree, grows in leeward (dry) areas

kokua - help

kona - south, direction from which winds and rain often come

koolau, north, windward

kuleana - homestead, plot of ground, territory, used to denote one's area of interest or primary activity

lanai - porch, terrace, patio

lani - heaven, sky

lauhala - pandanus tree leaf used in baskets and mats

laulau - bundle of food, usually pork, fish, etc. wrapped in taro leaves and ti leaves then steamed

lei - a garland or necklace of flowers

lomilomi - massage

luau - a traditional Hawaiian feast

luna - a plantation foreman or overseer

mahalo - thank you

makai - toward the sea

malihini - a newcomer to the islands

malo - loincloth worn by kane (men)

mana - the spiritual power which old Hawaiians believed existed in all things

manawahi - free, gratis

mauka - toward the mountains, inland

mauna - mountain

mele - song, chant

menehune - Hawaiian dwarf or elf

moana - the ocean

moe - sleep

muumuu - gown, Mother Hubbard-type dress the missionaries introduced to enforce modesty on Hawaiian women, now a colorful garment indispensable to any island woman's wardrobe

nani - beautiful

niu - coconut

nui - big, great

oe - you

okole - posterior, used to refer to the buttocks

okolehao - Hawaiian liquor distilled from the ti root

opu - stomach
pake - Chinese
palapala - book, printing, writing
pali - a cliff
paniolo - a Hawaiian cowboy
pau - finished, done
pilau - stench, smelly
pilikia - trouble
pipi - cattle, beef
poi - paste made from pounded taro root, a Hawaiian staple
puaa - pig
puka - hole
pupu - Hawaiian appetizer or hors d'oeuvre
pupule - crazy
wahine - female, woman, often used to identify women's toilet
wikiwiki - to hurry, make quick

A FEW WORDS ABOUT PIDGIN ENGLISH

As the unofficial language of Hawai'i, pidgin English is used everywhere. You will hear it on the streets, at the beaches, in the shopping centers, at offices, and even in the schools. It is the lingua franca of local islanders. Many locals can turn it on and off at will, others use it as their dominant mode of daily speech. It's been influenced by the various ethnic groups that have made Hawai'i home over the years. It takes some getting used to especially for the untrained ear. Visitors are advised to listen and enjoy and try to understand this local "lingo" but leave it to the local folks to actually use. Here's a sample:

any kine - anything
ass why - that's the reason, that's why
brah, bruddah - brother, good friend
buggah - guy, friend, also a pest or nuisance
bumbye - soon enough
chicken skin - goose bumps, when your skin gets the chills
chop suey - all mixed up
cockaroach - to steal or sneak away with something
da kine - a generally used term referring to everything, as in the right thing
fo'real - this is for real, no kidding
garans - guaranteed, for sure
get - used in place of verb "have"
get chance - possibility
heah - here
hele on - get moving
Howzit! - How are you?
ice shave - snow cone
junk - lousy, terrible
li'dat - like that
like - to want or want to
lolo - stupid, dumb

lua - toilet
make ass - to screw up, make a fool of oneself
manini - stingy, cheap
momona - fat
mo'bettah - better
musubi - rice balls
nah, nah, nah - no, just kidding
ni'ele - nosy
no can - cannot
no mo' - none
no shame - don't be shy
not! - you must be kidding, it cannot be
or what? - phrase added to any question
ono - delicious
pau - over, done, finished
plenty - lots, a great number
stink-eye - dirty look
talk story - talk, gossip
whatevah - applied to just about anything

BIG ISLAND PLACE NAMES

Halema'uma'u (Ha'lee'ma'oo'ma'oo) - crater, fire pit, within Kilauea Crater at Volcanoes National Park

Hilo (Hee'low) - county seat of Big Island (first night of new moon)

Holualoa (Ho'loo'ah'low'ah) - village in Kona District (long sled course)

Honoka'a (Ho'no'ka'aa) - small town on Hamakua Coast (rolling bay)

HILO BAY WITH MAUNAKEA

Ka Lae (Kah'lie) - southernmost point in Hawai'i (the point)

Kailua (Kai'loo'ah) - resort village in Kona (two seas)

Kapa'au (Kah'paa'ow) - village in North Kohala District (elevated portion of a heiau)

Kawaihae (Kah'wai'high) - village and bay on Kohala Coast (water of wrath; refers to people who fought over water supply in this arid area)

Kealakekua (Kay'al'lah'kay'koo'ah) - bay on Kona Coast where Captain James Cook landed and was killed (pathway of the god)

Kona (Ko'nah) - west coast district of Big Island (leeward side)

Laupahoehoe (Lau'pah'ho'ee'ho'ee) - village on Hamakua Coast (smooth lava flat)

Mauna Kea (Mau'nah Kay'ah) - 13, 769 ft. mountain, highest in Hawai'i (white mountain; often covered with snow in winter)

Mauna Loa (Mau'nah Low'ah) - 13, 677 ft. mountain, second highest in Hawai'i (long mountain; still active volcano, last erupted in 1984)

Na'alehu (Nah'ah'lay'who) - southernmost community in Hawai'i (volcanic ashes)

Onekahakaha (O'knee'ka'ha'ka'ha) - beach in Keaukaha area of Hilo (drawing sand)

Pahala (Pa'hah'la) - village in Ka'u District (cultivation by burning mulch)

Pahoa (Pa'hoe'ah) - village in Puna District (dagger)

Pololu (Po'low'loo) - valley in North Kohala (long spear)

Pu'ukohola (Poo'oo'ko'hoe'lah) - heiau (temple) at Kawaihae Bay (hill of the whale)

Waiakea (Wai'ah'kay'ah) - area of Hilo town near Hilo Bayfront (broad water)

Waiau (Wai'ow) - fresh water lake on Mauna Kea (swirling water)

Wailoa (Wai'low'ah) - river and pond in Hilo town (long water)

Wailuku (Wai'loo'koo) - river in Hilo town (water of destruction)

Waimea (Wai'may'ah) - village in Kohala District ranch country (red water)

Waipio (Wai'pee'o) - valley on Hamakua Coast (curved water)

GETTING THERE

Your first step in planning a trip to the Big Island should be to visit a professional travel agent. Better yet, if you don't already deal with one exclusively, visit two or three, if possible, regarding your travel plans. The travel industry, especially the airline industry, changes from day to day so much that it is virtually impossible for any travel agent to keep on top of everything. That's why it's important to check with more than just one on availability of flights, airfares, accommodations, tour packages, and all the details. It is also a good idea to do your homework before you consult a travel agent. The fact that you are reading this guidebook is a first step. By making yourself knowledgeable about travel to Hawai'i, and the Big Island, you can help your travel agent do a better job for you. In addition, it is wise to decide ahead how much to allow for expenses on your trip, how long you want to stay, where you want to stay, what you want to see and do, and all the other related details. You may wish to contact the Hawai'i Visitors Bureau and various Big Island resort associations listed in the "Helpful Information" section in this chapter. They'll send you all sorts of information and literature on hotels, attractions, what to see and do, etc. You can also visit your local library or bookstore and browse through some of the books listed in the HAWAIIANA READING FOR ADULTS section of this book.

CRUISE SHIPS

Before the advent of modern jet airliner travel, most visitors to Hawai'i traveled by elegant ocean passenger liner. Today, it is still possible to arrive via cruise ship. Several cruise ships call in regularly at Honolulu and other Hawaiian ports-of-call in their Pacific and around-the-world cruises. Some have regular scheduled roundtrip cruises to Hawai'i from various embarkation points. Foreign flag ships are prohibited by law from boarding passengers on the U.S. mainland and discharging them in Hawai'i and vice versa. Thus, many cruise ships have stops in Hawai'i ports while arriving from ports in Canada, Mexico, Tahiti or other Pacific ports. Princess Cruises ships *Island Princess, Sea Princess and Golden Princess* stop at Honolulu as does the Royal Viking Line's *Sagafjord* and *Royal Viking Sun*. Holland America Lines *Statendam, Rotterdam and Maasdam* stop in Hawai'i as does Cunard's *Queen Elizabeth II*. Royal Caribbean Lines *Legend of the Seas* has regular Hawai'i cruises in spring and fall. Carnival Cruise Lines, the big Miami-based firm, has recently added occasional Hawai'i cruises to its sailings on the *MS Tropicale*. Other cruise lines ships also include Hawai'i in their various sailings. Several of these ships include specific port calls in both Hilo and Kona on the Big Island. For the adventurous sailor-types, some freighters also carry small numbers of passengers from west coast ports to Hawai'i and beyond. Check with your travel agent for details.

American Hawai'i Cruises operate exclusively in Hawai'i with three-day to week-long, inter-island cruises with the *Independence*. The *Constitution* was taken out of service in 1996. The Independence visits Hilo and Kailua-Kona on the Big Island as well as other ports-of-call in the Hawaiian Islands. The ship generally spends a full day at each port before sailing in the evening. Shore excursions and various tours are available from dockside at each port. Ask your travel agent or contact American Hawai'i Cruises, 550 Kearny St., San Francisco, CA 94108, or call toll free 1-800-227-3666.

AIRLINE SERVICE TO HAWAI'I

By air, Hawai'i is only 5-5 1/2 hours from the West Coast. And with some 6 million visitors arriving in Hawai'i annually, competition among the airlines is fierce. There are all kinds of air fares and your travel agent can readily access the range via computer. Fares change rapidly, even by the minute, as do ticketing requirements and certain restrictions. A good travel agent will be able to help you sort out all the alternatives. There are several foreign airlines that stop at Honolulu International Airport on O'ahu. However, under federal law, they have no U.S. traffic rights, that is they cannot take passengers from one U.S. city to another, including Honolulu. You can fly a foreign airline and stop in Honolulu only if you are continuing on to an overseas destination.

There are presently several American air carriers serving Honolulu from various U.S. mainland cities. Telephone numbers are as follows:

AMERICAN AIRLINES - Reservations 1-800-223-5436, in Hawai'i 808/833-7600

AMERICA WEST AIRLINES - Reservations in Hawai'i, 1-800-247-5692

CONTINENTAL AIRLINES - Reservations 1-800-523-0000, in Hawai'i for information, 808-836-7730

DELTA AIRLINES - Reservations 1-800-221-1212, Hawai'i 808-955-7211

HAWAIIAN AIRLINES - Reservations 1-800-367-5320, Big Island 808-326-5615

NORTHWEST AIRLINES - Reservations 1-800-447-4747, Big Island 808-955-2255

TWA - Reservations 1-800-221-2000

UNITED AIRLINES - There is no central 800 number but one for each area of the U.S. See the yellow pages in your area. In Honolulu, the number for reservations and information is 547-2211 and on the Big Island it is 961-2811. United Airlines is the dominant air carrier to Hawai'i with about half of all traffic. They have more flights to more places, foreign and to the U.S. mainland, than any other airline. They currently provide direct mainland to Honolulu service with continuing service to Keahole Airport in Kona.

All United Hawai'i inbound flights (and mainland-bound return flights as well) pass through United's mini-hub at Honolulu International Airport. Their schedule sometimes changes with seasonal demand (Christmas-New Year's for example) when they may add direct flights to the Big Island from the west coast. If your schedule or plans do not allow you to take one of the United Airlines connecting Kona flights, you should have decided ahead of time whether you will enter the Big Island through Kona or Hilo and what local inter-island airline you will fly to get you to your final destination.

Be sure to have your baggage checked accordingly for Kona or Hilo. If you didn't have your baggage checked through to your final Big Island destination, you will have to retrieve them at the baggage claim area upon your arrival at Honolulu International Airport. From there, it is about a quarter of a mile walk or longer to the inter-island terminal which is next door to the overseas terminal. There is also a free Wiki Wiki Shuttle. If you walk over and have lots of luggage, rent one of the luggage carts inside the baggage claim area. For $1.50 you can push your luggage over to the inter-island terminal and save yourself some trouble.

Inter-island Airlines

Hawaiian Airlines and Aloha Airlines are the islands' primary air carriers and offer generally competitive fares. Have your travel agent check into group or family fares, special fares for children, senior citizens, military, and for the first and last flights of the day between islands. Both airlines also offer occasional special promotional fares and monthly unlimited air passes for flat rates. They also occasionally have flight coupon books on sale, with one coupon good for any inter-island one-way flight, at reduced rates. Inquire about the availability.

Hawaiian and Aloha offer several flights daily between Honolulu and Kona or Hilo, the Big Island's gateways. Aloha flies all Boeing 737 jets while Hawaiian flies DC-9 jets. Jet flights between Honolulu and Kona take 35 minutes, and between Honolulu and Hilo they take 40 minutes. On its mainland and overseas routes, Hawaiian flies DC-8's and DC-10's. If you came on Hawaiian Airlines from the mainland U.S. or overseas, your inter-island fare was probably already included in your ticket.

Hawaiian and Aloha Airlines however, have faced new competition the last couple of years from upstart Mahalo Air, a small commuter airline with service throughout the islands. Mahalo Air began initial Big Island service between Honolulu and Kona's Keahole Airport with several daily roundtrips. However, their anticipated service to Hilo has yet to materialize. Mahalo Air flies F-27 turboprop aircraft on its routes. If you don't mind taking longer to get to your destination you can save on their slightly lower fares. Their flights between Honolulu and the Big Island take about an hour or so each way.

The entry of Mahalo Air into Hawai'i's air market is the third attempt to establish a major air carrier in island skies in the last several years. Mahalo Air did prompt something of an airfare war in the islands by lowering fares and both Hawaiian and Aloha have responded in kind. It remains to be seen as to who will survive the stiff competition for inter-island travel. In the meantime, as long as fare wars continue, travelers benefit greatly.

One other change in Big Island air service worth noting was the recent takeover of service to Kamuela Airport by Trans Air, a small commuter airline based in Honolulu. Trans Air took over the Kamuela service when Island Air, an Aloha Airlines subsidiary, terminated the service due to low passenger loads. Trans Air was providing two round-trip flights daily (except Tues-Wed) between Honolulu and Kamuela using Cessna 402 aircraft.

One other thing to inquire about are the special inter-island airfare/room/car packages which the airlines offer. These vary from season to season but are almost always a bargain for short stays on the neighbor islands compared to purchasing each item separately. Contact information on the inter-island carriers is as follows:

ALOHA AIRLINES - For reservations and information call 1-800-367-5250; in Honolulu, 484-1111; and on the Big Island 935-5771.

HAWAIIAN AIRLINES - For reservations and information call 1-800-367-5320; in Honolulu, 537-5100, and on the Big Island 326-5615.

MAHALO AIR - For reservations and information call 808/833-5555 and on the Neighbor Islands 1-800-277-8333.

TRANS AIR - For reservations and information call 808/833-5557 and at Kamuela Airport on the Big Island, 808/885-5134.

There are several small air charter and helicopter tour operators on the Big Island and these are listed in ACTIVITIES AND TOURS, the "Air Tours" section.

Both the *Keahole Airport* in Kona and *Hilo International Airport* in Hilo provide modern terminal facilities. Kona's airport runway was recently expanded so it could service direct overseas/international jumbo jet flights. Hilo's runway can also handle large aircraft. But both airports are still waiting for regularly scheduled overseas flights to materialize. Kona does get some United Airlines mainland flights via Honolulu and occasional charters. Both airports were modernized in the 1970's but the Hilo airport has become something of a white elephant. At the time it was planned, Hilo's airport was seen by tourism officials as a second gateway to Hawai'i, providing some relief to congested Honolulu International Airport.

While Hilo's airport is called Hilo International, it's something of a misnomer as no international or overseas flights use it. Several U.S. carriers once served Hilo with direct mainland flights twenty years ago but all have since pulled out. Hilo never materialized as the second gateway to Hawai'i as envisioned. United was the last to leave in the early '80's, now centering their Big Island operations in Kona. Thus, Hilo ended up with an airport that is about three sizes too big. It has eight jetway arrival-departure gates but only three or four are used regularly. The cavernous waiting room inside the terminal is pleasant, colorful and comfortable, and conspicuously quiet until a Hawaiian or Aloha flight comes in. It's one airport you don't have to worry about crowds, there aren't any, except on long weekends and holiday periods when it seems like all of Hilo wants to go to Honolulu at the same time.

But the Big Island didn't lose out altogether. What was Hilo's loss was Kona's gain. Now that United Airlines flies from the mainland to Kona via Honolulu, visitor traffic to Kona has increased. In addition, the new resort developments along the Kohala Coast hold promise of further growth in the industry on the Big Island's sunny side. But more on that later.

Onizuka Space Center - Kona-Keahole Airport

If you're transiting through Kona's airport, or even driving by on the highway, make sure to stop and see the **Astronaut Ellison S. Onizuka Space Center**. This is a memorial to the Big Island's own native son and astronaut, born and raised on a Kona coffee farm, who was lost aboard the 1986 space shuttle disaster. The museum features memorabilia from Ellison's career in space exploration and includes hands-on displays and a piece of "moon rock" on loan from NASA. Open daily 8:30AM - 4:30PM; admission adults $2, children .50 cents. For information, contact Onizuka Space Center, P.O.Box 833, Kailua-Kona, HI 96745, (808) 329-3441.

WHAT TO PACK

As the golden rule of packing says, "Pack your bags, then remove half of that and you are ready to go." It's probably a fair assessment on the issue of what to take. All rules aside, you won't need too much to be comfortable in paradise. Dress is definitely casual, generally lightweight cotton and blend materials. Permanent press wash-and-wear clothing is best. The accent is on keeping cool in the tropics. Shorts and tee shirts are the mode here. The only evening dresses or coats and ties you might need would be for that elegant evening out at one of the more plush dining rooms at Kona or Kohala resorts. Otherwise keep it casual. The only warmer clothes you might need would be for visits to Waimea-Kohala ranch country, Volcanoes National Park, or Mauna Loa and Mauna Kea. Warm water-repellant jackets for hiking Volcanoes National Park or touring the ranch country would be very useful. Warm clothing suitable for below-freezing temperatures are in order if you plan to visit the summit of Mauna Kea where it can snow anytime of the year. Comfortable walking or hiking shoes are definitely a must for any short hikes in the parks or along the beaches. The local footwear is what mainland folks call "thongs," or rubber slippers. In Hawai'i they are called "zoris" or more simply "slippahs" (to borrow a pidgin word). They are great for wearing anywhere and everywhere, except for more formal occasions. You can buy a pair here for around $2-3 and up. A good sunscreen, a camera and film, and any other items of a personal nature could round out your packing. If you've forgotten something, you'll be able to get it here in the discount stores, supermarkets, drug stores and shopping centers.

TRAVELING WITH CHILDREN

Most youngsters will be able to handle the stress and pressure of traveling quite well if they are adequately prepared ahead of time. If they have never flown before, they need to be told what to expect, what it is like in a plane, what takes place on board a plane inflight. Youngsters have a natural curiosity and some basic information will increase their understanding and excitement about their trip to Hawai'i across the Pacific. One good thing to do would be to visit a library or bookstore together for some background information and reading on Hawai'i. A few children's books can do wonders to increase a youngster's perception and understanding of Hawai'i and the Big Island. See the section on HAWAIIANA READING FOR CHILDREN at the back of this book. And while you're at it, pick up a book or two for yourself. See HAWAIIANA READING FOR ADULTS for suggestions.

GOODY BAGS: Most youngsters take the waiting in airports and riding in airplanes for long hours quite well if they have enough to keep them occupied. While packing your luggage for the trip, include some special surprise goody bags for each youngster. Have enough surprises so that you can hand them out at intervals through the duration of the trip. Suggestions for things to include are small story books appropriate for the youngster, coloring books and crayons, game books, sticker books with sheets of colorful stickers, and even safe toys suitable for use on a plane or in confined places. You can even include snacks, small boxes of their favorite cereal, or even small cartons of juice with straw attached. Use your own imagination and create special goody bags that will keep your youngsters happy and content.

The flight attendants on the plane can sometimes provide complimentary gift bags for the kids. But you should come prepared with your own versions. It will all help make your own trip much more pleasant and satisfying.

ESSENTIALS: If you are traveling with an infant, make sure you have enough supplies of diapers, baby food, formula, etc. Soft teething rings and toys can help an infant clear the ears and equalize the air pressure if there is a problem. Older youngsters can do the same with chewing gum. Your carry-on luggage should include essential items, toilet articles, medicines, and even light changes of clothing in case your luggage is delayed or lost. Also, equally distribute important items and even clothing in all bags so the loss or delay of one bag won't be traumatic for one individual. Before you leave on your trip, be sure to check with your pediatrician especially if your child has a cold or is subject to ear problems. Inquire into the use of antihistamines or special medicines for childrens' use.

CAR SEATS: Hawai'i state law requires that all children age three and under must be placed in an infant restraint seat at all times when riding in an automobile. Most car rental companies have child car seats available but charge an $8-12 daily fee for use. Also, during peak travel seasons, demand may be high and reservations for car seats may not be completely reliable. And sometimes the car seat you get may not be that reliable either. So, you may want to consider bringing your own. An extra benefit of bringing your own car seat is that it may be usable on the airplane inflight. Check with your travel agent. If you check the car seat as baggage, put it in a box or use a large plastic bag and be sure to label it clearly.

CRIBS: Most hotels and condos provide infant cribs for a fee of $7-15 per night. Local rental shops also have them available for a few dollars per night if you opt to not bring your own portable crib.

Sara Baby Products at 74-5596 Pawai Place in Kailua-Kona's industrial area (326-4666) rents a full line of baby cribs, car seats, highchairs, strollers, playpens, etc. Another Kona area baby supply rental firm is Baby's Away, 329-7475, which carries a full line of baby needs.

BABYSITTING: Most hotels and condos have a babysitting service or list of available babysitters and will help you with arrangements. Fees usually run from about $10 per hour and up. There is also a baby-sitting service in the Kona area, **The Sitter Source,** 322-3587, which can assist with locating a sitter from their database of over 100 qualified babysitters. They charge $12 per hour plus a referral/booking fee.

EMERGENCIES/MEDICAL TREATMENT: There are several clinics and hospitals around the Big Island which can handle emergencies or walk-in patients. Your condominium or hotel desk can provide you with suggestions or check the yellow pages. In Kona, the Kaiser Permanente Medical Care facilities are at 75-184 Hualalai Rd. (327-2900); the Keauhou-Kona Medical Clinic is at 78-6740 Alii Dr., Suite 102 (322-2750).

For non-emergency medical care, Kona-Kohala Medical Associates, (329-1346) is at 75-137 Hualalai Road, Kailua-Kona. In Hilo, the Hilo Medical Group is at 1292 Waianuenue Ave. (969-1325). In Waimea/Kamuela, the Lucy Henriques Medical Center is right on Highway 19 near the Parker Ranch Shopping Center (885-7921) for both emergency and non-emergency attention. The Kona Hospital is in Kealakekua (322-9311) and Hilo Hospital is at 1190 Waianuenue Ave. (969-4111). There are also hospitals in Ka'u in Pahala town (928-8331), in Kohala at Kapa'au town (889-6211), and in Honoka'a town (775-7211). For emergency police/fire/ambulance service anywhere on the Big Island, dial 911. See "Important Phone Numbers" for additional listings.

BEACHES FOR CHILDREN: There are several safe beaches on the Big Island that are ideal for youngsters. In Hilo, Onekahakaha Beach Park in the Keaukaha area has a protected tidal pool enclosed by large rock boulders that slow the action of incoming surf. It is an ideal spot for the keikis (children) to swim, splash, and have a good time.

PARROTS

On the west side, Spencer Park at Kawaihae, South Kohala, provides one of the calmest beaches on the Big Island. Its small beach and sparkling clear water are perfect for the small ones. Hapuna Beach State Park below the Hapuna Beach Prince Hotel, South Kohala, is a large expanse of open sand great for the kids to run and play. The water is shallow here and the surf moderate but adults must be vigilant with youngsters in the water. Anaehoomalu Beach fronting the Royal Waikoloa Hotel, South Kohala, is a large sweeping crescent with fine sand, moderate surf and shallow water. Kamakahonu Beach fronting the King Kamehameha Kona Beach Hotel next to the Kailua-Kona Pier is also a fine small beach with gentle water that seems to have been made just for the keikis.

Never leave children unattended in the water because even the calmest of beaches occasionally have a surprise large wave roll in. A children's flotation device is strongly recommended in all cases. Also don't forget to liberally apply a good sunscreen before and after beachtime. And don't let the youngsters stay out in the sun for too long a period. Several short periods are better than one long period of being exposed to Hawai'i's strong sun. The same goes for you too mom and dad!

HOTEL-CONDO POOLS: It is essential to supervise your children at the hotel or condo swimming pool. Most hotel-condo pools usually aren't more than five or six feet at the deep ends and two or three feet at the shallow ends. Several of the newer hotels and resorts have Jacuzzi pools next to the regular pool. Vouching from my own daughters' experience, kids love the Jacuzzi. But be careful to not let them stay in the very warm water too long. Again, even at hotel-condo pools, use of a children's flotation device is highly recommended.

ENTERTAINMENT: Both Hilo and Kona, and even several of the small towns around the island, offer movie theaters showing the latest films. In Hilo, there are three theater complexes: Waiakea Theaters 1-2-3 in the Waiakea Town Plaza and the Prince Kuhio Theaters 1-2 in the Prince Kuhio Plaza and Kress Cinemas downtown. In Kona there are the Hualalai Theaters 1-2-3 and the World Square Theater at Kona Marketplace. Most of the hotels have cable television as well as in-house movies.

Most youngsters will be fascinated with exploring the beach and shores for bits of coral, seashells, and even looking for ocean tide pool life in the shallows. A guidebook to Hawai'i's shells, reef fish, and marine life may help them develop a better understanding of the beach and shore ecosystems. *Hawaiian Reef Animals* by Hobson & Chave, and *Hawaiian Fishwatcher's Field Guide* by Greenberg are two good references. Another excellent book especially for children is *Sand to Sea: Marine Life of Hawai'i* by Feeney and Fielding. A good place to see and feed the myriad schools of Hawai'i's colorful reef fish is at Kahalu'u Beach Park in Keauhou just south of Kailua-Kona. At the beach park next to the Keauhou Beach Hotel, schools of colorful fish swarm about in the shallow calm waters. It is a perfect place to view and hand feed the fish with bread, crackers, or something similar. Children will enjoy the experience of seeing the marine life up close. If they are old enough, they can use a mask and snorkel to gain an underwater view of the colorful reef life. If you have room in your luggage, plan on bringing along a light fishing rod and spinning reel. Children will enjoy trying their luck for some of the reef fish.

Kona also offers some good glassbottom boat cruises with special rates for children. *Captain Bob's Kona Reef Tours* offers a one hour cruise over shallow reef waters along the Kailua-Kona Coast, and you get to feed the fish too. The charge is $15 for adults and $7.50 for children (322-3102). Another glassbottom boat is the Captain Cook VIII operated by Hawaiian Cruises (329-6411). The Captain Cook cruises to the protected marine life preserve of Kealakekua Bay where guests can swim and snorkel in the pristine waters and enjoy watching the schools of reef fish. Non-swimmers can enjoy all the action and underwater scenery from the comfort of the glassbottom boat. The three hour cruise is $49 for adults and $24.50 for children.

In Hilo, a good place to check out marine life is at the Richardson Ocean Center located on Kalanianaole Avenue in the Keaukaha area. Here displays and aquariums explain much about the ecosystem and marine life of Hawai'i's beaches, reefs, and ocean. Lots of interesting fish are on display. There are also calm tidal pools to explore for such things as sea cucumbers, sea urchins, starfish, crabs, limpets, and other interesting forms of marine life. Youngsters can swim in the calm water too.

And as for fish, you can't beat the display of the Hilo fishing fleet's daily catch each morning at the Suisan Fish Auction. Here you can see the huge 100 + lb. yellow fin tuna and numerous colorful reef fish and seafood delicacies being sold. The auction is a genuine cross-cultural experience, with the bidding being done in pidgin English. It takes place each morning between 7 - 9AM (except Sundays) at Suisan Fish Market on the Wailoa River, Hilo Bay, adjacent to Banyan Drive hotels and Liliuokalani Park on the bayfront. Don't miss this when you visit Hilo!

Outside Hilo is one of the Big Island's least known attractions, perfect for kids of all ages. The Panaewa Rainforest Zoo is three miles south of Hilo off the Volcano Highway #11 on Mamaki Street. Watch for a sign indicating the turnoff. This facility, operated by the County of Hawai'i, is the only authentic rainforest zoo in the country. On display are animals from around the world representative of rainforest dwellers. Included are a beautiful Bengal tiger, monkeys, tapir, pygmy hippopotamus, land tortoise, parrots, and more. It's a pleasant place to stroll and picnic. There are no crowds and it's free!

Most restaurants provide a special keiki (children's) menu. And there are the usual attractions of several McDonald's around the island, some with a playground area. See the RESTAURANTS chapter of this book for dining details.

Finally, check with your hotel or condo desk and the local newspapers community activity file for additional children's activities around the Big Island. Many of the hotels provide special children's activities like hula dancing lessons, lei making, making a coconut leaf hat, playing Hawaiian games, and various other arts and crafts. During the summer and the major holiday seasons, many of the big hotels and resorts provide special supervised children's programs. For details, see the ACCOMMODATIONS sections for the area in which you are staying.

TRAVEL TIPS FOR THE PHYSICALLY IMPAIRED

When making your travel plans it is best to do so well in advance and to inform the hotels and airlines that you are handicapped and what services or special needs you require. A good travel agent should also be able to assist in planning for your needs. Most visitor industry facilities in Hawai'i are only too happy to accommodate the physically impaired. It would be wise to bring along your medical records in case of an emergency. And it is recommended that you bring your own wheelchair and inform the airlines accordingly.

ARRIVAL AND DEPARTURE: Both the Hilo and Kona airports on the Big Island are easily accessible for mobility impaired persons. Parking stalls are available at both terminals for the handicapped. Restrooms with wheelchair accessible stalls are also found in both terminals. The local airlines are very conscientious in accommodating the handicapped. Special lifts to the aircraft are provided wheelchair passengers, but again be sure to notify them in advance.

TRANSPORTATION: Only two Big Island rental car companies provide hand controls: Avis and Hertz. Avis requires two weeks advance notice and Hertz requires at least seven days. See the Rental Car listing for phone numbers or call their toll-free number in your local yellow pages. The Hawai'i County "Hele On" bus system provides a demand-response transportation service with lift-equipped vans within the Hilo and Kona areas only to accommodate individuals unable to utilize the standard transit buses. This "curb to curb" service is available from 7:00 AM to 4:30 PM Mondays through Fridays except County holidays. Requests for service must be made at least a day in advance. For information, call Coordinated Services in Hilo at (808) 961-3418 or Hele On Bus Office at 935-8343.

MEDICAL SERVICES AND EQUIPMENT RENTAL: As noted in the "Traveling With Children/Emergencies" section, Hilo Hospital telephone is (808) 969-4111, Kona Hospital telephone is (808) 322-9311. Some agencies can assist in providing personal care attendants, companions, and nursing aides while on your visit. Contact: Big Island Center for Independent Living in Hilo at (808) 935-3777; Interim Health Care in Hilo at (808) 961-4621 and in Kona at (808) 326-2722. Arrangements can be made for attendants in Hawai'i by calling one of the local offices.

The following companies provide medical equipment rentals. Pacific Rent-All in Hilo, 1080 Kilauea Avenue, (808) 935-2974, rents everything from hospital beds to wheelchairs; Kona Rent All at 329-1644 has a large line of rental equipment; Kona Coast Drugs, 75-5759 Kuakini Highway, Suite 104, corner of Hualalai & Kuakini, (808) 329-8886, rents a full line of wheelchairs, walkers, crutches, etc. Contact them in advance.

ACCOMMODATIONS: Most of the major Big Island hotels (at least the newer ones) and many of the condominium developments provide handicapped accessible rooms and facilities. However, because some have only a few, you need to request reservations well in advance. See the WHERE TO STAY chapter listing of hotels/condos and designation for handicapped accessibility.

ACTIVITIES: The Hawai'i Easter Seal Society can provide information on recreational activities for the disabled traveler. Contact them in advance in Hilo at (808) 961-3081. More information and phone numbers can be found in the ACTIVITIES AND TOURS chapter.

Additional information for the disabled traveler in Hawai'i can be obtained by contacting the Commission on Persons with Disabilities, State Department of Health, Hilo, Hawai'i 96720, (808) 933-4747, or the Commission on the Handicapped, Old Federal Building, 335 Merchant St., #215, Honolulu, Hawai'i 96813, (808) 548-7606.

SENIOR TRAVEL

Seniors traveling to and around the Big Island are advised to inquire with all airline, car rental firms, hotels, restaurants and paid attractions/activities as to whether any "Senior Discounts" are available. It's a good rule to always ask for any special discounts, rates, etc. that are provided especially for seniors. Your travel agent can be helpful on this also but don't hesitate to ask yourself if you make your own reservations. Many times there are "unadvertised" special senior rates.

The County of Hawai'i offers seniors a discount of 1/3 off the regular bus fares on its "Hele On" bus system. The bus system serves the entire Big Island with regularly scheduled services. For complete information and the latest fares, contact the "Hele On Bus," County of Hawai'i Transit Agency, 25 Aupuni St., Hilo, HI 96720, (808) 961-8343.

When making inquiries about senior discounts with travel agencies, tour operators, airlines, car rental firms, restaurants and the like, be ready to provide a valid photo/age I.D.

The University of Hawai'i at Hilo operates an annual program for the nationally-known "Elderhostel Program." In the Elderhostel Program, seniors have the opportunity to spend a week or more each summer on campus at UH-Hilo taking various courses and workshops in Hawai'i-Pacific culture, history, language, astronomy, vulcanology, oceanography, marine science and more. Fees cover tuition, room and board. Inquire with Elderhostel Program Director, University of Hawai'i at Hilo, 200 W. Kawili St., Hilo, HI 96720-4091; phone (808) 933-3555.

On the Big Island, additional senior information can be obtained from the County of Hawai'i's Senior Citizen Program, (808) 961-6939.

WEDDINGS AND HONEYMOONS IN PARADISE

A *honeymoon* on the Big Island can be "Paradise Found." And to make a romantic experience even more intimate, you can have your *wedding* here too. Many couples have chosen such settings as a Kona beach at sunset, the lush beauty of Liliuokalani Gardens in Hilo, on board a yacht sailing the majestic Kohala Coast, or for the traditional setting, any number of the Big Island's lovely little country churches. One is the beachside St. Peter's Church at Kahalu'u, in Keauhou-Kona.

Obtaining a marriage license is relatively easy. The legal age is eighteen for both parties and proof of age such as a certified birth certificate copy or baptismal record is required for those nineteen and under. The bride must have a rubella blood test and have the results certified by the lab,and physician ordering the test, using the prescribed form from the State of Hawai'i Department of Health. This form, along with an information packet, can be obtained from the Marriage License Section, Department of Health, State of Hawai'i, 1250 Punchbowl St., Honolulu, Hawai'i 96813 (808) 586-4545. Providing the proper form is used, the rubella test may be done by any government-approved laboratory on the mainland and signed by a physician licensed in any state. You can bring the test results with you to Hawai'i.

Once the test results are approved, you can obtain a marriage license from any authorized agent in Hawai'i. On the Big Island, call the Department of Health at 933-4210 for the name/address of a licensing agent in the area where you are staying. The license fee is $16.00. Both parties must appear in person and there is no waiting period once the license is issued. The license is valid for thirty days anywhere in Hawai'i.

WEDDING CHAPELS/SERVICES

The following is a listing of wedding chapels and services that can provide everything from a traditional church wedding to a lavish beachside exchange-of-vows at sunset at your choice of locations. Various packages are available and include such things as flowers, photography, video, music, champagne and even limousine. Costs will vary with how lavish and extravagant one wants a wedding to be.

Aloha Weddings in Paradise, Rev. B. R. Bates, P.O. Box 1626, Kamuela, Hawai'i 96743; 1-800-42ALOHA or (808) 322-6577

Beautiful Island Weddings, 77-6380 Kaheiau, Kailua-Kona, HI 96740; (808) 326-2264

Encore Talent, Kona, (808) 326-1636

Kinoole Baptist Church, 1815 Kinoole Street, Hilo, HI 96720; (808) 959-8012 or 959-3177

Kona Baptist Church, 78-7156 Puuloa Rd, Kailua-Kona, HI 96740; (808) 322-9119

Living Waters Assembly of God, 89 Maikai, Hilo, HI 96720; (808) 959-9524

Nani Mau Gardens, 421 Makalika Street, Hilo, HI 96720; (808) 959-3541

Paradise Weddings Hawaii ★, P.O.Box 383433, Waikoloa, HI 96738; 1-800-428-5844, (808) 883-9067, FAX (808) 883-8479; a full service wedding coordination operation which can arrange everything on the Big Island from location, minister, music, flowers-leis, photos-video, and wedding champagne and cake. Complete wedding packages with choice of location/site start at $295. Custom wedding arrangements are available, from intimate to outrageous. Get married on a sailboat cruise at sunset, at a quaint beachside chapel or mountain rainforest retreat. For details, contact professional wedding coordinator, Debbie Cravatta. **This is a very reputable service, highly recommended.**

Rev. Patrick Thompson, Kailua-Kona, HI (808) 322-3116

Salvador Enterprises, P.O. Box 1212, Hilo, HI 96721; (808) 959-4639

In addition, most of the major hotels and resorts have a social director who can often assist with your plans. Check with your travel agent on the various wedding-honeymoon packages currently offered by the hotels-resorts. There are usually different packages to fit different budgets. (Prices are subject to change without notice.)

HOTEL/RESORT WEDDING SERVICES

Hapuna Beach Prince Hotel, 62-100 Kauna'oa Drive, Kohala Coast, HI 96743; 1-800-882-6060, (808) 880-1111, FAX (808) 880-3112. The hotel has a special Romance Package available which includes three nights ocean view room, a bottle of champagne or gift basket and a room service breakfast for two for $995 per couple, extra nights at $375. The Suite Romance package is similar but includes suite accommodations for $2,345 per couple, extra nights at $800. There are three wedding packages with varying amenities and services included: Wedding Package #1-$725; Wedding Package #2-$1,150; Wedding Package #3-$1,700. Contact the hotel for specifics and latest information.

Hilton Waikoloa Village, 425 Waikoloa Beach Resort, Kohala Coast, HI 96743; 1-800-HILTONS, (808) 885-1234, FAX (808) 885-7592. At press time, the Hilton Waikoloa was about to open its new wedding pavilion on the grounds overlooking Waiulua Bay. The Hawaiian-style wedding chapel with Asian accents provides a beautiful tropical setting for that special day. The Hilton Waikoloa offers a honeymoon package along with a variety of wedding and romance packages including various amenities, services and activities. The wedding packages are Ginger, Jadeflower, Orchid, Maile or Pikake, named for exotic Hawaiian flowers. Wedding packages include a site fee, bottle of champagne, minister, two floral leis and two roses, and a canal boat ride with a "Just Married" sign. Other amenities and services are available. Call the resort for details and rates.

Keauhou Beach Hotel, 78-6740 Alii Drive, Kailua-Kona, HI 96740; 1-800-367-6025, (808) 322-3441, FAX (808) 322-6586. The Keauhou Beach has a basic 3 days/2 nights "Topless Honeymoon" package for $280 per couple, $140 per extra night. The package includes a convertible automatic rental car with a-c/unlimited mileage; deluxe ocean view room; bottle of champagne or arrival; chocolate-covered macadamia nuts; nightly turndown service; special gift from the hotel manager.

Royal Kona Resort, 75-5852 Alii Drive, P.O.Box 1179, Kailua-Kona, HI 96740; 1-800-452-4411, (808) 329-3111, FAX (808) 329-9532. The Royal Kona has a standard 4 day/3 night honeymoon package for $490, extra nights are $130. This includes full American breakfast every day, nightly orchid turndown service, champagne and chocolates upon arrival and a honeymoon remembrance gift.

Kona Surf Resort, 78-128 Ehukai Street, Keauhou-Kona, HI 96740, 1-800-367-8011, (808) 322-3411, FAX (808) 322-3245. The Kona Surf has a staff wedding coordinator who can assist with all the necessary arrangements. Their wedding packages are named after the fragrant seasonal flowers of the island, Ginger, Jasmine and Gardenia. The packages include various amenities such as flowers, champagne, photography or video, minister, and wedding site of Keauhou Gardens, Wedding Gazebo, Chapel Gardens or Kona Royal Chapel. The Ginger is $250, the Jasmine is $675 and the Gardenia is $1050. A standard honeymoon hotel package includes oceanfront room, rental car and champagne for $120 per night per couple; a similar deluxe suite package is $275 per night.

Kona Village Resort, P.O.Box 1299, Kaupulehu-Kona, HI 96745, 1-800-367-5290, (808) 325-5555, FAX (808) 325-5124. The Honeymoon Hideaway package includes accommodations in a private superior "hale" (bungalow) for 4 nights at $2,315 or 7 nights at $3,935 per couple, extra nights for $540. A deluxe hale package for 4 nights is $2,370 and 7 nights at $3,990, extra nights at $595. Also included are airport ground transportation, fresh-flower lei greeting and rum punch on arrival, a bottle of champagne, and choice of a three-hour morning snorkeling sail, a one-hour therapeutic body massage, a one-hour tennis lesson or one-hour dive excursion.

Honeymooners enjoy full American Plan breakfast, lunch and dinner as well as unlimited use of tennis courts, sailboats, outrigger canoes, snorkeling gear and glass-bottom boat cruises. A customized Deluxe Wedding package can also be arranged including flower leis and decorations, champagne, wedding cake, ceremony music, a minister to perform the wedding and the marriage license. Resort wedding gifts include 25 personalized wedding announcements and two classic full-lead Tiffany crystal champagne flutes. Receptions for up to 300 guests can also be arranged.

Mauna Kea Beach Hotel, P.O.Box 218, Kamuela, HI 96743; 1-800-882-6060, (808) 882-7222, FAX (808) 882-7657. The Mauna Kea has a basic special Romance Package available which includes a beach front room for three nights, a bottle of champagne or gift basket and a room service breakfast for two. Package rate is $995 per couple, extra nights at $375.

Mauna Lani Bay Hotel and Bungalows, P.O.Box 4000, Kohala Coast, HI 96743-4000, 1-800-327-8585, (808) 885-6622, FAX (808) 885-4556. Mauna Lani has a three-night honeymoon package featuring luxury accommodations with private lanai, a bottle of champagne upon arrival and a basket of fresh island fruit. The cost per couple is $1,025 for Ocean View or $1,260 with Ocean Front room. Extra nights are available at $395 and $450 per night respectively. Honeymooners may also custom-design their package by adding on any number of amenities or activities preferred.

The Mauna Lani also offers four special "To Mauna Lani...With Love" romance packages. All include five nights accommodations, various special meals, amenities and services. The packages range from "A Touch of Romance" for $2,921 per couple, "Raise the Mercury" for $3,300 per couple, "Hopelessly in Love" for $4,625 per couple, and the ultimate "Flaming Passion" at $23,275 per couple (this one includes five nights in an ocean front private bungalow).

Sheraton Orchid Mauna Lani, One North Kaniku Drive, Kohala Coast, HI 96743; 1-800-845-9905, (808) 885-2000, FAX (808) 885-8886. The Sheraton Orchid has a basic "Special Occasion" honeymoon or anniversary package. It includes deluxe accommodations in an executive suite; a split of champagne and two champagne flutes; full breakfast for two each day; and complimentary court fees at The Tennis Pavilion. Package price is $389 per night, two night minimum stay.

HELPFUL INFORMATION

INFORMATION COUNTERS: Official State of Hawai'i information counters are located in the arrival areas of both the Hilo (808-934-5840) and Kona (808-329-3423) airports. They have lots of brochures and information of all sorts and can help answer questions on Big Island travel.

HAWAI'I VISITORS BUREAU OFFICES: Maintains two offices on the Big Island: 250 Keawe Street, Hilo, Hawai'i 96720; (808) 961-5797, FAX (808) 961-2126; and 75-5719 W. Alii Drive, Kailua-Kona, Hawai'i 96740; (808) 329-7787, FAX (808) 326-7563. They provide additional literature and information on hotels, condos, tours, activities, etc.

BIG ISLAND RESORT ASSOCIATIONS: These organizations can provide further information relative to their resort area: *Destination Hilo*, P.O. Box 1391, 400 Hualani St. #20B, Hilo, HI 96721; 808/935-5294, FAX (808) 969-1984. *Destination Kona Coast*, P.O.Box 2850, Kailua-Kona, HI 96745, 808/329-6748; *Kohala Coast Resort Association*, P.O. Box 5000, Kohala Coast, HI 96743-5000; (808) 885-4915, FAX (808) 885-1044.

BIG ISLAND GROUP (BIG): This organization is composed of the County of Hawai'i, the Hawai'i Visitors Bureau and various hotels, resorts and visitor industry businesses who have joined together to promote the entire Big Island as a destination. Contact this group for information about the Big Island as well: Big Island Group, P.O. Box 5900, Kamuela, HI 96743; (808) 885-5900.

BIG ISLAND NEWSPAPERS: Prior to your visit, you may want to subscribe to one or the other daily to get information on upcoming events and to learn more about the Big Island in general. For the best wrap-up on local events and activities, it's recommended that you subscribe to both the Sunday and daily editions if you choose to subscribe at all. **Hawai'i Tribune-Herald** (covers entire Big Island), 355 Kinoole St., Hilo, HI 96720;(808) 935-6621; **West Hawai'i Today** (covers mostly Kona/West Hawai'i area), 75-5629R Kuakini Highway, Kailua-Kona, HI 96740; (808) 329-9311. There are also a couple of small press publications with specialized emphasis and coverage. **Coffee Times**, is a magazine format monthly with emphasis on Kona coffee culture, history, etc., available through Coffee Times, P.O. Box 1092, Captain Cook, HI 96704, 808/326-7637. **Ka'u Landing**, is a tabloid newspaper monthly with news and views on the Big Island's southern Ka'u District; available through Ka'u Landing, P.O. Box 160, Pahala, HI 96777, 808/928-6449.

TELEVISION: Most hotels and condos have TV's in-room. The major networks have Honolulu stations that telecast to the Big Island. These are KGMB (CBS) Channel 9, KHON (NBC) Channel 11, KITV (ABC) Channel 13, and KHET (PBS) Channel 4. In addition, there is Hilo's Community Resource Channel 2, and all major cable networks including CNN, ESPN, Discovery Channel, etc.

RADIO: Stations KKON-790 AM and KOAS 92.1-103.1 FM fill the air waves in Kona while KBIG-98 FM, KHLO-850 AM, KIPA-620 AM, KPUA-670 AM, and KWXX-95 FM do the same for the Hilo side. Maui and O'ahu (Honolulu) stations are picked up occasionally.

VISITOR PUBLICATIONS: Many free publications are available at shopping centers, hotels, supermarkets, etc. around the island. They are usually directed to visitors with lots of related advertising. They can be helpful in providing information on places to see and things to do. These publications often have discount coupons on everything from meals to tours to clothing. Some to look for are *This Week Big Island*, *Big Island Gold* and *Guide to the Big Island*.

WINDSURFING

IMPORTANT PHONE NUMBERS

All islands of Hawai'i are Area Code: 808

EMERGENCY: 24 hours daily 911

    Ambulance - Fire anywhere on Big Island 911
      Police - Hilo 935-3311
      Police - Kailua-Kona 326-4260
      Police - Waimea 885-0422
      Crime Stoppers . .Hilo 961-8300 Kona 329-8181
    Otherwise dial "0" for operator who will assist you.

Poison Control Center 1-800-362-3585

Crisis/Help Line . . . . Hilo 961-9111, Kona 329-9111

Sexual Assault Crisis Line 935-0677

Family Crisis Shelter . . . . Hilo 959-8400, Kona 322-7233

American Red Cross . . . . Hilo 935-8305, Kona 326-9488

Hawai'i Island Chamber of Commerce 935-7178

Hilo Hospital 969-4111

Kona Hospital 322-9311

Hawai'i Volcanoes National Park Headquarters 967-7311

Volcano Eruption Message/Information 967-7977

Hawai'i State Parks Division 933-4200

State of Hawai'i Information Office
    Hilo 933-4299
    Kona 329-9066

Hawai'i County
    Parks & Recreation 961-8311
    Office of Complaints & Information 961-8223
    Research & Development 961-8366
U.S. Coast Guard 935-6370

Weather Forecast
    Island of Hawai'i 961-5582
    Hawaiian Waters 935-9883

GETTING AROUND

FROM THE AIRPORT

Upon your arrival in Hilo or Kona, and after getting your luggage from the baggage claim area, you need to arrange transportation to where you are staying. Your options are a rental car, *bus/limousine* hotel shuttle, or a *taxi* cab. Unfortunately, due to a strong political lobbying effort from the Big Island taxi cab companies, the County of Hawai'i does not allow its own "Hele On" public bus system to service the airports.

Some of the local tour bus/limo companies do however provide airport to hotel service on a pre-arranged basis. Try Roberts Hawai'i (Kona, 329-1688; Hilo, 935-2858), Hawai'i Resorts Transportation Co. (Honoka'a, 775-7291) or Luana Limousine Service (Kona, 326-5466). Reservations should be made at least a day in advance or through your travel agent.

Approximate airport-hotel per person one way bus fares are: Kona Airport to Kailua-Kona or Keauhou area hotels $10-12; to the Kohala Coast resorts as follows, Royal Waikoloan Hotel and Hilton Waikoloa Village $18, Mauna Lani Bay Hotel and Sheraton Orchid Mauna Lani Hotel $20, Mauna Kea Beach Hotel and Hapuna Beach Prince Hotel $22. Hilo Airport to Banyan Drive hotels in Hilo $6.

Taxis from both the Hilo and Kona airports are expensive. Big Island taxis are metered but they practically double the transportation fare over buses and even make renting a car attractive, at least from the Kona airport.

In Hilo, from the airport to Banyan Drive hotels, a distance of two and a half miles, the standard charge is $7-9. Hilo's taxi services include ABC Taxi (935-0755), Ace One Taxi (935-8303/959-0114), A-1 Bob's Taxi (959-4800/969-7060), David's Taxi (961-6428), Hawai'i Taxi (959-6359) and Hilo Harry's Taxi (935-7091).

From the Kona Airport to Kailua-Kona area hotels, a distance of seven to ten miles, the fare is $15-17; to Keauhou area hotels, a distance of 12 to 14 miles, the fare is $26-28; to the Kohala Coast hotels which are spread out along the coast for 20 to 30 miles, the fares are as follows: Royal Waikoloan Hotel and Hilton Waikoloa Village $34-36, Mauna Lani Bay Hotel and Sheraton Orchid Mauna Lani Hotel $38-40, Mauna Kea Beach Hotel and Hapuna Beach Prince Hotel $48-50. Kona-Kohala-Waimea taxi services include Aloha Taxi (325-5448/883-9546), Alpha Star Taxi (329-6974/885-4771), C & C Taxi (329-6388/329-0008), Island Cruise Taxi-Limo (885-8687), Kona Airport Taxi (329-7779/883-9546), Marina Taxi (329-2481), Mauka Taxi (323-9000), Orchid Isle Taxi (326-7527), Paradise Taxi (329-1234), Sprint Discount Taxi (329-6974) and Waikoloa Taxi (883-8166).

Other distances on the Big Island from Kona Airport: to Hilo via the north route Highway 19 is 86 miles; to Kamuela via Highway 19 is 34 miles; to Volcano via Highway 11 is 100 miles; to South Point via Highway 11 is 60 miles; to Honoka'a via Highway 19 is 49 miles; and to Hawi in North Kohala via Highways 19/270 is 44 miles. From the Hilo Airport to Kailua-Kona via Highway 19 is 97.5 miles; to Honoka'a via Highway 19 is 42 miles; to Hawi in North Kohala via Highways 19/250 is 76 miles; to Kamuela via Highway 19 is 54.6 miles; to Volcano via Highway 11 is 28 miles; and to South Point via Highway 11 is 73 miles. The distance between Hilo and Kailua-Kona via the south route Highway 11 is 125 miles.

LOCAL BUSSES

Once settled in your hotel, you still need local transportation to get around. Taxis provide Hilo and Kailua-Kona area service and even standard tours, but again expense is a factor. In the Kailua-Kona and Keauhou areas, you can catch the "Alii Shuttle" bus which serves the entire length of Alii Drive from Kailua-Kona to Keauhou. The shuttle runs daily and takes 45 minutes in each direction. Its turn around points are the Lanihau Shopping Center in Kailua-Kona and the Kona Surf Resort in Keauhou. The shuttle makes stops along Alii Drive enroute at all major hotels and shopping centers. The fare is $1 each way; hours of operation are 7:45AM - 10PM, daily. Look for the white bus.

The other transportation alternative is the "Hele On" bus system operated by the County of Hawai'i. The public buses provide both Hilo and Kailua-Kona as well as island-wide service. Standard fare for short distances is $.75 within Hilo or Kailua-Kona, and gradually increases depending on how far you are going or to what town around the island. The around the island fare, Hilo to Kona, is a reasonable $6.00 one way.

Bus tickets are sold by the sheet at a 10% discount from the regular fare. Ten tickets per sheet cost $6.75. Certified senior citizens, handicapped and students are entitled to a special discount and can purchase ticket sheets for $5.00. Bus tickets are available at various stores, shops, and businesses around the island displaying the Hele On bus poster. There is a $1.00 per piece charge for luggage and backpacks. For bus schedules, contact County of Hawai'i, Mass Transportation Agency, 25 Aupuni Street, Hilo, HI 96720, (808) 935-8241.

LIMOUSINE SERVICE

If you want to splurge on transportation for that special occasion, wedding, honeymoon or for whatever reason, you can arrange for a personalized limousine for everything from airport-hotel service to a complete private around the island tour complete with champagne and catered lunch. The cost is obviously expensive but first-class for those who can afford it. Here's a listing of limousine service operators:

A Touch of Class Limousine, Kona, 808 325-0775

Aloha Aina Limousine, P.O. Box 2087, Kailua-Kona, HI 96745; 808 334-0633

47

Big Island Transportation & Tours, Kona/Kohala, 808 334-0606/883-0606

Luana Limousine Service, P.O. Box 2891, Kailua-Kona, HI 96745; 1-800-999-4001; 808 326-5466

Meridian Hawaiian Resorts Transport, Mauna Lani Bay Hotel and Bungalows, Kohala Coast, 808 885-7484

RENTAL CARS, VANS, 4-WHEEL DRIVES

The Big Island has some 1500 miles of paved county and state roads and highways. And those roads and highways pass through some of the loveliest and most diverse scenery in Hawai'i. The best way to see it all is by hiring your own car. There are several rental car companies located on the Big Island and most have stations in Hilo and Kona. A few have desks at major hotels and resorts. Some are national chains while others are local. One thing is certain: they all have a variety of cars available at a variety of rates, with special low-season, weekly discount, and holiday package deals. You can check out the following list and contact them yourself (many have toll free numbers) or you can have your travel agent do it.

Rental cars are your best bargain for transportation since they give you the independence and mobility to come and go as you please and to see and do what you want. Rates vary greatly among the car rental agencies as well as by season so it's wise to shop around. A survey of Big Island car rental agencies revealed the following rates, all with no mileage charges. The daily rate for an economy/compact ranges from $25-48. For a mid-size car, the daily rate ranges from $30-52. Full-size cars range from $38-59. Mini-vans range from $58-80 daily. Some agencies have various luxury cars available and they command premium rental rates. Many of the agencies offer special holiday and seasonal weekly rates and its always good to check on these. There are also special hotel room/car packages that are good values.

Keep in mind that these figures are only approximate. Special rates may apply during the "low" season in Hawai'i, usually from Labor Day until about Thanksgiving and again from Easter until about June 1. Hawai'i's peak season from December 1 until March 30 or so, finds demand and prices high on rental cars. The summer season although not as strong as winter generates a fair amount of demand and rates seem to fluctuate.

One thing that affects car rental rates is the extra charges for insurance coverage. These rates can run anywhere from $15 per day and up. This increases the daily rate drastically and most agencies strongly encourage you to buy the coverage. However, it is suggested that you check with your own insurance company at home to verify exactly what your policy covers. In fact, bring along your insurance company's address and telephone number just in case. Hawai'i is a no-fault state and without the insurance, if there is an accident, you are required to take care of all the damages before leaving the island.

Most of the car rental agencies have similar policies. They require a minimum age of 21 to 25 and a major credit card for a deposit or to hold your reservation. Most feature no mileage charges with you paying for the gas (from $1.65-2.00 or more per gallon). There is also a 4% sales tax.

For the adventurous who want to see some of Hawai'i's back roads and byways, you should consider renting a 4-wheel drive such as an Izuzu Trooper, Toyota Forerunner, Geo Tracker or similar vehicle. Harper Car & Truck Rentals in Hilo
rents 4-wheel drives with rates starting at $88 daily. Check with other car rental agencies for availability. These vehicles are approved for traversing such roads as Highway 200, the Saddle Road between Hilo and Waikoloa, Waipio Valley, South Point and other backroad areas. Check all rental conditions before renting a 4-wheel drive vehicle.

The Saddle Road is off limits to regular rental cars and driving on it is a violation of the rental car agreement. You would need a 4-wheel drive vehicle to reach such places as the summit of 14,000 ft. Mauna Kea, and other inaccessible backcountry or offroad locations, which are also off limits to regular rental cars.

One final note on renting a car on the Big Island. If you pick up your car at one airport, say at Kona, and drop it off at Hilo, most car rental agencies will charge you what is called a "drop" charge. This can run as high as $30-40. That's why it is usually best to pick up and return a rental car at the same location.

WARNING: Even paradise has its share of thieves so *never* leave your automobile unlocked at the beach, park, scenic site or parking lot. Also, take personal valuables with you. Secure your car and your valuables. And don't leave the keys in your car.

RENTAL CAR COMPANY LISTING:

AALA ALOHA CARS-R-US
Toll free 1-800-655-7989

AA PARADISE NETWORK
Toll free USA & Canada
1-800-942-2242

ALAMO RENT A CAR
1-800-327-9633
Hilo 961-3343
Kona 329-8896

AVIS RENT A CAR
1-800-321-3712
Hilo 935-1290
Kona 327-3000

BUDGET RENT A CAR
1-800-527-0700
Hilo 935-6878
Kona 329-8511

DOLLAR RENT A CAR
1-800-800-4000
Hilo 961-6059
Kona 329-2744/329-3161

HARPER CAR & TRUCK
RENTALS OF HAWAI'I
1690 Kamehameha Avenue
Hilo, HI 96720
Toll Free 1-800-852-9993
Hilo 969-1478

HERTZ RENT A CAR
1-800-654-3011
Hilo 935-2896
Kona 329-3566

PAYLESS CAR RENTAL
1-800-729-5377

NATIONAL CAR RENTAL
1-800-227-7368
Hilo 935-0891
Kona 329-1674

MOTORCYCLE, MOPED, MOTORSCOOTER RENTALS

Motorcycles, mopeds and motorscooters can be rented from the following (check for the latest half and full day rates):

Hilo Cycle Island, 741 Kanoelehua Avenue, Hilo, 935-4999; rents Harley Davidsons and bikes of all sizes.

DJ's Rentals, 75-5663A Palani Road, Kailua-Kona, across from King Kam Hotel, 329-1700 or on the Kohala Coast at Kings' Shops at Waikoloa Beach Resort, 885-7368; rents scooters/mopeds, small bikes and large Harley-Davidsons.

Kona Harley-Davidson, 74-5616 Luhia, Kailua-Kona, 326-9887; rents Harley-Davidsons and bikes of all sizes.

BICYCLE RENTALS

Dave's Bike & Triathlon Shop, 74-5588M Pawai Place, Kailua-Kona, 329-4522

Hawaiian Pedals, Kona Inn Shopping Center, Alii Drive, Kailua-Kona, 329-2294

Mauna Kea Mountain Bikes Inc., P.O.Box 44672, Kamuela, 96743, 885-2091

Mid Pacific Wheels, 1133C Manono St., Hilo, HI 96720, 935-6211

Red Sail Sports, Hilton Waikoloa Village, 885-2876 or
                Sheraton Orchid Mauna Lani, 885-2000

DRIVING ON THE BIG ISLAND

You'll find that driving on the Big Island is really no different than anywhere else, with one small exception. Big Island drivers are generally the most courteous and congenial among all the islands of Hawai'i. The majority of Big Island drivers drive with "Aloha" and will yield to others, allow others to make left turns in front of them, wave others through intersections and generally display other forms of courteous driving. But like everywhere too, there are a few who don't know how to drive courteously. You'll pick up fast on Big Island driving courtesy, but likewise, drive defensively at the same time.

You can drive completely around the Big Island, from Hilo to Kona, in a day, but it is a very tiring drive and not really practical for sightseeing and leisurely exploring. The circle drive is around 225 miles or so. The best thing to do would be to drive one leg between Kona and Hilo, say the northern route through Kamuela and Honoka'a, and then spend a night or two in Hilo taking in the sights of that area. Then the drive back to Kona could be completed another day via the southern route, through Volcanoes National Park and the Ka'u District to take in those sights. This routing could just as easily be reversed. The distance from Hilo to Kona around the north side through Kamuela is just about 100 miles. Around the south side through Ka'u it is about 125 miles. For an excellent road map of the Big Island, *Hawai'i, The Big Island* by cartographer James A. Bier is highly recommended. The cost is $2.95 at local bookstores or it can be ordered from Catalog Order Desk, The University of Hawai'i Press, Honolulu, Hawai'i 96822. If you're traveling with youngsters, plan on stopping at some of the town parks along the way to let the children stretch their legs and run off excess energy. Most of the parks have a playground area with swings, climbing bars, carousels, etc. It's a request I get frequently from my "backseat gang."

Hawai'i Warrior Markers: While driving around the Big Island, be on the lookout for the distinctive red and yellow cloaked Hawaiian Warrior marker-signs along the road. These signs have been erected by the Hawai'i Visitors Bureau to note special historic sites, places of interest to visitors, and scenic attractions. They are very easy to recognize and will help lead you to discover many additional interesting things while touring around the island.

A FEW WORDS ABOUT FISH AND OTHER SEAFOOD

About the only things harder for visitors to pronounce properly than the names of towns and streets are the names of fish. And whether you are dining out or buying fresh fish at the market, Hawaiian fish names can be confusing. Among the more common fish caught commercially and that you'll see at the market and on restaurant menus are Ahi (yellow fin tuna), Aku (blue fin tuna), Ono (wahoo), Mahimahi (dolphin fish), and several species of marlin. Other popular table fish include Opakapaka (pink snapper) and Onaga (red snapper) which provide delicate white flaky meat.

A short list of Hawai'i's more popular seafood delicacies follows:

A'AMA - A small black crab that scurries over rocks at the beach. A delicacy required for a Hawaiian luau.

A'U - The broadbill swordfish averages 250 lbs. in Hawai'i. The broadbill is a rare catch, hard to locate, difficult to hook, and a challenge to land.

AHI - The yellow fin tuna (Allison tuna) is caught in deep waters surrounding the Big Island. The pinkish red meat is firm yet flaky. This fish is popular for sashimi (raw, sliced thin, dipped in mustard-soy sauce) and costs $15-20 per lb. at New Year's when it is most in demand. They can weigh over 200 lbs.

ALBACORE - This smaller version of the Ahi averages 40-50 lbs. and is lighter in both texture and color.

AKU - This is the blue fin tuna, usually averaging 5-15 lbs.

EHU - Orange snapper

HAPU - Hawaiian sea bass

IKA - Hawaiian squid, used for many dishes

KAMAKAMAKA - Island catfish is a very tasty and popular dish, however, a little difficult to find at most restaurants.

LEHI - The Silver Mouth is a member of the snapper family with a stronger flavor than Onaga and Opakapaka and a texture resembling Mahimahi.

MU'U - A very mild white fish which is seldom seen on menus because it is very difficult to catch

MAHIMAHI - Also called dolphin fish but unrelated to the mammal of the same name. Ranges from 10-65 lbs. It is a seasonal fish and commands a high price when fresh. Traditionally one of Hawai'i's most popular seafoods, it is often imported from other Pacific and Far East areas to meet the demand. If it's on your dinner menu, ask if it is fresh (caught in Hawai'i) or frozen (imported). Excellent eating fresh and almost as good even if frozen, if prepared well.

ONAGA - Red snapper, considered a bottom fish as it is caught in quite deep water. Bright pink scales, tender white meat.

ONO - This one is a member of the barracuda family but the meat is flaky, moist, and "very good," which is what Ono means in Hawaiian.

OPAKAPAKA - Pink snapper has very light, flaky, delicate meat.

OPIHI - single shell limpet, mollusc that clings to rocks on the shore. Dangerous and difficult to gather as hazardous surf can sweep pickers into the ocean. Many have been drowned this way. But opihi are a must for an authentic Hawaiian luau.

PAPIO - This is a baby Ulua which is caught in shallow waters and weighs 5 - 25 pounds.

TAKO - better known as octopus. This a is very popular seafood prepared numerous ways and used in various dishes.

ULUA - Also known as Pompano, this fish has firm and flaky white meat. Often caught along the Big Island's steep rocky coastline. Ulua can weigh up to 100 lbs. A Papio is a young ulua usually under 25 lbs.

WANA - otherwise known as the sea urchin, many consider this a real delicacy. Simply scoop out the contents of the wana shell and enjoy!

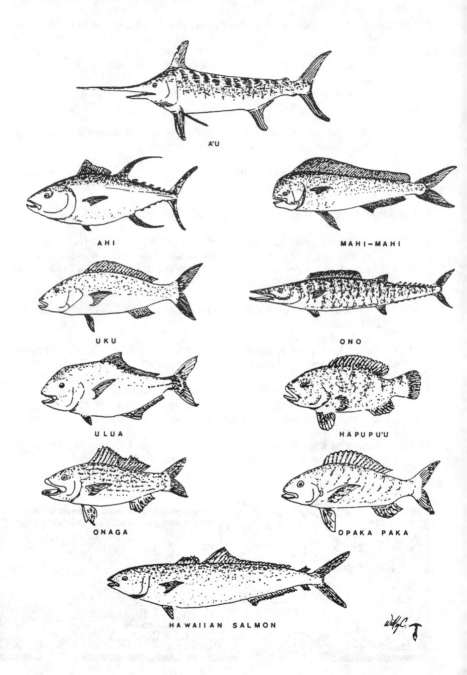

A'U

AHI

MAHI-MAHI

UKU

ONO

ULUA

HAPUPU'U

ONAGA

OPAKA PAKA

HAWAIIAN SALMON

54

GROCERY SHOPPING

You can expect to pay quite a bit more on the average for groceries on the Big Island compared to what you pay in most areas of the U.S. mainland. Big Island grocery prices average from 25-35% higher than mainland prices. And, like on the mainland, island supermarkets vary in price so it pays to shop around. Weekly advertised specials can change prices considerably. The following samples are average weekly advertised sale price ranges and may vary from store to store around the island. These prices were quoted a few months prior to publication so expect them to be higher as you read this.

> Kraft Mayonaise, 32 oz. - $2.19-3.29
> Kraft American cheese slices, 12 oz. - $1.99-3.57
> Lay's potato chips, 9 oz. - $1.69-1.99
> Bread, 1 lb. loaf - $1.39-2.79
> Skippy Peanut Butter, 18 oz. - $1.99-2.89
> whole fresh chicken - $.99-1.89 lb.
> Oscar Mayer beef hot dogs, 1 lb. -$2.89-3.75
> hamburger, extra lean $2.79-2.99 lb.
> chuck roast, 7 bone - $1.89-2.59 lb.
> New York steak - $5.89-6.99 lb.
> top sirloin steak - $3.99-4.57 lb.
> pork chops - $1.99-2.57 lb.
> pork spare ribs - $1.99-2.29 lb.
> Oscar Mayer bacon - $3.95 lb.
> head lettuce - $.99 lb.
> bananas - $.59-.79 lb.
> 1/2 gal. milk - $2.39-2.65
> 1/2 gal. orange juice - $1.99-3.79
> eggs-Grade A large, doz. - $1.63-1.91
> bathroom tissue, 4-roll pack - $.99-1.69
> 12-pack Coors/Bud beer - $6.99-7.49
> 12-pack Pepsi or Coke - $2.59-4.39

You'll find the range of grocery stores on the Big Island from simple Mom n' Pop country stores to modern convenient supermarkets. In Hilo, the major supermarkets are KTA Superstores, Safeway, Sure Save, and Sack n' Save. In Kona, the major supermarkets are KTA Superstores, Sure Save, Sack n' Save, Kamigaki Market and a soon-to-be Safeway is under construction at press time. In Waimea, the major stores are KTA and Sure Save while in Waikoloa it is Waikoloa Village Market (operated by KTA). Most of them advertise in the local newspapers, offering weekly specials and coupons.

Around the island, each town has a market or two and there are a number of stop and shop convenience stores such as 7-Eleven food stores. The Safeways in Hilo and Kona, the Sack n' Save and Sure Save stores in Hilo and the KTA stores in Hilo/Puainako, Waimea, Kailua-Kona and at Keauhou-Kona feature the latest in full service deli counters, ready to eat foods and bakeries.

On your trips around the island and through the towns, be on the lookout for one of the nondescript Mom n' Pop stores. These are the old fashioned small town family run stores, usually with grandma or grandpa still tending store and not infrequently by one of the younger members of the family who have returned to take over the family enterprise. With their homey country atmosphere, simple furnishings and fixtures, old ad displays on the walls, and ancient water coolers that keep beer and soda chilled, these old town stores allow you to step back into an earlier era of Hawaiian history. And often too you might luck out and get there as the homemade cookies, fresh sushi, or other country goodies are just out of the kitchen. And if nothing else, you might be able to get a "shave ice."

SPECIAL BIG ISLAND PRODUCTS

It's an island tradition that when you go traveling, you bring back some special gifts and goodies from the place you visit for friends and relatives back home. The Japanese call these special gifts "omiyage." For local folks from other parts of Hawaii, their Big Island visit wouldn't be complete without several extra boxes of goodies to take home. That's why at the airport baggage check in areas you'll see all manner of boxes and containers full of Big Island products destined for friends and relatives back home.

The Big Island doesn't disappoint when it comes to supplying local products for those back home to enjoy. These products are all grown or produced right here on the Big Island and are easily available at local supermarkets and gift stores around the island. Some of these products have already been mentioned in the "Best Bets" or other sections of this book. Naturally, most of these are edible food products with the exception of flowers. And while some of these products can be transported easily, a few are perishable and will require refrigeration and special handling.

One more note: pineapple isn't grown commercially on the Big Island but you can obtain it in local supermarkets and gift shops for shipping home. The pineapples come from either O'ahu or Maui.

Look for these special Big Island products:

Atebara Taro Chips from Hilo
Furukawa Kitch'n Cook'd Potato Chips from Kona
Miriam's Cookies from Kona
Donna's Cookies from the Hamakua Coast
Harrie's Lavosh from Hilo
Frank's Foods or Miko Meats Portuguese Sausage from Hilo
Kulana Foods Brand Big Island Ranch Beefsteaks from Hilo
Mauna Loa brand macadamia nuts and chocolates from Hilo
Big Island Candies brand macadamia nut chocolates from Hilo
Mountain View Stone Cookies from Mountain View
Amano fish cake and tempura (surimi) from Hilo
    (an essential ingredient for saimin noodles)

Hilo Macaroni Factory crackers from Hilo
    (Sorry they don't make macaroni anymore but the crackers are great!)
Niolopa brand tropical fruit jams and jellies from Hilo
Hawaiian Macadamia Plantations brand macadamia nuts, chocolates, cookies and
    other goodies from Honoka'a
Pure Kona Coffee (several brands available in local supermarkets) from Kona
Punalu'u Sweetbread from Punalu'u, Ka'u District
Anthuriums and orchids from Big Island flower farms and florist shops
Oshiro Tofu Products brand tofu from Hilo
Kelly Boy's sweetbread and cinnamon rolls from Hilo
Pueo Poi Factory laulau and poi from Hilo
Ishigo's Bakery breads and pastries from Honomu on the Hamakua Coast
Holy's Bakery frozen fruit pies from Kapa'au in North Kohala
Kohala Kim Chee from Hawi, Kohala
Big Island Taro Chips from Kalaoa on the Hamakua Coast
Hakalau Honey from Ouye Apiaries in Hakalau
Busy Bees Honey from Pahoa, Puna District
Orchid Island Cheure and Feta goat milk cheeses, Kurtistown
Volcano Winery Symphony, guava, passion chablis and lehua honey wines

KONA COFFEE MILLS/PLANTATIONS

While other areas of Hawai'i are now growing and producing coffee, the Big
Island is still the only place which grows and produces "pure Kona coffee" just
as it always has. Other islands may speak of their fine island-grown Hawaiian
coffee, but there is still only one "pure Kona coffee." Accept no substitutes!
And while you can pick up your supply at any Big Island supermarket and many
gift shops, you may want to actually visit one of the local coffee mills or
plantations to learn more about how Kona coffee is grown, roasted and milled,
and sip a complimentary cup while you're at it. Check out any of these Kona-
area plantations or coffee mills. Most have free daily tours and tastings.

Bay View Farms, (328-9658) in Honaunau, Kona; visit mill to see coffee
processing and coffee tasting.

Greenwell Farms, (323-2862) at 81-6560 Mamalahoa Highway 11 in Kealakekua; daily visitor tours of coffee groves and facilities.

Holualoa Kona Coffee Co., (322-9937) at 77-6261 Mamalahoa Highway 11 in
Holualoa area; visit coffee milling operation and coffee tasting.

Kahauloa Coffee Co. Plantation and Coffee Shack, (328-9555) at 83-5799
Mamalahoa Highway 11 a mile south of Captain Cook village.

Kona Coffee Emporium, (328-8424) on Mamalahoa Highway 11, three miles
south of Captain Cook village; coffee tasting daily 8AM - 6PM.

Kona Coffee Factory, (328-8239) at 83-5315 Mamalahoa Highway 11 in Captain
Cook; tasting daily 8AM - 6PM.

Langenstein Farm, (328-8356) at 84-4956 Mamalahoa Highway, Captain Cook; tours of processing plant, coffee and macadamia nut orchards and tastings.

Mauna Loa Royal Kona Coffee Mill and Museum, (328-2511) on the Kealakekua Bay Road to Napoopoo from Highway 11.

ANTIQUES

If you are an antique buff, you'll find some interesting antique shops around the island that are worth a browse. You'll find all sorts of antiques, collectibles and old attic items like vintage Aloha shirts and muumuus (women's dresses), soda and milk bottles, plantation-era items, ethnic-related things and lots more. The following is a list of antique shops worth browsing. If you're planning a stop at a particular shop, you might want to call ahead to check on the hours they're open as that can vary.

Antiques-Art-And - in Kealakekua, Kona, next to Kona Bakery (323-2239)

Dragon Mama Futon Shop - 266 Kamehameha Avenue, Hilo (934-9081)

Hanahou - 38 Kalakaua Avenue, Hilo (935-4555)

Honoka'a Market Place - 45-3321 Mamane Street, Honoka'a (775-8255)

Honoka'a Trading Co. - Mamane Street, Honoka'a (775-0808)

Hula Heaven - 75-5744 Alii Drive, Kona Inn Shopping Village, Kailua-Kona
    (329-7885)

Kohala Kollection - Kawaihae Shopping Center, Kawaihae (882-1510)

Mauna Kea Galleries - 276 Keawe Street, Hilo (969-1184)

Mid Pacific Store - 76 Kapiolani St., Hilo, opposite Lyman Museum (935-3822)

Paradise Antiques - 75-5695C Alii Drive, Kona Banyan Court Arcade, Kailua-
                    Kona (334-0533)
Plantation Memories - 179 Kilauea Avenue, Hilo (935-7100)

Seconds to Go Inc. - in Honoka'a (775-9212)

Shibuya Station - 78-7110 Kaluna, Kailua-Kona (322-0715)

Silk Road Gallery - Highway 19, Kawaihae Road in Waimea, Parker Square
                    Center (885-7474)

Statements - 74-5615 Luhia St., #A-1, Kailua-Kona (326-7760)

The Home Place - 197 Keawe Street, Hilo, below Spencer's Gym (935-7494)

Tinny Fisher's Antique Shop - on Highway 19, Mountain View (968-6011)

Treasuretique - 74-5600A Pawai Place, Kailua-Kona (329-3030)

Upcountry Connection Gallery - in Waimea, (885-0623)

The Village Inn Pahoa - in Pahoa (965-6444)

The Vintage Eye - Mamalahoa Highway, Kona (324-1800)

ART GALLERIES/HANDICRAFT SHOPS

Visitors to Hawai'i have a wide choice of souvenir and gift shops at shopping centers and resorts from which to choose mementos and gifts from their vacation in paradise for friends and family back home. See the WHERE TO STAY - WHAT TO SEE chapter for shopping details on each area of the island. However, for authentic made-in-Hawai'i arts and crafts, you need to be selective. Many of the souvenir and gift items in the shops are not necessarily "made-in-Hawai'i" but imported, mostly from the Far East, and passed off as "local." So, be selective. If in doubt as to a product's origin, ask the shop clerk. After all, it's your money. This section lists several art galleries and gift shops which carry a variety of local made-in-Hawai'i artworks and handicrafts by local island artisans.

Hilo/Hamakua

Akaka Falls Inn & Gift Gallery, 28-1676 Mainstreet in Honomu, on the road to Akaka Falls State Park, 963-5468; open daily 9AM - 4PM

Amaury Saint-Gilles Contemporary Fine Art, Paauilo, Highway 19, Hamakua Coast, 776-1800; open Mon-Sat 10AM - 5PM, Sundays/Holidays 10AM - 3PM

Big Island Woodworks, in the S. Hata Building, 308 Kamehameha Avenue, Hilo, 961-0400; open Mon-Sat 9AM - 5PM.

Creative Gifts & Crafts, 249 Keawe Street, Hilo, 934-0611; open Mon-Sat 8:30AM - 5:30PM

Cunningham Gallery, 794 Piilani Street, Hilo, 935-7223; open Mon-Fri 9AM - 5PM, Sat 9:30AM - 4PM

Dan Deluz Woods Inc., 760 Kilauea Avenue, Hilo, 935-5587

Dreams of Paradise, in the S. Hata Building, 308 Kamehameha Avenue, Hilo, 935-5670; open Mon-Sat 10AM - 9PM, Sun 11AM - 4PM

Handmade Treasures, 94 Keawe Street, Hilo, 961-0045; open Mon-Sat 9:30AM -5PM

Hawaii's Artist Ohana, Ishigo Building, Honomu, Hamakua Coast, on the road up to Akaka Falls, 963-5467

Kama'aina Woods, Lehua Street, Honokaa, down the hill from the post office, 775-7722; open Mon-Sat 9AM - 5PM

Mauna Kea Galleries, 276 Keawe Street, Hilo, 969-1184; open Mon-Sat 10AM - 5PM; closed Thursday and Sunday

Oasis Cafe & Crafts, 239 Keawe Street, Hilo, 961-6625; open Tues-Fri 9AM - 5PM, Sat 8:30AM - 4PM, closed Sunday and Monday; they operate a small deli/snack/coffee bar along with their gift shop

Sugawara Lauhala & Gift Shop, 59 Kalakaua Avenue, Hilo, 935-8071

The Warehouse Gallery, 875F Kanoelehua Avenue, Hilo, 935-6518

Waipio Valley Artworks, Kukuihaele, Hamakua Coast, 775-0958

Kohala

Ackerman Galleries, Kapa'au, Kohala, 889-5971; open daily 10AM - 5:30PM

Art Gallery at Waimea Design Center, Opelo Plaza, Kawaihae Road, Waimea, 885-6171; open Mon-Fri 11AM - 7PM and by appointment

Cook's Discoveries, Spencer House at Waimea Center, Waimea, 885-3633; open Mon-Sat 10AM - 6PM, Sundays/Holidays 10AM - 4PM

Dan DeLuz Woods Inc., 64-1013 Mamalahoa Highway, Waimea, 885-5856

Fine Art Galleries of Hawaii, Parker Ranch Center, Waimea, 885-7860

Gallery of Great Things, Parker Square Center, Kawaihae Road, Waimea, 885-7860

Hawaiian Moon Gallery, Hawi, North Kohala, 889-0880

Kailua Village Artists Inc., Royal Waikoloan Hotel, Kohala Coast, 885-6789

Kohala Koa Gallery, Hawi, North Kohala, 889-0055

Kohala Kollection Art & Antiques, Kawaihae Shopping Center, Kohala, 882-1510; open daily 11:30AM - 8:30PM

Mountain Gold Jewel Gallery, 65-1204A Lindsey Road, Waimea, 885-4653; open Mon-Fri 9AM - 5PM, Sat 10AM - 4PM

The Art Center at Mauna Lani, Mauna Lani Resort, Kohala Coast, 885-7779; open Mon-Sat 9:30AM - 6PM, Sunday 12 Noon - 6PM

Upcountry Connection, Mauna Kea Center in Waimea, 885-0623; open Mon-Sat 10AM - 6PM

Wyland Galleries, Hilton Waikoloa Village, Waikoloa Resort, 885-5258; Kings Shops, Waikoloa Resort, 885-8882

Kona

Banana Patch, 76-5942 Mamalahoa Highway, Holualoa, 322-3676; open Tues-Sat 10AM - 4:30PM

Cinderella's, Holualoa, Kona, 322-2474; open Tues-Fri 1-5PM, Sat 11AM - 5PM

Country Frame Shop & Gallery, Holualoa, Kona, 324-1590; open Mon-Fri 9:30AM - 4:30PM, Sat 9:30AM - 1:30PM

Grass Shack, Highway 11, Kealakekua, Kona, 323-2877

Hale O Kula Goldsmith Gallery, Holualoa, Kona, 324-1688; open Tues-Sat 10AM - 4PM

Holualoa Gallery, 76-5921 Mamalahoa Highway, Holualoa, 322-8484; open Tues-Sat 10AM - 5PM

Hulihee Palace Gift Shop, 75-5718 Alii Drive, Kailua-Kona, on grounds of Hulihee Palace, 329-6558; open daily 9AM-4PM

Kailua Village Artists Inc., 75-5660 Palani Road, King Kamehameha Kona Beach Hotel, Kailua-Kona, 329-6653; and in Keauhou Beach Hotel, 78-6740 Alii Drive, Keauhou-Kona, 322-3441

Kimura Lauhala Shop, Mamalahoa Highway, Holualoa, 324-0053; open Mon-Sat 9AM - 5PM

Mele O Polynesian Handcrafts, 75-5660 Palani Road, King Kamehameha Kona Beach Hotel, 326-2205

Neptune's Garden, 75-5669 Alii Drive, across from the pier, Kailua-Kona, 326-7490

Royal Monarch Gallery, 75-5663D Palani Road, Kailua-Kona, 329-7871

Sachi-Nifash Gallery, Holualoa, Kona, 322-2428

Studio 7 Gallery, Holualoa, Kona, 324-1335; open Tues-Sat 10AM - 4PM

Tai Lake Master Woodmaker, 76-5921 Mamalahoa Highway, Holualoa, 324-1598; open Tues-Sat 10AM - 5PM

The Myna Bird Tree, King Kamehameha Mall, 75-5626 Kuakini Highway, Kailua-Kona, 334-1412; open Tues-Sat 10AM - 8PM, Sun 12 Noon - 5PM

The Stenciled Cottage, 74-5600B Pawai Place, Kailua-Kona, 326-3224; open Mon-Fri only 10AM - 4PM

West Hawai'i Arts Guild, 75-5586 Ololi Road, Kona, 329-8535

White Garden Gallery, Holualoa, Kona, 322-7733; open Tues-Sat 10AM - 4PM

Wyland Galleries, Waterfront Row, 75-5770 Alii Drive, Kailua-Kona, 334-0037

Volcano

Kilauea Kreations, in Volcano Village behind Kilauea General Store, 967-8090

Volcano Art Center, Hawai'i Volcanoes National Park, Volcano, 967-7511

Woodcarver's Corner, 19-4005 Haunani Road, Volcano, 985-8518

BOOKSTORES

There are several good bookstores around the island worth browsing for that special Hawaiiana book as a memento of your visit to the Big Island. In addition to the following, several of the major resorts and hotels also have gift and sundry shops which carry books on Hawaii.

Basically Books - 46 Waianuenue Avenue, downtown Hilo, 961-0144

Book Gallery - Prince Kuhio Plaza, 111 E. Puainako, Hilo, 959-7744

Keauhou Village Book Shop - Keauhou Shopping Village, 78-6831 Alii Drive, Keauhou-Kona, 322-8111

Middle Earth Bookshoppe - 75-5719 Alii Drive, Kona Plaza Building, Kailua-Kona, 329-2123

Pueo Bookshop - Waimea Center, Highway 19, Waimea, 885-0039

Waimea General Store - Parker Square Shopping Center, Highway 19, Waimea, 885-4479

Waldenbooks - Prince Kuhio Plaza, 111 E. Puainako, Hilo, 959-6468 and Lanihau Center, 75-5595 Palani Road, Kailua-Kona, 329-0015

THEATRES-MOVIES-STAGE PRODUCTIONS

There are a number of movie theatres around the island which show popular first-run movies. Theatres in Hilo and Kailua-Kona are modern facilities and have nightly showings and weekend matinees. Theatres in the smaller outlying towns tend to be from an earlier era and often shows films only on weekends or selected evenings during the week. But even the smaller theatres show occasional first-run films or old classics and going to one of these classic theatres can be an experience in itself. Check local newspaper listings for current showings or call the theatres at listed numbers.

Akebono Theatre, Pahoa Town, Puna District, 965-9943.

Honokaa Peoples Theatre, Honokaa Town, Hamakua Coast, 775-0000.

Hualalai Theatres, at intersection of Hualalai Road and Kuakini Highway, Kailua-Kona, 329-6641.

Kahei Theatre, Hawi Town, North Kohala District, 889-6831.

Kona Marketplace Cinemas, Alii Drive, Kona Marketplace Shopping Center, Kailua-Kona, 329-4488.

Kress Cinemas, 174 Kamehameha Avenue, downtown Hilo, 961-3456.

Naalehu Theatre, Naalehu Town, Ka'u District, 929-9133.

Prince Kuhio Theatres, Prince Kuhio Shopping Plaza, Hilo, 959-4595.

Waiakea Theatres, Waiakea Square Shopping Center, Hilo, 935-9747.

Stage Productions/Performances

For information on stage productions, performances, concerts and the like, contact any of the following community theatres for details. Most of the community theatres have a seasonal schedule of events.

Aloha Community Players, Kainaliu, Kona, 322-9924.

Hilo Community Players, 141 Kalakaua, Hilo, 935-9155.

Kahilu Theatre, Parker Ranch Center, Kamuela, 885-6017.

Waimea Community Theatre, Kamuela, 885-5818.

University of Hawai'i-Hilo Theatre, 200 W. Kawili Street, Hilo, 933-3350.

SELF-SERVICE LAUNDRIES

Most hotels and condo units have a laundry service available, either the commercial send-out type or in-house coin-operated machines. Check with your front desk. For those in need of self-service laundries, there are a few located around the island. Hours of operation may vary.

Ed's Laundromat, Na'alehu Shopping Center, Na'alehu, Ka'u District, just off Highway 11 in town center, open daily 6AM - 10PM.

Hale Haloi, Kealakekua Shopping complex, Highway 11, next to Cap's Drive In, open daily 6AM - 10AM.

Heli Mai Laundromat, Kailua-Kona, Palani Road and Kuakini Highway a block above the King Kam Hotel, North Kona Shopping Center, 329-3494; open daily 5AM - 11PM.

Hilo Quality Cleaners Coin Laundry, 210 Hoku, Hilo, 961-6490; open Monday through Saturday only, 5AM - 10PM.

Jupiter Cleaners & Laundry, in the village of Kainaliu, Kona, 322-2929; open daily 6AM - 9PM.

Lole Wai Laundry, in the heart of Waimea across from the Waimea Shopping Center, 885-4696; open daily 5AM - 12 midnight.

Motherload Washerette, Honoka'a, just off the main street of town next to the Dairy Queen, 775-9788; open daily 6AM - 10PM.

Suds n' Duds Laundromat, Keaau Town Center, Keaau; open daily 7:30AM - 8:30PM, Sunday open until 7:30PM only.

The Wash Laundromat, Hawaiian Ranchos Center, Hawaiian Oceanview Estates, South Kona; open daily 6AM - 8PM.

Tyke's Laundromat, 74-5583 Pawai Place, Kailua-Kona, 326-1515; open daily, 6AM - 10PM; and at 1454 Kilauea Avenue, Hilo, 935-1093.

ANNUAL BIG ISLAND EVENTS

The following is only a partial listing of the many social, cultural, community, and sporting events that take place around the Big Island annually. The events are listed monthly only since the exact dates change yearly. Many events have numerous related activities like the annual Merrie Monarch Hula Festival in April which features hula dance and music, a parade, and arts and crafts demonstrations and displays of Hawaiiana. The same is true for many of the holiday celebrations, cultural fairs, and other events. For more specific information on dates, locations, etc., contact the Hawai'i County Research & Development Office at (808) 961-8366 in Hilo, or the Hawai'i Visitors Bureau-Big Island Chapter in Hilo at (808) 961-5797 or in Kona at (808) 329-7787. For additional listings of events see the local Big Island newspapers and visitor periodicals where you are staying.

JANUARY
"Hauoli Makahiki Hou" (Happy New Year celebrations) - Islandwide
Hilo to Volcano 31-Mile Ultra Marathon and Relay - Hilo
Keauhou Open Pro-Am Golf Tourney - Kona
Hawai'i County Band Jazz Concert - Hilo
Hawaiian Paradise Mountain Bike Challenge - Pohakuloa
Senior Skins Golf Tournament - Mauna Lani Resort
"Kung Hee Fat Choy" (Chinese New Year celebrations) - Island-wide

FEBRUARY
La Pa'ani (Hawaiian Sports Day) - Kona
Free Style Ski Meet - Mauna Kea ski slopes
Hawai'i County Band Guest Conductor Concert - Hilo
Big Island High School Basketball Tournament - Hilo
Annual Hilo Mardi Gras - Hilo
Annual Dr. Richard Mamiya Golf Tournament - Hilo Municipal Course

MARCH
Kona Marathon - Kona
Big Island Auto Show - Hilo
Big Island Plant Show/Sale - Hilo
International Hawai'i Ski Cup Meet - Mauna Kea ski slopes
Haili Men's Volleyball Tournament - Hilo
Kona Stampede Rodeo - Kona
Miss Aloha Hawai'i Pageant - Hilo
Hawai'i County Band Concert - Hilo
Prince Kuhio Day Holiday
Pele's Cup Mauna Loa Cross Country ski race - Big Island

APRIL
Moku-O-Hawai'i Volleyball Tournament - Hilo
Big Island School Band Festival - Hilo
Buddhist "Hanamatsuri" Festival - Island-wide
Boy Scout "Makahiki" Show - Island-wide
Hawai'i County Band Concert - Hilo
Paniolo Skier's Challenge - Mauna Kea ski slopes
Easter Sunrise Services - Island-wide
Merrie Monarch Hula Festival - Hilo
Merrie Monarch Hawaiian Quilt Show - Hilo
Saddle Road 100k Ultra Marathon and Relay - Hilo to Waimea
Pu'ukohola Educational Festival - Kawaihae
Pua Plantasia horticulture-flower show - Kailua-Kona

MAY
May Day-Lei Day Observances - Island-wide
Hulihe'e Palace Lei Contest - Kailua-Kona
John Kekua, Sr. Canoe Regatta - Hilo Bay
Kawaihae Canoe Regatta - Kawaihae
Kona Gold Jackpot Fishing Tournament - Kona
Kona Mauka Troller's Wahine Fishing Tournament - Kona
Visitor Industry Charity Walk - Kona
Kona Iki Troller's Jackpot Fishing Tournament - Kona
Hawai'i County Band Concert - Hilo
Golden Goddess Fishing Tournament - Hilo
Miss Filipina Hawai'i Pageant - Hilo
"I Luna Lilo" Mauna Loa Hike to summit - Volcanoes National Park
Annual Keauhou-Kona Triathlon - Kona
The Mauna Kea 200 Motorcycle Enduro - Hilo
Judi's Polynesian Dance Studio Recital - Hilo
Queen Liliuokalani Canoe Regatta - Kona
Memorial Day Observances - Island-wide

JUNE
King Kamehameha Holua Ski Meet - Mauna Kea ski slopes
Big Island Shoreline Fishing Tourney - Island-wide
Kamehameha Celebration Canoe Regatta - Kona

JUNE (Continued)
King Kamehameha Day (June 11) Celebrations/Parades - Island-wide
Lei-draping of King Kamehameha statue (June 11) - Kapa'au Courthouse, Kohala
Kauikeaouli Canoe Regatta - Kona
Kona Iki Trollers Fishing Tournament - Kona
Wailani Canoe Regatta - Hilo Bay
Big Island Massed Band Concert - Hilo
Miss Jr. Sampaguita Pageant - Hilo
Buddhist Obon Festivals - Island-wide Buddhist temples
Hawai'i Quarterhorse Show - Waiki'i Ranch, Kohala
Waiki'i Music Festival - Waiki'i Ranch, Kohala

JULY
Hapuna Rough Water Swim - Hapuna Beach, Kohala
Moku-O-Hawai'i Big Island Canoe Regatta Championship - TBA
Hawai'i County Band July 4th. Concert - Hilo
Annual July 4th. Naalehu Town Carnival & Rodeo - Naalehu
Annual Fourth Fest - Hilo and Island-wide
Cuisines of the Sun Food Festival - Mauna Lani Bay Hotel & Bungalows
Pu'uhonua O Honaunau Cultural Festival - Honaunau, Kona
Buddhist Obon Festivals - Island-wide Buddhist temples
Annual Big Island Bonsai Show - Hilo
Annual Hilo Orchid Society Show - Hilo
Annual July 4th. Parker Ranch Rodeo and Horse Races - Waimea
Kona Mauka Trollers Fishing Tournament - Kona
Okinawan Cultural Festival Haari Boat Races - Hilo
Big Island Slack Key Guitar Festival - Hilo
Mauna Kea Beach Hotel Annual Pro-Am Golf Tournament - Kohala
Turtle Independence Day - Mauna Lani Bay Hotel, Kohala
Keaukaha Canoe Race - Hilo Bay
Kona Ahi Jackpot Fishing Tournament - Kona
Annual International Festival of the Pacific - Hilo
Mountain Bike Race - Kulani Forest, Hilo
Keauhou-Kona Women's Golf Tourney - Kona
Kilauea Volcano Marathon and Rim Run - Volcano
Hawaiian International Billfish Pro-Am Tournament - Kona
Annual Hawai'i Anthurium Association Show - Hilo

AUGUST
Dan Nathaniel Sr. Canoe Race - Hilo
Hawaiian International Billfish Tournament - Kona
Hawai'i County Band Concert - Kona
Buddhist Obon Festivals - Island-wide Buddhist temples
Greater Mana to Kamuela Footrace 10K Run - Waimea
Kona Mauka Trollers Fall Fishing Tournament - Kona
Kona Fil-Am Women's Fast Pitch Softball Tourney - Kona
Great Waikoloa Open Golf Tournament - Waikoloa
Kona A'lure Women's Fishing Tournament - Kona
A.J. McDonald Canoe Race - Kona
Pu'ukohola Heiau Cultural Festival - Kawaihae

AUGUST (Continued)
Senior Citizens Softball Tournament - Hilo
Lydia Kamakaeha Canoe Race - Kawaihae
Kona Iki Trollers "Keiki" Fishing Tourney - Kona
Sand Castle & Sculpture Contest - Kona
Miss Latina Pageant - Hilo
Queen Liliuokalani Canoe Race - Kona
Horseshoe Pitching Championship - Kona
Kauikeaouli/Kona Gardens Canoe Race - Kona
Admissions Day Holiday Celebrations - Island-wide
National Park Service Day - Pu'uhonua O Honaunau, Kona
Ho'ola'a, Aloha Festival Royal Court Investiture - Volcano

SEPTEMBER
Big Island Bounty Food Fest - Sheraton Orchid Mauna Lani
Hawai'i County Fair - Hilo and Kailua-Kona
Big Island Aloha Week Festivals - Island-wide
Paniolo Parade - Waimea
Sam Choy Poke Contest - Waimea
Parker Ranch Roundup Rodeo - Waimea
Hilo Trollers Championship Fishing Tourney - Hilo
Senior Citizens Fishing Derby - Hilo, Kona
Keiki Deep Sea Fishing Tourney - Kona
Golden Marlin Jackpot Fishing Tourney - Kona
Duke's Kona Classic Fishing Tournament - Kona
Concert in the Park - Hilo
Iwalani O Ke Kai Jackpot Fishing Tourney - Kona
Senior Citizens Hawai'i Friendship Festival - Hilo, Kona
Kona Nightingale Donkey Race - Kona
Okoe Bay Rendezvous Marlin Fishing Tournament - Ka'u

OCTOBER
Aloha Festival Ho'olaulea - Hilo
Mauna Loa Macadamia Nut Festival & Parade - Hilo
Ironman World Triathlon Championship - Kona, Kohala
Octoberfest Harvest Festival - Hilo
Kona Coffee Cultural Festival & Parade - Kailua-Kona
Bario Fiesta - Hilo
Great Waikoloa Golf Tourney - Waikoloa
Kohala Coast Senior's Golf Classic - Waikoloa
Kohala Country Fair - Kohala
Taro Festival - Honoka'a/Hamakua Coast
Annual Kohala Club Rodeo - Waimea
Big Island "Karaoke" Singing Contest - Hilo
Concert in the Park - Hilo

NOVEMBER
Festival of Trees - Kona
Annual Kings Cup Amateur Golf Tournament - Waikoloa
Veteran's Day Observances - Island-wide
Kupuna Hula Competition - Kona
La Pa'aui (Hawaiian Sports Day) - Kona
Hawai'i Cattlemen's Bull and Horse Show Sale - Waikoloa
University of Hawai'i-Hilo Vulcans Basketball Classic - Hilo
Christmas in the Country - Volcano
Kilauea Lei Making Contest - Volcanoes National Park
Big Island Ultraman Endurance Triathlon - Island-wide
Christmas Arts and Crafts Fair - Kamuela
Christmas Parade - Kona
Concert in the Park - Hilo
YWCA Festival of Trees - Hilo

DECEMBER
Christmas Parades - Island-wide towns
Christmas Arts and Crafts Shows - Kona, Hilo
Christmas at Hulihe'e Palace - Kailua-Kona
Mauna Lani Bay Hotel Golf Tourney - Kohala Coast
Paniolo Golf Tourney - Kona
Christmas Fantasy - Honoka'a
Lyman House Museum's "A Christmas Tradition" - Hilo
Gingerbread Wonderland and Twelve Days of Hawaiian Christmas -
       Mauna Lani Bay Hotel, Kohala
Christmas Concert in the Park - Hilo
Mauna Kea Beach Hotel Golf Tourney - Kohala Coast
Annual Christmas Concerts - UH-Hilo Theatre, Hilo
Japanese New Year's Mochi (Good Luck) Rice Pounding - Island-wide

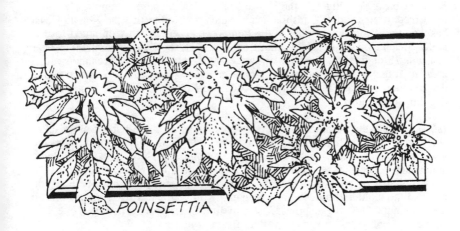

POINSETTIA

BIG ISLAND WEATHER

The Big Island's weather is a case of variety and extremes. The Big Island claims both the driest locality in the State as well as the wettest population center in the islands. Hawai'i lies well within the belt of northeasterly trade winds generated by the semi-permanent Pacific high pressure cell to the northeast. The climate of the island is greatly influenced by terrain. Its outstanding features are the marked variations in rainfall by elevation and from place to place, the persistent northeasterly trade winds in areas exposed to them, and the equable year around temperatures in localities near sea level.

Over the island's east windward slopes, rainfall occurs principally in the form of showers within the ascending moist trade winds. Mean annual rainfall, except for the semi-sheltered Hamakua district, increases from 100 inches or more along the coasts to a maximum of over 300 inches at elevations of 2000-3000 ft. and declines to about 15 inches at the summits of Mauna Kea and Mauna Loa. In general, the southern and western leeward areas are sheltered from the trades by the high mountains and are therefore drier. Mean annual rainfall may range from 20-30 inches along the coasts to 120 inches at elevations of 2500-3000 ft.

DRESSING FOR THE WEATHER: Comfortable summer type wear is suitable all year round on the Big Island. Dress is casual. However, a warm sweater or jacket would be useful for cool evening breezes or for visits to cool areas like Volcanoes National Park or Waimea ranch country. And if you plan hiking excursions, you may find light raingear useful. For treks to Mauna Kea or Mauna Loa, resort wear is definitely out. It can snow at any time of the year on either mountain and very cold weather can be experienced at any time at high elevations. Appropriate dress is in order.

KOHALA AND KONA: The driest area on the Big Island, and in the State with an average annual rainfall of less than 10 inches, is the coastal strip just leeward of the southern portion of the Kohala Mountains and of the saddle between the Kohalas and Mauna Kea. This is the area surrounding Kawaihae Bay on the Kohala Coast. Not long ago, the Hawai'i State Planning and Economic Development Department did a "Sunshine Map" study and found that the Kohala Coast has the highest sunshine rating in the state - even higher than such noted resorts as Ka'anapali on Maui and Waikiki on O'ahu. Kohala also maintains a near constant 78 degrees F. the year around. The Kailua-Kona and Keauhou resort areas average about 20 inches of rainfall annually. With such consistent sunny dry weather it is easy to see why the Kona and Kohala areas have become such popular destinations.

HILO: And then we have Hilo. Poor Hilo! It has been the butt of more jokes about its rain than there are umbrellas to sell. It seems that down through the years, people have taken a special delight in maligning Hilo for its rather damp atmosphere. They make up stories about how you don't tan in Hilo, you rust! They say that in Hilo, you have to keep moving and never look behind you because the mold and mildew may be gaining on you! They even say it rains all the time in the City of Rainbows. That is definitely not true. There was one day, oh a couple of years ago, when it didn't rain at all.

All kidding aside, it does rain an awful lot in Hilo, more than any other population center in the Hawaiian archipelago. Within the city of Hilo average rainfall varies from about 130 inches a year near the shore to as much as 200 inches in mountain sections. The wettest part of the island, with a mean annual rainfall exceeding 300 inches, lies about 6 miles up-slope from the city limits. Rain falls about 280 days a year in the Hilo area.

In fact, Hilo is recognized as the rainiest city in the United States by the U.S. Census Bureau's County and City Data Book. Hilo has the highest average annual rainfall, 128.15 inches, of any of the nation's cities with a population of 25,000 or more. Interestingly, Hilo's total rainfall in 1990 surpassed all previous records when 211.22 inches of rain were recorded. Needless to say, even Hiloans were in awe of Nature's abundance. But then as recently as 1995, Hilo recorded the fourth driest year of the century when just 85.87 inches of rain fell during the year.

But with such a soggy reputation, Hilo certainly doesn't need any more detractors. In fact, it really isn't as bad as one would think. Many of the showers are brief passing ones and according to statistics, three-quarters of Hilo's rain falls at night. Thus it doesn't spoil most daytime visitor activities. Also, the number of clear to partly sunny days far surpasses the number of totally cloudy-rainy days annually.

Another thing about Hilo's infamous rain is that it is equally distributed throughout the year. There is no distinct wet or dry season. Hilo's temperatures remain fairly constant also, averaging a high of 81 degrees F. and a low of 66 degrees F. the year round. And although the relative humidity in Hilo is in the moderate to high range as would be expected, the weather is seldom oppressive and uncomfortable due to the natural ventilation and cooling provided by the prevailing ocean breezes.

And like the Kona-Kohala climate that has provided such marvelous conditions for resorts and the visitor industry, Hilo's climate has created special conditions also. Only in Hilo and the surrounding area will you find the lush tropical beauty of the rainforest jungle, breathtaking waterfalls cascading down green gulches, and acres of gorgeous tropical flowers like anthuriums, orchids, bird-of-paradise, ginger, and others. The ample tropical rain makes Hilo and the windward side of the Big Island a real paradise. Even with its sodden reputation as a rainy old town, Hilo indeed is a special place for many people.

TRADE WINDS: Trade winds are an almost constant wind blowing from the northeast through the east averaging 5-15 mph and are caused by the Pacific anticyclone, a high pressure area. The cell remains fairly stationary in the summer (May through October) causing the trades to blow steadily 90% of the time bringing cooling relief for the generally warmer temperatures. In winter (November through April), interruptions diminish the winds constancy and they blow 40%-60% of the time with competing weather fronts, storms, etc.

KONA WEATHER: Hot, humid, and muggy weather is called Kona weather and is often due to an interruption of the trade winds. The trades are replaced by light variable winds and are most noticeable during the warmer summer months. Kona winds may also bring storm fronts and rain from the southwest, the opposite direction from which storms generally approach the islands. Kona storms are noted for their ferocity, bringing high winds, surf, and rain and have occasionally caused property damage.

HURRICANES: Hawai'i lies in the hurricane belt and is susceptible to these tropical cyclones from June through December. These storms carry severe winds of between 75 and 150 mph and are often marked by rain, thunder, and lightning. Most are spawned along the coast of Mexico and follow the trade winds in a westerly direction across the Pacific. Some are born close to the equator and move north. Since 1950, over a hundred hurricanes have been recorded in Hawaiian waters. Of these, only a few have passed nearby or directly struck parts of the Hawaiian Islands. Hurricane Iwa in 1982 and Hurricane Iniki in 1992 did extensive damage and that was mostly confined to the island of Kaua'i and to a lesser extent on O'ahu.

TSUNAMIS

Hawai'i is susceptible to tsunamis or tidal waves. Over the last century and a half, nine major tsunamis have caused moderate to severe damage and numerous deaths along affected coastlines. Although some tidal waves are locally generated from earthquakes, most of Hawai'i's tidal wave threats originate in South America or Alaska's Aleutian Islands. On the Big Island, Hilo is particularly vulnerable to tsunamis due to the funnel shape of Hilo Bay allowing an already speeding tidal wave to concentrate its force upon reaching land. An Aleutian Islands tsunami in 1946 rolled into Hilo pushing the water to 10 meters above sea level in some places. The death toll reached 83 and property damage was extensive. In 1960, a Chilean generated tsunami struck Hilo at a speed of 65 kilometers per hour and wreaked havoc along Hilo's bayfront destroying a major residential and business section. The water rolled in 11 meters high and 61 people were killed. There have been a few tidal waves generated by Big Island earthquakes as well. There is a statewide Tsunami Warning System in place and the Hawai'i Civil Defense System also coordinates disaster programs. Warning sirens and TV-radio broadcasts indicate approaching danger around all the islands. If you are on a beach or low lying coastal area when you receive such a warning, you must immediately seek higher ground as far away from the coast as possible.

EARTHQUAKES

Because of its volcanic origins, earthquakes are part of Hawai'i's geosystem. Volcanic eruptions on the Big Island are often preceded and accompanied by earthquakes. Few of these are generally strong enough to be felt or cause any damage. Major earthquakes are the result of fault action. Some of these faults are on the ocean floor while others are volcano related. Volcanic earthquakes are caused when sections of a volcano's inner works shift prior to erupting. It is usually associated with the inflation or deflation of a lava reservoir beneath the mountain as the lava swells or drains away.

TROPICAL PHOTOGRAPHY

Most folks who come to Hawai'i to vacation bring a camera to record some of those memorable and exciting scenes and experiences to enjoy again when they get back home. If nothing else, they take a lot of pictures to show off to their friends and relatives and to help them relive their dream vacation in Hawai'i.

And among the exotic places around the world in which to practice travel photography, Hawai'i certainly ranks among the best for beauty, adventure, and cultural attraction. Your picture taking journey through Hawai'i will be greatly enhanced with an awareness of some special factors that affect photography in the tropics. Good travel photographs are the result of forethought, organization, and good judgement before and during the trip. For those contemplating some photography while in Hawai'i, this is a good time to discuss some ideas garnered from several years of work in travel-photojournalism in paradise. Regardless of whether you use a sophisticated SLR (single lens reflex) camera, a compact "point and shoot" automatic type camera, or an instant picture camera such as a Polaroid, a little careful thought and planning will help you get travel pictures of which you'll be proud. The end results will be memorable pictures that will allow you to relive again and again the adventure and excitement of your visit to Hawai'i.

EQUIPMENT: Before you leave home on your trip, you should be intimately familiar with your camera's basic operations. You should run through a roll or two of film just prior to your trip to make sure that all systems are go. Be familiar with all the settings on your camera and install a fresh set of batteries. The majority of camera failures are due to dead batteries. There's nothing worse than being in the field ready for that picture of a lifetime only to have your camera fail due to a $3 set of batteries. Take along an extra set as well.

If you are using a single lens reflex camera (Nikon, Canon, Pentax, Minolta, etc.) you have a choice of lenses for your particular equipment. The standard lens is the normal 50mm which is a general purpose lens for most photographic situations. For those situations where you need more horizontal depth and width, such as panoramic scenes, you will need a wide angle lens. These lenses range from very wide 13-20mm to more narrow scope 24-35mm.

For candid portrait shots or scenes and action that are far away, you will need a telephoto lens. Telephoto lenses allow you to bring the scene or action closeup without moving closer to the subject. Telephotos are both medium, 85-105mm, and long range, 180mm to over 1000mm, in focal length. Zoom lenses cover several combined focal lengths, allowing one lens to replace several. There are wide angle zooms, 28-45mm to 43-86mm, and telephoto zooms ranging from 35-105mm to 360-1200mm. Closeup capability can also be achieved with an inexpensive set of screw-in closeup lenses which look very much like filters that fit over the front of a regular lens. Or you can invest in a macro lens built especially for extreme closeup work. For most practical purposes you'll probably find that a normal 50mm, a medium wide angle 24mm or a wide angle zoom, and a telephoto zoom of 75-200mm will cover most of your picture taking situations adequately. But, lens choice is a matter of what kind of photos you're after, personal taste, and budget.

FILM: There is a wide choice of films available. If you plan to shoot color (and what other way is there to capture the essence of Hawai'i?) you have a choice of color negative and color positive films. For snapshot prints to put in an album, you will want to choose a brand name film that ends with the suffix *-color*. These films produce negatives from which prints or enlargements are made. If you plan on projecting your photos using a slide projector, then you will want to use a brand name film with the suffix *-chrome*. These films produce a positive/-transparency image directly on the film, the so-called "what you see is what you get" image as you look through your camera's viewfinder. Films have varying ASA/ISO ratings, or film speeds, for varied light conditions and applications. The newer color print films range from 100 up to 1000 for average daylight to dim low light conditions. For positive/transparency films, the ASA/ISO ratings range from 25 up to 400 for average to low light conditions.

A good choice for all purposes would be a *-color* film rated at 100-200 and a *-chrome* film rated at 64-100. If you choose to shoot your pictures in black and white to make enlargements, a good choice would be ASA/ISO 100 or 400 speed film. These negative films will give good results with natural or artificial lighting.

A final thought on film is in order. How much do you bring with you? Well, like everything else, film is more expensive in Hawai'i, probably about 25% more than on the US mainland. You'd be better off to bring your own supply, however, you'll have no problem in buying film once here. Compared to airfare, lodging, and meals, film is cheap, so load up and shoot away!

ACCESSORIES: For taking pictures in extremely low light situations include a flash unit in your equipment. Besides providing general lighting when the available natural lighting is insufficient, flash allows you to fill in and highlight shadow areas on otherwise normal subjects. Flash units for SLR cameras are inexpensive and easy to use. Many automatic compact cameras have built in flash units, virtually taking the guesswork out of flash photography.

The most frequently used filters are the UV (ultra violet) and Skylight. These filters are designed to cut haze and reduce blue tones in some scenes. Professional photographers often keep them on lenses permanently to provide protection for the lens surface. The filters require little exposure adjustment and if your camera has a through-the-lens meter it will adjust automatically. In tropical photography, the Polarizing filter helps darken blue sky, makes clouds stand out more dramatically, and most importantly reduces reflections and glares from bright shining surfaces such as glass, water, sand, etc. For sky scenes, the Polarizing filter must be used at right angles to the sun. Another way to achieve this effect, without a Polarizer, is to increase the ASA/ISO film speed setting of your camera. If you are using ASA 64 slide film, for example, increase the setting to ASA 80. This will allow the camera aperture to compensate its exposure accordingly. For black and white films, red, orange, or yellow filters also produce varying degrees of enhancement.

Other accessories you should have are a sturdy camera bag, a light-weight tripod for telephoto and closeup shots, a cable release, a can of compressed air for dust removal, a soft lens brush, liquid lens cleaner, and tissues. An optional item you might consider would be a lead-lined film bag for transporting your film through airport security x-ray machines. Better yet is to avoid the cumulative effect of airport x-rays which can damage films, request a visual inspection of your film and camera equipment as you pass through security checkpoints. Most security personnel will cooperate if you request a hand-inspection.

SHOOTING ON LOCATION: Once you are finally in Hawai'i on location, you can begin to take advantage of all its unique and wondrous natural and geographic features to produce some excellent photographs. The dazzling colors and contrasting scenes of tropical flowers, golden beaches, puffy white clouds, cobalt blue sky, mystic jungles, stark lavaflows, green hills, blue-green ocean, dramatic sunsets, and multi-ethnic peoples will provide plenty of opportunity for picture taking. And because Hawai'i's sun is very strong, especially during the hours it is directly overhead, there are deep shadows and bright glare that interfere with photography. If you are shooting in heavily shadowed areas, use your flash to fill in dark areas, especially on people's faces. Be aware of shadows creeping into the composition as you look through the viewfinder to compose your shot. Use your flash indoors as well as outdoors under the shade of trees or on your shaded hotel lanai and even in shady areas of attractions you visit. If you are shooting a sunset with people in the foreground facing the camera, use your flash again to fill in otherwise the people will appear as silhouettes.

SPECIAL FACTORS: In Hawai'i you will be faced with two climatic extremes that can be hazardous to photography: rain and hot sun. Depending on the season and locale, rain can be frequent and heavy. However, with adequate raingear and plastic camera covers you can still shoot pictures even in the rain. One good point about rainy pictures is that soft subtle lighting can create special effects on your subjects and give your pictures a different accent and mood. Rainy days can also cause you to look inside for interesting subjects you may otherwise pass up.

At the other extreme is the glaring hot sun. The usual mid-day tropical sun is harsh, brilliant, and bright. In this light, as mentioned earlier, heavy shadows

almost always creep into photographs. Be aware of them and learn to compensate for them. If your camera has a built-in light meter, take a reading for both light and shadow areas of your scene and then average it out. Bracket your pictures one aperture stop above and below what the camera meter reads out to ensure that one of your photos will be perfect. Keep in mind that the early morning and early evening hours are best for picture taking because the light is usually soft, mellow, and golden, allowing dramatic picture opportunities.

Other potential problem sources for photographers in Hawai'i are the infamous three "S's": sun, sand, and salt spray. Any one of these can wreak havoc with your camera and film. The sun produces heat very fast in Hawai'i, especially in enclosed locked cars where folks often leave cameras and film unattended for long hours. Too much heat can ruin the emulsions of your film and adversely affect your camera's mechanism. The car will actually act like an oven and "bake" your film and equipment. So avoid leaving your camera equipment and film in a closed up car in the hot sun.

Sand from the beach is another problem. Fine gritty sand can get into the camera's mechanism, on the mirror, and lens. Sand can scratch and damage very easily. Protect your camera when you're on the beach. Don't put it down in direct contact with sand.

Finally, the fine misty salt spray from ocean surf is very corrosive to camera bodies and lenses. After shooting on or near the beach and ocean, thoroughly clean your camera with a soft cloth, lens cleaner and tissues.

Hawai'i provides unlimited picture taking possibilities. Go after them wherever they may be. But remember to use good judgement and be aware of the special factors that affect photography in the tropics. As time goes by you will be glad that you took the time to think, plan, and organize properly for your photography before and during your visit to this splendorous land called Hawai'i.

WHERE TO STAY -
WHAT TO SEE

INTRODUCTION

The Big Island has some 7000 hotel rooms, 2300 condominium units available for vacation rentals and anywhere from 300-500 or more spaces in bed and breakfast operations island-wide. The hotel room count includes standard resort and visitor center hotels as well as several small lodges, inns and varied accommodations in outlying towns and villages in the country. The range includes inexpensive to very expensive, from simple rooms with a shared kitchen and cooking privileges, to plush suites with inclusive meal packages and personal butler. The Big Island has three major visitor centers: the Kona Coast including *Kailua-Kona* and the Keauhou area, the Kohala Coast, and Hilo. Other accommodations are located in the Hamakua, North Kohala, Puna and Ka'u districts. This section contains a list of condominiums which have units in rental programs as well as hotels and related accommodations. In addition, there is a section on park campgrounds and cabins.

HOW TO USE THIS CHAPTER: To make it easy to locate information on accommodations, the various properties are first indexed alphabetically following this introduction. The listings are then arranged by geographic area beginning with the Kona Coast (including both the Kailua-Kona and Keauhou areas), followed by the Kohala Coast, and then Hilo, and the outlying country areas of Hamakua, North Kohala, Puna and Ka'u. Each geographic section begins with a description of the area, sights to see, shopping information, and then a listing of the accommodations. For each there is the local address, telephone and/or toll free number, and booking or rental agent(s) handling units at that property.

The Big Island, as does the rest of Hawai'i, has a summer off season (low) and a winter peak season (high) that affects supply and demand in accommodations, etc. The off season (low) is generally May 1 to November 30 and the peak season (high) is from December 1 to April 30. Within the low season, there are also two periods that are traditionally quite slow for Hawai'i's visitor industry. These are the times from Easter to approximately June 1 and from Labor Day to December 1. These "slack" periods are good times to take advantage of discounts on hotel rooms, car rentals, etc. The off season usually brings lower prices, discounts, special rates and room-car packages while peak season demand will keep room rates at a premium at most hotels and condominiums. Hilo hotels are not as prone to fluctuations in seasonal demand for accommodations as are the Kona and Kohala area hotels. However, room rates may vary somewhat by high and low season. Check to see what seasonal rates apply when booking your reservations as many properties' high-low seasons vary slightly. Rates in the hotel/condo listings cover the range of low and high season pricing. Some hotels/condos have a flat year-around rate so there is only one rate given.

Rates quoted for the hotels are the standard industry "rack rates" and most current available at the time of publication and are, of course, subject to change without notice. However, hotel "rack rates" are something that are seldom paid by guests since the majority of reservation bookings are done at discounted rates of one type or another. If you're doing your own booking, be sure to ask for the lowest possible rate quote or special discount being offered. A good travel agent can also assist in obtaining discounted rate quotes or specials. There are all sorts of special room/car packages, golf packages, tennis packages, honeymoon packages, "returning guest" packages, etc. So inquire before you confirm your rate. If you are a senior citizen, ask for "Senior Citizen Discounts," as more hotels and condos are offering such discounts for those 55 years and over.

Since the last edition of this book, hotel/condo room rates have changed little and some have even decreased. The tourism slowdown the past few years has been partly responsible and that means better room rates for Big Island visitors.

Accommodation rates listed in this section are for double occupancy (2 people) unless otherwise specified. Additional persons are charged from $10-15 per night at most places except the first-class properties where the extra person rate may be from $25-35 per night.

All properties have a swimming pool unless otherwise noted. Condos have kitchens and parking unless otherwise noted. The abbreviations o.f., p.o.v., o.v., g.v., and f.v. refer to oceanfront, partial oceanview, oceanview, gardenview and fairway view units. Additional listing codes are as follows: S-Studio, BR-Bedroom, PH-Penthouse, KF-Kitchen Facilities, Condo-Condominium unit, Cott.-Cottage, (W)-Accommodate wheelchairs.

Note: All hotels, motels, inns, condominiums, etc. in Hawai'i will add on a 10% tax on all accommodations charges. This includes a 4% sales tax and 6% hotel room tax.

Hotels and condominium listings marked with a ★ indicate a property that is an exceptional value due to location, cleanliness, services and amenities available, and general comfort, and not necessarily luxury. In the "What to See and Do" sections, a ★ indicates a worthwhile attraction or activity.

GENERAL POLICIES: All hotels and bed & breakfast operations are identified as such while all the rest are condominiums even though some don't use the term "condominium" in their name. Condominiums and rental agents usually require a reservation deposit equal to one or two night's rental to secure a confirmed reservation and some also require a security deposit. Some charge higher deposits during winter or peak season holidays like Christmas-New Year's. Generally a 30 day notice of cancellation is needed to receive a full refund although some charge a cancellation fee. Most condos and agents require payment in full either 30 days prior to or upon arrival.

Most condos also require a minimum stay of 3 nights and some have 5 and even 7 night minimums or longer in the winter and during peak holiday seasons. The peak winter season brings heavy demand for condo units and the restrictions, cancellation policies, and payment policies are much more stringent. It is not uncommon to book as much as two years in advance for the Christmas-New Year's season. If a condominium listing does not show a rental agent, you can address your correspondence to the manager. Some condo resident managers do not handle reservations and thus you should contact the rental agents listed for those properties. See the individual condo listings and/or the list of BOOKING AGENTS.

NOTE: The Big Island has experienced a housing shortage over the last few years, especially in the Kona and Kohala areas. Because of this the real estate market is in a very fluid state, affected by local and national economic influences. This affects the availability of short term "vacation rental" units at condominiums as many are being changed to long term residential. Thus, the prices/rates for condo rentals in this section are subject to change at any time as are the availability of "vacation rentals" at any condominium.

ACCOMMODATIONS INDEX

BED AND BREAKFAST LODGING

Bed and Breakfast operations on the Big Island have grown significantly over the past few years. The industry has expanded so rapidly that the County of Hawai'i and industry representatives have cooperated in establishing standards and guidelines for the operation of B&Bs. These popular accommodations are an alternative to the usual resort condominium and hotel room, and often less costly. B&Bs, as they're often called, provide a range of accommodations from clean simple rooms to, in some cases, luxurious well-appointed suites.

On the Big Island, B&Bs offer the chance to stay in everything from a renovated 1930's/40's-era sugar plantation home, a historic old missionary-era home, a cedar log house in cool quiet upcountry forest land, ranch homes and cottages in Parker Ranch country, or a modern home with lovely coastal views as well as more traditional family residences of Big Islanders. In most cases, B&Bs provide visitors a more homey atmosphere and a chance to get to know local folks more personally. They usually include, as the name implies, a continental-style breakfast which varies with each individual operation. B&Bs generally appeal to adventurous travelers who want a different lodging experience apart from the usual excitement of the hotel or resort center.

For directories, information and reservations at B&B operations on all islands of Hawai'i, contact the following reservations services:

A'anene B & B Reservations, P.O. Box 597, Volcano, HI 96785, 1-808-985-8673

All Islands B & B, 823 Kainui Drive, Kailua, O'ahu, HI 96734
1-800-542-0344 or 808 263-2342 or FAX 808 263-0308

Bed & Breakfast Hawai'i, P.O. Box 449, Kapa'a, Kaua'i, HI 96746
1-800-822-7771 or FAX 808 822-2723

B & B Honolulu, 3242 Kaohinani Drive, Honolulu, HI 96817
1-800-288-4666 or 808 595-7533 or FAX 808 595-2030

Go Native...Hawai'i B & B, P.O. Box 11418, Hilo, HI 96721
1-800-662-8483 or 808 935-4178

Hawai'i's Best B & B, P.O. Box 563, Kamuela, HI 96743
1-800-262-9912 or 808 885-4550 or FAX 808 885-0559

Hawai'i Island B & B Association, P.O. Box 1890, Honokaa, HI 96727
(No phone-provides listing of member B & B's on Big Island only)

Hawaiian Islands B & B, 1277 Mokulua Drive, Kailua, HI 96734
1-800-258-7895 or 808 261-7895 or FAX 808 262-2181

My Island B & B, P.O. Box 100, Volcano, HI 96785
808 967-7216/967-7110 or FAX 808 967-7719 (Big Island only)

Volcano Reservations, P.O. Box 998, Volcano, HI 96785
1-800-736-7140 or 808 967-7244 or FAX 808 967-8660

B&B Quality and Service

Hawai'i Island B&B Association members adhere to association standards of overall quality and cleanliness in B&B operation. Member B&Bs can be counted on to meet minimal standards of quality, cleanliness, service and maintenance of their operation and value for lodging dollars. Member B&B operators are identified in the listing by: **Member-HIBBA.**

Hawai'i's Best B&B is a booking service that handles exclusive upscale high quality B&B operations around the Big Island. Member B&Bs are guaranteed to provide a high quality B&B experience with overall excellent facilities, amenities and service. Member B&B operators are identified in the listing by: **Member-Hawai'i's Best.**

The rest of the B&B operations listed are independently owned and operated and not subject to booking service or association standards and are included here for the information and convenience of visitors.

Visitors considering staying at B&B operations should keep in mind that there can be great variance and differences between individual operations, regardless of the rates charged. There can be differences in accommodation level, room decor, furnishings, bathrooms, leisure facilities, breakfast provided, and overall quality of an individual B&B operation. Visitors should expect differences between operations charging $50 nightly with those charging $100 and more. For convenience, in the following listing, the rates given are generally the nightly rate for a double (two people).

The following is a listing of individual B & B operations by geographic area of the Big Island:

Kona

Da Third House, P.O. Box 321, Honaunau, HI 96726; 808 328-8410. This quiet peaceful studio with private entry and lanai has an unobstructed ocean view. Enjoy lush tropical grounds, minutes away from sandy beaches and snorkeling. Unit has king bed, refrigerator, microwave, TV, full bath. *Rates: $50-60 nightly.*

Dragonfly Ranch, P.O. Box 675, Honoanau, HI, 96726; 1-800-487-2159, 808 328-2159, Fax 808 328-9570. This private country estate is only three minutes from Honaunau Bay on Highway 160, about 20 miles south of Keahole Airport, Kona. The ranch is situated just above the Pu'uhonua O Honaunau National Historic Park. The main house offers two bedrooms with indoor bath and outdoor shower; there is an outdoor waterbed suite with private indoor room, kitchenette and bath; also a separate redwood cottage. Other features include fireplace, massage chair, cable TV/VCR, sundeck and nice views of Kona Coast. *Rates: Standard $60-70 nightly, Suites $100-160 nightly, Extra person $15*

Durkee's Coffeeland B & B, P.O. Box 596, Holualoa, HI 96725; 808 322-9142. This mountain side home nestles among coffee trees, palms, ferns, tropical fruit trees and flowers. It is in the heart of macadamia nut and coffee orchard country seven miles south of Kailua-Kona above scenic Keauhou Bay. Three rooms and a self-contained apartment available. Lanai views of the beautiful Kona Coast. Enjoy fresh Kona coffee from their own trees and roaster. *Rates: $65-75 nightly.*

Hale Hoa ★, reservations through Hawai'i's Best B&Bs, 1-800-262-9912, 808 885-4550 or Fax 808 885-0559. This is a Polynesian-style pole house overlooking Kealakekua Bay. It has a nicely appointed interior, tropical-inspired furnishings, separate bedroom and full kitchen. There is also a wrap-around veranda complete with jacuzzi. Sleeps up to four people; minimum 2 night stay. Member-Hawai'i's Best *Rates: $145 nightly*

Hale Malia ★, reservations through Hawai'i's Best B&Bs, 1-800-262-9912, 808 885-4550 or Fax 808 885-0559. This modern well-furnished home has two oceanfront rooms which open to a wide veranda overlooking the sea. There is also a room with a small side view. Each room sleeps two. On an oceanfront location just two miles south of Kailua-Kona town. Minimum 2 night stay. Member-Hawai'i's Best *Rates: $95-145 nightly.*

Hale Maluhia, 76-770 Hualalai Road, Kailua-Kona, HI 96740; 1-800-559-6627 or 808 329-5773, Fax 808 326-5487. Located just three miles upslope from Kailua-Kona village, this is a large rambling home on one acre with outdoor spa, lanai, rec room, CVR, library, etc. The "House of Peace" is wheelchair friendly. Member-HIBBA *Rates: $55 nightly, $40 for room w/shared bath, Cottage from $110*

Hale Pueo ★, reservations through Hawai'i's Best B&Bs, 1-800-262-9912, 808 885-4550 or Fax 808 885-0559. This contemporary home is located upslope at the 1800 ft. level on Mount Hualalai, 15 minutes from Kailua-Kona town. It features a downstairs guest studio with bright decor and ambiance. A pleasant lanai offers great views of the Kona Coast and sunsets. Sleeps four; minimum 2 night stay. Member-Hawai'i's Best *Rates: $80 nightly, $15 extra person.*

Holualoa Inn B & B ★, P.O. Box 222, Holualoa, Kona, HI 96725; Tel/fax 808 324-1121; reservations through Hawaii's Best B&Bs, 1-800-262-9912, 808 885-4550 or Fax 808 885-0559. This attractive cedar home is on a 40 acre estate in the small quiet village of Holualoa on the cool slopes of Mt. Hualalai in Kona. The estate is a former cattle ranch and coffee farm. The house features a rooftop gazebo providing magnificent views of the surrounding countryside, the Kona Coast, and incredible sunsets. There is a very quiet, relaxing atmosphere. There are four spacious and well-appointed guest rooms available, all with private bath. Minimum 2 night stay. Member-Hawai'i's Best *Rates: $125-165 nightly.*

Kailua Plantation House ★ , 75-5948 Alii Drive, Kailua-Kona, HI 96740; Tel/Fax 808 329-3727; reservations through Hawaii's Best B&Bs, 1-800-262-9912, 808 885-4550 or Fax 808 885-0559. This luxurious inn has five oceanfront or oceanview suites with private lanai. Rooms have private bath, TV, refrigerator, phone, etc. Outdoor pool and spa overlook the ocean. Located within walking distance of Kailua-Kona town; minimum 2 night stay. Member-Hawai'i's Best *Rates: $120-190 nightly.*

Kalahiki Cottage ★ , reservations through Hawai'i's Best B&Bs, 1-800-262-9912, 808 885-4550 or Fax 808 885-0559. This attractive one bedroom ranch cottage is located on a 15,000-acre working cattle ranch at Honaunau, Kona. It is filled with heirloom furniture and other treasures of the family's long history in Hawai'i. A sprawling veranda overlooks a 68 ft. swimming pool and jacuzzi. Forest covers the surrounding hills and guests will enjoy the country peace and tranquility. Sleeps two in cottage; room in host home nearby sleeps two extra; minimum 2 night stay. Member-Hawai'i's Best *Rates: Cottage $125 nightly; host home room $95*

Kealakekua Bay B & B ★ , reservations through Hawai'i's Best B&Bs, 1-800-262-9912, 808 885-4550 or Fax 808 885-0559. This is a private cottage on five landscaped acres a short walk from Kealakekua Bay. It has two bedrooms (sleeps up to 6), 2 1/2 baths, full kitchen and great view of the bay from the covered porch. Great for families or couples traveling together. The nearby host home also has a master bedroom with private entry, jacuzzi and nice view of the bay. A garden-level wing has two guest bedrooms, living area and private patio. Minimum 2 night stay. Member-Hawai'i's Best *Rates: Cottage $175 up to 4 people, $15 extra person; Guest rooms $85-125.*

Lions' Gate B & B, P.O. Box 761, Honaunau, HI 96726; 808 328-2335. This country home is in the Kona Coast's macadamia nut and coffee farm region with a very quiet, private setting. There is a jacuzzi, refrigerator, microwave, gazebo and TV room available for guest use. Just minutes away from Pu'uhonua O Honaunau National Historic Park and great snorkeling on the beach. Member - HIBBA *Rates: $60-75 nightly.*

Malama Llama B & B ★ , located 15 minutes from Kailua-Kona at the 2,000 ft. elevation on Mt. Hualalai. Reservations through Hawai'i's Best B&Bs, 1-800-262-9912, 808 885-4550 or Fax 808 885-0559. This is a secluded 5-acre farm with a garden-level apartment with private patio. Nice sunsets over the Kona Coast while llamas graze nearby. Sleeps up to five. Member-Hawai'i's Best *Rates: $85 nightly, $15-25 extra person.*

Merryman's B & B ★ , P.O. Box 474, 81-1031 Kepuka, Kealakekua, HI 96750; 1-800-545-4390, 808 323-2276; also through Hawai'i's Best B&Bs 1-800-262-9912, 808 885-4550 or Fax 808 885-0559. This is a comfortable cedar home located in the rural area of Kealakekua, Kona. The four spacious guest rooms are beautifully and comfortably furnished and offer either ocean or garden view. Two rooms share a bath, one suite has private bath and a downstairs room has private bath, entrance and deck. Large open living room and front-back lanais provide lots of room. Large open yard has lots of tropical fruit trees, plants and greenery plus a garden spa. Member-Hawai'i's Best and HIBBA *Rates: $75-95 nightly; $15 extra person.*

Puanani ★, reservations through Hawai'i's Best B&Bs, 1-800-262-9912, 808 885-4550 or Fax 808 885-0559. This contemporary home features lovely landscaped gardens and a two guest suites which open to a garden lanai, swimming pool, cabana and barbecue area. There are also great views of Kona Coast sunsets. Suites sleep three; minimum 2 night stay. Member-Hawai'i's Best *Rates: $75-85 nightly, $15 extra person.*

Rosy's Rest ★, 76-1012 Mamalahoa Highway, Holualoa, HI 96725; 808 322-REST; or through Hawai'i's Best B&Bs, 1-800-262-9912, 808 885-4550, Fax 808 885-0559. This country cottage home is in upcountry Holualoa area about five miles from Kailua-Kona town and has a panoramic view of the Kona Coast below. The downstairs guest apartment (sleeps 4) has full kitchen, bedroom, private bath and small porch. The separate upstairs studio (sleeps 2) has private bath, entrance, oceanview porch and refrige/microwave, TV/VCR. It's within walking distance to old Holualoa town shops, art galleries, etc. Member-Hawai'i's Best and HIBBA *Rates: $75-80 nightly*

Summer Breeze Cottages, P.O. Box 336, Captain Cook, HI 96704; 808 328-8451 or Fax 808 328-8452. Nestled in the hills above scenic Kealakekua Bay, this cottage offers views of Kona coffee country. The 2 BR cottage has an island decor. *Rates: $100 nightly, $575 weekly, credit cards.*

The Rainbow Plantation B & B, P.O. Box 122, Captain Cook, HI 96704; 1-800-494-2829, Tel 808 323-2393, Fax 808 323-9445. *Wir sprechen Deutsch; On parle francaise.* This country home is located on seven acres of macadamia nut orchards and forest land. The large guest rooms have private entrance, TV and refrige. Breakfast is enjoyed on the open oceanview deck. It's just minutes to beach snorkeling, restaurants, town and shopping. *Rates: $65-95 nightly.*

Three Bears' B & B, 72-1001 Puukala St., Kailua-Kona, HI 96740; Toll free U.S. 800 765-0480; tel/fax 808 325-7563. *Wir sprechen Deutsch.* Nice ocean views from the lanai of this cedar home. Located above Kona's Keahole Airport at 1600' elevation. Rooms have private baths, cable TV, micro oven, refrige and coffee maker. *Rates: $65-75 nightly, $10 extra person.*

Kohala

Belle Vue B & B ★, reservations through Hawai'i's Best B&Bs, 1-800-262-9912, 808 885-4550 or Fax 808 885-0559. *Wir sprechen Deutsch; On parle francaise; Italian too!* This is a spacious two-story cottage bordering open pasturelands of famous Parker Ranch in Waimea. There is a complete kitchen and cozy fireplace. Sleeps four; 3-night minimum stay. Walking distance to restaurants and shopping. Member-Hawai'i's Best *Rates: $115 nightly, $15 extra person.*

Hale Wailea ★, reservations through Hawai'i's Best B&Bs, 1-800-262-9912, 808 885-4550 or Fax 808 885-0559. This is a private home on a beach along the Kohala Coast near the luxury resorts. Located just 15 minutes from upcountry Waimea and restaurants/shopping. Sleeps up to four; 3-night minimum stay. Member-Hawai'i's Best *Rates: $150 nightly, $20 extra person.*

Hale Waipio ★, reservations through Hawai'i's Best B&Bs, 1-800-262-9912, 808 885-4550 or Fax 808 885-0559. This country home is a minute's walk from Waipio Valley Lookout on the Hamakua Coast and has expansive ocean views. Surrounded by pastures and sheltered by trees, the 2 BR home has kitchen, fireplace and deck. 20 minutes from Waimea restaurants/shopping. Sleeps 6; 3-night minimum. Member-Hawai'i's Best *Rates: $20 extra person, $110 nightly.*

Hawai'i Country Cottage ★, reservations through Hawai'i's Best B&Bs, 1-800-262-9912, 808 885-4550 or Fax 808 885-0559. This apartment is an attached wing of a country home and has its own entry, fireplace, paned windows and room to sleep four. Member-Hawai'i's Best *Rates: $65-75 nightly, $15 extra person.*

Hawai'i's Best B & B ★, P.O. Box 563, Kamuela, HI 96743; U.S. 1-800-262-9912, or 808 885-4550, Fax 808 885-0559. This booking service caters exclusively to upscale B&B's on the Big Island. The island's best lodgings, ranging from the most traditional host-home rooms to private country cottages, have been selected for inclusion in the "Hawai'i's Best" collection. Each home or cottage has been chosen for its distinctive personality, inspired attention to detail, and for the warm hospitality offered by its hosts. Each offers a beautiful setting, tasteful and comfortable accommodations, attentive service and a relaxed atmosphere. Host accommodations are available around the island in Kamuela, Hilo, Volcano, Kona and on the Kohala Coast. *Daily rates range from $65-150 double, with weekly rates available at most properties.*

Jenny's Country Cottage ★, reservations through Hawai'i's Best B&Bs, P.O. Box 563, Kamuela, HI 96743; 1-800-262-9912, 808 885-4550 or Fax 808 885-0559. This is a nicely restored cottage almost a century old. It features traditional koa furniture, a four-poster bed and decor reflecting a quiet country ambiance. Located just two miles from Kamuela town. Sleeps four. Member-Hawai'i's Best *Rates: $95 nightly, $10 extra person*

Kamuela Inn ★, P.O. Box 1994, Kamuela, HI 96743, 808 885-4243, Fax 808 885-8857. This country inn features 31 comfortable standard and kitchenette rooms all with TV. A new Mauna Kea Wing opened a last year added several comfortable, spacious, well-decorated rooms, two executive suites and a bright breakfast bar room. The original wing's rooms are smaller and a little more simple but very well kept and clean. Located in a quiet cool setting across from Edelweiss Restaurant off Highway 19 in Kamuela town. Near shopping, restaurants, area attractions, etc. and only 15 miles from Kohala Coast resorts and beaches. Reservations should be made well in advance.
Standard $54, Deluxe $67 Suite (max 3) with kitchen $83 Suite (max 4) with kitchen $93 Penthouse Suite $93
Mauna Kea Wing: King Beds $72-79, Two Twins $72, Executive Suites $165

Kamuela's Mauna Kea View B & B, P.O. Box 6375, Kamuela, HI 96743; 808 885-8425. This home offers wide open pastoral ranchland views backdropped with Mauna Kea. Rooms include a 2 BR unit with living room and kitchen and two separate rooms with shared bath. All have queen beds, color TV and phone. Convenient to area attractions and Kohala Coast resorts. Member-HIBBA *Rates: $55-75 nightly, $15 extra person.*

Kipuupuu ★, reservations through Hawai'i Best B&Bs, 1-800-262-9912, 808 885-4550 or Fax 808 885-0559. This private one-room cottage is on five acres of typical rural Waimea upland ranch country. It has a country motif decor, potbellied stove and a porch view that takes in the verdant horse pastures and rolling hills of the famed Parker Ranch country. Sleeps four; 2-night minimum stay. Member-Hawai'i's Best *Rates: $95 nightly, $15 extra person.*

Koa Lane Cottage ★, reservations through Hawai'i's Best B&Bs, 1-800-262-9912, 808 885-4550 or Fax 808 885-0559. This is a 1 BR cottage with European country decor set in the open pasturelands of Parker Ranch with great views of Mauna Kea. Sleeps four; 2-night minimum stay. Member-Hawai'i's Best *Rates: $95 nightly, $15 extra person.*

Makai Hale ★, reservations through Hawai'i's Best B&Bs, 1-800-262-9912, 808 885-4550 or Fax 808 885-0559. This country home is near Kawaihae on the Kohala Coast and offers consistently sunny weather. 'Four miles to area beaches. The two guest rooms have access to pool/jacuzzi deck. Sleeps five; 2-night minimum stay. Member-Hawai'i's Best *Rates: $65-95 nightly*

Merry Herbs Garden ★, reservations through Hawai'i's Best B&Bs, 1-800-262-9912, 808 885-4550 or Fax 808 885-0559. This charming and gracious country home captures the ranch lifestyle of old Hawai'i. Located on two quiet acres, the two bedroom wing has private entrance with expansive views of green pastures and Mauna Kea beyond. Open-beamed ceiling and picture windows accent a spacious living room. There is a dining table and refrige/microwave. Sleeps four. Member-Hawai'i's Best *Rates: $85 nightly, $15 extra person.*

Mountain Meadow Ranch B & B ★, P.O. Box 1361, Kamuela, HI 96743; 1-800-535-9376, 808 775-9376. Located halfway between Kona and Hilo in romantic Ahualoa above Honoka'a. Scenic pastures and majestic trees provide lots of country charm and atmosphere on this seven-acre estate. Enjoy area scenics like Waipio Valley, Parker Ranch, Manua Kea and Waimea town. There are 2 bedrooms, which can sleep up to three people each and a sofa sleeper in the outer room. TV/VCR, sauna, spa (solar powered). *Rates: $55 nightly, $350 weekly.*

Puu Manu Cottage ★, reservations through Hawai'i's Best B&Bs, 1-800-262-9912, 808 885-4550 or Fax 808 885-0559. This is a secluded country cottage located in open pastureland 3 miles from Waimea town. A converted horse barn, it has a cozy fireplace and French doors that open to large deck and views of Mauna Kea. A peaceful and romantic getaway. Sleeps four; 3-night minimum stay. Member-Hawai'i's Best *Rates: $105 nightly, $15 extra person.*

Waikii Cottage ★, reservations through Hawai'i's Best B&Bs, 1-800-262-9912, 808 885-4550 or Fax 808 885-0559. This country cottage is in a rural area at the 4,700 ft. elevation on Mauna Kea, 12 miles from Waimea on Highway 20. A cozy fireplace takes the chill out of the brisk mountain air and lovely English-style gardens grace the grounds. Sleeps four; 3-night minimum stay. Member-Hawai'i's Best *Rates: $95 nightly, $25 extra person.*

Waimea Gardens Cottage ★, reservations through Hawai'i's Best B&Bs, 1-800-262-9912, 808 885-4550 or Fax 808 885-0559. This streamside cottage has two private units on 1 1/2 acres. The cottage's Kohala and Waimea Wings have antique furnishings, patio French doors and decor which lend a pleasant country atmosphere. Each unit sleeps three; 3-night minimum stay. Member - Hawai'i's Best *Rates: $115 nightly, $15 extra person.*

North Hilo - Hamakua Coast

Akaka Falls Inn B & B, P.O. Box 190, Honomu, HI 96728-0190; 808 963-5468. This pleasant attractive B&B operation is located in an old plantation town storefront building right on main street in Honomu on the way to Akaka Falls State Park. Just two rooms are available. The operation combines a gift and art gallery with an ice cream counter-deli-snack bar. *Rates $50-65 nightly*

Hale Kukui , P.O. Box 5044, Kukuihaele, HI 96727; 1-800-444-7130 or 808 775-7130. There are a private studio, 2 BR and 3 BR cottages on four acres of high cliff oceanfront overlooking the Waipio Valley and towering coastline bluffs. Waipio Valley activities available include hiking in tropical rainforest, biking, swimming, surfing, horseback rides, mule wagon rides and 4x4 vehicle tours. Located in lush landscaped grounds with a tropical setting. Units have private bath and kitchen. *Rates: $75-95 nightly*

Hale Lamalani, 27-703 Kaieie Homestead Road, Papaikou, HI 96781; 1-800-238-8BED or Tel/Fax 808 964-5401. This special "House of Heavenly Light" is located 7.5 miles north of Hilo and two miles upslope at the 1000 ft. elevation on Mauna Kea. Great views of mountain, ocean, volcano and bay views from a refurbished 1940's-era plantation-style home. Three comfortable guest rooms have views, shared bath, sundeck and lanai. *Rates: $55 nightly.*

Luana Ola B & B Cottages, P.O. Box 430, Honokaa, HI 96727; 1-800-357-7727, 808 775-772 or Fax 808 775-0949. These charming private cottages overlook sweeping ocean views on the high coastline of Honokaa town. Each has kitchenette, full bath, large porch, laundry facilities, phones and are wheelchair accessible. Guests can walk into historic old Honokaa town to shops, dining, explore, etc. Member-HIBBA *Rates: $85 nightly.*

Mauka B & B, P.O. Box 767, Honoka'a, HI 96727; 808 775-9983. The guest unit is a cool, quiet studio with private entrance. It has TV-VCR, kitchenette and comfortable wicker furniture. It's just a half-mile to Kalopa State Park with a hundred acres of native Hawaiian rainforest and nature trails to explore. Member - HIBBA *Rates: $55 nightly.*

Our Place-Papaikou's B & B, P.O. Box 469, 3 Mamalahoa Highway, Papaikou, HI 96781; 1-800-245-5250, Tel 808 964-5250, Fax 808 964-3227. Located four miles north of Hilo on Highway 19. This is a large cedar home with four guest rooms. Common open lanai to each bedroom, overlooks a stream and tropical vegetation; Great Room features a library, fireplace, grand piano, cable TV/V-CR; no smoking indoors. Easy access to snorkeling-surfing, botanical gardens, Hawai'i Volcanoes National Park, shopping and dining in Hilo. Member-HIBBA *Rates: $55-80 nightly.*

Paauhau Plantation House ★ , P.O. Box 1375, Honoka'a, HI 96727; 808 775-7222. This is an old sugar plantation manager's estate set amid rolling yards, gardens and lovely trees all surrounded by acres of sugar cane lands. There are three self-contained cottages: Hale Kona and Hale Mauna Kea sleep 4 each and Hale Hilo sleeps up to 6. The rambling main house has a Master Suite that sleeps 4 and two Garden Rooms that sleep 2 each. *Rates: Garden Rooms $105, Master Suite $140, Hale Kona (max 4) $75, Hale Mauna Kea (max 4) $90, Hale Hilo (max 6) $90, Extra person $15.*

Suds' Acres, P.O. Box 277, Paauilo, HI 96776; 1-800-735-3262, 808 776-1611, Fax 776-1592. This is a guest cottage on a macadamia nut farm at 1800' elevation on the slopes of Mauna Kea with a Hamakua Coast view. The 2 BR cottage has bath, kitchen and living room and is just 5 miles from Honoka'a and 20 miles from Waimea. Sleeps up to 5 people. Member-HIBBA *Rates: $55-65 nightly, $10 extra person.*

Waipio Wayside B & B ★, P.O. Box 840, Honoka'a, HI 96727; 1-800-833-8849, Tel/Fax 808 775-0275; or through Hawai'i's Best, 1-800-262-9912, 808 885-4550 or Fax 808 885-0559. This is a refurbished 1938-era sugar plantation home. There are lots of tropical plants around the grounds and deck-gazebo for relaxation. There are five bedrooms: Moon Room with full-size bed and share bath; Plantation Room with twin beds and share bath; Chinese Room with full-size bed and half-bath; Garden Room with full-sized bed and share bath; Bird's Eye Room with full-size bed and private bath. Easy access to Waipio Valley, Waipio Ridge Walk, Kalopa Park, the Hamakua Coast and Kamuela. Member-Hawai'i's Best and HIBBA *Rates: Rooms w/private bath $80-100 nightly; room w/share bath $50-70; extra person $15.*

South Hilo - Hilo Town

Haili House Inn ★, 239 Haili St., Hilo, HI 96720; 808 969-7378. This renovated old home is on the edge of historic downtown Hilo. It is adjacent to Lyman House Museum and across from St. Joseph's Church, close to shops, restaurants, the farmers' market and other Hilo attractions. The 1922-vintage home has been carefully restored and offers clean comfortable rooms with nostalgic '40's-50's Hawaiiana decor. Five guestrooms have queen beds and either half or full-bath. *Rates: $69-89 nightly, $15 extra person, credit cards.*

Hale Kai ★, 111 Honolii Pali, Hilo, HI 96720; 808 935-6330, Fax 808 935-8439. This home perches on a bluff facing the ocean and Hilo Bay just two miles from downtown Hilo. There are three rooms with private baths and a separate apartment unit. All rooms face the ocean except the loft room which has a side ocean view. Guests enjoy the pool, jacuzzi and patio. Rooms have king or queen beds and cable TV. Easy access to area attractions. *Rates: Rooms, $85-120 nightly (2 night minimum) $15 extra person.*

Hale O Panaewa, HCR 1, Box 1-A, Hilo, HI 96720; 808 959-7432, Fax 808 982-9091. This secluded 1 BR guest cottage is situated on a nine acre macadamia nut orchard just four miles from Hilo and 25 miles from Volcanoes National Park. Enjoy cable TV, fireplace, king bed and petite kitchen. *Rates: $65 nightly.*

Hale Paliku ★, 40 Hina Street, Hilo, HI 96720; 808 969-7153, reservations through Hawaii's Best B&Bs, 1-800-262-9912, 808 885-4550 or Fax 808 885-0559. This is a 1930's era home just three blocks from downtown Hilo and two blocks above historic Lyman Museum. The living room offers a nice view of Hilo Bay and town area. Two guest rooms sleep four. The Mauka (mountainside) room has two twin beds while the Makai (oceanside) room has a king bed. Rooms have a shared bath; linens provided. Easy access to Hilo's restaurants, shopping and attractions. Member-Hawai'i's Best *Rates: $90 nightly, $15 extra person.*

Holmes' Sweet Home B & B, 107 Koula St., Hilo, HI 96720; 808 961-9089. This island home has two guest units each with private bath, lanai, sitting room and dining room; quiet private location, oceanview convenient. Member - HIBBA *Rates: $60-75 nightly, $10 extra person.*

Lihi Kai, 30 Kahoa Road, Hilo, HI 96720; 808 935-7865. This tropical Hawaiian home is on the oceanfront overlooking Hilo Bay. Two bedrooms share a bath and a half, swimming pool, TV. It's just two miles into town for shopping, dining and easy access to other area attractions. *Rates: $50 nightly.*

Maureen's B & B ★, 1896 Kalanianaole, Hilo, HI 96720; 808 935-9018. This lodging is the old Saiki family mansion (c. 1932) located in the Keaukaha area of Hilo, opposite James Kealoha Beach Park some four miles from town. Located just past the Mauna Loa Shores condo high-rise. The home is lovely redwood and cedar finished with a huge open-beam cathedral ceiling in the living room. Arched doorways and windows give this home a touch of New England. The home has dual staircases winding up to open balconies and guest rooms. Quaint antique furniture pieces, bookcases and artwork make this inviting lodging seem almost like a gallery. Five guest rooms accommodate 2 singles and 4 doubles, a total of 10 guests. With the beach right across the street, swimming, snorkeling and sunning are steps away. There is also cable TV/VCR. Children under 5 years old not accepted due to high stairs and balcony areas. Member-HIBBA *Rates: $40-60 nightly.*

Piihonua ★, reservations through Hawai'i's Best B&Bs, 1-800-262-9912, 808 885-4550 or Fax 808 885-0559. This is a spacious studio unit over the hosts' separate garage. Convenient access to Hilo's historic downtown district five minutes away plus area orchid and anthurium farms and nurseries, macadamia nut factory and botanical gardens. Well-maintained property, pleasant decor and good lodging value; sleeps four. *Rates: $75 nightly, $10 extra person.*

The Shipman House B & B, 131 Kai'ulani Street, Hilo, HI 96720; 1-800-MAP-THIS, or 1-800-627-8447, (808) 934-8002. This elegant Victorian-style home dates from 1900 and has been home to the Shipman family since 1901. The home is on both the State and National Historic Registers. Now owned by the Shipmans' great-grand daughter's family, it's one of Hilo's most unusual B&B's. The main home features a wide wrap-around lanai and three-story rounded tower with conical roof, reason for local children to call the home "the Castle." The home is on 5.5 acres including a magnificent tropical gulch and is landscaped with tropical fruit trees and flowering plants. One guestroom in the main house has twin beds; two guestrooms in the separate 1910 guesthouse each have a queen bed. All rooms have ceiling fans, private bath, TV and frige. Expanded continental breakfast is served on the lanai. Member-HIBBA *Rates: $130 nightly, $25 extra person.*

Wild Ginger Inn, 100 Puueo Street, Hilo, HI 96720; 1-800-882-1887, 808 935-5556. Strictly for budget travelers, this old inn dates from 1947 and has been operated as a hotel under various owners. Over the years the old place faded and grew a bit moldy. A coat of bright tropical pink paint has made the wood-frame building stand out. The 40 or so rooms provide only simple spartan accommodations, nothing fancy, great for budget travelers. Two blocks from downtown Hilo. *Rates: $39-59 nightly.*

Puna - Volcano

Aloha B & B, 13-3591 Luana, Leilani Estates, HI 96778; 808 965-9898, Fax 808 965-7434. This Hawaiian country home is located between Lava Tree Park and the Kalapana area near recent volcanic activity. The units are furnished with queen bed, refrige, coffeemaker, etc. It's a peaceful, quiet acreage nicely landscaped and has a large covered courtyard and pool. *Rates: $78 nightly.*

Carson's Volcano Cottage B & B, P.O. Box 503, Volcano, HI 96785; 1-800-845-LAVA, 808 967-7683. Accommodations at this quiet secluded location include one studio cottage and a three room-cottage. All have private bath, entrances and decks, and two have kitchenettes. Electric blankets and a heater are provided for cool Volcano evenings. Room decor reflects Polynesian, Oriental, Country and Southwest themes. A hot tub on the main house deck is available for all guests. Easy access to national park activities, golf course, restaurants. Deposit required to confirm reservation. *Rates: $65-125 nightly.*

Chalet Kilauea at Volcano B & B, P.O. Box 998, Volcano, HI 96785; 1-800-937-7786 or 808 967-7786, Fax 1-800-577-1849. *Parle francais.* This home is located on Wright Road in Volcano. Choose from rooms inspired by Oriental, African and European themes, a Treehouse suite or three separate nearby cottages: Ohia Holiday Cottage, Hapu'u Forest Cabin and Hoku Hawaiian House which sleep up to 6 people. Relax in the hot tub, enjoy the fireplace, peruse the library and wake up to a gourmet breakfast in the art deco dining room. The home is at the cool 3800 ft. elevation and just minutes away from Hawai'i Volcanoes National Park, village store and restaurants. *Rates: $95 and up nightly; Treehouse Suite $295 nightly, cottages $95-225 nightly.*

Champagne Cove at Kapoho Beach, RR2 Box 3943, Pahoa, HI 96778; 808 965-7426. This home is located at Kapoho Beach in the quiet secured Lyman Subdivision 45 minutes south of Hilo. Home has two 3 BR units suitable for groups of 6-7. Units are furnished with kitchen, linens, TV, private pool, etc. Enjoy ocean tidepools, swimming, snorkeling, fishing. Minimum stay of 4 days. *Rates: $75 nightly, $10 extra person.*

Country Goose, P.O. Box 597, Volcano, HI 96785; 1-800-238-7101, Tel/Fax 808 967-7759. This home has 1 BR with private bath and entry, king size bed and double futon quilt. Electric baseboard and heat-electric blankets take the chill off the crisp Volcano air. Very peaceful and quiet setting. Member-HIBBA *Rates: $70 nightly.*

Hale Iki ★, reservations through Hawai'i's Best B&Bs, 1-800-262-9912, 808 885-4550, Fax 808 885-0559. This back-country cabin is nestled in a fern forest in Volcano Village. It has a cozy interior complete with wood-burning stove and full kitchen. There is also an oversized tub and a view through tall bay windows to the rain forest. The sleeping loft which sleeps two is upstairs. Minimum stay is two nights. Member-Hawai'i's Best *Rates: $120 nightly*

Hale Ohia Cottages ★, P.O. Box 758, Volcano, HI 96785, 1-800-455-3803, 808 967-7986, Fax 808 967-8610; or through Hawai'i's Best B&Bs 1-800-262-9912, 808 885-4550, Fax 808 885-0559. This country cottage offers 3 BR and sleeps up to 5 people. There is a full kitchen, large living room and one tub-shower bath. Bedrooms have 1 double, 2 singles and a sleeping punee (sofa) in

livingroom. A large covered deck has table, chairs and barbecue for cookouts. Located one mile from national park entrance, near hiking trails, picnic areas, golf course, volcano observatory, etc. Member-Hawai'i's Best and HIBBA
Rates: $60-95 nightly, $15 extra person

Hydrangea Cottage and Mountain House ★, reservations through Hawai'i's Best B&Bs, 1-800-262-9912, 808 885-4550 or Fax 808 885-0559. This country cottage and house are on a 3-acre estate in the Volcano forestlands landscaped with pink and blue hydrangeas and a variety of other plants. Units are completely furnished including living room, kitchen and fireplace. The cottage sleeps 3 and the house has two master suites. Minimum 2 nights. Member-Hawai'i's Best
Rates: Cottage $120, Mountain House suites $135, $15 extra person.

Kilauea Lodge B & B ★, P.O. Box 116, Volcano, HI 96785; 808 967-7366, Fax 808 967-7367; also reservations through Hawai'i's Best B&Bs, 1-800-262-9912, 808 885-4550 or Fax 808 885-0559. A rustic old YWCA camping lodge and dormitory built in 1938 offers luxurious accommodations and an excellent restaurant with a full American-Continental dinner menu nightly. Set amidst the quiet cool country air of Volcano Village near Hawai'i Volcanoes National Park headquarters and visitors center. A new building set in the lush forest near the main lodge provides several comfortable beautifully decorated rooms with private baths. The main lodge offers rooms with private baths and fireplaces. Guests have breakfast in the dining room while enjoying the crackling warmth of the "Friendship Fireplace." There is also a nearby two bedroom/one bath cottage, "Tutu's House," ideal for families or small groups. Member-Hawai'i's Best
Rates: $90-120 nightly; Tutu's House cottage $135 nightly

Kilauea Volcano Kabins, P.O. Box 963, Volcano, HI 96785; 808 967-7773. This operation features nice cedar cabins among a fern tree forest, convenient to Volcanoes National Park, South Point, botanical gardens and east Hawai'i attractions. Cabins are complete with private bath, kitchen and woodburning stoves. *Rates: $45 nightly and up.*

Lokahi Lodge ★, P.O. Box 7, Volcano, HI 96785; 1-800-457-6924 or 808 985-8647; also reservations through Hawai'i's Best B&Bs, 1-800-262-9912, or 808 885-4550 or Fax 808 885-0559. This luxury four-room inn combines modern convenience with Volcano country charm. Located one mile from Volcanoes National Park entrance, this plantation-style home has heated rooms each with private bath. Wide veranda overlooks a lush native ohia forest. Each room sleeps four. Member: HIBBA and Hawai'i's Best *Rates: $75 nightly, $15 extra person.*

Mountain View B & B, P.O Box 963, Kurtistown, HI 96760; 808 968-6868, fax 968-7017. This large modern home is located about 15 miles south of Hilo in the rolling farm and forestlands of the Mountain View village area. The home is on a large lot surrounded by forest and lush greenery. The owner/operators are noted Big Island artists and instructors, Linus and Jane Chao, who have an art studio on the lower level where they conduct art classes. Inquire about special art class/room packages. The living and guest quarters are on the upper level. The Cherry Blossom and Heliconia Rooms have king or queen beds and private bath; the Plumeria and Lehua Rooms have twin beds and shared bath. There is easy access to shopping, dining and attractions of the East Hawaii-Hilo area and Hawaii Volcanoes National Park is just minutes away. Member - HIBBA *This B&B is smoke free and Chinese is spoken too. Rates: $55-75 nightly.*

My Island B & B ★, P.O. Box 100, Volcano, HI 96785; 808 967-7216/967-7110, Fax (808) 967-7719. This secluded operation is located in the pleasant cool climate of Volcano Village, not far from Hawai'i Volcanoes National Park visitors center. The house is a historic century-old missionary-style home set amidst a rambling botanical garden and fern forest jungle. The grounds have a fine collection of exotic plants from around the world. Rooms are neat, comfortable, and cozy with various bed arrangements: singles, doubles, triples, and families. Color TV and a library of Hawaiiana are available for entertainment. All the mac nuts you can eat. Member-HIBBA *Rates: $40-75 nightly.*

Ohia Cottage of Volcano B & B, HCR 2 Box 9591, Keaau, HI 96749; 808 966-4384. This country cottage is located in a quiet rain forest area. The fully furnished cottage includes TV, fireplace, and three cozy guest rooms with down filled bedding which sleep up to 5 people. *Rates: $45-75 nightly.*

Paradise Place B & B, HCR 2, Box 9558, Keaau, HI 96749; 808 966-4600. This home is in rural setting 1/2 mile from the ocean with views of Mauna Kea, the steaming volcano and tropical gardens. Rooms have private entrances and baths, kitchen with refrige, washer/dryer, TV room, patio and hammock. Centrally located to Volcanoes National Park and Hilo area attractions. *Rates: $65 nightly, $10 extra person.*

Pearl's Shell, P.O. Box 1324, 13-3432 Kupono St., Pahoa, HI 96778; 808 965-7015. This home has quiet, spacious rooms with private baths, entry and lanai patio. It features tropical garden setting, outdoor hot tub, kitchen privileges and full breakfast. Easy access to hot pools, Lava Tree State Park, light house and new black sand beach, hiking and biking trails. Member-HIBBA *Rates: $35-55 nightly.*

Rainforest Retreat, HCR1 Box 5655, Keaau, HI 96749; 808 982-9601/966-7712, Fax 808 966-6898. This private home is surrounded by native ohia forest, orchids and horse pastures. A Garden Studio has private entry and bath, king bed, TV, kitchenette and laundry facilities. The Ohia House is a separate cottage with a king and queen beds, TV, deck hot tub, etc. Located just off Highway 130 and 20 minutes from Hilo. Member-HIBBA *Rates: $65-90 nightly, $10 extra person.*

Victorian Rose B & B, P.O. Box 234, Volcano, HI 96785; 808 967-8026. This home is located five minutes from Hawai'i Volcanoes National Park entrance on the northeast border of the park. The one guest room has a queen bed, private bath and entry, microwave and refrigerator. *Rates: $65 nightly.*

Volcano B & B, P.O. Box 22, 19-3950 Keonelehua St., Volcano, HI 96785; 808 967-7779; Fax 808 967-7619. This is a peaceful country home located in the heart of cool lush Volcano Village, a mile from the entrance and visitors center of Hawai'i Volcanoes National Park. The house provides three single/double rooms with shared bath. The renovated 1935-vintage three story home is on 3/4 acre landscaped site with fireplace, sunroom, reading room, piano, cable TV/VCR; bicycles available. Access to national park provides year around hiking, biking, sightseeing and other recreational activities. Near village stores and restaurants. *Rates: $45-55 nightly, $10 extra person.*

Volcano Heart Chalet B & B, P.O. Box 404, Hana, HI 96713; 808 248-7725. This comfortable cedar home is surrounded by native ohia trees and tree ferns and has three themed decor rooms which sleep 2 guests each; shared baths, sitting room, kitchenette, laundry; near National Park attractions and restaurants. *Rates: $50 nightly.*

Ka'u

Becky's B & B, P.O. Box 673, Naalehu, HI 96772; 1-800-235-1233, tel/fax 808 929-9690. This is a sixty year old plantation home in the southernmost community of the USA. Green sand and black sand beaches nearby, South Point and near Volcanoes National Park. Located halfway between Hilo and Kona in the rural Ka'u countryside. One large room with two double beds and private bath, two other rooms with one queen bed, share bath. Member-HIBBA *Rates: $50-75 nightly, $10 extra person.*

Bouganvillea B & B, P.O. Box 6045, Ocean View, HI 96704; 1-800-688-1763, Tel/Fax 808 929-7089. This operation features pool, hiking, biking, ocean views and South Point and quiet country of rural Ka'u. Operators eager to share Hawaii and relaxing friendly atmosphere. Two guest rooms have private bath and entry. Guests can enjoy the swimming pool too. Member-HIBBA *Rates: $49-59 nightly, $15 extra person.*

Hobbit House ★ , reservations through Hawai'i's Best B&Bs, 1-800-262-9912, 808 885-4550, Fax 808 885-0559. This remote home is located near the southernmost town in the USA, Naalehu, in the Ka'u District. It sits on a hilltop with sweeping vistas all the way to the coast. The downstairs suite is filled with stained-glass art. It has all the comforts and amenities including a full kitchen. It's in such a quiet tranquil area that it is accessible only by a mile-long four-wheel drive road. Sleeps two. Member-Hawai'i's Best *Rates: $95 nightly*

South Point B & B , P.O. Box 6589, 92-1408 Donala Dr., Ocean View, HI 96737; 808 939-7466. This home offers guests quiet rooms all with private entrance and bath. Guests can enjoy breakfast on the wrap-around lanai while admiring the flowers and view of South Point vista and ocean. Nearby attractions include Ka Lae (South Point) where the first Polynesians landed in Hawai'i, hiking to remote Green Sands Beach, golf at Discovery Harbor or Seamountain courses, and Volcanoes National Park, an easy 45 minute drive away. Located near mileage marker 77 on Highway 11 south from Kona or Hilo. Turn into Donala Street near marker 77, go 50 feet and turn right to first driveway on right. *Rates: $55-65 nightly, 3 nights/$150.*

Wood Valley B & B, P.O. Box 37, Pahala, HI 96777; 1-800-854-6754, 808 928-8212, Fax 928-9400. This an old remodeled plantation home on 12 acres of pastureland with gardens and an outdoor bath with woodburning steamhouse. This isolated home gives a unique glimpse of old Hawaii. Best for adventurous budget-minded travelers. One guest room available. Member-HIBBA *Rates: $55 nightly.*

LODGES AND HOSTELS

The following lodge-hostels are strictly low budget accommodations for backpackers and travelers interested in simple no-frills economical lodging. There is one each in Hilo and Kailua-Kona.

Arnott's Lodge, 98 Apapane Road, Hilo, HI 96720; 1-800-368-8752, 808 969-7097, Fax 808 961-9638. This basic backpackers lodge is located in the Keaukaha area of Hilo near the beach parks. Private and bunk rooms share bathrooms, a common kitchen and TV room. Some units have private kitchen and bath. Free airport shuttle service.
Rates: 2 BR with kitchen/bath, sleeps five, $100 night
Double private room, $40 night; single private room, $30 night
Bunk rooms, $15 per person per night

Patey's Place Hostel, 75-195 Ona Ona, Kailua-Kona, HI 96740, 1-800-972-7408 or 808 326-7018. This budget accommodation is just two blocks from the ocean and near shops, restaurants and entertainment in the heart of Kailua-Kona town. Convenient to day tours to Volcano, coffee plantations, historic sites, etc.
Rates: $35 for private double room, $15 for share room.

PRIVATE ESTATES, RENTAL HOMES, VILLAS

ALI'I VILLA VACATIONS OF HAWAI'I
#4 Poipu Drive, Honolulu, HI 96825; 1-800-522-3030, 808 735-9000, FAX (808) 735-9895. This reservation service has a select list of privately owned beach homes, fairway villas and exclusive estates for groups of up to 10 people. *Rates: $225-1,500 daily.*

ELITE PROPERTIES UNLIMITED
PO Box 5273, Lahaina, Maui, HI 96761. 1-800-448-9222 U.S. & Canada, (808-665-0561). Family homes and luxury estates (3-7 bedrooms) available on all four major islands. Weekly and monthly rentals. One week minimum. Maid service, chefs and concierge services available.

GINGER

HALE (HAWAIIAN APARTMENT LEASING ENTERPRISES)
479 Ocean Ave. #B, Laguna Beach, CA 92651; 1-800-854-8843, or 714 497-4253/497-4474, FAX 714 497-4183. This reservation service has a wide range of 1 BR condos to 5 BR homes in Kailua-Kona, Keauhou-Kona, Waikoloa and Kohala areas, all amenities included. *Rates: $70-900 nightly.*

HALE O HAOLE
14-3508 Kauai Road, Pahoa, HI 96778; reservations 213 662-8411, Fax 213 662-4671. This is a fully furnished 2 BR/2 bath home just minutes from Hilo and Volcano. Sleeps up to 6 people. *Rates: $75 nightly.*

HIBISCUS HOUSE AT KAPOHO BEACH
14-4926 Kapoho Kai Dr., Pahoa, HI 96778; 1-800-869-0278. This large home has two separate 3 BR/2 bath units to accommodate 6-8 guests. Units have TV, phones, ceiling fans and tidepool. Quiet family vacation area with good snorkeling and swimming within 200 yds. *Rates: $70-110 nightly.*

HILO HARBOR VIEW HOME
195 Kahoa Street, Hilo, HI 96720; reservations 707 499-0420, Fax 707 443-2282. This new large fully furnished home overlooks Hilo Harbor and the ocean. Sleeps up to 6 people; non-smoking home. *Rates: $125 nightly.*

HILO PENTHOUSE
111 Honolii Pali, Hilo, HI 96720; reservations 808 935-6330, Fax 808 935-8439. This is a deluxe fully furnished 2 BR/ 2-1/2 bath unit with all the comforts and amenities including swimming pool, jacuzzi, laundry, etc. The unit sleeps up to 5 people; just two and a half miles from downtown Hilo attractions, shopping and dining. *Rates: $875 nightly.*

INSIDE HAWAI'I, INC.
3848A Pahoa Avenue, Honolulu, HI 96816; 1-800-722-5771, 808 737-7313, FAX 808 735-8857. This reservation service has over 50 units available ranging from 2-8BRs including private estates, beachfront homes and elegant resort condo units. *Rates: $200-2,000 per night.*

KAPOHO VACATION RENTALS
Kapoho Beach Lots, RR2 Box 3909, Pahoa, HI 96778; reservations 808 965-8341. This booking service has six fully furnished beach side homes available. Access to swimming pool and ocean front tide pools. *Rates: $60-100 nightly.*

KEALA HEALTH RETREAT
P.O. Box 297, Volcano, HI 96785; reservations 1-800-21KEALA, 808 967-8622. This two-unit operation includes all meals, health spa-fitness-wellness activities, massage, tours, ground transportation, etc. *Rates: $175-250 inclusive.*

KEALAKEKUA BAY ESTATE
P.O. Box 724, Captain Cook, HI 96704; reservations J.N. Properties, 808 328-8019, Fax 808 328-8014. This fully furnished rural country home is in a quiet area and enjoys beautiful ocean views. Sleeps up to 4 people. *Rates: $125-150.*

KONA VACATION RESORTS
77-6435 Kuakini Highway, Kailua-Kona, HI 96740, US 1-800-367-5168, Canada 1-800-800-KONA, Hawai'i 808 329-6488 or FAX 808 329-5480. This service has a wide range of vacation rental units available from studios to 4 BR homes. *Rates: $60-300 per night.*

LEE'S HOME AWAY FROM HOME
90A Pohakulani St., Hilo, HI 96720; phone/FAX 808 959-6940. This private home suitable for two guests is just five minutes from Hilo airport. *Rates: $50 nightly.*

LEILANI'S AT PUAKO BEACH
98 Puako Beach Dr., Kamuela, HI 96743; 808 882-7362. There are two studios and one guest cottage all with TV, laundry, microwaves, ceiling fans, bbq-decks and units are non-smoking; diving/snorkeling, beach activities. *Rates: $95-145 nightly, $10 extra person.*

MALUHIA HALE
77-6486 Akai Street, Kailua-Kona, HI 96740; reservations, 170 Emigrant Lake Road, Ashland, OR 97520; call collect 503 488-2826. This private home is just two blocks from White Sands Beach and has TV, swimming pool. 3 day minimum stay, can accommodate up to 8 people. *Rates: $190 nightly.*

MAUI & ALL ISLANDS CONDOMINIUMS & CARS
P.O. Box 947, Lynden, WA 98264; 1-800-663-6962, fax 604 856-4187. This booking service can make reservations for condos-hotels-houses and cars on all major islands of Hawai'i. They represent several properties in the Hilo, Kona and Kohala areas of the Big Island in all price ranges from budget to super luxury in addition to daily and weekly car rentals.

MELJIE HONEY'S VACATION HOME
167 Kapaa St., Hilo, HI 96720; 1-800-927-1922; This large private home can accommodate 8 guests and has TV, phone, spa, laundry, etc. Convenient to Hilo area attractions. *Rates: $125 nightly.*

PREMIER CONNECTION
33 Maruea Street, Suite 200, Wailuku, Maui, HI 96793, 808 244-4877. Privacy, elegance, and the ultimate in luxury for your Big Island vacation can be provided with a variety of exceptional hotel suites, homes, or mansion-like dwellings, available for short or long term stays. Prices reflect the quality of the accommodations and location. Agency can also arrange transportation, tours, flowers, and all details. *Rates: $200-2,000 daily.*

RESERVATIONS HAWAI'I
Paradise Management Corporation, Kukui Plaza #C-207, 50 South Beretania St., Honolulu, HI 96813; 1-800-367-5205, 808 538-7145. This company has over 700 listings on the Big Island ranging from condo units to vacation homes at a variety of rates available by day, week, month or longer.

SOUTH KOHALA MANAGEMENT
P.O. Box 384900, Waikoloa, HI 96738-4900, 1-800-822-4252, in Hawai'i 808 883-8500. FAX (808) 883-9818 Choose a home or condo unit for your ultimate luxury vacation from a select number of private residences. Listings include the

exclusive Fairways at Mauna Kea Resort, Mauna Lani Resort and Waikoloa Resort condos, and Puako Beach Oceanfront homes and private villas on the Kohala Coast. Homes and condos feature private swimming pools and jacuzzi, luxurious furnishings and many special amenities. Each home and condo is fully equipped to satisfy even the most discriminating traveller. There is also easy access to golf, tennis and a white-sand swimming beaches of the Kohala Coast in addition to award-winning resort dining. Varied rates.

TRIAD MANAGEMENT REALTORS
75-5629 Kuakini Highway, Kailua-Kona, HI 96740, 808 329-6402. This property management service has a variety of vacation rental homes available at varied rates.

VACATION LOCATIONS-HAWAI'I
Parker & Co. Realty, P.O. Box 1689, Kihei, Maui, HI 96753, 808 874-0077. Specializing in beachfront homes, golf course homes and estates around the Big Island. Write directly or call for locations, rates, and amenities. *Rates: $150-2,000 daily.*

VANGUARD VACATION RENTALS
76-6241 Alii Dr. #3, Kailua-Kona, HI 96740; 1-800-552-5642, 808-329-5737, FAX 808 326-5640. This reservation service has several oceanfront and ocean-view condos and homes, studios to 4 BR, available. *Rates: $50-400 nightly.*

WAIPIO RIDGE VACATION RENTALS
P.O. Box 5039, Kukuihaele, HI 96727; 808 775-0603. This renter has a 1 BR home, sleeps 5, fully furnished with refrige, microwave oven, coffee maker, fans, TV, etc. Located near the Waipio Valley. *Rates: $75 nightly, $385 weekly*

WHALING'S UPPER WAIOHINU VALLEY HIDEAWAY
P.O. Box 269, Naalehu, HI 96772; 808 929-9765. This private country bunga-low in the Big Island's remote southern area offers tranquil seclusion, panoramic coastal views, hot tub, 4x4 shuttle and tours. Accommodates up to 6 guests. *Rates: $100 nightly, $15 extra person.*

LONG TERM STAYS

Almost all condo complexes and rental agents offer the long term visitor moder-ate to substantial discounts for stays of one month or more. Long term rentals can be booked through the agents listed in the above section on PRIVATE ESTATES, HOMES, VILLAS or in the BOOKING AGENTS section.

MILITARY RECREATION CENTER

The Big Island is unique among Hawai'i's Neighbor Islands in that it has an official armed forces recreation center. This is the *Kilauea Military Camp* located at Hawai'i Volcanoes National Park. KMC, as it is called, has 55 rental cabins available plus dormitory facilities. The rustic well-kept cabins are 1 BR, 2 BR and 3 BR units fully equipped with fireplace, Television, full bath and some have kitchen facilities. The cabins are, however, available only to active duty regular military, reserve or national guard or retired personnel or Department of Defense civilian personnel.

The KMC "Mess Hall," actually a rustic cafeteria which serves standard but ample military chow, is open to any ID card carrying retired military personnel as well. The dining hall like the lodgings are not open to the public.

The cabin rentals are very reasonable and are based on rank and grade of the personnel. Advance reservations are required. Current rates are as follows:

Ranks E1-5: Studio $25; Standard 1 BR $27; Deluxe 1 BR $38; Standard 2 BR $35; Deluxe 2 BR $43; Standard 2 BR w/kitchen $45; Deluxe 2 BR w/kitchen $53; Standard 3 or 4 BR $50
Ranks E6-9, W1-3, O1-3: Studio $35; Standard 1 BR $37; Deluxe 1 BR $48; Standard 2 BR $45; Deluxe 2 BR $53; Standard 2 BR w/kitchen $55; Deluxe 2 BR w/kitchen $63; Standard 3 or 4 BR $60
Ranks W4, O4-10, Civilian: Studio $45; Standard 1 BR $47; Deluxe 1 BR $58; Standard 2 BR $55; Deluxe 2 BR $63; Standard 2 BR w/kitchen $65; Deluxe 2 BR w/kitchen $73; Standard 3 or 4 BR $70
Dormitory Rates, nightly per person: Open Bays $5-7.50; Rooms $7.50-10.00

KMC guests can enjoy a full range of recreation activities and programs in the national park including daily tours to various scenic attractions around the island of Hawai'i. Rental equipment is available including tennis rackets, bicycles, back packs, sleeping bags for camping, snorkeling gear and more. KMC also has billiards, ping-pong, video games, mini-golf and a fully equipped six-lane bowling alley. There are also Hawaiian music and hula, Hawaiian story-telling, lei making, and much more. There is a full service cafeteria-dining hall and a PX available. KMC is only about one mile from the national park visitors center and headquarters and Volcano House Hotel and restaurant. Volcano Country Club Golf Course is just across the highway.

For reservations contact Reservations Desk, Armed Forces Recreation Center, Kilauea Military Camp, Hawai'i Volcanoes National Park, Hawai'i 96718, or call (808) 967-8333 or FAX (808) 967-8343. From Honolulu, O'ahu, call locally 438-6707. When making reservations, you can also arrange a free shuttle bus pick-up at the Hilo Airport unless you want to rent your own car for the 45 minute trip to the camp. KMC guests must pay the standard national park one-time entry fee of $5 per vehicle or $3 per person (when using the KMC shuttle) upon entering the park.

CAMPING

The Big Island has numerous public parks in both coastal and inland areas. The parks are county, state, or federal operated and several are maintained as camp-grounds for those with their own tents and camping gear. Some also have varied housekeeping cabins or shelters that can be rented overnight or longer. There are no commercial camper or motorhome rental agencies on the Big Island.

BIG ISLAND CAMPGROUNDS

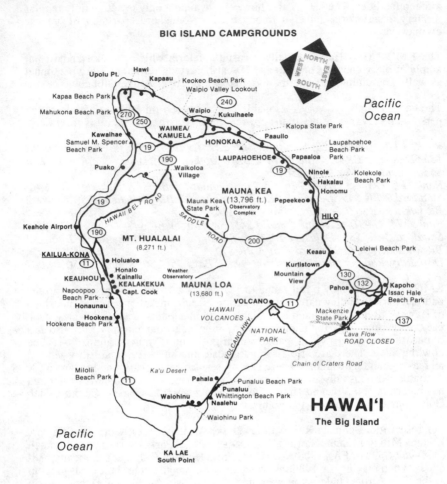

HAWAI'I
The Big Island

County of Hawai'i Parks

The County of Hawai'i maintains eleven parks around the island designated as campgrounds for those with their own tents and camping gear. The County has no cabins on these campgrounds. Facilities vary at the parks with some having full restrooms, showers and drinking water, while others may have more primitive pit latrines and no drinking water available. Check ahead on what facilities are available. Permits are required for campgrounds and for use of the pavilions, if available. Campsites are on a first-come, first-served basis, with advance reservations required, especially for peak seasons like the winter and summer holidays. Camping permits are issued for one week per park in summer months and two weeks per park in other months. Camping fees at County parks are Adults - $1 per day, Juniors (13-17) - $.50 per day, Children (12 and under) - no charge. For permits and complete information regarding County of Hawai'i parks, contact: Department of Parks and Recreation, County of Hawai'i, 25 Aupuni Street, Hilo, HI 96720, (808) 961-8311, or in Kona (808) 323-3046; hours, Mon-Fri 7:45AM -4:30PM.

State of Hawai'i Parks

The State of Hawai'i maintains a system of parks around the Big Island and six of them are designated for use as campgrounds. The parks have either a developed campground, camping shelters, housekeeping cabins, or group accommodations (barracks type) housing available for campers. However, the last few years have seen the quality of state-owned and managed park cabins deteriorate to the point where some are clearly unsuitable for use. Some are badly in need of maintenance work and are not recommended until they are upgraded. Intending campers are recommended to check first with the State Parks Office listed at the end of this section. There are no entrance, parking, picnicking, or camping fees. However, permits are required for camping and lodging in the parks where these are available. The maximum length of stay allowable under each permit for camping or lodging in any park is five nights.

Hapuna Beach State Recreation Area - on Queen Kaahumanu Highway 19, 2.3 miles south of Kawaihae on the Kohala Coast. Picnic pavilions are available. Six simple A-frame shelters are available and have a table, wooden platforms for sleeping bags, electrical outlets and shared cooking facilities, showers and toilets. This is one of best stretches of white sand beach on the island.

Kalopa State Recreation Area - at 2000 ft. elevation on Kalopa Road, 3 miles upland of Highway 19 about 5 miles south of Honoka'a on the Hamakua Coast. There are picnic pavilions, campgrounds, group cabins and a shared recreation/mess hall available. Nature hiking trails in native forest area.

Kilauea State Recreation Area - at 3700 ft. elevation on Kalanikoa Road off Highway 11 in Volcano Village, 29 miles south of Hilo and 1/2 mile east of entrance to Hawai'i Volcanoes National Park. Niaulani Cabin is a housekeeping cabin, sleeps six, furnished with bedding, linens, kitchen facilities, eating utensils, showers and toilets. Near hiking trails and attractions of the national park.

Camping

MacKenzie State Recreation Area - on Kalapana-Kapoho Road, Highway 137, 9 miles northeast of Kaimu Black Sand Beach. Picnic pavilions available; primitive campground, no drinking water.

Manuka State Wayside - on Highway 11, 19.3 miles west of Na'alehu in southern Ka'u district. This is a place to stop and rest and to picnic among a collection of native and exotic trees and plants. Open shelter camping and picnic pavilion; restrooms available but no drinking water.

Mauna Kea State Recreation Area - at 6500 ft. elevation on Saddle Road, 35 miles upland west of Hilo. Open picnic tables (can be windy here), housekeeping cabins and group lodges available. Dry shrub-land environment, good views of Mauna Kea and Mauna Loa, dry clear weather with cool nights. Near to Pohakuloa military training camp with sometimes busy military traffic.

Lodging fees for the accommodations available are as follows: Housekeeping cabins consist of single units and duplex cabins which can accommodate up to 6 persons each. Rates are on a per person per night sliding scale.

1 person - $10   2 persons - $7   3 persons - $6.50
4 persons - $ 6   5 persons - $5.50   6 persons - $5

Housekeeping cabins have a kitchen-living room, a bathroom and one to three bedrooms. Each unit is completely furnished with bedroom and kitchen furniture, electric range, refrigerator, hot shower, bathroom, bedding, linen, towels, dishes, and cooking and eating utensils. Electric heating is provided in cool mountain areas.

Group accommodations are available only at the Mauna Kea State Recreation Area and the Kalopa State Recreation Area. A maximum of 64 persons can be accommodated in group cabins at Mauna Kea and 32 persons at Kalopa. Rates are on a per person per night sliding scale and range from 1 person $8, 2 persons $6, 4 persons $5, 8 persons $3.50, 9-16 persons $3.25, 24 persons $3, up to 64 persons $2. Group accommodations consist of 8 person units provided with beds, bedding, linen, toilet facilities, hot shower, and fireplaces. Centrally located is a recreation-dining hall fully equipped for cooking and serving the entire group. Furnishings include a gas range, water heater, refrigerator, freezer, dishes, cooking and eating utensils, tables and chairs, as well as restrooms-showers and a fireplace. The pavilion is shared by all campers.

Advance reservations are required for any state park cabins. Keys for reserved cabins available from park caretaker or Division of State Parks office in Hilo, 75 Aupuni Street. Check in time is 2PM, check out time is 10AM. For complete information on obtaining a camping and lodging permit, contact: Department of Land & Natural Resources, Division of State Parks, Hawai'i District Office, P.O. Box 936, Hilo, HI 96721-0936, (808) 933-4200.

Hawai'i Volcanoes National Park

The national park maintains three drive-in campgrounds within Volcanoes National Park for campers with their own tents and gear. Each has pavilion-shelters with picnic tables and fireplaces but you need to bring your own wood or fuel supply. Check the discount stores in Hilo or Kona for camping supplies.

No permit is needed and there is no charge for camping. No reservations are taken, as all camping is on a first-come, first-served basis. Stays are limited to 7 days per campground per year. The park service also maintains three simple back-country cabins for hikers but you must register at park headquarters for overnight stays. No reservations are taken for the back-country cabins as use of them is first-come, first-served. However, these cabins are not heavily used and hikers can usually be accommodated. It is necessary to check on trail conditions and water supplies before undertaking a back-country hike. The cabins are located in remote desolate areas, some at high elevations where severe weather can occur, especially in winter. Check with park rangers for information.

One campground, Namakani Paio, also has simple A-frame cabins that can accommodate 4 people in one double bed and two singles. The cabins all share a central restroom and shower facility. Outside each cabin is a picnic table and an outdoor barbecue grill. You must provide your own charcoal and cooking utensils. Rates are $32 per night the year around and include bed linens, towels and blankets. It's recommended you bring extra blankets or sleeping bags (especially in winter) as the cabins are not heated and temperatures can drop to the mid-50's F. Reservations can be made through Volcano House Inn, P.O. Box 53, Hawai'i Volcanoes National Park 96718, (808) 967-7321.

For complete information on visiting, hiking, and camping Hawai'i Volcanoes National Park, contact: Superintendent, Hawai'i Volcanoes National Park, Volcano, HI 96718, (808) 967-7311.

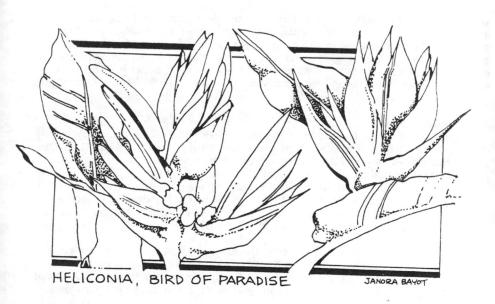

HELICONIA, BIRD OF PARADISE

JANORA BAYOT

NORTH &
SOUTH KONA DISTRICTS

AN INTRODUCTION

This section covers the two districts of West Hawai'i called North and South Kona, which take in some of the most stunning coastline of the Big Island, many important historic sites, and some of its most popular resorts. Since most Big Island visitors arrive at the Kona Airport, this area serves as their introduction to the Island of Hawai'i.

The North and South Kona Districts cover about two-thirds of the West Hawai'i coastline. From north to south, the two districts together stretch along some 60 miles of coastline. From the town of *Kailua-Kona*, located about mid-coast, the roads follow mostly coastal areas where possible. Highway 19 in the north and Highway 11 in the south pass through extremes in geographic terrain and climate. The roads are all paved and in excellent condition generally. It takes less than two hours to leisurely drive the 60 mile length of the North and South Kona Districts.

North Kona
North Kona takes in vast sweeps of plateau, mountain slopes, vast lava flows, and dry scrubland. The area is foothill country leading up to Mount Hualalai (8271 ft.) and Mauna Loa (13,679 ft.). It is rolling rocky countryside and very dry. The average rainfall is below 10 inches along coastal areas to 20-30 inches and more in inland upslope areas. The climate ranges from arid desert to tropical.

North Kona's main center is *Kailua-Kona* which is in fact the center for all of West Hawai'i. Other small villages and settlements include *Holualoa*, *Honalo*, and *Kainaliu*. These are coffee growing areas on the slopes of Mount Hualalai. Keauhou is an adjacent resort area just south of Kailua-Kona. The population of North Kona is not really concentrated in any one area, rather it is spread out in subdivisions and around the countryside on small ranches, farms, acreage, and homesites.

South Kona
South Kona hugs the southwestern coastal slopes and flanks of the huge towering volcano, Mauna Loa. The district's one main road, Highway 11 from Kailua-Kona town, passes through upslope areas rather than following the rugged cliffs of the coast, although some coastal areas are accessible. It's generally rolling hilly country, marked by an arid climate along the coast to tropical rainforest in the inland upper slopes. Rainfall varies by elevation. Highway 11 is generally a good road although some short stretches tend to be narrow and very winding. Caution is advised when traveling through South Kona.

South Kona's commercial center is the town of *Captain Cook*. Other villages include Kealakekua, Honaunau, Keokea, Napo'opo'o, and the Hawaiian fishing village of Miloli'i. Like North Kona, South Kona's population is spread out among the hills and slopes on small ranches, farms, acreage, and homesites.

The area is marked by lush rainforest in upland areas including beautiful tropical trees, plants, and other vegetation all along the road. Macadamia nuts, papaya, bananas, and *Kona coffee* are some of the products grown in orchards of the area. Lovely tropical flowers abound everywhere. In this sense, South Kona is more colorful and "tropical" than the more arid North Kona District.

Kona's Gold Coast

While it's been billed as the "Gold Coast" of the Big Island, the famed Kona Coast is still centered in the somnolent little fishing village of Kailua. Officially known as *Kailua-Kona*, it's just plain Kona to local folks. The Kona Coast covers 60 miles of rugged tropical coastline indented with numerous coves and isolated beaches, jutting fingers and towering cliffs of black lava rock and lush mountain slopes. Its some of the most splendid Hawaiian country you'll find anywhere in the islands. For a long time it was *the* resort destination for the Big Island before the rise of the magnificent South Kohala resorts just up the road.

In the old days, pre 1960 or thereabouts, Kona was a very quiet place. It was small and rural and tourists were few and far between. Kona could hardly be called a resort in those days. But the 60's and 70's brought tourism development and Kailua-Kona rapidly changed from a quiet fishing village to bustling tourist center in a few short years. A construction boom in Kona in the 70's followed by the rise of the nearby Kohala Coast luxury resorts in the 80's attracted many people and created demands for housing, roads, public services, etc. As a result, real estate values skyrocketed along with just about everything else. However, despite its tourist town image, Kona still has a Hawaiian country ambiance about it. Kona's allure rests in its verdant mountain slopes covered with coffee plantations, a deep blue sea filled with hungry marlin and tuna, and a strong tie to old Hawai'i as evidenced by the small town Mom & Pop general stores, old coffee plantation shacks and a relaxed laid-back atmosphere.

The lure of Kona has grown tremendously, thanks in part to a variety of media events and colorful celebrations. The most notable among these are the Hawaiian International Billfish Tournament held each August and the Ironman Triathlon World Championship held each October. These two events alone attract hundreds of participants and media types as well as thousands of spectators from around the world.

Local festivals are held throughout the year and create much interest in and attraction to Kona. These include the Kona Coffee Festival held each autumn to highlight the coffee harvest, King Kamehemaha Day Celebrations in June to honor Hawai'i's first monarch, and Admissions Day in August to honor Hawai'i's admission to the union as the fiftieth State. These and other celebrations all generate a number of parades, parties, and performances of local entertainment.

WHAT TO DO AND SEE

The Kona Coast has a reputation for generally consistent fine sunny weather with daytime temperatures averaging in the high 70's and low 80's F. year around. Rainfall along the Kona Coast varies by elevation but averages from 10-40 inches per year. It is no wonder that Kona is well known to sun and fun worshippers. The area abounds with a variety of activities ranging from the sedate to vigorous.

For adventurous history buffs, the fascinating heiau (temples) of old Hawai'i are a must. These sacred temples are the remnants of the old Hawaiian religion. They have been rebuilt with wood frame and grass thatched huts and fearsome looking carved tiki idols to lend an air of authenticity. In the old days, some of these temples were sites for human sacrifices to the gods. In Kona, there are two of these poignant reminders of the old way of life. One is ***Ahuena Heiau*** ★, located next to Kailua Pier and directly in front of the King Kamehameha Hotel. A walkway in front of the hotel leads directly to it. This site and the surrounding area is where Kamehameha the Great ruled his realm after he united the islands under one kingdom. The other is ***Pu'uhonua O Honaunau National Historic Park*** ★, the best preserved heiau in the islands, is located about 20 miles south of Kailua at Honaunau Bay. This shouldn't be missed as it represents so much of Hawai'i's ancient history and culture. National Park Service personnel are on duty to provide information and maps for a self-guided tour through the complex. The site has a restored temple, wooden tiki images, and canoe sheds. At various times of the year, local Hawaiian cultural groups put on authentic arts and crafts demonstrations highlighted during the Fourth of July period with a spectacular three day cultural festival. Call the park visitors center at 328-2288 for information.

Other historic attractions right in Kailua-Kona are ***Hulihe'e Palace*** ★ built in 1838 and used as a summer residence by Hawaiian royalty and ***Mokuaikaua Church*** ★, built in 1837 and the oldest church in the islands. These two historic buildings are opposite each other on Alii Drive in the heart of town. A $4 admission fee is charged at the palace to assist the Daughters of Hawai'i in maintaining the building and museum. The palace has some lovely antique Hawaiian furniture, original bedroom furnishings, and antique handmade Hawaiian quilts. It's open daily from 9AM-4PM. *Holualoa Village*, located on Mamalahoa Highway (old #180) and off Hualalai Road just minutes above Kailua-Kona town, is quietly emerging as Kona's leading arts and crafts center. The serene little coffee village boasts a considerable working artisans colony. Visitors will enjoy exploring any of the several art galleries and studios producing everything from raku-fired ceramics to original paintings to hand-crafted jewelry. Two of the better known are ***Holualoa Gallery*** featuring prints, sculpture, glasswork, ceramics and paintings of Matt and Mary Lovein, and ***Studio 7 Gallery***, which showcases mixed-media work by Hiroki Morinoue. ***Kimura Lauhala Shop*** in Holualoa is the place to shop for a fine selection of woven pandanus creations such as hats, purses and baskets plus other local authentic handicrafts. These are genuine Hawaiian-made articles, not imports. There are also some rustic village stores, shops and a couple of lodgings, the family-owned ***Kona Hotel*** and ***Holualoa Inn B&B***.

One of Kailua-Kona's more popular recreation spots is ***Magic Sands Beach*** (or Disappearing White Sands Beach) so called for the winter storms which often wash the sand away exposing the rocky coast, only to bring the sand back later. The beach provides good body surfing when sandy but the surf is tricky and dangerous for novices and non-swimmers.

Another popular activity is snorkeling and hand feeding the colorful reef fish at ***Kahalu'u Beach Park*** just five miles from Kailua town in the Keauhou area. Tiny and picturesque ***St. Peter's Catholic Church*** sits right on the beach here.

For the sailor types, glassbottom cruise boats and sailing or diving cruises operate daily trips over Kona's fabulous coral reefs to view the living undersea world.

Check your hotel activity desk for cruise schedules and reservations. And of course, if you want to seriously try your skills (and luck!) at hauling up one of the denizens of the deep for which Kona is justly famous, you can easily book a charter boat for a fishing trip. You can try your skill at landing a marlin, ahi (tuna), mahimahi (dolphin fish), ono (wahoo), or any number of other gamefish which abound in Kona's waters. For charter boat bookings, see your hotel activity desk or check the ACTIVITIES AND TOURS chapter.

South of Kailua-Kona on Highway 11 are the small towns of *Honalo*, *Kainaliu*, *Kealakekua*, *Captain Cook* and *Honaunau*. In Kealakekua, at 81-981 Halekii Street just off the highway is *Macadamia Nuts of Hawaii Factory* (322-2770) where you can enjoy free samples of the cookies and candy. Just outside of Kealakekua, look for the original *Little Grass Shack at Kealakekua* ★ right on the highway. The shop has a good collection of Hawaiiana, gifts, and local arts and crafts.

Along this stretch of coast south is *Kealakekua Bay* where Captain James Cook landed and met his fate at the hands of the Hawaiians in 1778. *Hikiau Heiau* is a restored temple site and located near the bay in the village of Napo'opo'o. A monument across the bay, accessible by boat, marks the exact spot where Captain Cook fell mortally wounded. Many of the snorkel/dive cruise boats come here to let guests dive in the clear waters of the Kealakekua Bay Marine Reserve sanctuary. The Captain Cook monument is also reached by a moderately difficult hiking trail from Highway 11 at Kealakekua town. To locate the trail, turn off Highway 11 (Hawai'i Belt Road) at Napo'opo'o Road to Kealakekua Bay (watch for sign). Just 100-yards from the turnoff is a dirt-gravel trail directly across from three big royal palm trees and running downslope between fence rows. You can park along the road. The trail is 1 1/4 miles down to the Cook monument and alternates between steep and level, rough rocky/loose gravel to solid footing. Allow at least three hours for a round trip. Be sure to take water, hat and sunscreen.

A couple of miles further down on the Napo'opo'o Road near the village and Kealakekua Bay is the *Mauna Loa Royal Kona Coffee Mill & Museum* (328-2511) where you can tour the museum displays for some history on Kona coffee farming and enjoy a free cup of fresh Kona coffee. The museum also has a gift shop.

PUUHONUA O'HONAUNAU NATIONAL PARK

The ***Kona Historical Society Museum*** ★, P.O. Box 398, Captain Cook, HI 96704 (808) 323-3222 is housed in the historic Greenwell Store located on Highway 11, one-half mile south of Kealakekua. Museum hours are 9AM - 3PM weekdays, closed holidays. The museum has regular historic displays featuring early Kona history and maintains a growing reference library and archives. The museum is part of the old Greenwell Ranch. Open to the public, admission by donation.

Next door is the ***Greenwell Coffee Farms*** where you can tour the coffee groves and learn about the famed Kona coffee industry. At the village of Captain Cook, look for the old country ***Manago Hotel*** where room rates are reasonable and local-style family meals are still served in the dining room. Just two doors away is the new home of ***Furukawa's Kitch'n Cook'd Potato Chips***, a long-time Kona favorite.

Also, just south of Captain Cook, look for a sign to the ***Amy B.H. Greenwell Ethnobotanical Garden***, P.O. Box 1053, Captain Cook, HI 96704, (808) 323-3318. This 10-acre botanical garden is being developed by the Bishop Museum of Honolulu as a living museum of traditional Hawaiian ethnobotany. The garden is open free to the public, 9AM - Noon daily for self-guided tours. Docent guided tours given on second Saturday of each month.

A little further south on Highway 11 is the ***Mauna Loa Polynesian Village and Marketplace*** ★ (328-2222), where you can experience the daily life of a typical Polynesian island village. The attraction showcases the arts and crafts, dance, music, foods and lifestyle of Polynesian island culture and is operated by a Tongan family. The village and marketplace is down below the Mauna Loa coffee shack/gift shop and its noted treehouse along the highway.

At Honaunau is the turnoff onto Highway 160 which leads down to the ***Pu'uhonua O Honaunau National Historic Park*** ★ at Honaunau Bay which was described earlier in this section. A side road from Highway 160 leads to *St. Benedict's Church* ★, which is Kona's famous "Painted Church." The church's interior is elaborately painted in religious scenes.

Highway 11 continues south into the Ka'u District and on to Hawai'i Volcanoes National Park, a distance of 97 miles and approximately a 2 hour and 45 minute drive. The route continues on to Hilo, another 28 miles or 40 minute drive.

WHERE TO SHOP

For those with shopping in mind, Kona has many possibilities. On Palani Road just above Kuakini Highway and the King Kamehameha Hotel are two shopping centers. On the north side is the ***Kona Coast Shopping Center***, anchored by ***KTA Superstore*** and ***Marshall's*** discount store, along with several other specialty shops and some local-style eateries. Opposite this on the south is the ***Lanihau Center*** featuring ***Long's Drugs*** and ***Sack 'n Save Supermarket***. There is also ***Baskins-Robbins Ice Cream***, ***Royal Jade Garden*** (Chinese food), ***Kona Grill*** (sandwiches/snacks) and a bakery-deli with the amusing name of ***Buns in the Sun***.

Below the Lanihau Center in the ***Kopiko Plaza***, there are more shops and restaurants including ***Kaminari Japanese Restaurant***, ***Yuri's Saimin*** and ***Kona Mixed Plate***. Adjacent to this plaza is ***Hilo Hattie's*** at 75-5597A Palani Road,

329-7200, a factory which produces colorful Aloha wear including those bright Aloha shirts, muumuus, pareaus, swimsuits, etc. They have free factory tours and a large inventory of garments from which to select at factory prices.

And for those who can't do without them, just above Kona Coast and Lanihau Centers near the main intersection of Highway 19 and Palani Road are Kona's newest big mainland retail discounters. *K-Mart* is just north of Palani Road off Highway 19 at Makalapua Center while *Wal-Mart* is just south of Palani Road on Henry Street off Highway 19. *Kamehameha Square* is a small shopping complex on Kuakini Highway near the intersection with Palani Road. It is located behind the Hotel King Kamehameha. In this center are *Ocean Seafood Restaurant* for Chinese seafood specials and *Bangkok Houses* for Thai-style fare. *Kona Wine Market, Island Preservations, Nature Walk Gifts, The Myna Bird Tree* and *Beachkomers Gifts* are some of the shops located here.

King Kamehameha Kona Beach Resort has a large shopping mall adjacent to its lobby. Anchoring the mall is a small branch of *Liberty House*, Hawai'i's chain department store (which will soon be overshadowed by a new Liberty House-Kona). This one features mostly resort wear and Aloha wear fashions, Hawaiiana, souvenirs, etc. Also in the mall are a number of shops including *Alii Artwear, Island Togs, Styles Resortwear* and *Jafar* for clothing and resort or Aloha wear. For the best in local coral jewelry and gifts try *Silver Reef Jewelry, Jewel Palace* and *The Shellery*. And for authentic Hawaiiana and Polynesian arts and crafts, *Mele'o Polynesian Handcrafts* has a wide selection. Also in the mall are *Atlantis Submarine Booking Office* and *King Kamehameha Divers*.

On Alii Drive across from the King Kamehameha Hotel and the Kailua-Kona Pier there are a number of small shopping centers and arcades with numerous shops. The *Seaside Shopping Mall* features *DJ's Cycle Rentals, Bubi's Sportswear, Kona Coast Sunglass Co., Tapa House of Polynesia, Goldfish Jewelry, Sandal Stop, Tropical Tees*. The *Kona Activities Booking Center* and *Nautilus II Submarine* booking office are also here. Upstairs is the *Kona Galley Restaurant* with nice views of the pier and sunsets over Kailua Bay.

In the *Kona Square Shopping Center* directly opposite the pier, try *E-Z Discount Store* for sundries, *Island Silversmith* and *Gems of the Sea* for jewelry and gifts, and *Mermaids Boutique* for swimwear and resortwear. *The Exploration Company* is an activity booking and outfitter service. *Kona Amigos Restaurant* is located upstairs.

In the *Kona Banyan Court Center*, you'll find *Unison Kona* for T-shirts and official Ironman Triathlon wear, *Kona's Finest Woods* for local woodcraft and gifts, *Big Island Jewelers, Pearl Gallery* for pearl jewelry, *Paradise Antiques* for some unusual Hawaiiana collectibles and *Kona Water Sports* for water sports activities rentals. You'll also find *Sibu Cafe*, Kona's only restaurant featuring Indonesian cuisine.

In the *Kailua Bay Inn Shopping Plaza* just opposite Hulihee Palace and the seawall, check out *Kona Arts & Crafts* for Hawaii-made products, *Kona Gold Jewelry* for jewelry, *Kona Jog & Gift Shop* for gifts, *Sunset Traders* for clothing and gifts. The arcade also has eateries like *Aki's Cafe, Golden Sun Restaurant* and *Bad Ass Coffee Co. Espresso Bar*. Just behind the complex across the alley is *ABC Store* for sundries, *Pacific Vibrations* for swimwear and ocean sporting goods and *Tropical Squeeze* for snack bar refreshments including coffee, juices, soda and fresh fruit smoothies and ice cream.

In the *Kona Plaza Shopping Arcade* is *Middle Earth Bookshop*, the *Hawai'i Visitors Bureau-Kona Office*, *Cloud Nine Boutique* and *Cassandra's Greek Taverna* cafe. Out front along Alii Drive is *Kona Marketplace* and *Crazy Shirts* for T-shirt fashions. Upstairs is *Pancho & Lefty's Mexican Restaurant*.

Kona Marketplace next-door wing also has a number of interesting shops worth exploring, including *Paradise Clothing*, *Kona Flea Market*, *A Little Extra*, *Goodies of Hawai'i*, *Kona Bazaar*, *The Eclectic Craftsman*, *BT Pottery & Jewelry* and others.

There are also many interesting shops in the *Kona Inn Shopping Village*. Besides retail shops the center features such restaurants and snack shops as *Fisherman's Landing*, *The Captain's Deck*, *Kona Inn Restaurant*, *The Royal Thai Cafe*, *Cuz'uns*, *Mrs. Barry's Kona Cookies* and *Don Drysdale's Club 53*. Take some time and stroll through this complex and browse such places as *Tropical Touch Boutique*, *Alley Gecko's*, *Aloha Spirit*, *Kona Inn Jewelry*, *Golden Orchids*, *Island Life Tee Shirts*, *Hawaiian Fruit & Flower Co.*, *Flamingo's*, *Hula Heaven Hawaiiana*, *Big Island Hat Co.*, *Kona Inn General Store*, *Sgt. Leisure* and many more.

Down Alii Drive, a block or so south of Kona Inn Shopping Village, is *Waterfront Row*, across from St. Michael's Church, a complex that is a combination dining-shopping center. The food arcade features *The Chart House*, *Jolly Roger*, *Bad Ass Coffee Espresso Bar*, *Happi Yu Japanese Steak House* and *Yu Sushi* on the lower level and *Michaelangelo's Italian & Seafood Restaurant* upstairs. Shops include *Crazy Shirts*, *Pure Kona Art*, and *Wyland Galleries*. There is validated underground parking available.

The parking lot on the corner of Alii Drive and Hualalai Road next door to St. Michael's Church is the site for the *Kailua Farmers' Market* which is held every Wednesday-Friday-Saturday-Sunday, 6AM - 3PM. Here you'll find all sorts of fresh local produce, fruit, veggies, baked goods, arts & crafts, and more.

At the *Alii Sunset Plaza* next to the Kona Alii Condo, there aren't any shops but there are plenty of places to eat. Over the past couple of years the plaza has quietly become something of an international cuisine dining center in Kona with many varieties of cuisine available. There are several restaurants here including *King Yee Lau Chinese Restaurant*, *Restaurant Yokohama*, *Yasu's Kona Sushi*, *Rico's Mexican Restaurant* and *Thai Rin Restaurant* along with *Island Lava Java Espresso Bar*, *A Piece of the Apple* and *Mona's BBQ*.

South of Kailua-Kona at Keauhou, *Keauhou Shopping Village* is located off Highway 11 at the intersection of Kamehameha III Road and Alii Drive.

It's anchored by *KTA Supermarket*. Shops include *Alapaki's* for fine Hawaiian gifts, handmade originals, wood carvings, etc. plus *Keauhou Golf Shop*, *Showcase Gallery* and *Keauhou Village Book Shop* and others. A new phase to the center was recently added and is anchored by *Long's Drugs* and *Ben Franklin Crafts*. Eateries include *Drysdales Two*, *Bad Ass Coffee Co. Espresso Bar*, and *Daylight's Donuts*.

ACCOMMODATIONS -

NORTH AND SOUTH KONA

INTRODUCTION: The resorts and hotels of the Kona Coast are primarily located in the immediate *Kailua-Kona* town area and spread out along Alii Drive for five miles south leading to a cluster of hotels and condos in the Keauhou area. The accommodations range from first-class hotel and luxury condominiums, to standard budget hotels, to an exclusive hideaway South Seas-style beach resort featuring individual island "hales" (cottages). Unlike other resort areas of Kaua'i, O'ahu, and Maui, Big Island resorts generally don't have broad sandy beaches due to the fact that Hawai'i is still a young island and has not yet developed many fine sandy beaches. At least this is the case on the Kona Coast, where many properties listed as being on the "beach" or "beachfront," are not necessarily on a nice sandy beach. In fact, it is often the exact opposite with the "beach" being very rough rugged lava rock interspersed with sandy areas. However, there are some good beaches in the area. See the ACTIVITIES AND TOURS chapter for details on area beaches.

Whether you decide to stay right in Kailua-Kona town, or in one of the condos along Alii Drive, or even in the nearby Keauhou area, you will still be close to all of the Kona Coast's attractions, dining options, and shopping. Most of the activities and resort attractions are within a 10 mile radius of Kailua-Kona or no more than a short ride away, regardless of where one stays.

The lone exception to that rule would be the Kona Village Resort, and next door Four Seasons Resort, located in North Kona, twelve miles north of Kailua-Kona town. These exclusive resorts are quite secluded on the coast and most visitors who choose to stay there usually do so for the privacy, seclusion, and complete relaxation which these resorts provides.

By staying in the Kailua-Kona or Keauhou areas, you have easy access to all the activities, attractions, dining, and shopping opportunities of these resort centers. The dining experiences available along the Kona Coast vary considerably. There is a good selection of resort dining rooms and family restaurants in town as well as a variety of local-style eateries featuring ethnic favorites. See the RESTAU-RANTS chapter for details.

The Kailua-Kona area offers a distinct resort-town atmosphere and attracts the majority of Big Island visitors. With its multitude of hotels, shopping arcades and centers, varied restaurants, shops, historic sites, and busy charter fishing boat harbor, it is the Big Island's preeminent tourist center.

There is a lot of hustle and bustle along Alii Drive which is the main street of the town and follows the Kailua Bay coastline and continues south to the Keauhou area.

111

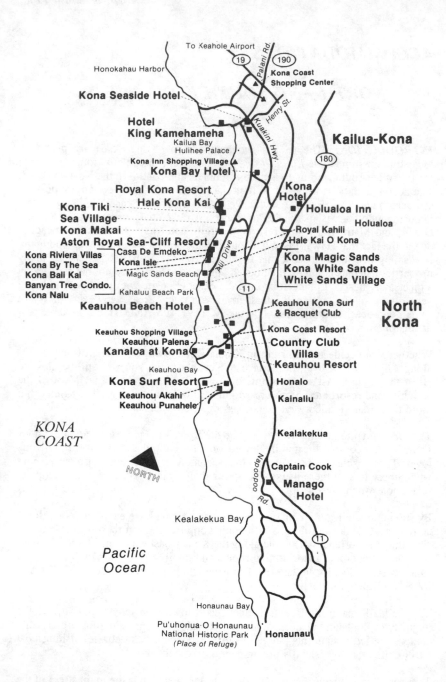

To Keahole Airport

Honokahau Harbor

Kona Seaside Hotel

Kona Coast
Shopping Center

**Hotel
King Kamehameha**
Kailua Bay
Hulihee Palace
Kona Inn Shopping Village
Kona Bay Hotel

Kailua-Kona

Royal Kona Resort
Hale Kona Kai

Kona
Hotel

Kona Tiki
Sea Village
Kona Makai
Aston Royal Sea-Cliff Resort

Holualoa Inn

Holualoa

Royal Kahili
Hale Kai O Kona

Kona Riviera Villas
Kona By The Sea
Kona Bali Kai
Banyan Tree Condo.
Kona Nalu

Casa De Emdeko
Kona Isle
Magic Sands Beach
Kahaluu Beach Park

Kona Magic Sands
Kona White Sands
White Sands Village

Ali Drive

Keauhou Beach Hotel

Keauhou Kona Surf
& Racquet Club

**North
Kona**

Keauhou Shopping Village
Keauhou Palena
Kanaloa at Kona

Kona Coast Resort

**Country Club
Villas**
Keauhou Resort

Keauhou Bay

Kona Surf Resort
Keauhou Akahi
Keauhou Punahele

Honalo

Kainaliu

Kealakekua

*KONA
COAST*

NORTH

Captain Cook

**Manago
Hotel**

Napoopoo Rd.

Kealakekua Bay

*Pacific
Ocean*

Honaunau Bay

Pu'uhonua O Honaunau
National Historic Park
(Place of Refuge)

Honaunau

Kailua-Kona evolved from a quiet country village that became noted for its excellent marlin and tuna fishing into the busy resort town of today. And while the town has changed considerably, it still has that special Hawaiian quality of embracing and respecting the past, enjoying the present and not rushing too fast into the future. It's a resort town true enough but it's still small enough to appreciate and enjoy. And yet it offers visitors those things they want most of a in a vacation in Hawai'i: good choice and value in accommodations, a wide range of restaurants, numerous opportunities for shopping and activities galore.

The Keauhou area is somewhat different than Kailua-Kona town. It is a cluster of hotels and condominiums located five miles south of town at the end of Alii Drive. The properties are either on the "beach" (again, no real sandy beach but rather rocky lava rock coastline here) or are situated around the golf course at the Kona Country Club. Keauhou has the quiet ambiance and casualness one would expect of a resort. The generally good accommodations and facilities of the area make it a desirable vacation destination whether one is interested in golf, tennis, sightseeing, shopping or just getting away from it all. And other than resort shops in the hotels, the only other shopping in the immediate area is at the *Keauhou Shopping Village* noted earlier.

BEST BETS:

King Kamehameha Kona Beach Hotel - This is a good standard quality hotel right on a small sand beach (perfect for kids) on Kailua Bay, in the heart of Kailua-Kona resort town and near to everything.

Country Club Villas - This condo complex is located at the Kona Country Club golf course in Keauhou and is an ideal location, especially for golfers, and still accessible to everything else in Kona.

Kanaloa at Kona - A very nicely maintained condo complex with well furnished, spacious, and comfortable units with beachfront location but no sand beach.

Keauhou Beach Hotel - This is one of the more underrated of Kona's hotel properties, yet its rooms are very clean, comfortable, and it has a relaxing atmosphere. Renovations in the lobby and dining room areas have improved appearances.

Kona by the Sea - This is a conveniently located complex right on the beach about two miles from Kailua-Kona town center. The rooms are very neat, clean and spacious. Nice pool area with adjoining grass yard for young children. Good value for family groups.

Royal Kona Resort - This is one of Kona's original large tourist hotel properties. Even though it has no real sandy beach, like most Kona hotels and resorts (it does have a tiny manmade sand cove), it has a pleasant atmosphere and is a nice place to stay. The rooms are very clean and quite comfortable. Ask for a room in either the Village or Beach Buildings as the Main Building has lots of noise and music at night from the lounge. It's just a short walk to the center of Kailua-Kona town.

Kona Village Resort - If you want privacy, seclusion, and just plain old peace and quiet, this is for you. A South Seas atmosphere pervades the village with its authentically-styled island cottages reflecting the architecture of Fiji, Samoa, Tonga, Tahiti, New Guinea and other Pacific Islands.

Note: Kona and Kohala resorts and hotels have varied rates by low season (approximately May 1 to November 30) and high season (December 1 to April 30). Listed rates for hotels and condos cover the range of low and high seasons. Check what seasonal rates apply when booking your reservations and inquire about any discounts (many of which are not publicized). Especially during the low season, hotel/condo rooms can be had for less than advertised rates.

KONA COAST ACCOMMODATIONS

Alii Villas
Aston Royal
  Sea-Cliff Resort
Banyan Tree Condo
Casa De Emdeko
Country Club Villas
Four Seasons Resort
  Hawaii at Hualalai
Hale Kona Kai
Hale Pohaku
Kahaluu Bay Villas
Kailua Bay Resort
Kailua Village
Kanaloa at Kona
Keauhou Akahi
Keauhou Beach Hotel
Keauhou Kona Surf
  & Racquet Club
Keauhou Palena
Keauhou Punahele

Keauhou Resort
King Kamehameha
  Kona Beach Hotel
Kona Alii Condo
Kona Bali Kai
Kona Bay Hotel
Kona Billfisher Condo
Kona By The Sea
Kona Coast Resort
Kona Hotel
Kona Islander Inn
Kona Isle
Kona Luana
Kona Magic Sands
Kona Makai
Kona Mansions
Kona Nalu
Kona Onenalo
Kona Palms
Kona Plaza Condos

Kona Reef
Kona Riviera
  Villa Condo
Kona Seaside Hotel
Kona Surf Resort
Kona Tiki Hotel
Kona Village Resort
Kona West
Kona White Sands
  Apartment Hotel
Malia Kai
Manago Hotel
Mauna Loa Village
Royal Kahili
Royal Kailuan
Royal Kona Resort
Sea Village
White Sands Village

ALII VILLAS
75-6016 Alii Drive, Kailua-Kona, HI 96740, (808) 329-1288. Agent: Golden Triangle Real Estate (808) 329-1667; Hawaiian Apartment Leasing 1-800-854-548843; Hawai'i Resort Management 1-800-553-5035, Hawai'i (808) 329-9393; Knutson & Associates 1-800-800-6202, Hawaii (808) 329-6311; West Hawaii Property Services (808) 322-6696. This condo has only ten units in rental programs. It is a beachfront location with palm trees, flowers and garden setting less than a mile from town. Units are generally clean and well kept although this is strictly a budget-condo operation.
1 BR g.v. $65-75 day, $420-450 week; 1 BR o.v. $75 day, $525 week; 2 BR o.f. (2,max 4) $110-125 day, $735-750 week

ASTON ROYAL SEA-CLIFF RESORT
725-6040 Alii Drive, Kailua-Kona, HI 96740, (808) 329-8021. Agent: Aston Hotels & Resorts 1-800-922-7866, in Hawai'i 1-800-321-2558; FAX (808) 922-8785. This is a 148 unit condo-hotel about a mile and a half south of Kailua-Kona

town. The air-conditioned spacious units are excellent for families and are fully furnished including kitchen with microwave, small appliances and full in-unit laundry facilities. Guest facilities also include parking, both fresh and saltwater pools, tennis court and barbecues. The complex is a terrace arrangement making the lower units closer to the shoreline and very private and quiet. The only drawback is the need for new furnishings, carpets, and general refurbishing of the units as they are showing some age and wear in what would otherwise be a luxury-category condo. Spend 7 nights with Aston Hotels and get a 20% discount, inquire when booking. *Studio $145-160, 1 BR (2,max 4) $165-215, 2 BR (2,max 6) $195-245, Oceanfront Villa $455-505*

BANYAN TREE CONDOMINIUM
76-6268 Alii Drive, Kailua-Kona, HI 96740, (808) 329-4220. Agent: Village Realty 1-800-927-1577; Kona Vacation Resorts, 1-800-367-5168, Canada 1-800-800-KONA, FAX (808) 329-5480. This small 20 unit condo has just 10 units available for rental. All are 2 bedroom/2 bath oceanfront units that will accommodate up to four people. Some units may accommodate up to six, $10 per extra person. Covered parking, heated swimming pool for winter, ceiling fans, no air-conditioning. Minimum stay of four days required. *2 BR $115-140 day, $690-840 week, $2484-2520 month*

CASA DE EMDEKO ★
75-6082 Alii Drive, Kailua-Kona, HI 96740, (808) 329-6488. Agents: Hawai'i Resort Management 1-800-553-5035, Hawai'i (808) 329-9393; Kona Vacation Resorts, US 1-800-367-5168, FAX (808) 329-5480; Village Realty (808) 329-1577; Knutson & Associates 1-800-800-6202, Hawai'i (808) 329-6311; Golden Triangle Real Estate (808) 329-1667; West Hawaii Property Services (808) 322-6696.

This lovely three story white-washed building is located on the water although there is no sand beach here. The 40 available units are spacious, comfortable, and well-appointed. The central garden-courtyard is well maintained with tropical plants. The oceanside swimming pool features a "sandy beach" surrounding the pool. *1 BR g.v. $75-90, $510-525 week, 1 BR o.v. $75-100, $595-600 week, 2 BR o.v./o.f. $115; $805 week, Extra person $10*

COUNTRY CLUB VILLAS (W)
78-6920 Alii Drive, Kailua-Kona, HI 96740, (808) 322-2501. Agents: Hawaiian Apartment Leasing 1-800-854-8843; Hawai'i Resort Management 1-800-553-5035, Hawai'i (808) 329-9393; Keauhou Property Management 1-800-745-KONA, FAX (808) 326-2055; Knutson & Associates 1-800-800-6202, Hawai'i (808) 329-6311; Ron Burla & Associates (808) 329-2421; Triad Management 1-800-345-2823, FAX (808) 326-2401; Village Realty 1-800-927-1577; West Hawaii Property Services (808) 322-6696.

This condominium is located on the Kona Country Club golf course with easy access to other Keauhou resorts, dining, shopping, etc. Amenities include TV, private lanai on each unit, 2 tennis courts, and on request maid service. All units have golf course views with Kona Coast beyond. Minimum 5 nights. *2 BR/3 BR Suites only: 2 BR o.v. (2,max 4) $130-140, $800 week, $2600 month; 3 BR o.v. (2,max 6) $130-180, $780-1020 week, $2808-3400 month*

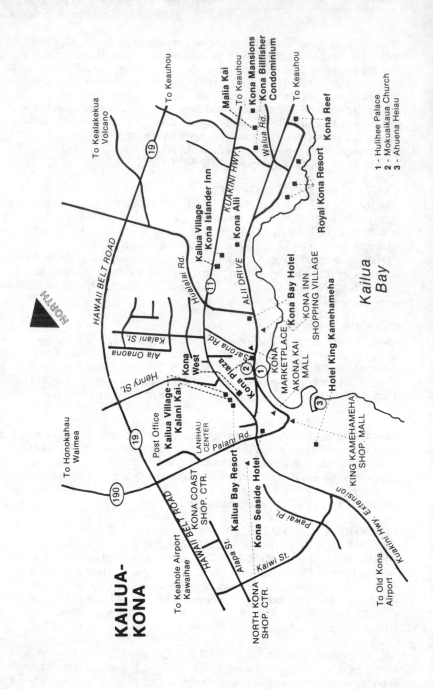

KAILUA-KONA

NORTH

To Honokahau Waimea
To Keahole Airport Kawaihae
To Kealakekua Volcano
To Keauhou

HAWAII BELT ROAD
HAWAII BELT ROAD

Post Office
Kailua Village Kalani Kai

Kona Village Kalani Kai
Kona Islander Inn
Kona Alii

Hualalai Rd.
Henry St.
Kalani St.
Ala Onaona

Kona West
Kona Plaza

KUAKINI HWY.
ALII DRIVE

Walua Rd.

Malia Kai
Kona Mansions
Kona Billfisher Condominium
To Keauhou
To Keauhou

Kona Reef

Royal Kona Resort

LANIHAU CENTER
KONA COAST SHOP. CTR.
Alapa St.
Palani Rd.
Sarona Rd.

Kailua Bay Resort
Kona Seaside Hotel
NORTH KONA SHOP. CTR.
Kaiwi St.
Pawai Pl.

KONA MARKETPLACE
Kona Bay Hotel
KONA INN SHOPPING VILLAGE
AKONA KAI MALL
Hotel King Kamehameha

KING KAMEHAMEHA SHOP. MALL

Kuakini Hwy. Extension

To Old Kona Airport

Kailua Bay

1 - Hulihee Palace
2 - Mokuaikaua Church
3 - Ahuena Heiau

To Keauhou

FOUR SEASONS RESORT HAWAII AT HUALALAI

P.O. Box 1119, Kailua-Kona, HI 96745; 1-800-334-6284, Tel (808) 325-8000, Fax (808) 325-8100. This is the Kona Coast's newest resort hotel and was scheduled to open in early fall, 1996. It's located on a remote stretch of beachfront land immediately next door to the venerable Kona Village Resort just north of the Kona airport.

The Four Seasons has 243 rooms and suites in 32 beachfront and four golf course bungalows. There are one, two and three-bedroom suites, some with private plunge pools. The resort is surrounded by the Jack Nicklaus-designed golf course, an 18-hole, par-72 championship layout. The Hualalai course has been designated the home of the Senior PGA Tournament of Champions for ten years beginning in 1997. The resort also features a driving range, putting and chipping greens, eight court tennis complex, and Hawaiian interpretive center depicting the story of the land and its people through historic and cultural displays. The resort features the Oceanfront Restaurant, Poolside Bar & Grill and Golf Club Restaurant & Bar.

In addition to a variety of resort activities, there is a special "Kids for All Seasons" program for children aged 5-12 offered the year-round.
Rates were unavailable at press time.

HALE KONA KAI ★ (W)

75-5870 Kahakai Road, Kailua-Kona, HI 96740. 1-800-421-3696, (808) 329-2155. Agents: Kona Vacation Resorts, 1-800-367-5168, Canada 1-800-800-KONA, FAX (808) 329-5480; Triad Management 1-800-345-2823, FAX (808) 326-2401; Hawai'i Resort Management 1-800-553-5035 or (808) 329-9393. This 39 unit condo is air-conditioned with on request maid service, TV, BBQ facility. No room telephones. Corner units are larger with bigger lanai area but all units are very nicely furnished. Minimum stay required is three days. Located right on the water and immediately next door to the Royal Kona Resort, but there is no sand beach; within walking distance to the village. *1 BR (2,max 4) $75-85, $510 week, $1530 month   Extra person $10*

HALE POHAKU

76-6194 Alii Drive, Kailua-Kona, HI 96740. Agent: Kona Vacation Resorts, 1-800-367-5168, Canada 1-800-800-KONA, FAX (808) 329-5480. This small 6 unit complex offers oceanfront privacy, individual lanais, ceiling fans, full kitchens, swimming pool, paddle tennis and entertainment area.
2 BR (2,max 4) $140, $840 week, $2520 month

KAHALUU BAY VILLAS

78-6715A Alii Drive, Kailua-Kona, HI 96740, (808) 322-0013. Agent: Kona Vacation Resorts, 1-800-367-5168, Canada 1-800-800-KONA, FAX (808) 329-5480. This luxury complex is a short walk along Alii Drive to Kahaluu Beach Park where there is good snorkeling. Spacious units have separate master bedrooms, full kitchens, ceiling fans, private lanais, pool, gazebo, parking and barbecue area.
1 BR o.v. $90, $540 week, $1620 month;
2 BR o.v. $140, $840 week, $2520 month

KAILUA BAY RESORT
75-5669 Kuakini Highway, Kailua-Kona, HI 96740, (808) 329-2260. This 15 unit condo does not have air-conditioning. In room TV and swimming pool with spa are available. Located one long block from the rocky beach of Kailua Bay and near the center of Kailua-Kona town shopping, restaurants, etc. Minimum 3 months lease. *1 BR $780-850, 2 BR $850-1000*

KAILUA VILLAGE
At the intersection of Hualalai Road and Kuakini Highway near the town center. Agent: Hawai'i Resort Management 1-800-553-5035, Hawai'i (808) 329-9393, FAX (808) 326-4137; Knutson & Associates 1-800-800-6202, Hawai'i (808) 329-6311. This multi-story complex is one block from the ocean and within easy walking distance of the town center, restaurants, shopping, attractions, Kailua Pier, etc. The 1 BR units have window a/c, and access to swimming pool, parking, elevators. *1 BR o.v. $55-79, Week $385-490, Month $1155-1470*

KALANIKAI CONDOMINIUMS
75-5681 Kuakini Highway, Kailua-Kona, HI 96740, (808) 329-5241. Agents: West Hawai'i Property Services, Inc. (808) 322-6696; Paradise Management 1-800-272-5252; Property Management 1-800-358-7977, FAX 808 329-1200. This condominium is located in the heart of the village and within walking distance of resort activities, shopping, and restaurants. Amenities include air-conditioning and BBQ facilities. Units have mountain views. *1 BR $59-75 day, $350-455 week, $1400 month*

KANALOA AT KONA ★
78-261 Manukai St., Kailua-Kona, HI 96740, 1-800-777-1700, (808) 322-9625, FAX (808) 322-3818. Agents: Colony Hotels and Resorts, Inc. 1-800-777-1700; Hawaiian Apartment Leasing 1-800-854-8843; Keauhou Property Management 1-800-745-KONA, FAX (808) 326-2055; Kona Vacation Resorts, 1-800-367-5168, Canada 1-800-800-KONA, FAX (808) 329-5480; Outrigger Hotels Hawaii, 1-800-OUTRIGGER (688-7444); Property Network 1-800-358-7977, FAX 808 329-1200.

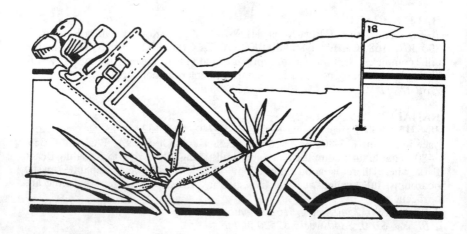

This 120 unit condo is located oceanfront in Keauhou but there is no sandy beach. The luxurious units are spacious and fully equipped including lanai wet bar, Koa wood interiors, ceiling fans, and TV. Kanaloa is bordered on one side by the sparkling blue Pacific with a secluded bay for snorkeling and sunning and on the other by the Kona Country Club golf course. Tennis courts, Edward's at the Terrace Restaurant, cocktail lounge, BBQ facilities, and recreation-meeting room are on property.
1 BR $130-150, $775-850 week; 2 BR $135-195, $850-1100 week; 3 BR $180-250, $1350 week   Extra person $15

KEAUHOU AKAHI
78-7030 Alii Drive, Kailua-Kona, HI 96740, (808) 322-2590. Agents: Triad Management 1-800-345-2823, FAX (808) 326-2401; Village Realty (808) 329-1577; Golden Triangle Real Estate (808) 329-1667. This 48 unit complex is located on the Kona Country Club golf course with far ocean views. There are laundry facilities in each unit, full kitchens and on property swimming pool. It is 7 miles from the village. Minimum one week stay.
1 1/2 BR o.v. $400-550 week, $1200-1650 month

KEAUHOU BEACH HOTEL ★
78-6740 Alii Drive, Keauhou-Kona, HI 96740, (808) 322-3441, 1-800-367-6025, local 1-800-446-8990, FAX (808) 947-7338. This is an older but generally well-maintained 310 room property located next to the rocky coastline. There is a very small sand beach and lovely tidal pools for youngsters to explore for marine life at low tide. Night lighting on the tidal pools brings out all sorts of marine life for easy viewing from the hotel's wrap-around lanai next to the tidal pools. The hotel features air-conditioning, TV, sauna, exercise room, room refrigerators, tennis courts, and Kuakini Terrace Restaurant for casual ala carte and daily buffet dining. Rooms are very clean, spacious, and comfortable and most have nice views of Keauhou coastline. The property has a very relaxing and pleasant ambiance.
g.v. $100, part o.v. $110, o.v. $130, Deluxe o.v. $150, Deluxe o.f. $170, Suites $245-415, Extra person $15

KEAUHOU KONA SURF & RACQUET CLUB ★
Alii Drive, Kailua-Kona, HI 96740, (808) 322-9231. Agents: Clark Realty 1-800-929-7667, (808) 329-5300; Golden Triangle Real Estate (808) 329-1667; Hawai'i Resort Management 1-800-553-5035, Hawai'i (808) 329-9393; Hawaiian Apartment Leasing 1-800-854-8843; Keauhou Property Management 1-800-745-KONA, FAX (808) 326-2055; Kona Vacation Resorts, US 1-800-367-5168, Canada 1-800-423-8733, ext. 329, FAX (808) 329-5480; Knutson & Associates 1-800-800-6202, Hawai'i (808) 329-6311; Ron Burla & Associates (808) 329-2421; Village Realty 1-800-927-1577; West Hawai'i Property Services, Inc. (808) 322-6696. This is a large complex of 190 units which are very nicely furnished with TV's plus great views of the golf course fairways or ocean. The complex has wonderful recreation facilities including 3 lighted tennis courts and a poolside community center.
2 BR $ 85-135, $550-945 week, $1800-2835 month; 3 BR $160, $1000 week, $3100 month

KEAUHOU PALENA CONDOMINIUM
78-7054 Kamehameha III Road, Kailua-Kona, HI 96740, (808) 322-3620.
Agents: Clark Realty 1-800-929-7667, (808) 329-5300; Golden Triangle Real
Estate (808) 329-1667; Keauhou Property Management 1-800-745-KONA, FAX
(808) 326-2055); Village Realty 1-800-927-1577; West Hawai'i Property (808)
322-6696; Kona Vacation Resorts, US 1-800-367-5168, Canada 1-800-423-8733,
ext. 329, FAX (808) 329-5480.

This condo is on the eleventh fairway of the Kona Country Club golf course with
easy access for golfing visitors. Units are fully equipped including ceiling fans
and TV. The den makes into an extra bedroom enabling these units to sleep four
comfortably. It's located near the end of Alii Drive in the Keauhou area.
1 BR (2,max 4) $80-95 day, $480-625 week, $1710-2100 month

KEAUHOU PUNAHELE CONDOMINIUM ★
78-7070 Alii Drive, Kailua-Kona, HI 96740, (808) 322-6585, reservations (206)
742-2440. Agents: Hawai'i Resort Management 1-800-553-5035, Hawai'i (808)
329-9393; Hawaiian Apartment Leasing 1-800-854-8843; Keauhou Property
Management 1-800-745-KONA, FAX (808) 326-2055; Village Realty 1-800-927-
1577; West Hawai'i Property Services, Inc. (808) 322-6696; Golden Triangle
Real Estate (808) 329-1667; Century 21 1-800-255-8052; Kona Vacation Resorts,
US 1-800-367-5168, Canada 1-800-423-8733, ext. 329, FAX (808) 329-5480;
Triad Management 1-800-345-2823, FAX (808) 326-2401

This large complex (93 units) has only a few available in rental programs. It is
the last complex at the end of Alii Drive in the Keauhou area and on the Kona
Country Club golf course with ocean view across golf course. Units are not air-
conditioned but are roomy and generally well-appointed with high ceilings
keeping units cool and breezy. The units are clean and well-kept and the grounds
are well-groomed. Located 7 1/4 miles from the village but Keauhou Shopping
Center is only half a mile away. *2 BR $115, $690-725 week, $2070 month; 3 BR
$130-155, $780-930 week, $2790-2850*

KEAUHOU RESORT CONDOMINIUMS (W)
78-7039 Kamehameha III Rd, Kailua-Kona, HI 96740, 1-800-367-5286; (808)
322-9122, FAX 322-9410. Agent: Hawai'i Resort Management 1-800-553-5035,
Hawai'i (808) 329-9393. This condo has 48 townhouse units available with TV,
two swimming pools and is on the golf course; maid service included. Minimum
stay of five days.
1 BR $65-90, deluxe $75-100; 2 BR $85-115, deluxe $95-135, Extra person $10

KING KAMEHAMEHA KONA BEACH HOTEL ★ (W)
75-5660 Palani Road, Kailua-Kona, HI 96740, (808) 329-2911; toll free
US/Canada 1-800-367-6060; FAX (808) 923-2566. This 458 room hotel is one
of Kailua-Kona's landmark hotels, located on sandy calm Kamakahonu Beach on
Kailua Bay behind the pier at the head of the town's main street, Alii Drive. All
rooms are air-conditioned with TV. Restaurants, cocktail lounges, tennis courts,
lobby shopping mall, and meeting rooms are available.
Standard $110, Deluxe $195, 1-2-3 BR Suites $ 300-500, Extra persons $10 each.

KONA ALII CONDOMINIUMS

75-5782 Kuakini Hwy., Kailua-Kona, HI 96740, (808) 329-2000. Agents: Hawai'i Resort Management 1-800-553-5035, Hawai'i (808) 329-9393; Kona Vacation Resorts, 1-800-367-5168, Canada 1-800-800-KONA, FAX (808) 329-5480; West Hawai'i Property (808) 322-6696; Hawai'i Apt. Leasing US 1-800-854-8843, California 1-800-472-8449, Canada 1-800-824-8968; Paradise Management 1-800-272-5252. Units are fully furnished with private lanai and major appliances. Bedding for up to 4 persons. Tennis court, top floor sun deck, private sandy beach, bar-b-que area. Short two minute walk into Kailua village for shopping, restaurants and resort activities.

1 BR o.v. (2,max 4) $65-105, $455-625 week, $1600-1710 month;
2 BR o.v. (2,max 4) $88-135, $500-810 week, $2430 month

KONA BALI KAI (W)

76-6246 Alii Drive, Kailua-Kona, HI 96740, (808) 329-9381; Agents: Always Sunny Condos, 1-800-692-2638, 206 479-2729 or FAX 206 479-5130; Colony Resorts Inc., 1-800-777-1700, FAX (808) 322-3818; Hawaiian Apartment Leasing 1-800-854-8843; Kona Vacation Resorts, US 1-800-367-5168, Canada 1-800-423-8733, ext. 329, FAX (808) 329-5480; Property Network 1-800-358-7977, FAX 808 329-1200; Village Realty 1-800-927-1577; West Hawaii Property Services (808) 322-6696. This condo has 86 units available on Holualoa Bay, Kona. All units have full kitchen and TV, some with air-conditioning, plus sauna, jacuzzi, pool, health club, barbecue facilities, convenience store/deli are available. Located three miles from town.

Studio o.f. $75, $450 week, $1350 month; 1 BR o.f. $95-105, $570-630 week, $1890-2052 month; 2 BR/3 BR o.f. (2,max 4) $95-130, $630-850 week, $2100-2700 month

KONA BAY HOTEL (W)

75-5739 Alii Drive, Kailua-Kona, HI 96740; (808) 329-1393, US/Canada 1-800-367-5102, FAX (808) 935-7903. This older hotel has 145 guest rooms available, all air-conditioned. In room TV, swimming pool, Banana Bay Cafe, cocktail lounge, and shops all available. Located across from the Kona Inn Shopping Village only one block from Kailua Bay, centrally located in town.

Standard $59, Superior $69, Studio/kitchen $74, Oceanview $84, Extra person $10

KONA BILLFISHER CONDOMINIUM

75-5841 Alii Drive, Kailua-Kona, HI 96740, (808) 329-9277. Agent: Hawai'i Resort Mgmt. 1-800-553-5035, Hawai'i (808) 329-9393, FAX (808) 326-4137; Triad Management 1-800-345-2823, FAX (808) 326-2401. This condo has 20 units in rental programs, all air-conditioned with TV and bar-b-que area. It is located across the street from the Royal Kona Resort and is also within easy walking distance of the town center, shopping and several restaurants.

1 BR (2,max 4) $60-75, $420-525 week, $1260-1575 month
2 BR (2,max 6) $80-95, $520-665 week, $1500-2000 month

KONA BY THE SEA ★

75-6106 Alii Drive, Kailua-Kona, HI 96740, (808) 327-2300. Agent: Aston Hotels & Resorts 1-800-922-7866, Hawaii 1-800-342-2558, FAX (808) 922-8785. This is a well maintained, quiet, four-story condominium complex with 78 units available for vacation rentals. The bright nicely appointed and very spacious rooms are air-conditioned with TV and fully-equipped kitchen. And while the complex is located on a rocky beach, there is a swimming pool, jacuzzi, adjoining grass yard for small children, sandy area with barbecue grills and lounge chairs. The shore area attracts lots of surfers as the surf builds and breaks directly in front of the complex, a great place to watch the surfers if you don't take to the board yourself. There is also a public salt water pool beyond the rockwall at the end of the property, accessed by a public walkway. However, the heavy surf can break up and over the pool's edge so caution is required. Spend 7 nights with Aston Hotels and get a 20% discount, inquire when booking.
Studio suite $175-195, 1 BR (2,max 4) $195-250, 2 BR (2,max 6) $245-285

KONA COAST RESORT/KEAUHOU GARDENS ★

78-6842 Alii Drive, Keauhou-Kona, HI 96740, 1-800-359-2566, (808) 324-1721, FAX (808) 322-8217. Agent: Hawaiian Apartment Leasing 1-800-854-8843; Keauhou Property Management 1-800-745-KONA, FAX (808) 326-2055. This lushly landscaped development has a number of rental units available. They are spread out among the complex on a lovely slope surrounded by the fairways of the Kona Country Club with the ocean just beyond. The units are luxuriously furnished with plush furniture, bedding, and overall very tastefully appointed. There is a recreation area, with tennis, two pools, jacuzzi, gas BBQ area, and wet bar. *1 BR g.v. $95-110, $700 week, $2400 month; 1 BR o.v. $125, $750 week, $2600 month; 2 BR o.v. $140-150, $900 week, $2900-3100 month*

KONA HOTEL ★

P.O. Box 342, Holualoa Road, Holualoa, Kona, HI 96725, (808) 324-1155. Located approximately 7 miles from Kailua-Kona town in a prime coffee farming area on the slopes of Mount Hualalai. This charming upcountry 11 room hotel has been run by the Inaba family for many years. It is one of Kona's original lodgings and still run with an old fashioned family atmosphere. Nothing fancy but basic accommodation for guests wanting budget accommodations. Guests share a community bathroom and entertain themselves in the small lobby-TV room. This hotel has a quiet and sedate old-fashioned Hawaiian country ambience. *Standard $18-26*

KONA ISLANDER INN

75-5776 Kuakini Highway, Kailua-Kona, HI 96740, (808) 329-3181. Agents: Aston Hotels & Resorts 1-800-922-7866, Hawai'i 1-800-321-2558, FAX (808) 922-8785; Clark Realty 1-800-929-7667, (808) 329-5300; Hawai'i Resort Management 1-800-553-5035, Hawai'i (808) 329-9393; Property Network 1-800-358-7977, FAX 808 329-1200; West Hawaii Property Services, 1-800-799-KONA, FAX (808) 324-0609. This condo/hotel has just 51 rental units available. Rooms have air-conditioning, refrigerator, TV and there is a pool and jacuzzi. There is a convenience shop with beverages, snacks, etc. in the lobby. While this is an older complex in Kailua-Kona (dating from 1969) it is clean and quiet and is conveniently located to all the dining, shopping and attractions of the village and within easy walking distance of most things. The complex occupies a narrow strip between other buildings and stretches from Kuakini Highway to Alii Drive with the lower end just across Alii Drive from Kailua Bay. This is a good location if you don't have a rental car and want to explore Kona on foot. Spend 7 nights with Aston Hotels and get a 20% discount, inquire when booking. *g.v. $83-93, o.v. $98-108   Extra person $15*

KONA ISLE CONDOMINIUM
75-6100 Alii Drive, Kailua-Kona, HI 96740, (808) 329-2241, FAX (808) 326-2401. Agents: Knutson & Assoc. 1-800-800-6202, (808) 329-6311; Ron Burla & Associates (808) 329-2421; Hawai'i Resort Management 1-800-553-5035 or (808) 329-9393; Triad Management 1-800-345-2823, FAX (808) 326-2401; West Hawaii Property Services (808) 322-6696. This is an oceanfront complex, some units with oceanview. The beautifully manicured grounds are very spacious and pleasant. There are BBQ facilities and tables poolside and lounge chairs near the oceanfront seawall. There is no sand beach here, it is too rocky. Laundry facilities are in each unit. Located 2 1/2 miles from the village. One week minimum stay. *1 BR g.v. $375-490 week, $1125-1470 month; 1 BR o.f. $475-595 week, $1425-1785 month*

KONA LUANA
75-5958 Alii Dr., Kailua-Kona, HI 96740, (808) 329 6488. Agent: Kona Vacation Resorts, 1-800-367-5168, Canada 1-800-800-KONA, FAX (808) 329-5480. This small complex less than a mile from Kailua town offers full ocean front views over the Pacific with full furnishings, laundry facilities, lanai and wet bar. *2 BR o.f. $130 day, $780 week, $2340 month*

KONA MAGIC SANDS
77-6452 Alii Dr., Kailua-Kona, HI 96740, (808) 329-6488. Agents: Hawai'i Resort Management 1-800-553-5035, Hawai'i (808) 329-9393; Kona Vacation Resorts, 1-800-367-5168, Canada 1-800-800-KONA, FAX (808) 329-5480; West Hawaii Property Services, 1-800-799-KONA, FAX (808) 324-0609. Located next to famous Magic Sands Beach Park with swimming and body-surfing available. There are just 10 studio units available.   Features TV, Jameson's By the Sea Restaurant, cocktail lounge, and on request maid service. Some rooms have telephones.   3 day minimum stay. *Studios-standard $65-85, $420-455 week, $1260-1600 month; Extra person $10*

KONA MAKAI
75-6026 Alii Drive, Kailua-Kona, HI 96740, (808) 329-6488. Agents: Golden Triangle (808) 329-1667; Hawaiian Apartment Leasing 1-800-854-8843; Kona Vacation Resorts 1-800-367-5168, FAX (808) 329-5480; Paradise Management 1-800-272-5252; Property Network 1-800-358-7977, FAX 808 329-1200; Village Realty 1-800-927-1577; West Hawai'i Property Services, Inc. (808) 322-6696. This complex has just 15 units in rental programs. Amenities include jacuzzi, BBQ, tennis courts, sauna and exercise room. Oceanfront but no sandy beach. 3 day minimum stay.
1 BR p.o.v. $75-90, $540 week, $1620 month
1 BR o.v. $95, $570 week, $1710 month
2 BR g.v. (2,max 4) $120, $720 week, $2160 month
2 BR o.v. (2,max 4) $130, $780 week, $2340 month

KONA MANSIONS (W)

75-5873 Walua Road, Kailua-Kona, HI 96740, (808) 329-2374. Agents: Hawaiian Apartment Leasing 1-800-854-8843; West Hawaii Property Services, 1-800-799-KONA, FAX (808) 324-0609. This complex is located across from the Royal Kona Resort and within walking distance of the village. There are no good views from this complex. Units do have TV and on request maid service available. Easy access to all other resort town activities. There are only a few units in rental programs. 5 day minimum. *1 BR (2,max 4) $65-85, $455-550 wk, $1600-1800 month*

KONA NALU

76-6212 Alii Drive, Kailua-Kona, HI 96740; (808) 329-6488; Agents: Kona Vacation Resorts, 1-800-367-5168, Canada 1-800-800-KONA, FAX (808) 329-5480. This small complex is located on the waterfront two miles from Kailua town. Units are completely furnished and well maintained; large lanais, laundry facilities, pool, covered parking, a/c. *2 BR o.f. $150, $900 week, $2700 month*

KONA ONENALO

77-6516 Alii Dr., Kailua-Kona, HI 96740, (808) 329-6488. Agent: Kona Vacation Resorts 1-800-367-5168, Canada 1-800-800-KONA, FAX (808) 329-5480. This comfortably furnished condo comes complete with lots of living area, full kitchen, washer/dryer, and convertible den for extra sleeping area and many other conveniences plu oceanside pool and jacuzzi. *2 BR o.f. (2,max 4) $150 day, $900 week, $2700 month*

KONA PALMS

77-6611 Alii Dr., Kailua-Kona, HI 96740, (808) 329-6488. Agent: Kona Vacation Resorts, US 1-800-367-5168, Canada 1-800-800-KONA, Fax (808) 329-5480. This property is about 3 1/2 miles south of Kailua-Kona town and offers an unobstructed view of the ocean. Units have ceiling fans, washer/dryer and are fully furnished with a/c plus ceiling fans.
1 BR o.v. $90-95, $540-580 week, $1620-1660 month

KONA PLAZA CONDOMINIUMS

Alii Drive, Kailua-Kona, HI 96740, (808) 329-1132. Agents: Clark Realty 1-800-929-7667, (808) 329-5300; Century 21 1-800-255-8052, FAX (808) 329-6693; Kona Vacation Resorts, 1-800-367-5168, Canada 1-800-800-KONA, FAX (808) 329-5480. This complex has 75 air-conditioned units in the heart of the village on Alii Drive across from the Kona Inn Shopping Village. Restaurants, shopping, Kona Pier, hotels are all within walking distance. Guests have access to a rooftop sundeck. *1 BR $75-80, $450-480 week, $1350-1728 month; 2 BR o.v. $100, $600 week, $2160 month*

KONA REEF

75-5888 Alii Drive, Kailua-Kona, HI 96740, (808) 329-6488. Agents: Hawaiiana Resorts 1-800-367-7040, Canada 1-800-877-7331, FAX (808) 537-3701; Hawaiian Apartment Leasing 1-800-854-8843; Knutson & Assoc. 1-800-800-6202, (808) 329-6311; Kona Vacation Resorts, US 1-800-367-5168, Canada 1-800-423-8733, ext. 329, FAX (808) 329-5480; Village Realty 1-800-927-1577. This condo has 51 units available as vacation rentals. All rooms are air-conditioned with TV. Facilities include pool, jacuzzi, party pavilion, barbecue, etc. The complex is nearby to shopping and restaurants. Minimum stay of two nights required.

Oceanfront location but no sandy beach. *1 BR o.v. $75-100, $525-600, $1575-2052 month; 1 BR o.f $95-115, $570-690 week, $1710-2484 month; 2 BR o.f. $145, $870 week, $3132 month*

KONA RIVIERA VILLA CONDOMINIUMS ★
75-6124 Alii Drive, Kailua-Kona, HI 96740, (808) 329-1996, FAX 325-2178. Agent: Knutson & Associates 1-800-800-6202, Hawai'i (808) 329-6311. This condo is located on the beach with private lanai on each unit, nearby to tennis courts, golf, snorkeling, plus village shopping and restaurants. There are about 10 units available, accommodating up to four persons. Minimum stay of 3 nights required. *1 BR g.v. $65-75, $385-455 week, $1350-1650 month; 1 BR o.v. $70-90, $420-560 week, $1500-2000; 1 BR o.f. $100, $700 week, $2520 month*

KONA SEASIDE HOTEL
75-5546 Palani Road, Kailua-Kona, HI 96740, (808) 329-2455.
Agent: Sands, Seaside and Hukilau Hotels, 1-800-367-7000,
Hawai'i 1-800-451-6754, FAX (808) 922-0052. This 228 room property partially fronts Kailua Bay. Most rooms are air-conditioned and all have TV. Stan's Restaurant, cocktail lounge, and meeting rooms available. This is in the heart of the village with shopping and restaurants all within walking distance. Kailua Pier is one block away. This is a good budget hotel with clean rooms and simple decor. *Standard $80, Deluxe $105, Kitchenette $100   Extra person $10*

KONA SURF RESORT HOTEL   (W)
78-128 Ehukai St., Keauhou-Kona, HI 96740, (808) 322-3411, 1-800-367-8011, FAX (808) 322-3245. This 530 room hotel, one of Keauhou Resort's major properties, sits handsomely on a peninsula bluff above Keauhou Bay and overlooks the fabulous Kona Coast. The rocky coastline has no sand beach but the hotel has fresh and saltwater pools. Spacious rooms are air-conditioned and have TV. Restaurants include The Makee Restaurant and Pele's Court plus cocktail lounges. Other amenities include the adjacent Kona Country Club golf course, tennis courts, shops, and Kona's most complete convention facilities. Lovely tropical botanical gardens surround the hotel grounds, highlighted by a lovely wedding chapel and pond. *Std. $109,   g.v. $130,   o.v. $160,   o.f. $185,   suites $375-550, Extra person $20*

KONA TIKI HOTEL
P.O. Box 1567, Kailua-Kona, HI 96745, (808) 329-1425, FAX (808) 327-9402. This small apartment hotel has just 17 total units with parking, swimming pool, and ceiling fans. No room telephones. Strictly for the budget minded traveler who wants no frills. *Standard $54, Deluxe with kitchenette $59   Extra person $8*

KONA VILLAGE RESORT ★ (W)
P.O. Box 1299, Kaupulehu-Kona, HI 96745. Reservations: toll free 1-800-367-5290, (808) 325-5555, FAX (808) 325-5124. This is perhaps the Big Island's most unique resort. It is situated on the beach at Kahuwai Bay and stretches along the coast in either direction. The resort is comprised of 125 separate thatch-roofed hale (ha-lee) bungalows as the guest rooms. The hale reflect the traditional design and decor of the South Pacific Islands including Hawai'i, Tahiti, Fiji, New Zealand Maori, New Caledonia, New Hebrides, Samoa, Palau, and the Marquesas. All guest hale have full modern conveniences including full bath, ceiling fans, comfortable tropical furniture and beach hammocks. This is a no-nonsense escapist resort for those seeking complete relaxation, solitude, and the feel of a South Seas Paradise. No room phones, no radios, no TV to disturb the peace and quiet. The resort is clustered along the beach with lush landscaping of trees, flowering plants and birds abound everywhere. Guests walk back and forth to the restaurants and activities at the resort center. A large pond is home to a collection of ducks, geese and rare waterbirds. For the uninitiated, the most disturbing things about this resort will be the sound of birds singing in the mornings and the rumble of surf at your front door. This is indeed a magical place. Room rates reflect Full American Plan with all meals included for two people. The weekly luau is unrivaled for quantity and diversity of authentic Hawaiian luau food including roast pig cooked in an earth oven. Located 15 miles north of Kailua-Kona on the beach at Kaupulehu well off the main highway. The Kona Village has a complimentary program for children during school holiday periods and in the summer. *Standard Hale $395, Moderate Hale $480, Superior Hale $540, Deluxe Hale $595, Royal Oceanfront Hale $680. Extra person $160, children ages 6-12 $110, ages 2-5 $55, infants $25*

KONA WEST
75-5680 Kuakini Hwy., Kailua-Kona, HI 96740, (808) 329-6488. Agent: Kona Vacation Resorts 1-800-367-5168, Canada 1-800-423-8733, ext. 329, FAX (808) 329-5480; West Hawaii Property Services (808) 322-6696. This is a small complex near the heart of town on the Kuakini Highway within walking distance of shopping, restaurants, etc. Units are furnished with stove top burners, small refrige and air-conditioning. There are on-site laundry facilities, swimming pool and jacuzzi. *Studio g.v. $45-70 day, $300-420 week, $950-1260 month; Studio o.v. $75 day, $450 week, $1350 month*

KONA WHITE SANDS APARTMENT HOTEL
P.O. Box 594, 77-6467 Alii Drive, Kailua-Kona, HI 96745, (808) 329-3210, FAX (808) 326-4137. Agent: Hawai'i Resort Management 1-800-553-5035, Hawai'i (808) 329-9393. This small 10 unit apartment-hotel has just 5 units available in rental programs. Units have kitchenettes, TV, ceiling fans and individual private lanais, but no room telephones. This complex is directly across from White Sands Beach. Strictly a no-frills budget-class lodging. 3 day minimum. *Standard $65-70, Extra person $10*

MALIA KAI ★
75-5855 Waiua Road, Kailua-Kona, HI 96740, (808) 329-1897. Agent: Triad Management 1-800-345-2823, FAX (808) 326-2401. This complex is very conveniently located, about 2 blocks from the center of the village. It is across the street from the Royal Kona Resort. The central courtyard is a profusion of tropical plants and flowers with a small relaxing swimming pool. It is a very quiet comfortable location. Units are simply furnished with ceiling and table fans, no air-conditioning. The only negatives of this property are the narrow stairway leading up to each unit's split-levels and kitchens that show some age and wear. *1 1/2 BR $65-80, $390-480 week, $1170-1440 month*

MANAGO HOTEL ★ (W)
P.O. Box 145, Captain Cook, HI 96704, (808) 323-2642, FAX 323-3451. This is another old-fashioned family hotel operated by the Manago family since its founding in 1917. There are 64 rooms, some with shared bathroom facilities. The hotel features a homey family-type environment and the restaurant serves local family-style meals. Cocktail lounge on grounds. No room telephones. Located right on Highway 11 eight miles from Kailua-Kona in the busy town of Captain Cook at 1400 ft. elevation above the Kona Coast overlooking Kealakekua Bay and Pu'uhonua O Honaunau National Historic Park. The Manago enjoys sunny days and cool quiet evenings. *Standard $35-38, deluxe $38-52, Extra person $5*

MAUNA LOA VILLAGE ★
78-7190 Kaleopapa Road, Keauhou-Kona, HI 96740, 1-800-829-9661, (808) 324-0620, FAX (808) 322-1609; Colony Hotels 1-800-777-1700; Village Realty, 1-800-927-1577. This complex is in the Keauhou area, located just above the Kona Surf Hotel and Keauhou Bay. The 469 units are arranged in hexagonal pod-like clusters. Lovely tropical color schemes accent the tasteful decor and contemporary furnishings of each unit. The grounds are well landscaped with numerous bubbling streams and pools, fountains, gardens and a swimming pool for every 18 units. Easy access to Holua Tennis Center, golf at next door Kona Country Club and other resort activities and attractions. *1 BR (2,max 4) $85-140, $510 week, $1836 month; 2 BR (4,max 6) $165-180, weekly/monthly rates on request*

ROYAL KAHILI CONDOMINIUM
78-6283 Alii Drive, Kailua-Kona, HI 96740, (808) 329-2626. Agent: Kona Vacation Resorts, 1-800-367-5168, Canada 1-800-800-KONA, FAX (808) 329-5480; Triad Management 1-800-345-2823, FAX (808) 326-2401; Property Network 1-800-358-7977, FAX 808 329-1200; West Hawaii Property Services (808) 322-6696. This complex is across the street from the ocean but has a private oceanfront picnic area and barbeque area. Laundry facilities are in each unit. It is located 3 miles from the village. The rental units are in the B-wing with no views. *2 BR $75-125 $450-750 week, $1300-2250 month*

ROYAL KAILUAN
75-5863 Kuakini Highway, Kailua-Kona, HI 96740; (808) 329-3318. Agent: Property Network 1-800-358-7977, FAX 808 329-1200; Village Realty 1-800-927-1577. This condo complex is located within walking distance of the Kailua-Kona village. Some units have ocean views, ceiling fans or a/c, enclosed lanai, etc. The complex has swimming pool and laundry facilities. *1 BR $70, $420 week, $1512 month*

ROYAL KONA RESORT ★

75-5852 Alii Dr., Kailua-Kona, HI 96740, (808) 329-3111, FAX (808) 329-9532. Reservations: 1-800-774-KONA (5662).

This 445 room hotel is a well-known Kona landmark and one of Kona's original modern tourist hotels. It sits on a rocky precipice jutting into Kailua Bay and affords a commanding view of the town and bay area. The rooms are very neat, clean and air-conditioned with TV, refrigerators, and complimentary coffee-tea making facility. Amenities include the Lanai Restaurant, plus cocktail lounge, swimming pool, tennis courts, shops, and meeting rooms. The most quiet rooms are in either the Village or Beach Buildings away from the Main Building with its noisy-at-night lounge music. Check on their special room-car packages, often cheaper than buying both separately.
Standard $150, o.v. $175, o.f. $210, Suites $230-410, $15 extra person

SEA VILLAGE ★

75-6002 Alii Dr., Kailua-Kona, HI 96740, (808) 329-1000. Agents: Hawaiian Apartment Leasing 1-800-854-8843; Knutson & Assoc. 1-800-800-6202, (808) 329-6311; Kona Vacation Resorts 1-800-367-5168, FAX (808) 329-5480; Paradise Mgmt. 1-800-272-5252; Property Network 1-800-358-7977, FAX 808 329-1200; West Hawaii Property Services, 1-800-799-KONA, FAX (80) 324-0609.

This 131 unit condo has 50 guest units available. TV, kitchen, tennis court, maid service are available but no room telephones. Minimum stay of three days. Units are very nicely furnished, clean, spacious, and comfortable. The central grounds are beautifully maintained and landscaped. Pool area with BBQ facilities is right on water's edge but there is no beach here as it is too rocky. Nice views of Kailua Bay and the village. 3 day minimum stay.
1 BR g.v. $ 90-105, 1 BR o.v. $100-115, 1 BR o.f. $110-125
2 BR g.v. $115-130, 2 BR o.v. $125-140, 2 BR o.f. $135-150

WHITE SANDS VILLAGE ★ (W)

74-6469 Alii Drive, Kailua-Kona, HI 96740. Agents: Hawaiian Apartment Leasing, 1-800-854-8843; Kona Vacation Resorts 1-800-367-5168, Canada 1-800-800-KONA, FAX (808) 329-5480; Triad Management 1-800-345-2823, FAX (808) 326-2401.

This 108 unit condo complex has just a few units available in rental programs. The units are air-conditioned with nicely coordinated furnishings and color schemes. Tennis courts, TV, and on request maid service are available. The central courtyard has a complete kitchen and BBQ area near the pool. The complex is across the street from White Sands Beach Park. 3 day minimum stay.
1 BR p.o.v. $90, $540 week, $1620 month
2 BR g.v. (2,max 4) $110, $660 week, $1980 month
2 BR p.o.v. (2,max 4) $115, $690 week, $2070 month
2 BR o.v. (2,max 4) $130, $780 week, $2340 month

SOUTH KOHALA DISTRICT

THE KOHALA COAST

The **South Kohala District** embraces parts of the Kohala Mountains, the plateau and plains of Parker Ranch, and extends west to the Kohala Coast. The district includes the towns of Kamuela, Waikoloa Village, Kawaihae, and the resorts of the Kohala Coast. Highway 19, the Hawai'i Belt Road that circles the Big Island, connects Kamuela from Honoka'a and continues on down to Kawaihae and the Kohala Coast's Queen Ka'ahumanu Highway. Going south out of Kamuela, Highway 190 is a scenic route which passes through rolling upcountry ranchlands on its way to Kailua-Kona. Some 15 miles out from Kamuela on Highway 190 is the Waikoloa Road turnoff which passes through Waikoloa Village and on down to the Kohala Coast.

It is necessary to clarify some confusion surrounding the town of Kamuela, or Waimea as it is also called. Kamuela is the name for the Waimea post office. It was named, according to some anyway, for Samuel Parker, son of the founder of Parker Ranch. Kamuela is Hawaiian for Samuel. However, the town itself is named Waimea which in Hawaiian means red water. The two names, Kamuela and Waimea, refer to the same place on the Big Island: the home of the famous Parker Ranch. To make matters even more confusing, there is a town on Kaua'i also named Waimea. That's why the post office people, anyway, prefer the name Kamuela for the Big Island town. However, many Big Islanders use the two names interchangeably when talking of the same place. And being a Big Islander myself, I may do it in this book too. Easy isn't it?

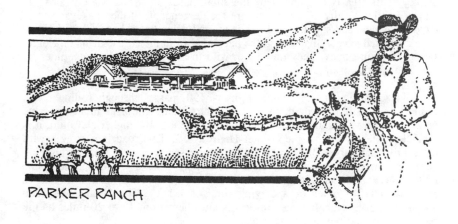

PARKER RANCH

Kamuela town lies at the foot of the Kohala Mountains. It is also on the edge of a large plain or plateau that stretches to the base of towering Mauna Kea. The plateau also slopes, gradually, to both the east and west. Driving through this typically Hawaiian ranch country, you'll be amazed at how lush and green the pastures and gardens are. Naturally, there are lots of cattle and horses roaming the large open pasture lands. The rolling grasslands with the forested hills in the distance will remind you of many areas of the great American West such as Wyoming or Colorado. Kamuela is also a truck-farming community and much of the produce consumed in the state is grown here. The cool climate produces many varieties of vegetables such as lettuce, cabbage, carrots, beans, etc.

Most of the rest of the South Kohala District is a virtual desert or near desert. Lying in the lee of Kamuela and the Hamakua Coast tradewinds to the east, most of the downslope district receives very little rain. It is one large tract of dry brown scrubland from the mid-island plateau of 3000 ft. elevation running down to the bone-dry *Kohala Coast*. The land is mostly hot, dry, windy and rolling grassland with little vegetation other than drought-resistant kiawe and haole-koa trees. Old lava flows disrupt the landscape here and there and most folks are surprised and totally unprepared for the stark conditions found here.

The road system through South Kohala is generally excellent. The Kohala Coast Highway 19, the Queen Ka'ahumanu Highway, which connects *Kailua-Kona* with the Kohala Coast and Kamuela, was completed only in the mid-1970's. At a cost of many millions, the road has returned its investment many times over as it has allowed the development of the famed *Kohala Coast* super-resorts which we'll be discussing shortly. Highway 19 in this area is a generally straight highway with fairly unobstructed views of the sloping uplands of Kohala and many vast old lava flows through which it passes. And because of its nearness (less than a mile) in most places to the coast, it is quite warm on the road most of the time.

In the area just above the Kona Village Resort, about 14-15 miles north of *Kailua-Kona*, be on the lookout for yellow road signs with the silhouette of a donkey. This area is frequented by the small herds of "Kona Nightingales" as they are called locally. These beasts are the descendants of the donkeys used in the old days to pack supplies and goods up and down the old coastal trail. They were also used to carry bags of coffee harvested from the coffee farms on Kona's steep mountain slopes. They now roam wild in this area and can sometimes be seen near the highway.

The old scenic upcountry route, Highway 190, passes through rolling ranch country and is still used by many since it offers a different panorama on a drive between *Kailua-Kona* and *Kamuela*. And because it is at a higher elevation, it is a much cooler drive that the coastal Highway 19. This road is narrower with more hills and curves but it is definitely more scenic for a casual sightseeing drive. Beautiful scenic views of the South Kohala Coast are frequent along this route. On either route, the distance between Kailua-Kona and Kamuela is approximately 40 miles or a driving time of 1 hour. The distance between Kamuela and the Kohala Coast resorts is anywhere from 12 to 20 miles as the resorts are spread out along the coast.

A few years ago, the State of Hawai'i's economic development department produced a statewide "Sunshine Map" and study. That project confirmed what the old Hawaiians knew long ago: the Kohala Coast has the highest sunshine rating in the islands - even higher than such sun resorts as Ka'anapali on Maui and Waikiki on O'ahu. Kohala Coast weather is consistent: average annual rainfall is 8.7 inches over the last 35 years or so records were kept. Temperatures average in the mid-60's for lows and mid to upper 80's for highs with 78 degrees the average year around. It's no wonder that Kohala lays claim to, and rightfully so, the title of the "sunniest coast" in Hawai'i.

Kohala is one of the least pretentious but most elegant resort destinations in Hawai'i. What first looks like an apparent developers mirage at long range reveals itself on close inspection to be a stunning oasis of luxury resorts, golf courses, tennis complexes, and all the amenities of a palatial playground in the middle of a vast dry inhospitable lava desert.

This lonely desolate stretch of land combines golden beaches, rugged lava flows, hot dry desert, incredibly blue sea, and luxury resorts, all the stuff of dreams. And so it is that the Kohala Coast has become Hawai'i's leading destination with its complex of plush super-resorts. But more on that shortly.

South Kohala has a pastoral side that is best observed in the upcountry town of *Waimea*, or *Kamuela* as it is also called. This quiet, cool town (3000 ft. elevation) is the center of paniolo (cowboy) country. Waimea is the headquarters for the famous *Parker Ranch*, the state's largest and one of the largest ranches in the United States. Over 50,000 head of Hereford cattle are raised on over 220,000 acres of pastureland. Each year Parker Ranch produces 10 million pounds of beef, more than one-third of Hawai'i's total. Waimea is a ranch town and its atmosphere reflects a country lifestyle. Located on the flatlands of the Waimea plateau and surrounded by rolling hills, the area is a welcome contrast to the warm sunny skies of the Kohala Coast.

WHAT TO DO AND SEE

Visitors to Waimea will find a lot to explore in this cool green upcountry town. A major attraction is the *Parker Ranch Visitor Center* ★ located in the *Parker Ranch Shopping Center*. Here visitors can discover the fascinating history and operations of Parker Ranch and the Hawaiian paniolo (cowboy) lifestyle still in existence today.

A large screen video presentation highlights day-to-day ranching activities of the 100 or so ranch hands and cowboys employed by Parker Ranch. Visitors can also browse through the museum which depicts the six generations of the Parker family and see items used during 140 years of ranching history. The visitor center is open daily except Sunday, 9AM-5PM. Admission is $5 for adults, $3.75 for children 4-11 years. Phone: (808) 885-7655.

Another ranch attraction is the historic Parker Ranch homes at *Pu'uopelu* ★. Just outside Waimea on Highway 190 is the entrance to Pu'uopelu, the residence of the present ranch owner. This is the setting for *Mana*, the quaint 140 year old restored New England-style house built by John Palmer Parker I. The interior is made entirely of native Hawaiian koa wood. ***Pu'uopelu***, the 100 year old main ranch residence, features an outstanding art gallery with an impressive collection of original paintings plus many other objects d'art and antiques. Pu'uopelu is open daily except Sunday, 9AM-4:30PM. $7.50 adult admission, $5.00 for children 4-11 years. Phone: (808) 885-5666.

Of interest to World War II/Pacific War vets and history buffs is a large stone marker on Highway 190 near the entrance of Pu'uopelu. The marker notes the surrounding grounds of Parker Ranch which were used as "Camp Tarawa 1943-45" by the 2nd and 5th U.S. Marine Divisions which trained here.

The ***Kamuela Museum*** (885-4724) in Waimea is at the intersection of routes 19 and 250 (Kohala Mountain Road). It is the largest privately owned museum in Hawai'i. Interesting collections of ancient Hawaiian weapons, World War II relics, furniture of Hawaiian royalty, and many other antiques and art objects are on display. Open daily, 9AM-5PM. The admission fee is adults $5, children under age 12, $2.

On the ***Kohala Coast***, at Kawaihae Bay is ***Pu'ukohola Heiau National Historic Site*** ★, well worth a visit. This massive heiau (temple) was built by Kamehameha the Great in 1791 upon the advice of a priest who told Kamehameha that he would conquer all the islands of Hawai'i if he did so. By 1795, Kamehameha did conquer in battle all the islands of Hawai'i except Kaua'i, which later acceded to his rule and recognized him as the ruler of all Hawai'i. At the time Kamehameha built his heiau, his chief Big Island rival was his cousin, Keoua Ku'ahu'ula, also a chief. Kamehameha invited Ku'ahu'ula to his temple dedication to make peace and Ku'ahu'ula fatefully accepted. As Ku'ahu'ula and his party landed at the beach below the heiau, Kamehameha's warriors swept down and killed them all. Ku'ahu'ula's body was carried up to the temple and was offered as the principal sacrifice to Kamehameha's war god. Thus the heiau was dedicated according to ancient Hawaiian religious custom. Just below the heiau site is ***Spencer Beach Park***, a popular place for camping, swimming, snorkeling, and picnicking. The beach has calm quiet water and fine sand perfect for youngsters. There are also restrooms, a pavilion, picnic tables, basketball court, and showers.

About three miles south of Kawaihae on Highway 19 is the entrance to the *Hapuna Beach State Park*, recognized as the Big Island's best beach and, rated by <u>Conde Nast Traveler Magazine</u> as the best beach in the country in 1993.

Restrooms, pavilions, picnic tables, and showers are available. The beach has moderate surf and shallow water good for body surfing but not for board surfing. At the north end of the beach on the hills overlooking the area, is the 350-room luxury *Hapuna Beach Prince Hotel*. Next door is *Mauna Kea Beach* on *Kauna'oa Bay*, itself one of the loveliest white sand crescents on the Big Island. Behind the beach is *Mauna Kea Beach Hotel*, the "Grand Dame" of the Kohala Coast hotels. Limited public parking is available at the Mauna Kea Beach Hotel but public access to this lovely beach is maintained.

A mile south of Hapuna Beach on Highway 19 is the *Puako Road* turnoff where there is public access to the beach areas of Puako. A couple of miles further south is the turnoff to *Mauna Lani Resort* location of the *Sheraton Orchid Mauna Lani Hotel, Mauna Lani Bay Hotel and Bungalows*, and *The Islands, Mauna Lani Point and Mauna Lani Terrace* condos. The ancient fishponds at *Kalahuipua'a* next to the Mauna Lani Bay Hotel have been restored and can be seen on a walk through the hotel grounds. This beautiful site is now operated as a working aquaculture preserve stocked with mullet fish. Just north of the Sheraton Orchid Mauna Lani is *Holoholokai Beach Park* and a trail leading to the *Puako Petroglyph Fields*. Here visitors can see detailed rock carvings of human figures, mythical figures and symbols done by the old Hawaiians on the lava rocks.

Five miles further south on Highway 19 is the turnoff to *Anaeho'omalu Beach Park* and *Waikoloa Beach Resort* location of the *Royal Waikoloan Hotel* and the *Hilton Waikoloa Village* and the condo complexes *The Shores at Waikoloa and Vista Waikoloa*. Anaeho'omalu Beach is a lovely sweeping wide crescent of golden sand fronting a fishpond. There is good snorkeling and swimming at this beach as the water is generally not too rough. Picnic tables and restrooms are available. The Royal Waikoloan Hotel sits behind the beach and fishpond areas with easy access to the beach.

Segments of the *King's Highway* ★, the centuries old footpath that winds along the *Kohala Coast*, can still be walked in this area. Hawaiian petroglyph fields lie scattered throughout the area.

The Waikoloa Road intersects Highway 19 (Queen Ka'ahumanu Highway on the Kohala Coast) and connects the old Waimea to Kailua-Kona upcountry road, Highway 190. At *Waikoloa Village*, there is the *Waikoloa Highlands Center*, a small full-service shopping center with a supermarket, restaurant, shops, gas station, post office and a golf course. The village is growing as a retirement and vacation community for sunseekers and golfers as well as a residential community for employees of Kohala Coast resorts. Its near proximity of 7-10 miles to the Kohala Coast resorts makes it a popular spot. The distance between Kamuela and Waikoloa is approximately 18 miles.

Five miles north of the Waikoloa Road, Highway 19 intersects with Highway 200, the "Saddle Road" which connects Hilo with West Hawai'i via the plateau between Mauna Kea and Mauna Loa. About six miles above this intersection on the Saddle Road is *Waiki'i Ranch* nestled in the rolling hills at 4,500 ft. elevation. This is an exclusive residential area of country homes and acreage.

WHERE TO SHOP

Presently, South Kohala is not noted for its shopping. In fact, at the Kohala Coast resorts, there is little beyond the standard pricey resort shops. Each of the major hotels, Mauna Kea Beach, Hapuna Beach Prince, Mauna Lani Bay Hotel, Sheraton Orchid Mauna Lani, Hilton Waikoloa Village and the Royal Waikoloan all have their own resort wear, jewelry, photo and general gift shops are located on the premises.

At Waikoloa Resort, the *King's Shops* complex has a full-range of first-class resort shops and eateries. Among the tenants are *Benetton, Endangered Species, Noa Noa, Ocean Splash, Under the Koa Tree, Island Shells* and others. Restaurants include *Hama Yu Japanese Restaurant, Big Island Steak House, Hawaiian Chili by Max and Subway*. The complex also features museum exhibits showcasing the area's cultural history. For most shopping needs on the Kohala Coast, one has to go all the way upcountry, from 10-20 miles, to Kamuela. The other alternative is to drive the 25-35 miles south into Kailua-Kona. However, Waimea doesn't disappoint serious shoppers. It has a surprising variety of fine shops and goods available for a small ranch town.

The *Parker Ranch Shopping Center* in the center of town has a number of interesting local shops. The center is anchored by *Sure Save Supermarket*. The ranch's own *Parker Ranch Store* is the place for official Parker Ranch T-shirts and western-wear accessories. There is also *Alihi Creations* which features Hawaiiana and special gifts from all over, *Keep In Touch* for T-shirts and gifts, *Blue Sky Art & Apparel* for clothing and crafts, *Malia Kamuela* for fashionable women's clothes, *Reyn's* for fine men's Alohawear, *Big Island Coffee Co.* for a selection of Big Island coffees and others. Also located here are *Su's Thai Kitchen and Morelli's Pizza*. In back of the complex, next to Morelli's back entrance, is *Kamuela Meat Market* which distributes local Big Island ranch-raised beef and beef products. If you're staying in a condo or home and doing the shopping for your kitchen or barbeque grill, this is the one place on the Big Island to buy prime cuts of Big Island ranch beef including steaks, filets, roasts and hamburger. They have a full line of butcher meats. You won't find any other butcher shop or grocery store on the island handling exclusively Big Island ranch-raised beef. You can also call and place an order at 885-4601; open Monday 1:30-5PM, Tuesday-Friday 9AM - 5PM, Saturday 9AM - 1PM.

Just across Highway 19, is the *Waimea Center* anchored by *KTA Superstore* for groceries, along with several eateries, *McDonald's*, *TCBY Yogurt*, *Subway*, *Great Wall Chop Suey*, *Kamuela Deli*, *Maha's Cafe* and *Yong's Kal-Bi*. For unique made-in-Hawaii gifts, try *Cook's Discoveries* which carries a wide selection of koa wood pieces, jewelry, clothing, specialty food products and more. The center also has *Pueo Bookshop, Kamuela Kids, Kamuela Hat Co.* and several other boutiques and general shops.

On Highway 19 out toward the west edge of town is *Parker Square Shopping Center*, a shopping complex with an old ranch motif. The complex houses *Waimea Coffee & Co.* coffee bar (885-4472) and *Waimea General Store* (885-4479) a general gift shop that also carries arts and crafts, kitchenware items, and all sorts of unique gifts. *Gallery of Great Things* (885-7706) pretty much lives up to its name. It's more like strolling through a museum, or an archeologist's lab. There are numerous antiques and art pieces from all over the Pacific area including Hawai'i, Micronesia, New Guinea, the Solomon Islands, Bali in Indonesia, and more. It is a fascinating collection of authentic Pacific art: tribal masks, wood carvings, primitive weapons, paintings, and more. It's all beautiful and with prices to match! For art lovers and collectors this shop is a must! *Bentley's* (885-5565) is a general gift shop and feature decorative home furnishings and seasonal accessories. Other shops include *Marc's Fine Jewelry* for local handcrafted jewelry, *Silk Road Gallery* for a selection of Asian antiques, and *Sweet Wind Books & Reads* a psychic/futuristic bookstore.

Also near the west edge of Kamuela town on the Kawaihae Road is *Opelu Plaza*, a small shopping and commercial development which features *Mean Cuisine* (885-6325) a bakery-deli specializing in wonderful fresh-baked bread and pastries, fresh-made sandwiches, soups, salads, and gourmet box lunches called "Yuppie Bentos,"; open daily except Sunday, 6AM-8PM. *Merriman's*, a gourmet dining room that has won wide acclaim for fine Hawaiian regional cuisine, is also located here. They are open for lunch Monday-Friday 11:30AM - 1:30PM; dinner nightly 5:30 - 9PM; and Sunday brunch 10:30AM - 1:30PM.

On the east side of town, toward Honoka'a, there are several small shopping complexes and commercial centers spread out along the highway. Some are relatively modern and one or two are located in quaint old "Mom & Pop" type store buildings. There are a couple of local-style eateries among the assorted shops, *Nori's Saimin Too* in the Ululani Plaza and *Don's Pake Kitchen* in an old gas station/general store building. Also of interest is the Hawaiian Homestead Farmers' Market held each Saturday morning, 7AM - Noon, on the grounds of the Hawaiian Homes Administration just east of Waimea town. The market features seasonal fruits and vegetables, flowers, homemade goodies and local handicrafts at bargain prices direct from the farmers or craftspersons.

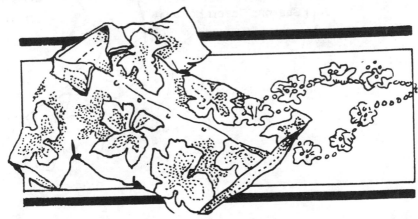

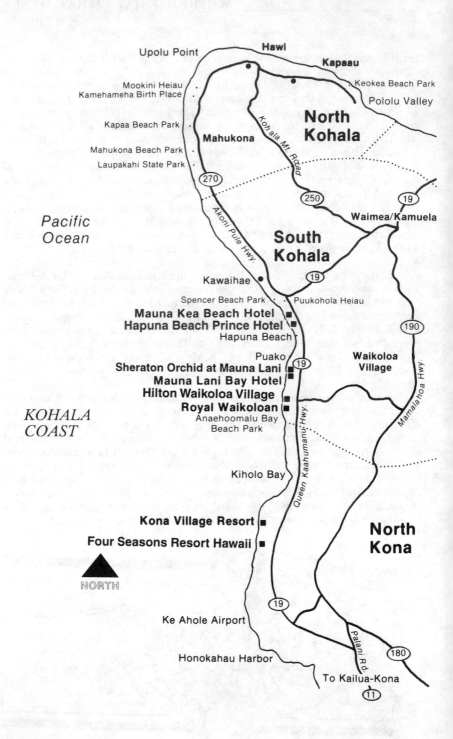

ACCOMMODATIONS-SOUTH KOHALA DISTRICT

South Kohala's accommodations are located along the famed Kohala Coast and in the town of Waimea (Kamuela) or at Waikoloa Village. The Kohala Coast resorts are of course where all the excitement and activity are: luxurious hotels and condos, fabulous golf courses, complete tennis facilities, and all the amenities of world-class super-resorts. The Kohala Coast is celebrated for its resort properties which include the Mauna Kea Beach Hotel, the Hapuna Beach Prince Hotel, the Mauna Lani Bay Hotel and Bungalows, the Sheraton Orchid Mauna Lani, the Hilton Waikoloa Village, the Royal Waikoloan Hotel and resort condominiums.

Waimea, boasts a couple of clean comfortable motel-type accommodations in the Parker Ranch Lodge and the Kamuela Inn. Both places offer good value accommodations at reasonable rates. In addition, there are some good quality B & B operations as well (see B&B listings). Waikoloa Village has condo rentals in the growing retirement-vacation community only a few minutes drive from the Kohala Coast resorts.

For those wanting to experience the ultimate in luxury, comfort, and sumptuousness, any of the Kohala Coast resorts will fit the bill. These resorts cater to every whim and fantasy and can make your dream vacation a reality. They are the ultimate in resorts in Hawai'i and will provide a memorable experience. The cost of course will be considerable. Among these are the Big Island's all time leading and renowned resort, its newest, its most expensive as well as its largest. The Kohala Coast resorts are simply some of the most splendid playgrounds in Hawai'i. Dining and restaurant options on the Kohala Coast are strictly limited to resort facilities. However, the resorts boast several award-winning restaurants and dining rooms noted for their culinary expertise, diversity of cuisine and personal service. Away from the resorts, one can find local-style favorites and some fine American-Continental cuisine in Kamuela and Kawaihae restaurants. See the RESTAURANTS chapter for details.

'ILIMA

BEST BETS:

Hapuna Beach Prince Hotel, a luxury hotel, is part of the famed Mauna Kea Resort on the north end of the Kohala Coast and overlooks Hapuna Beach.

Hilton Waikoloa Village is the largest resort on the Big Island and fully lives up to the "Hilton" expectation of offering all the activities, services, amenities and more needed for a complete vacation experience.

Kamuela Inn - If you are seeking a quiet haven away from the gaudiness of the tourist resorts, you'll find at this simple country inn in the pleasant upcountry coolness of Waimea town.

Mauna Kea Beach Hotel - The legendary "Grande Dame" of the Kohala Coast hotels reopened at Christmas, 1995, after a year-long renovation program. It still sparkles.

Mauna Lani Bay Hotel and Bungalows - This elegant sophisticated hotel provides a regal vacation experience for those who like to indulge in the good life.

Mauna Lani Point Condominiums - This is perhaps Mauna Lani Resort's most luxurious condo and is located near the coast and in the middle of some of the most stunning golf course fairways on the Big Island.

Royal Waikoloan Hotel - This property has about the best beach location of any of the Kohala Coast resorts and is a class act overall.

Sheraton Orchid Mauna Lani - This is a very plush luxury hotel situated on a lovely ocean cove with white sand beach surrounded by Mauna Lani's golf course.

The Islands at Mauna Lani is a super-luxury development of impeccable huge condos at Mauna Lani Resort.

The Shores at Waikoloa- This luxurious complex has spacious units and full amenities that make any stay a totally enjoyable experience.

KOHALA COAST ACCOMMODATIONS

Elima Lani	Parker Ranch Lodge
Hapuna Beach Prince	Puako Beach
Hotel	Apartments
Hilton Waikoloa Village	Royal Waikoloan
Mauna Kea Beach	Sheraton Orchid
Hotel	Mauna Lani
Mauna Lani Bay Hotel	Shores at Waikoloa
Mauna Lani Point	The Islands at Mauna Lani
Mauna Lani	Vista Waikoloa
Terrace Condo	Waikoloa Villas

ELIMA LANI

P.O. Box 384389, 68-3883 Lua Kula St., Waikoloa, HI 96738; Reservations U.S. and Canada 1-800-367-5004 or (808) 883-8288, FAX (808) 883-8170, toll free U.S./Canada FAX 1-800-477-2329. This 216-unit condo complex has lovely garden-style landscaping and great views overlooking Waikoloa Golf Course. The 2 BR units have two baths, full kitchen, living, dining area and lanai. No a/c in cool upland climate of Waikoloa. Complex has swimming pools, spas and tennis and golf; easy access to shopping at Waikoloa Shopping Village. The Waikoloa Resort hotels, restaurants and beach activities are minutes away. From Elima Lani, guests can easily explore Waimea, Waipio-Honoka'a and east Hawai'i, or Kohala, Kailua-Kona and west Hawai'i.

Studio suite $85-89; 1 BR $90-105; 2 BR (2,max 6) $109-125 nightly; weekly/monthly rates on request

HAPUNA BEACH PRINCE HOTEL ★

62-100 Kauna'oa Drive, Kamuela, HI 96743-9706, 1-800-882-1111, (808) 880-1111, FAX (808) 880-3200. This luxury-class resort hotel, one of the newest on the "Sunshine Coast," is next door to the Mauna Kea Beach Hotel. The property occupies 32 oceanfront acres above the north end of Hapuna Beach. The hotel has 350 spacious guest rooms including 36 plush suites each with private lanai and either ocean front or ocean view. The Hapuna Suites are private luxury units and the deluxe 3 BR unit has full kitchen, living room, dining room, den and private swimming pool. The hotel has a large swimming pool, health and fitness center, spa and boutiques. Restaurants include Ocean Terrace, Hakone, Bistro, Coast Grille and Arnie's at the nearby Hapuna Golf Course Clubhouse. Hotel guests enjoy championship golf at both the Arnold Palmer-designed Hapuna Golf Course and the famed Mauna Kea Beach Course. Tennis buffs have access to the Mauna Kea Tennis Park Complex. There are also numerous water-sports like ocean swimming, snorkeling, scuba-diving, sailing and deep-sea fishing plus hiking, jogging, horseback riding and more. The hotel also has complete convention and meeting facilities and services.

Partial Ocean View $325, Ocean View $375, Ocean View Prime $435, Ocean Front $460, Ocean Front Suites $900, Hapuna Suite 1-BR $5,000, Hapuna Suite 2-BR $5,500, Hapuna Suite 3-BR $6,000 Extra Person $45

HILTON WAIKOLOA VILLAGE ★

69-425 Waikoloa Beach Drive, Kamuela, HI 96743, (808) 885-1234, 1-800-HILTONS, FAX (808) 885-2900. At 1,238-rooms, this is the Big Island's largest resort hotel. Somehow it seems to accent the Big Island itself, as everything here is done on a grand scale. The hotel occupies 62-acres of tropically landscaped acres on the otherwise parched sunny lavascapes of the Kohala Coast. Guestrooms are located in three towers. The Ocean Tower has 600 rooms, the Palace Tower has 397 rooms, and the Lagoon Tower has 282 rooms. There are also 52 luxury suites and five Presidential suites throughout. *Seven floors are designated non-smoking.* The grounds are marked by lush gardens, meandering streams and waterfalls, pools and lagoons. The resort is like an oasis with water the focus. The four-acre ocean-fed lagoon is a giant living aquarium with a rainbow of tropical reef fish and marine life. Occupying part of the lagoon is the famed Dolphin Quest program which features several Atlantic bottlenose dolphins. Dolphin Quest provides hands-on educational experiences for hotel guests in working and playing with the dolphins.

Guests travel through the resort via canal boats that cruise over a mile of water-ways or quiet tram trains which shuttle from one end of the resort to the other. Guests can also stroll the mile-long open-air museum walkway filled with a vast collection of Pacific and Asian artworks. The hotel also provides several boutique and resort shops with everything from sundry items to handcrafts and resortwear fashions. The Kohala Spa is a 25,000-ft. health spa with everything from whirlpools, weight rooms, aerobics, sauna and steam baths to a full-service beauty salon and full spa treatments. Golfers can enjoy the championship layouts of the Robert Trent Jones Jr. designed Beach Course or the challenging Tom Weiskopf and Jay Morrish designed Kings Course. Tennis buffs have access to eight courts, including two clay courts. Pool fanatics can indulge in the Ocean Tower pool, the Kohala River Pool with a series of waterslides, or the Kona Pool, complete with waterfalls, whirlpools and a giant 175-ft. waterslide. Other activities which can be arranged by the tours/activities desk include varied in-hotel tours, horseback riding, catamaran sails, snorkel-dive cruises, deep-sea fishing, petroglyph tours, scenic flights and much more. For youngsters aged 5-12, there is also "Camp Menehune," a daily program (9am-4pm) of activities with everything from arts and crafts to hula dancing and swimming ($45 per child fee includes lunch).

Hotel guests have a wide selection of restaurants including Donatoni's for fine Italian cuisine, Imari for authentic Japanese food, Kamuela Provision Company for island-style cuisine with Asian/Pacific accents, Orchid Cafe for poolside coffee-shop dining, Palm Terrace for daily varied buffet-style dining and Hang-Ten for casual beach and lagoon-side snacks and sandwiches. The Hilton's emphasis on attentive Aloha-style service in all areas makes this a family-friendly resort. They also cater to large and small meetings and conferences with out-standing support facilities.

Garden View $210-280, Golf/Mountain view $210-280, Ocean $235-310, Deluxe Ocean $260-340, Hilton Towers Floor $310-390, Suites $550-1,455 Presidential Suite $3,750

SPINNER DOLPHINS

MAUNA KEA BEACH HOTEL ★ (W)
62-100 Mauna Kea Beach Drive, Kamuela, HI 96743-9706. (808) 882-7222.
Reservations: 1-800-882-6060, FAX (808) 880-3112.

This 310 room property is located on the beach on Kauna'oa Bay and is the
original Kohala Coast resort. The hotel was developed in the mid-1960's as
Hawai'i's foremost luxury hotel and is the standard by which other fine resort
hotels in Hawai'i, and elsewhere around the world, are measured. There's not
much more to be said about the resort which consistently wins acclaim from
various organizations and the travel-hospitality industry and media for its high
standards of service, quality and recreational facilities. The hotel reopened at
Christmas, 1995, after being closed for a year while undergoing a major renovation program. There is no doubt that the Mauna Kea is still the hotel on the
Kohala Coast. It's nice to see some things don't change.

Modified American Meal Plan is available. Guest have access to all resort
activities including golf at Mauna Kea Resort's two courses, the Mauna Kea Golf
Course and Hapuna Golf Course, tennis at the MKB Tennis Park, swimming
pool, and all water sports at Kauna'oa Beach fronting the hotel. The MKB
tradition of award-winning fine cuisine is available at its restaurants including The
Batik for classic European cuisine from Provence, The Pavilion for Mediterranean inspired cuisine, The Terrace for a sumptuous daily buffet luncheon, The
Hau Tree/Gazebo for light fare daily and a weekly Clambake seafood extravagan-
za and the 19th. Hole at the golf course clubhouse. There is also a weekly
authentic Hawaiian luau on the hotel grounds.

*Mountain View $280, Mountain View Premier $350, Beach Front $420, Deluxe
Ocean View $435, Ocean View Premier $500, Junior "27" Suite $525, Beach
Front 1 BR $575, Mountain View Suite $750, Series "27" Suite $925, Beach
Front 1 BR Suite $975, Ocean View 1 BR Suite $1050*

MAUNA LANI BAY HOTEL AND BUNGALOWS ★ (W)
68-1400 Mauna Lani Drive,, Kohala Coast, HI 96743-9796, (808) 885-6622.
Reservations 1-800-367-2323/327-8585, FAX (808) 885-1484.

This sleek and elegant 350 room property sits on 29 oceanfront acres amidst a
stark black lava flow on beautiful Makaiwa Bay Beach on the Kohala Coast at
Kalahuipua'a. All rooms have ocean views except for 27 which have views of
Mauna Loa and Mauna Kea. Guestrooms are very spacious at 550+ sq. ft. and
luxuriously appointed with oversize TV, refrigerator, air-conditioning, mini-bar,
double sink bathrooms and many other features. The Bay Terrace and Canoe
House restaurants provide superb dining, along with the casual poolside Ocean
Grill, plus the Honu Bar for light suppers and appetizers, meeting and banquet
space for groups up to 600, resort shops and more. With the ultimate in luxury
and service in mind, the Mauna Lani has five private bungalows available, each
with its own swimming pool, whirlpool spa and personal butler and concierge
staff to cater to the guest's every whim. The Mauna Lani also has fully-equipped
1 BR-2 BR-3 BR Ocean Villa condo units ideal for families.

Activities are varied at Mauna Lani. The Francis I'i Brown Golf Course has received wide acclaim for excellence from the golfing world. The 36-hole layout includes North and South courses. The fairways wind through lavaflows and along the rugged coastline and are almost too spectacular to believe. One sports editor said of it, "If they ever put a golf course in the Smithsonian, this will be it." It's been designated one of the ten most beautiful golf courses in the world by *Travel Weekly*; the South course 17th hole was designated as one of three "Pearls of the Pacific" by *Golf Digest*. The Mauna Lani Golf Course is home to the annual Senior Skins Game tournament each January featuring some of golf's greatest senior players. *Tennis Magazine* has recognized the resort as one of the "Top 50 Greatest U.S. Tennis Resorts" for its fine Tennis Garden facilities. The hotel health club provides full services and work-out equipment; there is also a beauty salon. Guests can also choose from scuba diving, snorkeling, sailing, windsurfing, deep-sea fishing, glassbottom boat tours and sunset cocktail cruises.

The Mauna Lani has a complimentary childrens' program, "Camp Mauna Lani," which is offered from late June through Labor Day for ages 5-12; the hotel also has a seasonal Eco-Teen Adventures program for ages 13-17 at nominal charges. The teen program includes on-site events as well as two and three-day excursions along the Kohala Coast with overnight adventures.

Mountain side $260, Garden View $295, Part Ocean View $355, Ocean View $395, Deluxe Ocean View $430, Ocean Front $465, Deluxe Ocean Front $495, Corner Ocean Front $520, Suites $795, Bungalows $3,025-3,850, Ocean Villas 1 BR $395, 2 BR $425-485, 3 BR $630

MAUNA LANI POINT CONDOMINIUMS ★
68-1310 Mauna Lani Drive, Mauna Lani Resort, Kohala Coast, HI 96743. Reservations: Classic Resorts 1-800-642-6284, or (808) 885-5022, FAX (808) 661-0147. Agents: Hawaiian Apartment Leasing 1-800-854-8843.

This 116-unit complex sits next to the ocean amidst the fairways of Mauna Lani's renowned Francis I'i Brown South Golf Course. It is perhaps one of the Big Island's least known luxury vacation resorts.

The units have either garden fairway or ocean fairway views. The extra-large units are very well appointed and include large private lanais, living and dining areas, full kitchens, microwave, TV, laundry facilities, air-conditioning, double soaking tubs and many other amenities. Each unit has carport parking.

Guests get preferred tee times at either of the North or South golf courses and reserved court time at the Racquet Club for tennis on hard or grass courts. There is also a private beach club with restaurant at Makaiwa Bay's lovely white sand beach. Guests also have access to a whirlpool, sauna, swimming pool and barbecue pavilion. Three day minimum stay required. Extra person $15.

1 BR f.v. $220-260; 1 BR o.v. $260-320
2 BR f.v. $285-345; 2 BR o.v. $330-420
3 BR o.v. $450-520

MAUNA LANI TERRACE CONDOMINIUM ★

Mauna Lani Resort, Kohala Coast, HI 96743. Agent: Hawaiian Apartment Leasing 1-800-854-8843; South Kohala Mgmt. 1-800-822-4252, (808) 883-8500, FAX (808) 883-9818.

These magnificent luxury units are located adjacent to the Mauna Lani Bay Hotel at Mauna Lani Resort. The large spacious units are sparkling and well maintained throughout with the tasteful decor and furnishings expected of a luxury unit. The units are incredibly large and roomy, providing lots of space to move around, relax and enjoy the special luxurious ambiance of Mauna Lani. All units are air-conditioned with ceiling fan in living room, private lanais, wet bars, and complete laundry facilities. There is easy access to the resort's world class golf and tennis, health club, and water sports. Minimum stay of five nights in high season, three nights in low season.

1 BR (2,max4) $260-295
2 BR (2,max6) $330-385
3 BR (2,max8) $475-525

PUAKO BEACH CONDOS (W)

3 Puako Beach Drive, Kamuela, HI 96743; reservations at P.O.Box 1128, Pahoa, HI 96778, (808) 965-9446 and South Kohala Management, 1-800-822-4252, (808) 883-8500, FAX (808) 883-9818. This 40 unit condo has only a few units available for vacation rentals. The condo is located in the quiet Puako Beach area near Hapuna Beach Park on the Kohala Coast. Rooms have TV and kitchen and there is twice weekly maid service. *$140-160 nightly*

ROYAL WAIKOLOAN HOTEL ★

69-275 Waikoloa Beach Drive, Kamuela, HI 96743-9763; for reservations (808) 885-6789, FAX (808) 885-7852.

This 547 room hotel is located directly behind the beautiful 1/2 mile crescent shaped Anaeho'omalu Bay Beach and lagoon amidst a stark black lava flow. The rooms are small but attractively furnished, air-conditioned and have TV.

There is also a separate 20-room Royal Cabana Club, operated as an upscale or concierge section of the hotel with a separate staff and special services such as complimentary continental breakfast and sunset cocktails. The lobby is spacious and opens out onto a lanai overlooking the pool and gardens. The hotel features the Royal Terrace and Tiare Room Restaurants, cocktail lounges, tennis courts, access to Waikoloa Resort golf courses, shops, and meeting rooms. With Anaeho'omalu Beach and its lovely fishponds fronting the hotel, this is one of the loveliest settings along the Kohala Coast. It is a natural for varied water-sports activities which are readily accessible to guests through *Ocean Sports Waikoloa*, located on the beach. A special free childrens' program, "Keiki's Hoolaulea," is offered during summer.
Garden View $120, Mountain View $135, Ocean View $170,
Ocean Front $200, Royal Cabana $250, Suites $350-750
Extra person, $20

SHERATON ORCHID MAUNA LANI HOTEL ★

One North Kaniku Drive, Kohala Coast, HI 96743. (808) 885-2000, 1-800-845-9905 or 800-325-3589, FAX (808) 885-1064. Formerly the Ritz-Carlton, the hotel is one of Sheraton's premier "Luxury Collection" and is located at the world-class Mauna Lani Resort. The hotel occupies a beachfront site and is surrounded by fairways of the resort's North Golf Course. It has 541 guest rooms and features The Cafe, The Grill and The Dining Room restaurants plus lounges and an entire range of luxury guest amenities and services. The hotel has an emphasis on activity with the focal point being an attractive white sand beach and swimming lagoon. *Red Sail Sports* operates a beach equipment and water sports concession. There is also a large freshwater pool, jacuzzi, a magnificent 15 court tennis pavilion complex including grass and exhibition courts and a health and fitness center. Extensive conference facilities provide space for both large and small group meetings. There is a hands-on activities program offered for youngsters during holiday and seasonal vacation periods.
Gardenview $240-285, Part Oceanview $275-325,
Oceanview $310-400, Oceanfront $350-455,
Club Rooms $410-495, Suites $525-2,800 Extra person $35

THE ISLANDS AT MAUNA LANI ★

P.O. Box 4959, Mauna Lani Resort, Kohala Coast, HI 96743-4959; Agents: Classic Resorts, 1-800-642-6284, Hawai'i 808/885-5022. This 46-unit super-luxury townhouse complex is surrounded by golf course fairways and tropical landscaping and five acres of saltwater ponds, streams and waterfalls filled with fish and marine life. The 2 BR units are incredibly spacious with full kitchen, living room, dining room, bathrooms and private lanais and carports, plus laundry room. They are tastefully furnished with contemporary island-style decor and furniture. Amenities include jacuzzi, swimming pool and barbecue areas. Guests have access to Mauna Lani Resort beaches, golf, tennis and restaurants. This condo provides the ultimate in a VIP condo vacation experience; two-night minimum stay. Rates include a full-size car picked up at Kona Airport and a grocery starter package with breakfast items.
2 BR Deluxe Garden View $325-375; 3 BR Deluxe Garden View $425-475

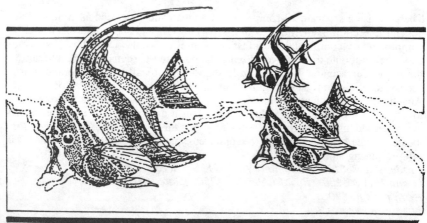

KIHIKIHI   JBay

THE SHORES AT WAIKOLOA ★

HC02 Box 5460, Waikoloa, HI 96743. (808) 885-5001. Agents: ASTON Hotels & Resorts 1-800-922-7866, Hawai'i 1-800-321-2558, FAX (808) 922-8785; Hawaiian Apartment Leasing 1-800-854-8843; Marc Resorts Hawaii, 1-800-535-0085, FAX 808-922-2421; South Kohala Mgmt. 1-800-822-4252, Hawai'i (808) 883-8500, FAX (808) 883-9818. There are 64 units available in rental programs. These are 1-2-3 BR, all fully air-conditioned, full kitchens, TV, washer/dryer, private lanai and wetbar as standard features. The units are very spacious and well furnished with lots of extra room and large bathrooms. Perfect for families. Guests have easy access to pool, barbecue facilities, tennis courts and adjacent Waikoloa Beach and King's Golf Courses. Guests can enjoy dining at any of several resort restaurants at the Royal Waikoloan or Hilton Waikoloa Village. Golf course fairway location in Waikoloa Beach Resort.
1 BR (2,max 4) $199-245, 2 BR (2,max 6) $235-350,
2 BR (2,max 6) Golf Villa $305-355, 3 BR (2,max 8) $360 and up

THE VISTA WAIKOLOA ★

Waikoloa Beach Drive, Waikoloa Beach Resort, Waikoloa, HI 96743; Agent: Hawaiian Apartment Leasing 1-800-854-8843; Marc Resorts Hawaii, 1-800-535-0085, FAX 808-922-2421; South Kohala Management, 1-800-822-4252, (808) 883-8500, FAX (808) 883-9818. This luxurious development has 122 units, some in vacation rental programs. The multi-building complex is located right on Waikoloa Beach Drive between the Royal Waikoloan and Hilton Waikoloa Village and next to the golf course fairways. The units are completely furnished with full kitchens, a/c with access to pool, spa and resort recreational facilities.
2 BR (2,max 6) $180-200 Garden View, 2 BR (2,max 6) $195-275 Golf Villa
3 BR (2,max 8) $220-250 Ocean View

WAIKOLOA VILLAS

P.O. Box 3498, Lua Kula Drive, Waikoloa, HI 96743; (808) 883-9144. Agent: Clark Realty 1-800-929-7667, (808) 929-5300; Marc Resorts Hawaii, 1-800-535-0085, FAX 808-922-2421; Hawaiian Island Resorts, 1-800-367-7042, FAX (808) 544-1868. This condo has 41 units available in rental programs. Units have full kitchens, telephones, ceiling fans, TV, meeting room, in-unit laundry facilities and weekly maid service. Golf course is nearby. Minimum stay of 2 days required.
1 BR $65-85, $455-550 week, $1600-1800 month
2 BR $125-169, $750 week, $2250 month
3 BR $145-209, $870 week, $2610 month   Extra person $10

WAIMEA COUNTRY LODGE ★

P.O. Box 2559, Highway 19, Kamuela, HI 96743, in Hawai'i 1-800-707-4111; (808) 885-4100, FAX (808) 885-6711. This small 21 unit country motel features spacious rooms all with TV and king or queen beds. Clean pleasant furnishings, TV, and phone with nice meadow and mountain views of Kamuela ranch country. Located right in heart of Kamuela town adjacent to Paniolo Country Inn Restaurant and near shopping, other restaurants, area attractions, etc. It's only a 15 mile drive to the Kohala Coast resorts and beaches.
Standard $68, Superior $73, Deluxe kitchenette $78   Extra person $10

SOUTH HILO DISTRICT

HILO: A LOOK ON THE BRIGHT SIDE

Mention has already been made of Hilo and its notorious rainy reputation ("Big Island Weather"). Granted, it's probably Hawai'i's most underrated and least glamorous place. It has what public relations experts call "an image problem." Even though it does rain a lot - some 130 inches annually - its sordid reputation is really undeserved as there is so much more to the Big Island's county seat (pop. 45,000) and gateway to lush and lovely East Hawai'i than its jaded rainy reputation. Of course, I admit, I am biased. I live here, by choice and good fortune. Hilo has had so many jokes made about its rain and more stories fabricated about its wet climate that even some Hilo folks believe them! But whatever is said about their fair town, Hilo folks remain decidedly cheerful, open, friendly, and optimistic. Afterall, these are the people who have endured everything Mother Nature has thrown at them: earthquakes, tidal waves, and threatening eruptions and lava flows from Mauna Loa. They are not about to let a little rain get them down, or other folks' unfair jokes about their town. When you've survived all of these, you know a good thing when you have it and for them Hilo is it, rain or shine.

Known informally to some as Bay City or Crescent City (for its curving beach on Hilo Bay) and even the City of Rainbows (an obvious attempt to brighten its image) Hilo dates back to early Hawai'i. It was long the government and commercial trade center of the island and serviced the sugar plantations that were the main industry of early Hawai'i until its decline in the 1960's-70's. The abundant rains still produce a lush green tropical landscape but, in spite of it, the sugar industry is dead. Several plantations have gone out of business in the last twenty years and former cane lands are being planted in macadamia nuts, papayas, bananas, tropical flowers and garden crops which hold more economic promise and are more environmentally sound.

Today's Hilo remains a colorful small town that attracts the island's country folks and still provides shave ice (snow cones), sodas, and Saturday movies for island youngsters just as it did a generation or two ago. It remains as the governmental, commercial, and social hub of the island's east side. Though it is a generally conservative town, as small towns are inclined to be, it is learning to cope with an ever changing economy and lifestyle, however some might argue that point.

And while Hilo's once-promising tourist industry has given way to the booming Kona-Kohala resort areas on the west side, Hilo has not given up entirely. As mentioned, the area's agriculture is learning to diversify with the exit of sugar and Hilo is gaining recognition as a residential small college town with the growth and expansion of the state supported *University of Hawai'i* at Hilo and adjoining *Hawai'i Community College*. The schools share a lovely campus and a cosmopolitan enrollment of some 5000 students from around the islands of Hawai'i, the U.S. mainland and all over the Pacific Rim. The University of Hawaii-Hilo's University Research Park is home to the Joint Astronomy Center which operates two observatories on Mauna Kea and the headquarters of the Caltech Submillimeter Observatory, also on Mauna Kea, operated by the California Institute of Technology. Along with the development of the Prince Kuhio Plaza shopping center and other local improvements like the renovation of several old buildings throughout downtown Hilo, there is a reflection of confidence in the business community in Hilo's future.With its distinctly tropical climate, Hilo has become the center for the world's largest tropical flower industry. Anthuriums, those heart-shaped long-lasting blooms that fetch $3-5 each in winter, are marketed by the thousands worldwide from numerous farmer co-ops and flower farm exporters. The orchid industry features numerous varieties of lovely cut flowers, sprays, and potted plants that are exported worldwide also.

Downtown Hilo is a conglomeration of vintage wood frame and stucco finished buildings, many dating from the turn of the century. A walk through town reveals an interesting collection of general retail shops, offices, flower and fruit stalls, seed shops, an old fashioned soda fountain or two, barber shops, lunch shops, and Mom & Pop stores. Many of these places give the impression of it still being the 1930's. You can sample everything from a bag of cracked seed (delectable Chinese preserved and dried fruits and fruit seeds, a sort of Oriental candy), to a local gourmet plate lunch, to a bag of fragrant tropical fruits or a bouquet of tropical blooms. In addition, you may chat with the friendly Hilo folks who make downtown Hilo a rich cross-cultural experience. And where else can you get a haircut for $6.00 these days? Or use parking meters that still take, would you believe, nickels, dimes and pennies?

The last few years have seen much improvement and change in downtown Hilo as new businesses have renovated old shop buildings. Several new restaurants and coffee shops, gift shops, art galleries, boutiques and more have added new life to a once decaying downtown. Even the venerable Palace Theater on Haili Street is undergoing a facelift with plans to serve as a cultural and performing arts center. Added to such attractions as the East Hawai'i Cultural Center and the *Farmers Market* (Wednesday-Saturday-Sunday mornings) at the corner of Mamo and Kamehameha Streets and its easy to see why people are rediscovering downtown Hilo. Much of the change and renovation has been brought about through the efforts of downtown merchants, new businesses moving in and the Hilo Main Street Program have assisted with various development projects. While making downtown Hilo more attractive to people, great care has been placed on preserving its unique historical tradition. And after experiencing the real Hilo and its notorious rain, perhaps you'll come to see that Hilo does indeed have its place in the sun. Some see Hilo as a salve to soothe and comfort those with tortured soul and psyche who seek relief in a definitely slower and perhaps saner pace of life. With its warm showers, lush tropical splendor, and friendly caring folks, Hilo is indeed a balm for troubled souls and aching hearts. You see, the old line about Hilo's rain is really relative. It's all in how you look at it. Hilo's rainy reputation has kept the visitor counts to a minimum which some folks don't mind. Because of it, Hilo has been slow to change. And perhaps that's good. It has helped Hilo to retain its essential hometown charm and personality, a valuable asset these days. Yes, there is a bright side to Hilo. And you really need to discover it for yourself. Oh, and when you come, bring your umbrella. It looks like a shower today!

WHAT TO DO AND SEE

Hilo and vicinity receive little attention from the visitor industry as a destination. However, a locally organized group is working to publicize the area's attractions. *Destination Hilo*, can be reached at P.O. Box 1391, Hilo, Hawai'i 96721; telephone 808/935-5294. And partly because of Hilo's anonymity, it presents an "unspoiled paradise" image, if there is such a thing. There is so much to see, experience, and enjoy in this perennial Hawaiian hometown that you'll need more than a day or two to see it all. A description of some of the major attractions follows.

Liliuokalani Park ★ is located on Banyan Drive in the Waiakea Peninsula adjacent to the hotels and on the shore of Hilo Bay. This authentic Japanese garden park was named in honor of Hawai'i's last reigning monarch, Queen Liliuokalani. It was built in the early 1900's as a memorial to the immigrant Japanese who developed the old Waiakea Sugar Plantation. The park features several magnificent Japanese stone lanterns, pavilions, an arching footbridge, a tea house, and reflecting lagoons. It is one of Hawai'i's loveliest cultural parks. Free. This is a must see place in Hilo.

Banyan Drive Trees ★ line Hilo's hotel row and give it the name "Banyan Drive." Most of these handsome spreading trees were planted fifty or more years ago by such VIPs as President Franklin D. Roosevelt, Amelia Earhart, Babe Ruth, Fannie Hurst and other notables of the era. There's even one planted by a then-aspiring politician named Richard Nixon. Each tree is marked accordingly.

Coconut Island in Hilo Bay is a small island just offshore from Liliuokalani Park. A footbridge just opposite the Hilo Hawaiian Hotel leads to it. It is a great place for watching local fishermen angling and the kids swimming and diving from an old bridge platform. There are picnic tables and shelters available. Coconut Island is often used for cultural events by local groups. Worth a stroll in evening at sunset if you are staying at a nearby hotel.

BANYAN TREES   J. BAYOT

Merrie Monarch Festival Office may not be worth a visit necessarily but if you need information or want to order tickets for this annual April "Superbowl of Hula" (they sell out months in advance) contact them at: Merrie Monarch Festival, c/o Hawai'i Naniloa Hotel, 93 Banyan Drive, HI 96720; 808 935-9168.

Old Mamalahoa Highway Scenic Drive ★ is just five miles north of Hilo at the intersection with Kalanianaole School. Old Highway 19 follows the rugged rainforested Hamakua Coast for four miles before linking back with the newer Highway 19. The scenic route takes in numerous gulches and coves as it winds through lovely coastal country with scenic views of the rugged Hamakua Coast and lush rainforest jungles. Shower trees, royal poinciana, breadfruit, coconut, African tulip, and royal palms line the route much of the way. The old route passes through aged sugar plantation villages with melodious names such as Papaikou, Onomea, Pepeekeo, and Kawai Nui. It's definitely an easy and scenic drive well worth taking.

Rainbow Falls and Boiling Pots are above old downtown Hilo and just off Wainuenue Avenue on Rainbow Drive at Wailuku River State Park. This small park features walking trails, restrooms, and magnificent views of Rainbow Falls, best viewed early in the morning when the sun strikes the falls, sending rainbows over the spray and pool. A little further up the road, above Hilo Hospital, the Wailuku River is marked by giant holes and recesses, called Boiling Pots, in the lavarock gorge. The Pots create a series of deep swirling pools, falls, and rapids during heavy rain periods. There is no safe swimming in this treacherous and deep gorge. There are restroom facilities, picnic tables, and a scenic overlook of the Wailuku River Gorge. Free.

Suisan Fish Market Auction ★ is located on Hilo Bay at the mouth of the Wailoa River on Lihiwai Street, and within walking distance of the Banyan Drive hotels. The auction is a colorful cultural experience and a must for Hilo visitors. Laid out is the tuna fishing fleet's catch of 50-100 lb. yellow fin tuna (ahi), plus numerous colorful tropical fish, squid, and other seafood delicacies. The auction is conducted in a spirited multi-lingual pidgin-English that gives an exotic atmosphere to the scene. The auction begins at 7:00 A.M. Monday through Saturday. Closed Sunday. Free. Don't leave Hilo without first experiencing this activity!

Hilo Farmers' Market ★ is a general fruit-vegetable produce, tropical flower and flea-market operation on Wednesday-Saturday-Sunday mornings until noon at the corner of Mamo Street and Kamehameha Avenue in downtown Hilo across from Mo'oheau Park. Bargains galore!

University of Hawai'i at Hilo and Hawai'i Community College Campus is located between Lanikaula and Kawili Streets in Hilo. The University and Community College, which share a common campus have a combined enrollment of some 5000, offer two and four year degree programs. The University utilizes its special geography and resources to offer programs of study in such unique fields as Hawaiian Studies, Pacific Islands Anthropology, Marine Science, Oceanography, Aquaculture, Volcanology, Geothermal Energy, Astronomy and others. The Community College specializes in the Liberal Arts, Business Education and vocational-technical trades. The serene campus is landscaped with many species of tropical trees and plants. Its theatre hosts numerous public performances, concerts, shows, and plays throughout the year and the Campus Center art gallery has ongoing displays. The campus annually hosts several Elderhostel Program senior citizen courses for U.S. mainland visitors as well as a broad range of summer session offerings. Visitors are welcome. For information, contact the Office of University Relations, UH-Hilo (808) 933-3567, or HCC Provost's Office, (808) 933-3611, (both colleges at the same address) 200 W. Kawili St., Hilo, Hawai'i 96720-4091.

Hilo Stars, the local entry in the Hawai'i Winter Baseball League plays in a four-team league with Honolulu, Kauai and Maui. The Hawai'i Winter Baseball League is sanctioned by major league baseball and features top players from United States A and AA minor leagues plus young players from professional teams in Korea and Japan. The league plays from October to December. For information, contact Hawai'i Winter League Baseball, 1210 Auahi Street, #231, Honolulu, HI 96814 or call 808 592-2255 or in Hilo 808 969-9033.

Lyman Museum and Mission House ★ is an old New England style missionary home built in 1839 for the Rev. David and Sarah Lyman, the first Christian missionaries to arrive in Hilo. In addition to the original Lyman House, the Museum next door holds a unique collection of memorabilia of early Hilo and Big Island life. Included are items from the pre-western old Hawaiian era, the Hawaiian Monarchy era of the 1800's, and the early 1900's. Numerous artifacts from the different cultures that populated Hawai'i are also on display. Museum hours are Monday to Saturday, 9:00AM to 5:00PM, at 276 Haili Street, 935-5021. Admission fee is $4.50 for adults, $3.50 for children ages 13-18, $2.50 for children ages 6-12. Mission House tours are given several times daily beginning at 9:30AM.

LYMAN HOUSE MUSEUM

Hilo Sampan Company ★ 70 Kekuanaoa St. #340, Hilo, HI 96720, 808/935-6955 or Fax 808/934-0281. This company operates a few of the old open-air jitneys or "sampan busses" that are leftovers from Hilo's early form of public transport dating from fifty and more years ago. The old '40's-50's model Chevys, Chryslers and DeSotos make the rounds of Hilo's major attractions and shopping centers on daily hourly runs, 8AM-4PM. Passengers can get on or off at any of several points along the route. Fares are $2 for a one-way ticket and $7 for a daily unlimited pass. Monthly passes are available. This is a great way to cruise through Hilo town, get some culture, history and color, and see the sites.

Downtown Hilo Walking Tours ★ with Kalakaua Park as the town center are the focus of a free tour scheduled for the third Saturday of each month at 9AM. The tours are sponsored by the Lyman Museum and American Association of University Women. Kalakaua Park, in the center of downtown Hilo, was originally conceived as a civic center by King Kalakaua. The park has roots to one of the first missionary stations as early as 1825. Other nearby places of historical interest included in the walking tour are Niolopa (once the Hilo Hotel), the old and new library buildings, the old federal building, Lyman Museum and others. Reservations can be made through Lyman House Museum (808/935-5021). The tours are free and begin at the museum, 276 Haili Street, Hilo.

East Hawai'i Cultural Center is located in downtown Hilo at 141 Kalakaua Street, opposite Kalakaua Park and the Post Office. The center is housed in the Old Police Station, a historic building constructed in 1932 and placed on the National Register of Historic Buildings and Places. It resembles a Hawaiian "hale" (house) of the 1800's with its hipped roof. The Center is dedicated to culture and the arts in East Hawai'i. Ongoing art gallery shows and exhibits are free and open to the public. Community theater performances are sponsored by the Center throughout the year as well as special events and activities. For information, call 961-5711. Open daily except Sunday, 9AM - 4PM.

Panaewa Rain Forest Zoo ★, located a couple of miles south of Hilo just off the Volcano Highway 11 on Mamaki Street, is one of Hilo's least known and most delightful free attractions. It is one of the few natural tropical rainforest zoos in the United States. The small facility is operated by the County of Hawai'i and features several rainforest species in natural environment enclosures. Among the animals on display are an African pygmy hippopotamus, water buffalo, rain forest monkeys, a tapir, various jungle parrots, a rainforest tiger, and endangered Hawaiian birds like the Nene Goose, Hawaiian 'Io (hawk), Pueo (owl) and Hawaiian Stilt. The zoo is a pleasant walk through natural Hawaiian rainforest with numerous flowering trees and shrubs. Colorful peacocks strut openly. The zoo is adjacent to the Panaewa Equestrian Center, horse stables, and racetrack-rodeo grounds. Open daily, 9:00 AM to 4:30 PM, 959-7224. Free.

Mauna Loa Macadamia Nut Factory ★ is located three miles south of Hilo on the east side of Volcano Highway 11 and back in through the orchards a couple of miles. Look for road signs marking the entrance. A visitors center provides free samples of Hawai'i's popular gourmet nut and a wide variety of macadamia nut products are available for purchase. There is also a free narrated factory tour. Open daily from 9 AM to 5 PM. Call 966-8612 for information.

Wailoa State Park-Wailoa Center is adjacent to Suisan Fish Market on the Wailoa River and behind Kamehameha Avenue and the Hilo Bayfront. Wailoa Park comprises the lands surrounding the Wailoa River and Waiakea Fish Pond. There are lots of picnic tables and several covered pavilions. Fishermen in rowboats are often seen floating around the pond angling for the abundant mullet fish. There are also a Vietnam Veterans War Memorial and a Tsunami (Tidal Wave) Memorial in the park. The Wailoa Center in the park features various free art exhibits, seasonal showings, and cultural displays by local artisans. Check the schedule at the Center for current show. Wailoa Park is a good place for a pleasant picnic lunch.

Flower farms and botanical gardens are numerous in the Hilo area and many welcome visitors. Farm and nursery visits are usually free, but private botanical gardens charge admission.

Check your hotel desk or the visitor brochures and newspapers for listings of Hilo area orchid and anthurium farms. The following are a few of my favorite places to see Hawai'i's tropical beauty up close:

Hawai'i Tropical Botanical Garden ★, just north of Hilo on the four mile scenic drive (old Highway 19). Nature trails meander through tropical rainforest, cross streams and waterfalls, and follow the rugged coast. Extensive collections of palms, bromeliads, gingers, exotic ornamentals, and rare plants. Open daily 8-5. Phone 964-5233. Adult admission is $12, children 16 and under are free. Well worth the ticket price when you see what they have created out of former overgrown wild jungle. A garden of joy for nature photographers.

Nani Mau Gardens ★, 421 Makalika Street, Hilo, just south of town off Volcano Highway. You can't miss the turn off the highway, just look for beautiful floral beds and displays on both sides of Makalika Street. From the highway, it's a half-mile to the gardens. There are some 20 acres of tropical foliage, flowers, trees and plants along with a waterfall, pond and Japanese Garden. Visitors can stroll on their own or opt for a tram tour through the grounds. The orchid greenhouse is spectacular with many varieties of orchids in bloom. There is a large gift shop also. Open daily, 8-5. Phone 959-3541. Adult admission is $6.50 and children 16 and under are $4.

Rainbow Tropicals ★, on Mamaki Street just off Volcano Highway 11 just south of Hilo, Open daily 8:30-5. Self-guided tour of orchid, anthurium, and tropical plant gardens. Phone 959-4565. Free.

Hilo Tropical Gardens, 1477 Kalanianaole, Hilo, Open daily 8:30-5. Stroll through gardens of exotic tropical flowers including orchids, anthuriums, gingers, etc. Phone 935-4957. Free.

WHERE TO SHOP

Hilo can be a great place to explore and shop for special mementos or gifts. It has everything from modern shopping centers with the latest boutiques, fashion shops, and department stores, to nondescript little arts and crafts and specialty shops in old downtown Hilo. Some of the shopping centers and specialty shops worth checking are listed below.

Shopping Centers in Hilo have everything from major department stores (Sears, Penny's, Liberty House), to discount stores (Longs Drugs, Payless, Woolworths and a soon-to-open Walmart), to fashion stores, shoe stores, bookstores, jewelry stores, etc. Many fashion and department stores carry Hawaii-made Aloha clothing for those who want to get into colorful Aloha shirts and muumuus. Shopping centers include *Prince Kuhio Plaza* at intersection of Kanoelehua (Volcano Highway 11) and Puainako Streets; *Hilo Shopping Center* at corner of Kekuanaoa and Kilauea Avenue; *Kaiko'o Mall* on Kilauea Avenue is becoming less of a shopping mall and more of a government office and service center as retailers relocate to Prince Kuhio Plaza; and *Puainako Town Center* on Kanoelehua opposite Prince Kuhio Plaza.

Sugawara Lauhala & Gift Shop, 59 Kalakaua Street, 935-8071, and *Huki Like*, 71 Banyan Drive in front of the Hilo Hawaiian Hotel, are the places to visit if you are looking for authentic Hawaiian handicraft items. Look for genuine locally made Hawaiian lauhala (pandanus) woven slippers, hats, baskets, handbags, mats, and related goods. Also in downtown Hilo, you'll find *Oasis Cafe & Crafts*, 239 Keawe Street, 961-6625, to be an unusual combination of a local handcrafts store and a snack-deli-coffee bar operation. Next door is *Creative Gifts & Crafts* also with a selection of local handcrafts.

Doris' Island Delights, 935-7113, 1261 Kilauea Avenue, Hilo Shopping Center, carries a variety of island food products and gifts. They pack and ship as well.

Hawaiian Handcraft Shop Factory, 760 Kilauea Avenue, 935-5587, is the place to go for fine handcrafted wood products. Check out the carvings, bowls, platters, trays, and other items made from local koa, monkeypod, milo, breadfruit, and other Hawaiian woods.

Hilo Hattie's Fashion Center, 111 E. Puainako in the Prince Kuhio Plaza, 961-3077, is the original Aloha-wear factory. Features all locally made Hawaiian Aloha shirts, shorts, dresses, and muumuus. Showroom, factory tours, purchases directly from factory.

In downtown Hilo on Keawe Street between Waianuenue and Kalakaua, the "Keawe Collection of Shops" provide some interesting browsing and gift ideas. *Handmade Treasures*, corner of Waianuenue and Keawe, has a wide selection of special gift ideas and gourmet food items. Just down Keawe Street, *KD's Gifts & Crafts* features children's clothes and special gifts. *The Most Irresistible Shop in Hilo* (also in Prince Kuhio Plaza) is just that. It is loaded with all sorts of specialty items for every room in your house as well as many gift ideas and local items.

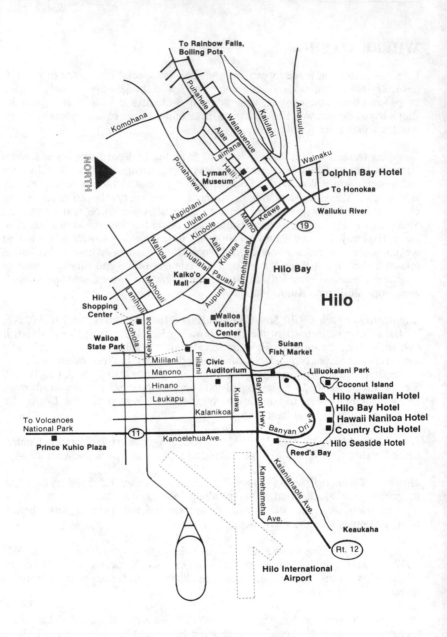

In the Hilo Shopping Center, corner of Lanikaula and Kilauea, *Oriental Designs* is a specialty T-shirt shop with lots of local designs and other take home gift ideas. Try *Pickle Barrel* for a bento (box) lunch, sandwich, saimin or other local-style goodies. *The Orient Connection* is an oriental food store for those with a fancy to take home some of the local and imported oriental products.

At 308 Kamehameha Avenue downtown, you'll enjoy exploring the restored landmark *S. Hata Building* with its handsome bell tower out front.   This carefully restored facility now houses a number of professional offices and interesting shops such as *Dreams of Paradise* art gallery, *Paradise Gourmet* which features Big Island food products, *Big Island Woodworks* for fine wood-crafts, *Thundering Seas Jewelry* and *Kipuka Smoke Shop* as well as *Skylight Garden Cafe*.   Kam Avenue has many old and new shops and small businesses representing a revitalization of the downtown core.   *Mo'oheau Park and Bandstand* and *Mo'oheau Bus Terminal* are also located here on the bayfront.

And for those with a flair for adventure, in downtown Hilo each Wednesday, Saturday and Sunday from about 7AM - Noon, take in the *Hilo Farmers' Market*, a fresh produce and general flea market operation on the corner of Mamo Street and Kamehameha Avenue across from Mo'oheau Park. It's a colorful gathering that will give you a glimpse of local folks at their best, just being themselves. You might even find some bargains!

ACCOMMODATIONS - HILO

Most of Hilo's hotels are located along Banyan Drive on the Waiakea Peninsula which extends out into Hilo Bay. These hotels are on the bay but there are no sandy beaches as the lavarock coastline is too rough and rugged. The Waiakea Villas Hotel is located adjacent to Wailoa State Park and Waiakea Fishponds in a relatively quiet secluded garden location a mile from the Banyan Drive area hotels.

For great views of Hilo town, Hilo Bay, and the twin towers of Mauna Kea and Mauna Loa, you should stay at one of the Banyan Drive hotels. For the best views, the Hawai'i Naniloa or the Hilo Hawaiian are tops. The Banyan Drive hotels also offer the best values in accommodations for visitors considering their amenities, facilities, and location.

For pre-arranged sightseeing coach/bus tours, pick-ups are easiest at Banyan Drive hotels, although arrangements can be made at the other hotels as well. If you have your own car, it doesn't matter where you stay in Hilo as you can easily find your way around to the important sites. And even the public "Hele On" bus service can take you to points around town.

As for shopping and dining, again wherever you stay in Hilo, you won't be far from shopping centers and/or dining options. Hilo is not a large town. Banyan Drive provides several hotel restaurants and local restaurants and eateries are not far away. See the RESTAURANT chapter for details.

BEST BETS:

Dolphin Bay Hotel - This is a budget-class lodge with clean simply furnished rooms near downtown Hilo.

Hawai'i Naniloa Hotel - This is Hilo's landmark property. There has been a "Naniloa" hotel in Hilo for, well, almost as long as there have been visitors to Hawai'i. It is still a fine place to stay while in Hilo.

Hilo Hawaiian Hotel - This lovely building faces directly onto Hilo Bay and Coconut Island. It has a relaxing Hawaiian ambiance and is just a nice place for a visit.

HILO ACCOMMODATIONS

Country Club Hotel   Dolphin Bay Hotel
Hawai'i Naniloa Hotel   Hilo Hawaiian Hotel
Hilo Bay Hotel   Hilo Seaside Hotel

COUNTRY CLUB HOTEL (W)
121 Banyan Drive, Hilo, HI 96720; Phone/FAX (808) 935-7171. All 130 units are air conditioned, some with TV. Stratton's Restaurant, cocktail lounge, and meeting room are on premises. Located across the street from Naniloa Country Club golf course and on shores of Hilo Bay. There is no beach as the shoreline is rugged lavarock. Within walking distance of Coconut Island, Liliuokalani Park, and Suisan Fish Auction. *Standard $45 Deluxe $75 Extra person $10*

DOLPHIN BAY HOTEL ★
333 Iliahi Street, Hilo, HI 96720. (808) 935-1466. This small 18 unit hotel is located in a quiet old residential area of Hilo four blocks from the downtown area and three blocks from Hilo Bay. There are few amenities other than fans and TV; no room telephones. Kitchen facilities are included in all units. The rooms are bright, airy, spacious, and very clean.
Standard $50-65, 1 BR Suite $75-85, 2 BR Suite $85, Extra person $10

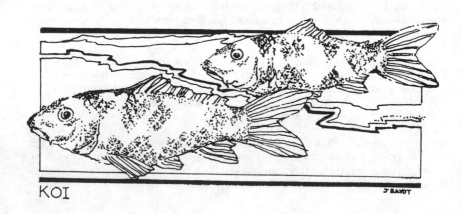

KOI

J BAYOT

HAWAI'I NANILOA HOTEL ★ (W)
93 Banyan Drive, Hilo, HI 96720; (808) 969-3333, 1-800-367-5360, FAX (808) 969-6622. This lovely 325 unit tower is a Hilo landmark overlooking Hilo Bay. The spacious rooms are 100% air conditioned with TV. The hotel features the Sandalwood Restaurant for continental-regional dining and Ting Hao Seafood Restaurant for Mandarin Chinese cuisine. There is a cocktail lounge and karaoke bar, complete health spa and fitness center and resort pool. There is no beach as the shoreline is rugged lavarock. It is located across from the Naniloa Country Club golf course and in heart of Banyan Drive hotel area; walking distance to Coconut Island, Liliuokalani Park, Suisan Fish Auction. This is one of Hilo's nicest hotels.
Standard $100, Superior $120, Deluxe $140, Suites $190-570, Extra person $15

HILO BAY HOTEL (W)
87 Banyan Drive, Hilo, HI 96720; 1-800-367-5102, (808) 935-0861, FAX (808) 935-7903. This is a 145 unit standard hotel located right on Hilo Bay. The rooms are all air-conditioned with TV. Uncle Billy's Restaurant, cocktail lounge, gift shops, and lovely tropical gardens are on grounds. There is no beach as the shoreline is rugged lavarock. It is located across from the Naniloa Country Club golf course; walking distance to Coconut Island, Liliuokalani Park, and Suisan Fish Auction. *Standard $59, Superior $69, Deluxe $79, Oceanfront $84, Studio/kitchen $74, Extra person $10*

HILO HAWAIIAN HOTEL ★ (W)
71 Banyan Drive, Hilo, HI 96720; 1-800-367-5004, (808) 935-9361, FAX (808) 961-9642. This beautiful 285 room hotel fronts directly on Hilo Bay just behind Coconut Island. There is no sand beach as the shoreline is rugged lavarock. The spacious comfortable rooms are air-conditioned with TV. The Queen's Court Restaurant, cocktail lounge, meeting room, and shops are on grounds. It is located across from the Naniloa Country Club golf course; walking distance to Coconut Island, Liliuokalani Park, and Suisan Fish Auction. *Gardenview $99, Superior $119, Oceanview $129, Suites $150-315, Extra person $15*

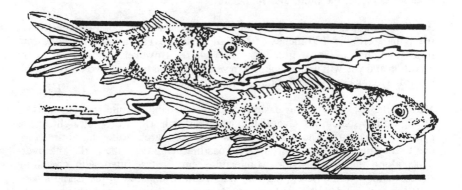

HILO SEASIDE HOTEL
126 Banyan Drive, Hilo, HI 96720; 1-800-367-7000, (808) 935-0821, FAX (808) 922-0052. This 145 room hotel is located just opposite Reeds Bay small boat harbor and the Ice Pond swimming hole but there is no good beach here. The rooms are standard but clean and feature ceiling fans and TV. The Hukilau Restaurant, cocktail lounge, and meeting rooms are on premises. It is adjacent to the Naniloa Country Club golf course; walking distance to Suisan Fish Auction, Liliuokalani Park, and Coconut Island.
Standard $80, Deluxe $95, Extra person $10

NORTH HILO / HAMAKUA DISTRICTS

INTRODUCTION

Just north, outside the town of Hilo, and running the length of the Big Island's east side some 40 miles to Honoka'a and another 10 miles beyond to Waipio Valley is the *Hamakua Coast*. The Hamakua Coast overlaps the districts of North Hilo and Hamakua. Up until a couple of years ago, when the sugar industry closed down, this region's vast sugar plantations annually produced thousands of tons of raw cane to feed the sugar mills located along the coast. Now the once productive plantations are being planted in macadamia nut orchards, ginger and taro fields and other crops which have taken over the former sugar cane lands.

Along the Hamakua Coast are numerous gulches and ravines filled with gushing streams and waterfalls, verdant tropical rain forest vegetation, and scattered stands of forest. Weathered old sugar plantation villages appear amidst the fields presenting a vestige of Hawai'i's past. A generation or two ago, most of the Big Island's population lived in such plantation camps.

Driving the length of the Hamakua Coast can be a most enjoyable experience with beautiful scenic vistas of ocean, farmlands and tropical rain forest. The route passes through a number of small towns and settlements along the way, each with a melodious Hawaiian name: Papa'ikou, Pepe'ekeo, Honomu, Hakalau, Laupahoehoe, O'okala, Pa'auilo, and Pa'auhau.

As is the immediate Hilo area, the Hamakua Coast is generally quite wet receiving well over 100 inches of rainfall annually. This accounts for the rain forest and lush fields of greenery everywhere. However, rainfall varies by elevation and you will notice changes in vegetation and terrain as you travel north towards Honoka'a. It does become somewhat drier.

Most of the coastline on this eastern side of the island is quite rugged, marked by high cliffs sometimes several hundred feet high which drop straight to the pounding ocean surf. There are very few safe beach areas along this entire coast due to the rugged rocky nature of the coastline. However, the parks and overlooks along the way provide wonderful scenic vistas, often with cascading streams and waterfalls dropping into the ocean. Compared to the island's west side, the east is indeed a Paradise and a Garden of Eden, it is so lush and green.

WHAT TO DO AND SEE / WHERE TO SHOP

The Hamakua Coast doesn't offer a whole lot in the way of activities or shopping. Being a predominately rural agricultural area, it is marked by several small villages and settlements and a fair number of scenic sites. Some of the small villages have one or two unique shops, maybe an antique shop or two, and usually a Mom n' Pop general store.

Five miles north of Hilo is the old Highway 19 scenic route, *Mamalahoa Highway* ★, that winds along the coast for four miles. It is a short but very scenic drive along the twisting old coastal highway which was the only route around the island in the pre-World War II days. Also on this old scenic route is the *Hawai'i Tropical Botanical Garden* ★. See the section on HILO in the WHAT TO DO AND SEE chapter for other details.

About 11 miles north of Hilo is the village of *Honomu*, a typical old sugar plantation town. The town's main street is all of two blocks long and houses some interesting shops in the original shop buildings. At one end you'll find the *Akaka Falls Flea Market* store and at the other *Ishigo's Store & Bakery*, an old family run "Mom & Pop" operation. In between are an ice cream shop, a forlorn old movie theater, *Woodshop Gallery*, and *Akaka Falls Inn & Gift Gallery* which combines a bed & breakfast inn with an ice cream counter-coffee-snack bar and an interesting gift shop with local-made arts and crafts. Explorers can check out the unique old Japanese churches lined up along main street too. A stroll down this old main street will provide a glimpse of the Hawai'i of just a generation or two ago. It's not hard to imagine the residents of this quiet little town rising each morning to toil in the green fields of sugar cane on the slopes rising behind the town.

From Honomu, take Route 22 on out from town. The paved road rises sharply through the hilly fields above town on its 3.6 mile route to *Akaka Falls State Park* ★. Here under a rainforest canopy, the ocean tradewinds are cool and delightful. The 66 acre park is a refreshing stop after the uphill drive. Restrooms and picnic tables are available. The main attraction is the fascinating walk down into the ravines where mountain streams are gushing and waterfalls are splashing. Beautiful stands of bamboo, ginger, and many flowering trees and plants delight walkers. It's a gorgeous tropical greenhouse. The walk is highlighted by inspiring views of the 420 ft. cascades of Akaka Falls and nearby Kahuna Falls tumbling into deep gorges. If you like tropical splendor, don't miss this attraction.

Continuing on Highway 19 north out of Honomu about two and a half miles and just past the 16 mile marker, is the turnoff to the entrance of the *World Botanical Gardens*. This is a new development on 300 acres of old sugar cane fields to establish a world-class botanical garden. The gardens opened in mid-1995 and are being planted with thousands of species of tropical plants and trees. The garden trails and nature walks include a lookout point at the spectacular triple cascades of Umauma Waterfalls. There are also a visitors center and shuttle-bus being planned along with other improvements as development moves ahead.

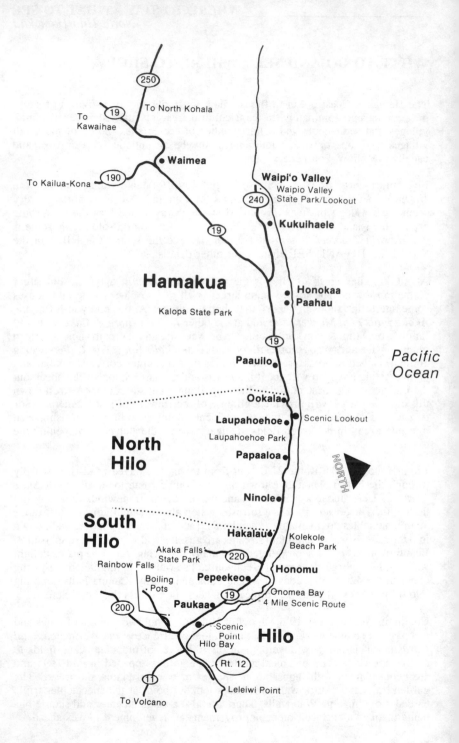

To North Kohala

To Kawaihae

To Kailua-Kona

Waimea

Waipi'o Valley
Waipio Valley
State Park/Lookout

Kukuihaele

Hamakua

Kalopa State Park

Honokaa
Paahau

Paauilo

Pacific
Ocean

Ookala

Laupahoehoe   Scenic Lookout

Laupahoehoe Park

**North
Hilo**

Papaaloa

NORTH

Ninole

**South
Hilo**

Hakalau

Kolekole
Beach Park

Akaka Falls
State Park

Rainbow Falls

Boiling
Pots

Pepeekeo

Honomu

Onomea Bay
4 Mile Scenic Route

Paukaa

Scenic
Point
Hilo Bay

Hilo

Rt. 12

To Volcano

Leleiwi Point

160

Further north it is about 12 miles to **Laupahoehoe Point**. There is a scenic overlook alongside the highway before you get to the gulch leading down to the point. The point itself is a lava peninsula extending into the ocean. There is a grassy park area with picnic tables, restrooms, and shelters. Small boat launching facilities are available and from the point there are scenic views of the Hamakua Coast. A monument stands on the point in memory of the 24 teachers and school children who were swept to sea in a 1946 tidal wave that devastated a school which occupied the site.

It's another 10 miles or so to **Pa'auilo**, another fading sugar plantation village. Be sure to stop just south of the village at **Donna's Cookies** for the best home-made cookies on the Big Island.

From Pa'auilo, it is only six miles to **Honoka'a**, the largest country town on the Hamakua Coast. Honoka'a has an old west look about it with weathered store-fronts lining Mamane Street and even an occasional Hawaiian paniolo (cowboy) strolling down the town's main street. Visit the **Hawaiian Macadamia Nut Plantation Factory** located just below town at the end of the main street, watch for the signs. There are numerous macadamia nut and chocolate creations on display, as well as many other products in the gift shop, and free factory tours. For more gift ideas, check out **Kama'aina Woods**, located on Lehua Street. Hand turned bowls of koa, milo, and other native Hawaiian woods are crafted in the factory here. There is another woodshop, **Hamakua Woodworks**, on Mamane Street plus other country town shops like **S. Hasegawa Dry Goods, Hirata Shirtmaker, Filipino Store** and the usual small town hardware store, a second hand shop, bakery, and eateries like **Jolene's Kau Kau Korner and Herb's Place**, and **Hotel Honoka'a Club**.

Back on Highway 19 above town, don't miss a Honoka'a institution, **Tex's Drive-In**, famous for fresh hot malasadas (deep-fried Portuguese doughnuts, a sheer delight anytime), and other local fast-food items as well.

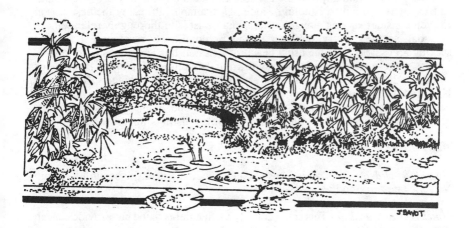

Out of Honoka'a, take Route 240 north nine miles to the tiny village of **Kukui-haele**. You can visit **The Last Chance Store** for cold sodas and snacks and see what a small country village general store is like. **Waipio Wood Works Art Gallery** is a great place for handcrafted Hawaiian wood products, paintings, prints, photos, glasswork, pottery, jewelry, baskets, batik art, and general Hawaiiana created by island artists. Also, in this shop you can book a tour with **Waipio Valley Shuttle** (775-7121), to take a narrated one and a half hour 4x4 drive down into the magnificent **Waipio Valley** ★, just a half mile further on.

The tour details the history and culture of the valley from past to present, and includes information on taro growing, the main economic activity at present. The shuttle tour is $31 per person, children under 12 are $15. You can also see the Waipio Valley via horseback rides booked through **Waipio Na'alapa Trail Rides** (775-0419) or **Hawaii Resorts Transportation** (775-7291). These are two-and-a-half hour horseback tours on the floor of Waipio Valley.

The steep winding road into the valley begins at **Waipio Valley State Park** ★. *CAUTION NOTE*: Under no circumstances should you attempt to drive your rental car down the dangerously steep valley road. Only 4x4 vehicles are allowed. In addition to the steep road, there are numerous streams which must be crossed on the valley floor and regular rental cars will not make it.

Waipio Valley Park provides a covered picnic pavilion and restrooms at the top of the valley and spectacular views from an overlook of the six mile long valley interior with its almost vertical 2000 ft. walls, and also of the northern coastline of the Big Island. The valley fronts the ocean with a wide black sand beach and heavy pounding surf. This beach is not safe for swimming due to hazardous undercurrents.

ACCOMMODATIONS - NORTH HILO AND HAMAKUA

Visitors will not find any world class accommodations in this area of the island. In fact, there are only a handful of lodgings available. Probably the best reason to even consider staying along the Hamakua Coast is to thoroughly relax, enjoy, and soak up the country ambiance of this predominately rural area. For those seeking an escape from the usual beach resorts and hustle and bustle of tourist centers, this area of the island provides lots of appeal. For those looking for strictly budget accommodations, this area will also fill the bill nicely. The North Hilo and Hamakua areas can actually provide some wonderfully quiet and peaceful vacation experiences and memories in one of the Big Island's most beautiful areas. Also check the Bed & Breakfast listings for this area.

BEST BETS:

Hamakua Hideaway - This is a rustic country cottage near the beautiful Waipio Valley State Park and valley overlook.

Hotel Honoka'a Club - This small country town hotel is dated but provides cheap basic accommodation where there's not much other choice in the immediate area.

NORTH HILO AND HAMAKUA ACCOMMODATIONS

Hamakua Hideaway
Hotel Honoka'a Club
Waipio Tree House
Waipio Valley Hotel

HAMAKUA HIDEAWAY

P.O. Box 5104, Kukuihaele, Hamakua Coast, HI 96727. (808) 775-7425. Located in the small country village near Waipio Valley lookout. Accommodations are one rustic self-contained cottage, **The Cliffhouse**, and a separate room, **The Treehouse Suite**. Cliffhouse sleeps up to four people, Treehouse sleeps two. Cliffhouse has a full kitchen, bathroom, and fireplace and sits on a pali (cliff) with wonderful views of Hamakua Coast up past Waipio Valley and to the southern coast. Treehouse has bath and kitchen. Hikes or guided jeep trips into Waipio Valley available nearby. *Cliffhouse $75 Treehouse $65 Extra person $10*

HOTEL HONOKA'A CLUB

P.O. Box 185, Mamane Street, Honoka'a, HI 96727; (808) 775-0533/775-0678. This rambling old wooden building has been a Honoka'a landmark for years. It is centrally located on the main street of town off Highway 19. The hotel has just 14 rental rooms available with TV, full bathroom, queen size beds, and each features a distant ocean view. Restaurant and parking on grounds. There is nothing fancy about this hotel but it provides basic accommodation in an area where there is little else. The back-packing no-frills adventurous traveler will find it accommodating. *Standard $35, Deluxe $44*

WAIPIO TREE HOUSE

P.O. Box 5086, Honoka'a, HI 96727; Tel/Fax (808) 775-7160. This is a fantasy lodging for an adventurous few and one of the most unusual lodgings on the Big Island. **The Tree House** is for real, located in a huge monkeypod tree in Waipio Valley. The facility has a double and single bed, refrige, hot plates, electricity and running water. There is a Japanese ofuro hot tub, hikes on jungled valley trails, swimming in quiet pools and splashing waterfalls or horseback and mule-drawn wagon rides. The Tree House can accommodate 3 adults or 2 adults and 2 children. There is a separate private cottage, **The Hale**, available which sleeps up to six people. The Hale has full kitchen, livingroom and loft. **Kahu** is a larger private unit for up to 10 guests. Guests supply their own food at both units. **Note:** There can be a few days each year (about 10) when these units are inaccessible because of high river water. Should guests be unable to leave, food and lodging during their delay are complimentary. For the adventure-minded only! *Tree House $175-225, The Hale $175-225, Kahu $200-250 Extra person $35, kids under 12 free.*

WAIPIO VALLEY HOTEL

25 Malama Place, Hilo, HI 96720; (808) 775-0368 in Waipio. This too is one of the Big Island's most unusual accommodations. Located on the floor of Waipio Valley it is a very simple rustic inn providing only the bare essentials: a bed, toilet, and a cold shower. Guests bring their own food and other essentials and share cooking facilities. The hotel is run by taro farmer, Tetsuo Araki, who spends lots of time tending his taro patches in the valley. He also lives in Hilo

and drives back and forth. Contact him at the hotel at (808) 775-0368 in Waipio or in Hilo at (808) 935-7466. If you don't have the necessary 4-wheel drive transport to get down the hazardous valley road, you can either hike (2 miles from top of valley to the hotel) or get a ride with the Waipio Valley Shuttle tours mentioned above. This is a great place to hike and explore the wonders of a tropical rain forest valley. Don't forget the mosquito repellant! Five guest rooms with twin beds are available. Reservations should be made at least 3-4 weeks in advance. *Rates: $15 per person per night.*

NORTH KOHALA DISTRICT

INTRODUCTION

The North Kohala District occupies the northern two-thirds of the Kohala Mountains peninsula, the Big Island's top end. This is one of the smallest districts on the island. To get there, take the Akoni Pule Highway 270 which follows the west coast from Kawaihae (and from the South Kohala resorts) and the intersection of the cross island Highway 19. North Kohala can also be reached from Kamuela via the Kohala Mountain Road, Highway 250, which in my opinion is the most scenic drive on the Big Island.

The Akoni Pule coastal highway passes through some of Hawaii's driest country where rainfall is less than ten inches annually. Kohala's hot dry winds blow across fields of dry grass and acres of hardy keawe trees. The road also passes through Kohala Ranch country and the North Kohala towns of Hawi and Kapaʻau.

Of the two, the Kohala Mountain Road, Highway 250, is the more scenic drive. Running from the town of Kamuela on the South Kohala plateau, the road immediately ascends the Kohala Mountains. Scenic views of the plateau ranging across to the base of Mauna Kea and sweeping vistas of the slope down to the South Kohala coast are at every angle as the highway climbs to over 3000 ft. elevation. There is a scenic overlook with a panoramic view of South Kohala about five miles from Kamuela town. The road passes through beautiful rolling Kahua Ranch and Kohala Ranch lands where herds of cattle graze and numerous sheep frolic in the lush green meadows. This is the heart of Kohala's "paniolo" (cowboy) country. And because the Kohala winds blow with such regularity up here, the highway is lined with evergreens that serve as a windbreaker. This adds to the real "country lane" atmosphere of the Kohala Mountain Road which is emphasized by the panoramic views of green hills and mountains, grazing cattle and sheep, and the sweeping views of the Kohala-Kona Coasts. The Kohala Mountain Road is my favorite drive on the Big Island.

As the road nears the town of *Hawi*, it descends rapidly and another road branches off to Kapaʻau town. In Hawi, the Kohala Mountain Road joins the Akoni Pule Highway allowing a complete circle drive around the North Kohala District. Route 270 continues on through the towns of Hawi and Kapaʻau and angles south along the eastern coast of the peninsula. It passes through a few old sugar plantation settlements and past the old Kohala Mill, which went out of business in 1970. The road terminates at Pololu Valley Lookout about eight miles from Hawi.

The small settlements, villages and abandoned old mill in this area of North Kohala are all that's left of a once viable sugar plantation industry. The cane fields have long since lain fallow but some are being replanted to macadamia nuts, flowers, ornamental plants, etc. The closing of the sugar mill created an economic wasteland here as sugar was its only business for almost a century.

The last several years has seen these North Kohala communities rebound from disaster to the point where development, growth, and improvement is happening again. Much of it is attributed to the rise of the plush resorts in neighboring South Kohala which provide jobs and a sense of security for North Kohala residents.

WHAT TO DO AND SEE / WHERE TO SHOP

North Kohala is a predominately rural area, with lots to see but little to shop for in the towns. This is Kamehameha Country and, as mentioned in the A HISTORY OF HAWAI'I section earlier, is the birthplace of King Kamehameha the Great who united the islands of Hawai'i under one rule in 1795. Because of this, North Kohala is filled with the lore of Kamehameha.

In front of the county courthouse in Kapa'au is a statue of *King Kamehameha* ★ which has an interesting history. The statue was originally commissioned as a monument for Honolulu. It was cast in bronze in the 1880's in Paris and, after a rather turbulent history, including being sunk in the South Atlantic Ocean near Cape Horn at Port Stanley in the Falkland Islands, ended up here at the Kapa'au Courthouse in 1912. Before this statue was salvaged from the icy waters of the Atlantic, a duplicate model was cast and that one now stands in front of the Judiciary Building, Aliiolani Hale, across from Iolani Palace in Honolulu. Since the original statue was no longer needed in Honolulu, it was placed in North Kohala. This final resting place for the original Kamehameha statue in quiet lonely North Kohala seems fitting. The meaning of the name Kamehameha is "the lonely one." Each June 11, Kamehameha Day, local residents drape the statue with beautiful flowing flower leis.

Across from King Kamehameha's statue in Kapa'au, the *Ackerman Gallery* shop outlet features island arts and crafts, antiques and unique gifts. The gallery's main shop and studio is less than a block down the road. *Kohala Country Store* carries varied lines of clothing, accessories and special gifts. In the same building *Don's Family Deli* has ice cream treats, sandwiches, and light lunches. Just down the block in 1939 Sakamoto Building is *Tropical Dreams Ice Cream Shop* for ice cream and deli bar treats and *Kamehameha Pharmacy*.

Highway 270 continues east of Kapa'au to *Pololu Valley*, a distance of nine miles. Before reaching the end of the road at the valley, however, there is a turnoff for *Keokea Beach Park*. This is a secluded little beach park reached by a two mile winding road through an old sugar village. The beach is very rocky and not recommended for swimming. There are picnic pavilions and restrooms here. The bay of this beach is framed by interesting picturesque cliffs 75-100 feet high. If you brought a picnic lunch this is a good place for a restful stop.

The road continues on to its termination and turnaround at *Pololu Valley* ★. The Pololu Valley is second only to the famed Waipio Valley just a short distance down the east Kohala Coast. From the parking area and overlook there is a majestic view of the valley walls and floor as it reaches back toward the Kohala Mountains. Perhaps most eye-catching are the two or three rock islets that stand just off the mouth and beach of the valley. These islets are actually chunks of the Big Island that were separated at some time in the far past probably by some volcanic activity. They present interesting subjects for photography buffs. The beach of Pololu Valley is composed of fine black lava sand. However, the surf here is quite dangerous as the undertow is very strong and swimming is not advised. The trail leading down to the valley floor and the beach is a nice hike but can be hazardous in or just after rain and caution is advised.

Back in *Hawi* town most places of interest are just at the intersection of Highways 250 and 270. Check out *Nakahara Store* for a look at an old-fashioned country general store. The store is a relic of Kohala's plantation days. A block from the highway intersection toward Kapa'au in an old store building you'll find *Vea Polynesian Gifts* which carry Polynesian handmade arts and crafts and collectibles. In the same location is *Sugar Moon Clay Works,* a pottery gallery and gift shop. On the Kawaihae side of the highway intersection is *As Hawi Turns*, a boutique which features a blend of romantic European and local Hawaiiana apparel and crafts from local artisans. Next door is *Kohala Coffee Mill* espresso shop for fresh Kona coffee and snacks. Across the street in the old Takata Store building is *Kohala Koa Gallery* which shares space with *Bamboo Restaurant & Bar.* Next door is *Matthew's Place*, a small local-style diner. Along the mainstreet are a few other shops like *Pumehana Flowers, Hawaiian Moon Gallery, and Frank's Furniture & Second Hand.*

Just two miles west of Hawi on Route 270, is the turnoff for the *Upolu Airport Road* which leads down two miles to the coast and the tiny airstrip at Upolu Point, the northernmost point on the Big Island. The airport road is a bumpy narrow asphalt single-lane strip.

At the airstrip, a sign points the direction west along the coast to the ancient settlement that is *King Kamehameha's Birthplace* ★ and the adjacent *Mo'okini Luakini Heiau* ★. The 1 1/2 mile bumpy, rutted and very dusty road from the airstrip along the coast to the restored birthplace site is unimproved dirt and driving it can be hazardous. There can be several deep ruts and mud bogs which may or may not be passable. Drive at your own risk! If you can't get through, you can always park the car and walk the rest of the way.

While restoration work on these two sites is ongoing, both are beautiful and impressive. Kamehameha's birthplace is a large square shaped rock wall enclosure about 75 yards per side, and encloses various other foundations and structures. It sits about 50 yards from the beach in an open sloping area. The wind and sun are both strong here.

Mo'okini Luakini Heiau is located just off the same road as the birthplace site. It occupies the summit of a hill and as such dominates the immediate area. The temple is where the ali'i nui, the kings and ruling chiefs, fasted, prayed, and offered human sacrifices to their gods. The temple was built about 480 A.D. and is one of the largest on the Big Island, measuring 267 ft. by 250 ft. on the west and east walls, and 135 ft. and 112 ft. on the north and south walls. The walls are 30 ft. high and 15 ft. wide. The structure is in the shape of an irregular parallelogram.

The stones used in constructing the temple are of smooth water worn basalt. Legend has it that the stones come from Polulu Valley on the east side of the Kohala peninsula, a distance of some 10-14 miles. It is said that each stone was passed by hand from man to man the entire distance, a feat requiring from 15,000 to 18,000 men. By this method, so says the legend, the temple was built in a single night, from sunset to sunrise.

Mo'okini Luakini was constructed under the direction of High Priest Kuamo'o Mo'okini and was dedicated to the battle god, Ku. The priestly order of Ku, through the Kahuna Nui, provides the guidance and direction of the temple. Throughout its 1500 year history, members of the Mo'okini family have served as Kahu (guardian) of the Mo'okini Luakini. The latest member of the family to inherit the title of Kahuna Nui (high priestess and councilor to a high chief) is Leimomi Mo'okini Lum, a direct descendant of High Priest Kuamo'o Mo'okini.

Today, the heiau and adjoining Kamehameha Birthplace are open to visitors to stroll the grounds and learn about the history and culture of old Hawai'i. Various celebrations and cultural days are held here on special occasions such as King Kamehameha Day (June 11).

About eight miles south of Hawi and twelve miles north of Kawaihae on Route 270 is the turnoff for *Lapakahi State Historical Park* ★. Located right on the Kohala Coast, Lapakahi Park is the site of a restored ancient Hawaiian fishing village. It is a chance to stretch your legs and walk through a once inhabited, living village and get a sense of what life in old Hawai'i was like. It's well worth your time.

The park provides a self-guided walking tour and follows well laid out trail of wood chips and mulching that make for easy walking. You'll notice a number of stone wall foundations for houses which served the Hawaiians as protection against the almost constant Kohala winds. Within the walls, the people built their "hales" (houses), canoe sheds, and other structures. The sites are all clearly marked and can be identified with the trail guide brochure picked up at the entrance to the park. Following the trails and learning from the displays and sites, you'll come to appreciate how the old Hawaiians lived in harmony with the land and sea. The park has remnants of a family heiau, a fishing shrine, lamp stand, salt pans (depressions carved in rocks) where sea water was left to crystallize into salt, old fire pits, a water well, and plantings of sugar cane, sweet potatoes, bananas, and gourds, all important to Hawaiian life.

At Kawaihae Village, just north of the intersection of Highways 270 and 19, you'll find the town center, as such, at *Kawaihae Center.* This is a small shopping complex housing a number of shops like *Black Pearl Jewelry, Kohala Divers, Kohala Collection Art & Antiques* and eateries such as *Tres Hombres Beach Grill and Cafe Pesto.* On Highway 270 across from the boat harbor/docks is *Kawaihae Harbor Grill.*

ACCOMMODATIONS - NORTH KOHALA DISTRICT

Accommodations are limited in the remote North Kohala District. Readers wishing to stay in the area are advised to check the **Bed and Breakfast Lodging** section of this book for B&B reservation services as to what may be available in the North Kohala area. The closest other accommodations would be in Waimea about 20 miles south or further south at the Kohala Coast resorts, see **Accommodations - South Kohala**, for details.

KOHALA VILLAGE INN
55-514 Hawi Road, intersection of Highways 270 & 250, Hawi, North Kohala, HI 96719; reservations (808) 889-0105 or 889-0419. If you're looking to stay in the wind-swept regions of North Kohala, this is the only accommodation available.

After several changes of ownership the last few years, and a stint as a residential complex, this country-style inn is open once again offering basic, no-frills country lodging. There is nothing fancy about the place. The budget-priced rooms are clean and simple. There are ten guestrooms, ranging from singles to doubles which can accommodate up to six people. All rooms have private bath and TV (except the singles). The inn owners also operate the Kohala Village Restaurant next door and offer a meal discount for inn guests. If you're looking for a complete change-of-pace in lodging with no-frills, this may be the place for you. Easy access to nearby Pololu Valley for hiking, horseback riding, Mookini Heiau, King Kamehameha Birthplace and statue (at Kapa'au), seasonal whale watching, and the country charm of a very small town and friendly folks.

Rates: Single Rooms $47-55, Double Rooms (3 max) $59, Double Rooms (5 max) $72, Double Rooms (6 max) $79

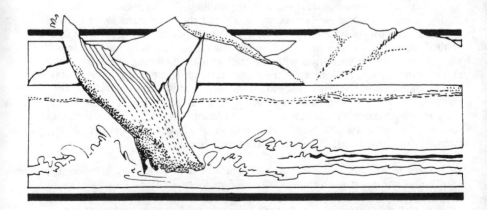

THE SADDLE ROAD AREA

This section is added for informational purposes even though there are no towns or villages, no stores or services of any kind other than a state park, and for the most part no permanent inhabitants through the entire area. It is included because it passes through some incredibly surreal country of stark lava flows, cinder cones, ranch lands and towering volcanic peaks and is the route used to its primary attractions: the world renowned telescope observatories at the summit of Mauna Kea mountain and the weather observatory on Mauna Loa.

Caution!: Driving on Saddle Road, Highway 200, is prohibited in regular rental cars due to hazardous driving conditions and an unstable roadway and is in violation of car rental contracts. Only 4x4 vehicles are recommended for driving on the Saddle Road. While the Saddle Road is paved its entire length it is very narrow and winding in some areas.

The Saddle Road is so-called because it passes through the plateau adjoining the massive Mauna Kea and Mauna Loa. From Waimea/Kamuela to Hilo via the Saddle Road is a distance of 60 miles and from Kailua-Kona to Hilo it is 87 miles. However because of the narrow winding road conditions (especially near the Hilo side) and the extreme caution needed when driving it, this route often takes longer to drive than other routes around the island.

The drive does present some different scenery however. The towering peaks of Mauna Kea and Mauna Loa are seen from a closer perspective on the drive over the plateau separating them. This of course is possible assuming clouds don't obscure one's vision from the Saddle Road elevation. The early morning hours are generally clear while from mid-day on into the afternoon, clouds roll upslope from the eastern Hilo and Hamakua districts and tend to fill up the plateau area between the mountains. From the Waimea and Kona side, the road passes through vast tracts of ranch grazing lands extending down from Mauna Kea's lower slopes. This is generally dry, windy and wide-open countryside. On the Hilo side, the road passes through several miles of heavy rainforest vegetation above the town which gives way to extensive fern and ohia lehua forest of the mountain's mid-elevation slopes. Interspersed here and there are rough and rugged lava flows until at the 3000 ft. level on the central plateau it appears to be one huge lava flow. On the lower slopes of Mauna Kea, ranch grazing lands stand out as large green patches against the upper level brown barrenness of the mountain and the lower level grey and mottled green of the fern and ohia lehua forest and lava flows.

Midway on the Saddle Road from either the Kona/Waimea (28 miles) or the Hilo side (27 miles) is the turnoff for the Mauna Kea Summit Road. This road leads to the summit of the 13,796 ft. mountain. At the 9200 ft. elevation level (6.5 miles up the summit road) is the ***Ellison Onizuka Center for International Astronomy*** ★. A visitors center has displays and programs of interest on Mauna Kea and astronomy. The visitors center is open Friday from 1 - 5PM and Saturday-Sunday from 8AM - 5PM. Every Friday, Saturday and Sunday night a public information presentation is held from 7 - 9PM and includes a "star gazing" tour using an 11-inch telescope. Official Mauna Kea summit day tours through

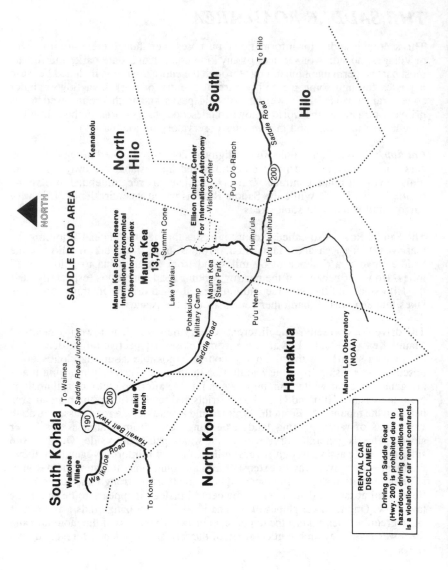

NORTH

SADDLE ROAD AREA

Keanakolu

North Hilo

South Hilo

To Hilo

Saddle Road

200

Pu'u O'o Ranch

Ellison Onizuka Center
For International Astronomy
Visitors Center

Humu'ula

Pu'u Huluhulu

Mauna Kea Science Reserve
International Astronomical
Observatory Complex
Mauna Kea
13,796

Summit Cone

Lake Waiau

Pohakuloa
Military Camp

Mauna Kea
State Park

Saddle Road

Pu'u Nene

Mauna Loa Observatory
(NOAA)

Hamakua

To Waimea

Saddle Road Junction

200

Waiki
Ranch

190

Hawaii Belt Hwy.

South Kohala

Waikoloa
Village

Waikoloa Road

To Kona

North Kona

**RENTAL CAR
DISCLAIMER**

Driving on Saddle Road
(Hwy. 200) is prohibited due to
hazardous driving conditions and
is a violation of car rental contracts.

the University of Hawai'i 88-inch observatory are given on Saturday and Sundays only at 2:30PM. Participants should meet at the visitors center at 1PM to join the tour to the summit. Visitors must provide their own 4-wheel drive transport to the summit. All programs are free and open to the public. For more information, call the center at (808/961-2180) for a recorded message.

The Onizuka Center also serves as the base camp housing the many scientists and astronomers engaged in research projects utilizing the telescopes at the summit. This center is at the 9200 ft. elevation level and is more conducive to a comfortable existence for those working long hours in the extremely thin air at the nearly 14,000 ft. summit. The center is named in honor of Astronaut Ellison Onizuka, a native son of the Big Island, who died in the 1986 Challenger spaceshuttle tragedy.

Above the Onizuka Center, the "John A. Burns Way" extends another 6.6 miles to the final cinder cones at the summit. A paving project on the hazardous gravel road has been underway over the last couple of years and due to extreme conditions on the mountain, progress has been slow. The road is cut into the side of the steep mountain slopes and winds around giant cinder cones. This part of the drive is an eerie yet spectacular journey across a moonscape panorama. There is nothing but fine volcanic dust, pumice, and jagged rocks and lava flows. There is little in the way of vegetation above 10,000 ft. on Mauna Kea. The extreme dryness of the entire summit area is precisely why the observatories were built here. Mauna Kea offers some of the finest and most consistent conditions for optical and infrared astronomy of any site in the world. Here at the summit, the observatories are above 40% of the earth's atmosphere, water vapor in the air is at a minimum and the number of cloud-free nights for viewing through the telescopes is higher than anywhere else in the world.

It is no wonder then that Mauna Kea has become known as the premier site for optical and infrared astronomy in the entire world. The major observatories currently in operation are the University of Hawai'i 88" optical-infrared instrument, the NASA 3-meter infrared instrument, the Canada-France-Hawai'i 3.6-meter optical-infrared telescope, the United Kingdom 3.8-meter infrared telescope, the Caltech 10.4-meter submillimeter observatory, and the James Clerk Maxwell 15-meter submillimeter facility. The twin telescopes of the W.M. Keck Observatory are like a giant high-tech pair of binoculars. They are 10-meter optical-infrared multiple-mirror instruments that make the Keck instruments the largest telescopes of their kind in the world. The 82' wide, 100' tall antenna dish of the Very Long Baseline Array is part of the 5,000-mile wide radio telescope which stretches from the Virgin Islands to Hawai'i with dish sites across the mainland. But more facilities are either planned or under construction and due for completion by the end of the century. The Smithsonian Institute is building a high tech multi-dish radiotelescope with an array of six 6-meter dishes, called the Smithsonian Submillimeter Array. Astronomy research groups from Japan are building the Subaru Japan National Telescope, a 7.5-meter optical-infrared facility. Also planned for Mauna Kea is the Gemini Northern Telescope, half of a pair of 8-meter mirror telescopes with the other half at Cerro Pachon, Chile, in South America. The Gemini project is a joint partnership between the U.S., United Kingdom, Canada, Chile, Argentina and Brazil. An Italian telescope, a 3.5-meter optical instrument named for the famed Renaissance astronomer, Galileo

Galilei, will also be built atop Mauna Kea by the Universities of Padua and Bologna of Italy. Even without these new facilities, Mauna Kea Observatory has more viewing surface and light-gathering power than any other site on earth. Little wonder the Mauna Kea Science Complex is so well known and envied in the astronomy world.

For information on visiting *Mauna Kea Observatory* or visitor center tours, call *Mauna Kea Support Services* in Hilo (808/935-3371). Visitors must provide their own 4x4 (4-wheel drive) transport to the Onizuka Center and to the summit. For those wishing to visit the summit but not wanting to drive themselves, there are two tour operators with Mauna Kea summit tours. Both *Waipio Valley Shuttle/Mauna Kea Summit Tours* (808/775-7121) and *Paradise Safaris* (808/322-2366) offer full day summit tours with lunch included. See ACTIVITIES AND TOURS for details.

Caution Note: Youngsters under 12, pregnant women and anyone with respiratory or cardiac problems are advised **not** to go to Mauna Kea's summit. The very thin air (60% of normal oxygen) can cause altitude sickness and nausea. Even scientists working at this elevation experience difficulties. Also be advised that Mauna Kea's weather can change suddenly and dramatically, especially in winter months. From November to March, it can snow anytime and blizzard conditions are possible. Even the summer months can bring below freezing temperatures at the summit.

About two miles above the Saddle Road on the Hilo-side of the Mauna Kea Summit Road is an unmarked gateway and dirt road leading off to the northeast. This is the **Mana Road** which passes through the open range and hill country of Parker Ranch and Mauna Kea's upper flanks, areas of rainforest and the Hakalau National Wildlife Refuge wilderness area. You absolutely must have a 4-wheel drive off-road vehicle for this backcountry drive. The Mana Road goes through government and private ranchlands and is very narrow, rough, bumpy and filled with ruts and mud bogs, especially after rains. It is however, a spectacular drive through some serene backcountry little seen by island residents or visitors alike. There are vistas of beautiful range grasslands with herds of grazing cattle and stands of huge native koa trees and rainforest. There are many places to stop and marvel at the beauty and enjoy a quiet picnic lunch. The drive through Mana Road leads to Waimea and takes about four-hours. As it is a remote backcountry area, there are no services of any kind until you reach Waimea.

The **Mauna Loa Access Road** leads off the Saddle Road in the opposite direction of the Mauna Kea Summit Road. This drive of just over 17 miles to the 11,000 ft. level of *Mauna Loa* passes through nothing but stark barren lava flow country. There are sweeping views back across the Saddle Road plateau and to Mauna Kea on cloudless days. But other than that, the 34 mile round trip on this road is a drive across a moonscape rock desert. At the end of the Mauna Loa Access Road is the National Oceanic and Atmospheric Administration (NOAA) Mauna Loa Weather Observatory which keeps track of developing weather over Hawai'i using sophisticated instruments and satellite communications. A hiking trail from the end of the road here continues on up to Mauna Loa's summit and to a hiker's cabin. Hikers can connect there to a trail system leading downslope on the other side to Hawai'i Volcanoes National Park headquarters. But it is not a hike for novices or unprepared casual hikers. It is a very strenuous hike over very rugged terrain. Only experienced backpackers with full supplies should attempt the route. Check the section on "Camping - National Park" for details.

Along the Saddle Road is Pohakuloa Military Camp, a large reserve used by the army for live firing exercises and military maneuvers. Be on the alert for large slow military trucks on the Saddle Road and an occasional convoy of military vehicles or even a tank!

Mauna Kea State Park is one of the island's better maintained parks and is also located on the Saddle Road. It has the area's only overnight accommodations, very rustic self-contained rental cabins offering only basic lodging. The cabins have refrige, stove, hot showers, towels and linens. You provide your own food. The area is remote and isolated and is not overused by the camping public. See the "Camping - State Parks" section for details. There are no other accommodations in the Saddle Road area. The park is on the plateau at the foot of Mauna Kea and the area abounds in introduced wild game birds like pheasant, quail and partridge as well as many species of native Hawaiian bird life. Visitors can enjoy the peace and solitude of this remote area and stroll through the trails and backroads of the park area to gain a perspective of this most unusual part of Hawai'i.

PUNA DISTRICT

INTRODUCTION

The *Puna District* comprises the area immediately south and southeast of Hilo town. It is a wide open area of lava lands, rugged coasts, and rain-forest slopes leading up to Hawai'i Volcanoes National Park which straddles the Puna-Ka'u border. Within Puna are the country towns of *Kea'au, Kurtistown, Mountain View, Pahoa, Volcano,* and a few other small settlements. In addition, there are a number of heavily populated country residential subdivisions. Puna is bisected by the main Hilo to Volcano Highway 11 and by Highway 130 which branches off from Highway 11 to Pahoa town.

Puna is noted for orchid, anthurium, papaya, banana, macadamia nut, and other tropical products. Numerous farms and orchards are found throughout the district. The combination of adequate rainfall and warm sunny conditions make it ideal for cultivating tropical fruits and flowers.

About the eastern one-third of *Hawai'i Volcanoes National Park* is located within the Puna District. And since January, 1983, this east rift zone, as it is called, has been the site of a series of ongoing volcanic eruptions and spectacular lava flows from Kilauea Volcano's vents of Pu'u O'o and Kupaianaha. The first three years of Kilauea's eruption were episodic outbreaks of dramatic lava fountaining and bursts from Pu'u O'o vent which gradually formed a cinder cone several hundred feet high. The eruptive activity of the last few years has come from the large lava pond and vent called Kupaianaha, located at the 2200 foot elevation level. Both of these vents are in remote inaccessible areas. Viewing of eruption activity is best done by plane or helicopter. See "Air Tours" for information.

173

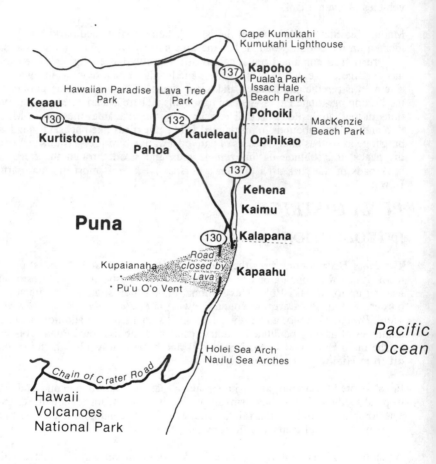

NORTH

Cape Kumukahi
Kumukahi Lighthouse

Kapoho
Puala'a Park
Issac Hale
Beach Park

Pohoiki

MacKenzie
Beach Park

Hawaiian Paradise
Park

Lava Tree
Park

Keaau

130

Kurtistown

132

Kaueleau

Pahoa

Opihikao

137

Kehena

Kaimu

Puna

130

Kalapana

Road
closed by
Lava

Kupaianaha

Kapaahu

Pu'u O'o Vent

Pacific
Ocean

Holei Sea Arch
Naulu Sea Arches

Chain of Crater Road

Hawaii
Volcanoes
National Park

174

This almost continuous volcanic eruption is unprecedented in recent history. For several years the volcano has steadily erupted and sent lava flows rolling downslope in search of the sea and in the process, causing considerable damage to man-made structures as well as destroying thousands of acres of Hawaiian forests. The entire village and residential areas of Kalapana have been totally destroyed by the various lava flows. Area residents have been forced to evacuate their homes and relocate elsewhere. Altogether, almost 200 homes have been destroyed since 1983.

Some 25 square miles of land have been covered by lava up to 50-70 feet deep. Damage estimates run into the millions with some 2 1/2 miles of roads, 2 miles of waterlines and 2 miles of utility lines wiped out by the lava flows. The lava courses its way downslope some seven miles to the sea at Kalapana through an extensive underground system of lavatubes. Over 100 acres of new land have been added to the Big Island's coastline since this eruption activity began in 1983.

Highway 130, which passed through Kalapana, has been cut off at various points and it is no longer possible to drive through Kalapana and on out the coast to the south entrance of Hawai'i Volcanoes National Park. Even the famed Kaimu and Kalapana Black Sand Beaches and Kamoamoa Beach Park have been covered with lava and are no longer accessible. Visitors can travel Highway 130, the Chain of Craters Road, from inside Volcanoes National Park, but it deadends now just west of the Kalapana area due to the lava cutoff. Visitors must return to the national park via the Chain of Craters Road.

WHAT TO DO AND SEE / WHERE TO SHOP

For most visitors, the biggest attraction is the volcanic activity. During the current eruption phase it was possible to drive near the former south entrance of Volcanoes National Park on Highway 130. National Park rangers now operate a mobile visitors center van at the end of the road here. The rangers provide maps and information on hiking trails to the current eruption site and lava flows. You should check first to see if conditions are safe for hiking the area.

From this point, a varying trail hike along the coast for a quarter to a mile long afforded a dramatic view of the lava flow entering the sea. Great steam clouds were visible and at night the sky glowed from the fiery lava as it entered the water. If the eruption activity is still ongoing, as you use this guidebook, you can possibly see the lava flows enter the sea. However, no one can predict or guarantee eruption activity, not even the scientists at the national park observatory.

As noted earlier, *Kaimu Black Sands Beach Park* and *Kalapana Black Sand Beach* were both destroyed and made inaccessible by 1990 lava flows. These famous beaches, long popular with photographers and visitors, are no more. Just west along the coast from the former Kalapana area, lava flows in 1992 also destroyed the famed *Kamoamoa Park and Campground*.

To reach the other side of the lava flows at Kalapana, you have to backtrack through Pahoa and go through the main entrance of Hawai'i Volcanoes National Park and follow Highway 130, the Chain of Craters Road to the Kamoamoa area (minimum 2 hour drive from Kalapana). At the road's end, park rangers have a mobil information center. If the eruption is still current, there may also be trails of varying lengths leading to viewing sites to see the lava enter the sea. As the molten lava enters the sea it explodes and shatters into fine pumice and cinders which are carried by the surf along the coast. This volcanic residue accumulates in such great quantities that it creates new black sand beaches along this rocky coast. If you do any hiking, be sure to have good footwear for the sharp jagged lava rock trails, carry water, sunscreen and a hat.

Another of Kalapana's more famous attractions, the historic *Star of the Sea Painted Church* ★, was rescued from lava flow destruction in 1990 and moved to a new location alongside Highway 130 just above the Kalapana area. This wooden frame structure dates from the early 1900's and was built by an early Belgian Catholic missionary priest who also did the intricate paintings of religious scenes on the walls and ceiling. It is now a community center.

Other sights in the Puna District that are easily accessible include the Opihikao and Kapoho areas. These areas are off the main Highway 130 and form a loop using Highway 132 (Kapoho Road) and Highway 137 (Opihikao Road) leading from Pahoa town to the coast down to Kalapana and back to the main Hwy. 130.

Highway 132 (Kapoho Road) passes through papaya and orchid fields to the site of the former *Kapoho Village*, which was completely covered by a fiery lava flow in 1960. A historic plaque marks the site. At the end of the Kapoho Road you can drive right up to the *Cape Kumukahi Lighthouse* which, according to local lore, was spared by Madame Pele to protect Hawaiian fishermen at sea. The lava flowed around and past the lighthouse grounds but did not touch the lighthouse itself. Also on the Kapoho Road is *Lava Tree State Park* where hollow lava impressions of tree stumps are visible. The lava flowed around the living trees and baked them, leaving a hollow lava shell.

The end of Kapoho Road near the Cape Kumukahi Lighthouse intersects with Highway 137, known as the Opihikao Road. Highway 137 follows the coast south toward Kalapana. While driving on this road, be aware that it is very narrow and winding in places. There are large orchards of papaya and macadamia nut trees in the area as well as some magnificent views of rugged coastline. Along this stretch are *Issac Hale Park* which has a natural geothermal pool for bathing heated by underground steam vents and *Mackenzie State Park* which features a restored section of the old "*King's Highway*," the former around-the-island trail used long ago. *Kahena Beach* is a lovely black sand beach at the base of a cliff but swimming is considered dangerous due again to heavy surf and currents. *Puala'a Park* just south of the junction of Highways 132 and 137 on the Kapoho Coast is a new county park opened in 1993 to replace the lost Kalapana beach parks. The beaches and parks in this area have suffered from severe overuse and overcrowding of late due to the loss of the Kalapana and Kaimu beach parks to the lava flows. So, expect all parks in the area to be well used. Also on the Opihikao Road there is an area called "*Pu'u Lapu*," a haunted hill where your car will appear to coast uphill without power.

And speaking of going uphill, the 32 mile drive from Hilo to Volcano Village near Hawai'i Volcanoes National Park is all uphill. The drive on Highway 11 goes from sea level in Hilo to 4000 ft. at Volcano. Along the way, the route passes through the abandoned cane fields of the former Puna Sugar Company and its old mill near *Kea'au*. Further on upslope, the cane fields give way to groves of eucalyptus trees and vegetation of the tropical rainforest. Fields of wild ginger, orchids, and other exotic plants fill the roadsides and meadows of the scattered country homesites and small ranches of the area. Finally, stands of the rugged and hearty ohia lehua tree with its deep red blossoms become apparent nearer the Volcano area.

For tropical flower aficionados, there are numerous orchid and anthurium farms and nurseries throughout the Puna District and many welcome visitors. On the main Highway 11 at the 22 1/2 mile marker in the Glenwood area, is *Akatsuka Orchid Gardens* (967-8234), one of the largest variety orchid farms in Hawai'i with many varieties of orchids on display and for sale. *Yamamoto Dendrobiums Hawai'i* (968-6955), *Bergstrom Orchids* (982-6047), and *Hawaiian Heart Inc.* (968-6322) are but a few of the orchid and anthurium farms in the Keaau-Mountain View area that welcome visitors. In Pahoa, try *Hawaiian Greenhouse Inc.* (965-8351), *Puna Flowers & Foliage* (965-8444), or *Puna Ohana Flowers* (965-8456), and in Kurtistown stop at *Hata Farm* (966-9240) for all types of tropical flowers and plants. In addition, as you drive along be on the lookout for farm and nursery signs welcoming visitors to stroll the gardens.

The small towns and villages of the Puna District don't offer much in the way of shopping opportunities. The towns of Kea'au and Pahoa, the largest of the district, have more shops and stores than the rest but most cater to the needs of residents rather than visitors. Each town and village has a Mom and Pop general store which can always provide sodas, snacks, and local favorites. For something quite different, stop in Mountain View at *Mountain View Bakery* (968-6353) for some of their famous "Stone Cookies." These cookies were made for dunking in coffee! When you bite into one, you'll understand their name. Good! At the Glenwood area at the 20-mile marker is *Hirano Store* (968-6522) where you can buy cold drinks, sandwiches, snacks, gas and general store supplies.

ORCHIDS

177

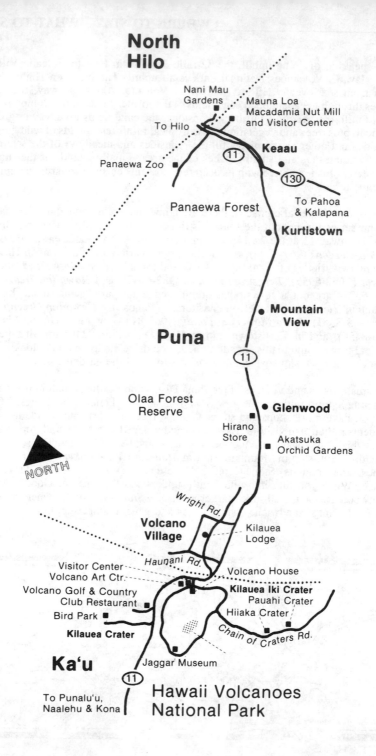

North Hilo

Nani Mau Gardens

Mauna Loa Macadamia Nut Mill and Visitor Center

To Hilo

(11) **Keaau**

Panaewa Zoo

(130)

Panaewa Forest

To Pahoa & Kalapana

Kurtistown

Mountain View

Puna

(11)

Olaa Forest Reserve

Glenwood

Hirano Store

Akatsuka Orchid Gardens

NORTH

Wright Rd.

Volcano Village

Kilauea Lodge

Haunani Rd.

Visitor Center
Volcano Art Ctr.

Volcano House

Volcano Golf & Country Club Restaurant

Kilauea Iki Crater

Pauahi Crater

Bird Park

Hiiaka Crater

Kilauea Crater

Chain of Craters Rd.

Ka'u

Jaggar Museum

(11)

To Punalu'u, Naalehu & Kona

Hawaii Volcanoes National Park

178

Along the old Volcano Highway in *Volcano Village*, which is just a mile from the national park entrance, there is the **Volcano Store and Diner** (967-7210) where picnic supplies or snacks, sandwiches and plate lunches can be purchased. They have gas pumps if you're in need. In the same area is **Kilauea General Store** (967-7555) which provides deli snacks, sandwiches, groceries and gas. On the Ka'u side of the national park entrance a mile and a half, turn into the Volcano Golf Course and drive to the **Volcano Vineyards and Winery** (967-7772) for samples of the delightful Symphony wine and tropical fruit wines produced here.

ACCOMMODATIONS - PUNA DISTRICT

BEST BETS: *Kilauea Lodge* - This is such a lovely place in the delightfully cool and crisp (especially in winter!) climate at Volcano Village; rooms have charming graceful decor, and some have a fireplace to take the nip from the mountain air. The restaurant also has a good reputation.

PUNA ACCOMMODATIONS
Hale Ohia Cottage and Kilauea Lodge (For other Puna area accommodations, see the "Bed & Breakfast" listing earlier in this chapter)

HALE OHIA COTTAGE
P.O. Box 599, Volcano, HI 96785. (808) 967-7986. This lovely cottage offers 3 bedrooms and sleeps up to 5 people. Cottage has well equipped kitchen, large living room and one tub-shower bath. Bedrooms have 1 double, 2 singles and a sleeping punee (sofa) in living room. There is a large covered deck with table, chairs and hibachi barbeque for cookouts. Located one mile from Hawai'i Volcanoes National Park in Volcano Village. Near hiking trails, picnic areas, national park facilities, golf course, volcano observatory, etc. Cottage is 26 miles from Hilo. *$60 nightly, $360 weekly, Extra person $15*

KILAUEA LODGE ★
P.O. Box 116, Volcano Village, HI 96785. (808) 967-7366, FAX 967-7367. A rustic old YWCA camping lodge and dormitory built in 1938 has been renovated and reopened in 1988 as a lodge and general restaurant. Set amidst the quiet cool country air of Volcano Village near Hawai'i Volcanoes National Park headquarters and visitors center. There are 12 guest units with private bathrooms and fireplaces and one private cottage. The restaurant offers full American-Continental dinner menu nightly 5:30-9PM. *Standard $85-125, Deluxe Cottage $105*

KA'U DISTRICT

INTRODUCTION

The Ka'u District comprises one of the largest geographic districts on the Big Island and at the same time one of the more remote and least populated as well. It takes in about one-fifth of the island's land which represents some 800 + square miles. The district includes most of the massive Mauna Loa (13, 680 ft.) and the western two-thirds of Hawai'i Volcanoes National Park. Along this southern coast of the Big Island is **Ka Lae**, *South Point*, the southernmost point in the United States. The district is mostly dry lava desert, windblown grasslands and rugged rocky coastline. Inland there are cattle pastures and macadamia nut orchards.

Ka'u is serviced by the main around the island road, Highway 11, which onnects the remote area to Volcano and Hilo to the east and Kona to the west. Sparsely populated, Ka'u has only three small towns: *Pahala*, *Na'alehu*, and *Waiohinu*.

WHAT TO DO AND SEE / WHERE TO SHOP

The Ka'u District's biggest attraction is no doubt *Hawai'i Volcanoes National Park*, the bulk of which lies within the district's boundaries. The park does overlap into the Puna District to the east. But for visitors, the national park headquarters, visitor center, volcano observatory, campgrounds, Volcano House Inn, and related sites are centrally located at Kilauea Caldera in Ka'u near Volcano Village.

Visitors from Hilo will drive to the park via Highway 11, a distance of 35 miles, through the Puna District described in the previous section. Visitors from the Kailua-Kona area will have to travel a distance of 96 miles via Highway 11 around the South Point area. This is a rather long drive through some pretty desolate stretches of open lava lands, dry scrub land, and the Ka'u desert. The road is paved but has some short stretches in the South Kona area where it is winding and narrow. Otherwise the road is excellent and if you have your own rental car you should plan at least a day trip to Volcano. If you have time, plan on an overnight or longer visit which will allow you to explore the area in more depth. Allow a minimum of two and a half hours for the drive from Kailua-Kona to the national park. It's best to get an early start. The drive up to the park passes through South Kona's coffee farm, fruit orchard, and flower farm country gradually turning away from the coast and heading further inland as it turns around Mauna Loa's southernmost slopes. The land here, some 8-10 miles inland from the coast and at 2000 ft. elevation, is damp and cool, a contrast to the drier resort areas of Kona and the lands traversed along the way. The terrain is marked by lush vegetation and stands of tropical forest. Ranch grazing lands appear intermittently along with macadamia nut orchards in an otherwise sparsely populated area. Along this route is *Manuka State Park*, a lovely and well-maintained arboretum with a variety of plants and trees. Picnic tables and restrooms are provided. *Ka Lae*, South Point, is reached via South Point Road which branches off from Highway 11 at the extreme southern tip of the Ka'u District.

LAYSAN ALBATROSS

The narrow road courses its way some twelve miles to the South Point Peninsula where it terminates. It passes by the **Kamao'a Wind Farm**, a wind powered electricity generation facility utilizing huge wind turbines. This stark, windswept, hot, dry and grassy area is the southernmost point geographically in the United States. The first Hawaiians are believed to have landed here and settled the area around 400 A.D. There are old canoe mooring holes and the ruins of a fishermen's heiau (temple). Fishermen still use South Point to moor their boats but they must hoist them up and down the high cliffs to the relatively calm waters below. The foundations of an old World War II military camp are also found in the area.

Green Sand Beach, composed of green olivine crystals giving it a marked green hue, is located five miles east of South Point but is accessible only by hiking or with a 4x4 vehicle as the coastal road is extremely rough and rugged over rocky terrain. The beach is at the bottom of a steep cliff, reached by a hazardous trail, and is not safe for swimming due to rough surf and strong currents.

The small town of **Na'alehu**, proclaims itself to be "the southernmost town in the USA" and has a large sign stating the claim alongside the town shopping center. At the shopping center, located right on the highway in mid-town, there is a coffee shop, grocery store, and snack shop for refreshments. Across the road from the shopping center is the **Punalu'u Sweetbread Visitor Center**. This is a bakery and snack shop that produces some 4,000 loaves weekly of its popular "Portuguese Sweetbread." The snack shop has fresh Kona coffee, sweetbread, pastries and other refreshments.

The neighboring town of **Waiohinu** boasts the **Mark Twain Monkeypod Tree** planted by the famous author during his 1866 visit. The original tree toppled in a storm several years ago but the roots have sprouted new saplings and the tree lives. Just down the road is **Kauahaao Church**, a century old New England colonial styled church. Passing through these very small Hawaiian country towns will give you a sense of having stepped back into an earlier time where the fast-paced modern world hasn't quite made any inroads yet. It's all a very pleasant and refreshing experience to know that places like these tiny quiet villages still exist. They are indeed havens of refuge in an all too busy world.

At **Punalu'u**, eight miles further on toward the national park, there is **Punalu'u Beach Park** and **Seamountain Golf Course**. At **Punalu'u Black Sand Beach Park**, spend a few minutes to watch the shoreline for sea turtles which are often seen feeding on sea weed on the rocks and coral. The turtles are quite common in this area. Five miles from here is the very small town of **Pahala**. If you are looking for a grocery store or gas station turn off the highway at the sign for the town; the Ka'u Hospital is right at this intersection also. The Ka'u Sugar Mill just off the main center of the town was the last operating mill on the Big Island until it too closed in 1996. The plantation's closing has brought more hardship to the residents of this quiet remote region. The once lovely green fields of sugarcane which formed a beautiful background vista as one traveled along Highway 11 are now being planted to macadamia nuts. It is hoped macadamia nut orchards can replace sugarcane and provide jobs for the area residents. From Pahala it is 25 miles on to the national park through generally dry desert and lava rock country.

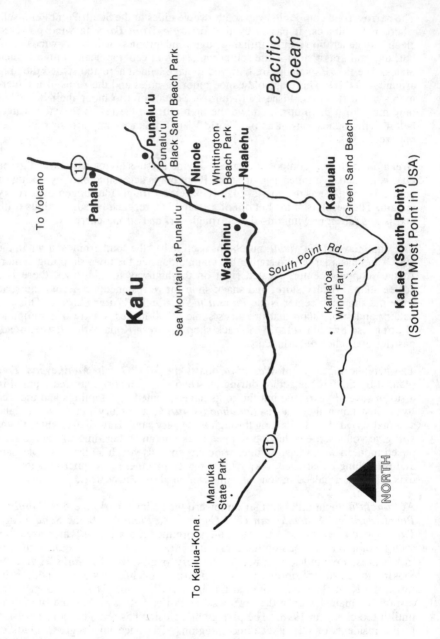

Ka'u

Pacific Ocean

To Volcano

Pahala

Punalu'u
Punalu'u Black Sand Beach Park

Ninole

Whittington Beach Park

Naalehu

Kaalualu

Green Sand Beach

Sea Mountain at Punalu'u

Waiohinu

South Point Rd.

Kama'oa Wind Farm

KaLae (South Point)
(Southern Most Point in USA)

Manuka State Park

To Kailua-Kona

NORTH

Near the national park entrance and leading off from Highway 11 is Volcano Golf Course Road. Past the golf course clubhouse a mile to the end of the road is the southernmost winery in the U.S., *Volcano Winery*. The winery produces delightful tropical fruit wines such as guava chablis, passion chablis, passion-star chablis, lehua blossom honey wine and Volcano Blush as well as its main vintage, Symphony and Symphony Dry, from a new grape developed by the University of California-Davis School of Viticulture. The Winery operates a tasting room and gift shop on site and is open daily, 9AM - 5PM. It's well worth a visit to the Big Island's only working winery. For information, contact Volcano Winery, P.O. Box 843, Volcano, HI 96785; 808 967-7479.

Hawai'i Volcanoes National Park ★ is one of the island's most popular visitor attractions and a must for visitors. On any given day, there can be several hundred or a few thousand visitors passing through the park. The marvels of the park should not be missed by anyone.

The park *Visitor Center* is located a mile west of Volcano Village just inside the main entrance. Here visitors will find a natural history museum detailing information on the national park, a free eruption movie shown several times daily, and park rangers on duty to provide information. Entry fees into the national park are: $5 per car with the pass good for 7 days; $15 for a yearly pass; $3 for walk-in visitors or on bicycle, moped, etc.

The *Volcano Art Center* (967-7179) is located adjacent to the visitors center and provides historic information on the park as well as beautiful arts and crafts produced by local artisans. Artwork can be purchased here. The Art Center also stages and conducts art shows, performances and art and photography workshops the year around. Some of the programs allow visitors and residents a chance to interact with artists who receive their inspiration from working within Hawai'i Volcanoes National Park. Occasionally, a resource artist will lead a walk through some spectacular area of the park to describe and demonstrate the use of natural

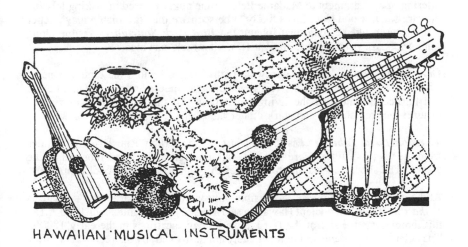

HAWAIIAN MUSICAL INSTRUMENTS

materials and/or atmosphere of the park environment in creating artwork. The walks focus on protecting and enhancing the fragile national park environment. Call the center for information.

The gigantic, and still steaming fire pit, *Halemaumau*, a 3000 ft. diameter 1300 ft. deep lava vent lies on the floor of *Kilauea Caldera*. *Kilauea Iki*, is a huge cinder cone vent that last erupted in 1959. Both of these vents are easily viewed from *Crater Rim Drive* and can be reached on foot by easy hiking trails. At the *Jaggar Volcano Observatory*, volcanologists study the latest seismograph readings that would foretell of an impending eruption. Here visitors can view the crater and see the steam vents hissing and sulfur banks smoking and marvel at what the forces of nature have created. Educational displays explain the natural history of volcanoes and related geology. There are vast fields of lava, once molten rivers of liquid rock, spewed out from the earth's center. Two types of lava emerge from Hawai'i's volcanoes: pahoehoe with its black and relatively smooth surface (much like cake batter) and 'a'a, which solidifies in a jumble of small clinker like rocks with sharp edges and rough surfaces. Kilauea Volcano is the legendary home of the Hawaiian fire goddess, *Madame Pele*.

Native Hawaiians have long had a healthy respect for her and even today, ceremonial offerings are cast into Halemaumau fire pit while chants, songs, and dances are performed in her honor. It is said that Madame Pele has a fondness for gin.

One of the outstanding features of Hawai'i Volcanoes National Park is its fine system of hiking trails. The trails begin at various points along the Crater Rim Drive and Chain of Craters Road. Hikers can choose from trails that offer outstanding closeup views of volcanic craters, steaming lava vents and colorful sulfur banks, to sweeping vistas of Kilauea's lava flows and sloping flanks, to a cool pastoral trail leading through a rare bird sanctuary.

Along other trails of the park, hikers may see some rare and endangered flora and fauna. Among these are the sacred ohelo berry, held in high regard as an offering of appeasement to Madame Pele, or the pukiawe used in making leis and the rare sandalwood tree. Birds likely to be seen are the Hawaiian honeycreeper and the wren-like 'elepaio that inhabit the *Bird Park Sanctuary*. Visible along some trails are petroglyphs, ancient Hawaiian rock carvings.

Devastation Trail, a raised boardwalk path, located behind the cinder cone of Kilauea Iki, winds through the vast fields of lava cinders and pumice that buried and burned off most of the living vegetation. All that is left is a myriad of picturesque tree stumps and stark cinder landscape.

Thurston Lava Tube Trail is located just off the Crater Rim Drive two miles from the visitors center. Here one can walk through a giant lava tube much like a cave. The short trail leading to it passes through a pleasantly cool fern forest.

At the park's south entrance, accessible only via the Chain of Crater's Road, is *Waha'ula Heiau*, an ancient Hawaiian sacrificial temple. Built about 1250 A.D., this temple was the site of the last known human sacrifices in the early 1800's. The heiau was surrounded, but fortunately not destroyed, by the recent lava flows from Kilauea's volcanic eruptions. The park visitors center at this site was however totally destroyed in summer, 1989.

In addition to traditional campgrounds, the national park's premier place to stay is the venerable and historic **Volcano House**. The Volcano House is located across from the visitors center at the main entrance. The Volcano House was first built in the 1860's as an overnight station for visitors who rode on horseback all the way from Hilo to see the splendors of the volcano. It's had a number of distinguished visitors down through the years including Mark Twain who visited here in 1866. Twain described the hotel as "a neat little cottage with four bedrooms, a large parlor and dining room."

The hotel has been rebuilt several times since 1866 and now features 37 comfortable rooms with private bath and even heat, an unusual feature for hotels in Hawai'i. The Volcano Art Center noted earlier is, in fact, part of the old Volcano House Hotel from 1877. The hotel today features a lobby fireplace that has burned continuously for more years than anyone can remember. It's sort of a Volcano House tradition and the fire burns day and night to help keep guests comfortable.

The wood paneling and cozy decor create a rustic country lodge atmosphere that gives the Volcano House its special charm. The **Ka Ohelo Dining Room** is the inn's restaurant. It is about the only lodging in the world that perches on the edge of an active volcano.

ACCOMMODATIONS - KA'U DISTRICT

BEST BETS: **Volcano House** - simply because it is one of Hawai'i's better known landmark accommodations and the only place in the world where you can sleep comfortably next to an active volcano. **Shirakawa Motel** - a simple yet comfortable motel-type accommodation in a very quiet, rural area especially nice for those seeking solitude.

KA'U - ACCOMMODATIONS

Shirakawa Motel
Volcano House
Seamountain at Punalu'u Colony I

SHIRAKAWA MOTEL ★ (W)
P.O. Box 467, Na'alehu, HI 96772. (808) 929-7462. Advertised as "The Southernmost Motel in the U.S.", this 13 unit country motel offers simple accommodations for relaxation, peace and quiet. It is nestled amidst the cool climate of a coffee tree grove and lush vegetation. The Shirakawa family combine the warmth of true old-fashioned Hawaiian hospitality with simple yet modern conveniences. No TV. This is a no frills, simple getaway for those wanting the solitude of the countryside.
Standard $30-35, Kitchenette unit $42 Extra person $8-10

VOLCANO HOUSE (W)

P.O. Box 53, Hawai'i Volcanoes National Park, Hawai'i 96718. (808) 967-7321, FAX (808) 967-8429. This 42 room hotel has a rustic country lodge atmosphere with generally spacious well-kept rooms. The quiet cool volcano climate is invigorating and a pleasant change from Hawai'i's standard beach and tourist center accommodations. The Ka Ohelo Dining Room features American-Continental cuisine, and cocktail lounge, gift shop, and meeting room are available. The national park headquarters and the visitors center are directly opposite.
Ohia Wing $79, Non-crater view $105, Crater view $131 Extra person $10

SEAMOUNTAIN AT PUNALU'U COLONY I (W)

P.O. Box 460, Pahala, HI 96777. 1-800-488-8301 or 1-800-344-7675, (808) 928-6200/928-8301, FAX (808) 928-8075/928-8008.

This condominium/hotel has 62 rental units available. Located in the fairly remote Punalu'u area of Ka'u, the development is situated at the Seamountain Golf Course and near the ocean front and Punalu'u Black Sand Beach and Ninole Cove. The beach is hazardous due to heavy surf and strong currents and swimming can be dangerous. The nearest town is Pahala, five miles away. All units have kitchen facilities, TV and fans. Cocktail lounge, swimming pool, tennis courts, golf course, meeting rooms are on grounds or nearby. Two day minimum stay.
Studio g.v. $75, Studio o.v. $85, 1 BR g.v. $99,
1 BR o.v. $95-126, 2 BR g.v. $125, 2 BR o.v. $150-161 Extra person $10

RENTAL AGENTS

ALWAYS SUNNY CONDOS
3627 Wheaton Way, #100
Bremerton, WA 98310
1-800-692-2638
206 479-2729
Fax 206 479-5130

Kona Bali Kai

**ASTON HOTELS
& RESORTS**
2255 Kuhio Avenue
Honolulu, HI 96815
1-800-922-7866
Hawai'i 1-800-321-2558

Aston Royal Sea Cliff Resort
Aston The Shores at Waikoloa
Kona By The Sea
Kona Islander Inn

CENTURY 21
75-5909 Alii Drive
Kailua-Kona, HI 96740
1-800-255-8052
(808) 329-0021

Keauhou Punahele
Kona Plaza

CLARK REALTY
75-5722 Kuakini Highway
Kuakini Tower, #103
Kailua-Kona, HI 96740
1-800-929-7667
(808) 329-5300
FAX (808) 329-8102

Kona Islander Inn
Kona Plaza
Keauhou Palena
Keauhou Kona Surf
  & Racquet Club
Waikoloa Villas

CLASSIC RESORTS
50 Nohea Kai Drive
Lahaina, HI 96761
1-800-642-6284
(808) 667-1400
from Hawai'i and Canada

Mauna Lani Point
The Islands at Mauna Lani

**COLONY HOTELS
& RESORTS**
841 Bishop St.
Honolulu, HI 96813
1-800-777-1700

Kanaloa at Kona
Kona Bali Kai
Mauna Loa Village

**ELITE PROPERTIES
UNLIMITED**
PO Box 5273, Lahaina, Maui, HI
96761. 1-800-448-9222 U.S. &
Canada, (808-665-0561)

Luxury residences & family homes.
Three to seven bedrooms. Weekly
& month rentals. Maid service and
concierge service available.

**GOLDEN TRIANGLE
REAL ESTATE**
75-5865 Walua Road #F1
Kailua-Kona, HI 96740
(808) 329-1667

Alii Villas
Casa De Emdeko
Keauhou Akahi
Keauhou Kona Surf
Keauhou Palena
Kona Makai

HAWAI'I APARTMENT LEASING ENTERPRISES
479 Ocean Ave. #B
Laguna Beach, CA 92651
US/Canada 1-800-854-8843
(714) 497-4474/497-4253
FAX (714) 497-4183

Alii Villas
Country Club Villas
Kanaloa at Kona
Keauhou Punahele
Keauhou Kona Surf
 & Racquet Club
Kona Bali Kai
Kona Coast Resort
Kona Makai
Kona Mansions
Kona Reef
Mauna Lani Point
Mauna Lani Terrace
Sea Village
Shores at Waikoloa
White Sands Village

HAWAI'I RESORT MANAGEMENT
75-5776 Kuakini Hwy, Suite 105C
Kailua-Kona, HI 96740
1-800-553-5035, (808) 329-9393
Fax (808) 326-4137

Alii Villas
Casa De Emdeko
Country Club Villas
Kailua Village
Keauhou Kona Surf &
 Racquet Club
Keauhou Punahele
Keauhou Resort
Kona Alii
Kona Billfisher
Kona Islander Inn
Kona Isle Condo
Kona Magic Sands
Kona White Sands Apt-Hotel

HAWAIIAN PACIFIC RESORTS
1150 S. King St.
Honolulu, HI 96814
1-800-272-5275

Hilo Hawaiian Hotel

HAWAIIANA RESORTS
1270 Ala Moana Blvd.
Honolulu, HI 96814
1-800-367-7040
(808) 591-8785

Kona Reef

KEAUHOU PROPERTY MANAGEMENT COMPANY
P.O. Box 390282
Kailua-Kona, HI 96739
1-800-745-KONA
Hawai'i (808) 326-9075
Fax (808) 326-2055

Country Club Villas
Kanaloa at Kona
Keauhou Kona Surf
Keauhou Palena
Keauhou Punahele
Kona Coast Resort

KNUTSON & ASSOCIATES
75-6082 Alii Drive, #8
Kailua-Kona, HI 96740
1-800-800-6202
(808) 329-6311
FAX: (808) 326-2178

Alii Villas
Casa De Emdeko
Country Club Villas
Kailua Village
Keauhou Kona Surf
 & Racquet Club
Kona Isle
Kona Reef
Kona Riviera
Sea Village

KONA VACATION RESORTS
77-6435 Kuakini Highway
Kailua-Kona, HI 96740
1-800-367-5168, (808) 329-6488

Alii Villas
Banyan Tree
Casa de Emdeko
Hale Kona Kai
Hale Pohaku
Kahaluu Bay Villas
Kanaloa at Kona
Keauhou Palena
Keauhou Punahele
Keauhou Surf & Racquet
Kona Alii
Kona Bali Kai
Kona Luana
Kona Magic Sands
Kona Makai
Kona Nalu
Kona Onenalo
Kona Plaza
Kona Reef
Kona West
Royal Kahili
Sea Village
White Sands Village

MARC RESORTS HAWAII
2155 Kalakaua Avenue, 7th. FL.
Honolulu, HI 96815-2351
1-800-535-0085

The Shores at Waikoloa
Vista Waikoloa
Waikoloa Villas

OUTRIGGER HOTELS HAWAII
2375 Kuhio Avenue
Honolulu, HI 96815
1-800-OUTRIGGER (688-7444)
FAX: 1-800-622-4852

Kanaloa at Kona

CLASSIC RESORTS
50 Nohea Kai Drive
Lahaina, HI 96761
1-800-642-6284
(808) 667-1400
from Hawai'i and Canada

Mauna Lani Point
The Islands at Mauna Lani

**COLONY HOTELS
& RESORTS**
841 Bishop St.
Honolulu, HI 96813
1-800-777-1700

Kanaloa at Kona
Kona Bali Kai
Mauna Loa Village

**ELITE PROPERTIES
UNLIMITED**
PO Box 5273, Lahaina, Maui, HI
96761. 1-800-448-9222 U.S. &
Canada, (808-665-0561)

Luxury residences & family homes.
Three to seven bedrooms. Weekly
& month rentals. Maid service and
concierge service available.

**GOLDEN TRIANGLE
REAL ESTATE**
75-5865 Walua Road #F1
Kailua-Kona, HI 96740
(808) 329-1667

Alii Villas
Casa De Emdeko
Keauhou Akahi
Keauhou Kona Surf
Keauhou Palena
Kona Makai

SOUTH KOHALA MGMT.
P.O. Box 384900
Waikoloa, HI 96738
1-800-822-4252
(808) 883-8500
FAX (808) 883-9818

Mauna Lani Terrace
Shores at Waikoloa
Vista Waikoloa

TRIAD MANAGEMENT
P.O. Box 4466
Kailua-Kona, HI 96745
1-800-345-2823
(808) 329-6402
FAX (808) 326-2401

Country Club Villas
Hale Kona Kai
Keauhou Akahi
Keauhou Punahele
Kona Billfisher
Kona Isle
Malia Kai
Royal Kahili
White Sands Village

VILLAGE REALTY
75-5742 Hualalai Rd 1st FL
Kailua-Kona, HI 96740
(808) 329-1577
1-800-927-1577

Banyan Tree
Casa De Emdeko
Country Club Villas
Holua at Mauna Loa
Kanaloa at Kona
Keauhou Kona Surf
Keauhou Palena
Keauhou Punahele
Kona Alii
Kona Bali Kai
Kona Makai
Kona Plaza
Kona Reef
Royal Kailuan
White Sands Village

WEST HAWAI'I PROPERTY SERVICES, INC.
Keauhou Shopping Village
78-6831 Alii Drive, #237
Kailua-Kona, HI 96740
1-800-799-KONA
(808) 322-6696
Fax 808 324-0609

Alii Villas
Country Club Villas
Kalanikai
Keauhou Kona Surf
Keauhou Palena
Keauhou Punahele
Kona Alii
Kona Bali Kai
Kona Islander Inn
Kona Isle
Kona Magic Sands
Kona Makai
Kona Mansions
Kona West
Royal Kahili
Sea Village

RESTAURANTS

INTRODUCTION

Like so many other things, the Big Island is blessed with a wide variety of restaurants, cafes, coffee shops, drive-ins and island-style eateries. And like most things in life, there are disputes and friendly disagreements as to what and where is the best. For Hawai'i is no different from anywhere else when it comes to eating: everybody has his/her own personal favorite.

The Big Island has restaurants of all types serving a wide variety of food from local ethnic to mainland continental, from fresh to frozen, from fast food to superb gourmet. It's doubtful that anyone can attest to having dined in every restaurant on the Big Island. This writer certainly does not. However, this section profiles a good number of Big Island dining spots that have actually been tried and proven. In addition, a great effort has been made to gather the opinions and experiences of many other people in order to get as wide an input as possible. Your comments and opinions are also welcome. See the READER RESPONSE.

On the following pages, you will find the restaurants first indexed alphabetically and then also by food type. The restaurants are then divided by geographical area, separated by price range, and listed alphabetically in those price ranges. These are: "INEXPENSIVE," under $10 per person, "MODERATE," $10 to $25 per person, and "EXPENSIVE," $25 and up per person. The price ranges were decided by comparing an average dinner meal, exclusive of tax, alcoholic beverages and desserts. Due to changes in menus, management, supplies or other factors, restaurant prices are obviously subject to change at any time. If you are a senior citizen, be sure to ask about a "Senior Citizen Discount" as more restaurants are extending such a courtesy.

For simplicity, the restaurant listings do not include McDonalds, Burger King, Jack in the Box, Kentucky Fried Chicken, Taco Bell, Dairy Queen, Pizza Hut or similar fast-food outlets or 7-Eleven Food Stores and other convenience stores located around the Big Island. Most folks are aware of the type of food to be had in such fast food operations and they do not merit a separate listing in this book.

In the following listings, those restaurants marked with a ★ indicate an exceptional value in quality of food and service, decor and ambiance, or unique and unusual cuisine and dining experience or a combination of these factors and not just cost alone.

Great effort has been given to ensure that those restaurants so marked as an exceptional value have in fact earned the accolade. This has been done through personal visit and evaluation of a meal or by close and careful consultation with reliable patrons, sometimes both. In spite of this, restaurants, like everything else, can and do change over time. What may have been an enjoyable dining experience last week or last month, may well be a complete disaster the next time around. The consistency factor of good food and service for the level of dining carries much weight in the evaluation and consideration. Those restaurants marked as an exceptional value have proven themselves consistent on these last points noted.

Readers are encouraged to check ahead with restaurants and call them for specific hours and days of service as this is one area noted for rapid and frequent change. Several restaurants seem to change their hours seasonally and from time-to-time based on a variety of factors. Some restaurants may offer lunch and dinner hours one week, and then be open for dinner only the next, and then change back to both lunch and dinner hours the following week, things of that sort. So, it is advised to check with a given restaurant before traveling any distance to be sure they are open when you expect them to be and to avoid disappointment.

Finally, as you travel around the Big Island, you may come across a restaurant or dining place not listed in this book. The reason is either that the specific restaurant opened after this book went to press or, for whatever reason, the author deemed the establishment unworthy to be included in this book.

BEST BETS

TOP RESTAURANTS

The criteria for being listed as a top restaurant is the excellence and quality of food preparation and presentation, a pleasant relaxing dining atmosphere, and gracious courteous service where the guest is everything. Only a choice few Big Island restaurants make this category and those that do are really excellent overall. Almost without exception, any meal will be superb. Of course, any restaurant can have an "off" night but that is certainly a rare occurrence at these restaurants. As with fine dining anywhere, you can expect to pay dearly for it. Meals at the following restaurants can run anywhere from $50-100 or more per person depending upon entree selected, appetizer, soup and salad, wine or alcoholic beverages, dessert, and of course, gratuity. But generally a gourmet meal at any of these fine restaurants will be a memorable part of your Big Island experience. Dinner jackets for gentlemen may be required dress for some of these restaurants.

Batik	-	Mauna Kea Beach Hotel
Bay Terrace	-	Mauna Lani Bay Hotel
Hale Samoa	-	Kona Village Resort
The Gallery	-	Mauna Lani Resort
The Pavilion	-	Mauna Kea Beach Hotel
Tiare Room	-	Royal Waikoloan Hotel

TOP RESTAURANTS IN A CASUAL ATMOSPHERE

The following restaurants are less expensive, but a dinner meal can still cost $25 or more per person depending on what is ordered. The dining experience is superior in a less formal atmosphere.

Canoe House   - Mauna Lani Bay Hotel
Coast Grille   - Hapuna Beach Prince Hotel
Edelweiss   - Waimea
Hale Moana   - Kona Village Resort
Imari   - Hilton Waikoloa Village
Kilauea Lodge   - Volcano Village
Merriman's   - Waimea
Palm Cafe   - in Kailua-Kona

BEST BUFFETS

Buffets are a great way to enjoy a wonderful meal at a generally more moderate price compared to an a la carte menu. In addition, buffets often include a wide selection of various Hawaiian ethnic and international foods than can be a delightful experience in cross-cultural dining. You may not otherwise get to sample some of these diverse delicacies and dishes. The following are the best buffets on the Big Island.

Bay Terrace   - Mauna Lani Bay Hotel (Sunday brunch)
Hale Moana   - Kona Village Resort (Lunch daily)
Kona Beach Restaurant - King Kamehameha Kona Beach Hotel (Sunday brunch)
Kuakini Terrace   - Keauhou Beach Hotel (Dinner)
Queen's Court   - Hilo Hawaiian Hotel (Fri-Sat dinner)
The Terrace   - Mauna Kea Beach Hotel (Lunch daily)
Hau Tree Clambake   - Mauna Kea Beach Hotel
                         (Saturday seafood dinner buffet)

TOP "LOCAL STYLE" RESTAURANTS

The Big Island abounds in inexpensive local-style restaurants where you can sample and enjoy the diverse range of Hawaiian-ethnic cuisine. Most of the establishments are not fancy in decor or looks, but often the service is even better than at the big expensive restaurants. This is true of the family-operated restaurants where courtesy and friendliness are just the way they do business. So if you enjoy inexpensive food that is colorful, plentiful and just plain good, and you don't mind simple decor and surroundings while you eat, you'll have a fun time exploring the world of Big Island local-style restaurants. Some of the best are listed below.

Manago Hotel   Captain Cook (Oriental)
Ocean View Inn   Kailua-Kona (Oriental)
Peacock House   Kealakekua (Chinese)

Royal Jade Garden	Kailua-Kona (Chinese)
Sam Choy's Restaurant	Kailua-Kona (Hawaii/Pacific)
Teshima's	Honalo, Kona (Japanese)
Uncle Gil's Saimin	Kailua-Kona (Japanese noodles)
Don's Grill	Hilo (varied local)
Hukilau Restaurant	Hilo (seafood)
Kay's Lunch Center	Hilo (Korean)
Kimo's Ono Hawaiian Food	Hilo (Hawaiian)
Kow's Restaurant	Hilo (Chinese)
Leung's Chop Suey	Hilo (Chinese)
Nori's Saimin	Hilo (Japanese noodles)
Seaside	Hilo (Seafood)
Ting Hao Mandarin	Hilo (Mandarin Chinese)
Naalehu Coffee Shop	Naalehu (American-Oriental)
Don's Pake Kitchen	Waimea (Chinese)
Mean Cuisine	Waimea (International)
Morelli's Pizza	Waimea (Italian/pizza)
Nori's Saimin Too	Waimea (Japanese noodles)
Paniolo Country Inn	Waimea (BBQ-Mexican)

NIGHTCLUBS AND ENTERTAINMENT

Consult the local visitor publications and newspapers to see what entertainers or groups are currently playing what clubs. The following are some of the more popular nightclubs and lounges which have nightly entertainment in the form of contemporary rock or disco music or more relaxed easy listening Hawaiian music. My personal favorite watering hole is the Billfish Bar at the King Kamehameha Kona Beach Hotel. The bar sits poolside and has nice views of Kailua Pier, Kamakahonu Beach fronting the hotel and glorious sunsets over Kailua Bay.

Kona

Banana Bay Cafe	-	Kona Bay Hotel
Billfish Bar	-	King Kamehameha Kona Beach Hotel
Fisherman's Landing	-	Kona Shopping Village
Huggo's	-	on Alii Drive
Makai Bar	-	Keauhou Beach Hotel
Nalu Terrace	-	Kona Surf Resort
Windjammer Lounge	-	Royal Kona Resort

Kohala

The Second Floor	-	Hilton Waikoloa Village
Batik	-	Mauna Kea Beach Hotel
Canoe House Lounge	-	Mauna Lani Bay Hotel
Petroglyph Bar	-	Royal Waikoloan Hotel

Hilo

Crown Room	-	Hawai'i Naniloa Hotel
Uncle Billy's	-	Hilo Bay Hotel
Lehua's Bay City Bar & Grill	-	11 Waianuenue Ave., Hilo

ALPHABETICAL INDEX

FOOD TYPE INDEX

JANORA BAYOT

CONTINENTAL-INTERNATIONAL

DRIVE INS

FAMILY DINING

FILIPINO (Philippines)

FRENCH

GREEK

DRIVE-INS

To economize on space, drive-ins, fast food operations and plate lunch shops on the Big Island, of which there are several, are listed separately in this section rather than detailed and listed with regular restaurants in each area of the island. Big Island drive-ins generally offer similar fare for breakfast, lunch, and dinner. Food ranges from egg-pancake items for breakfast, to sandwiches, burgers, saimin, and a variety of local style beef, pork, chicken, fish dishes, etc. for lunch-dinner. The emphasis is on quantity and fast service. Quality varies from mediocre to magnificent, and from day to day, at many of the drive-ins. But generally you can count on a good meal for a reasonable price, most of the time for about $5. One local Big Island favorite is "loco moco" which is essentially a bowl of rice with a hamburger patty and egg on top. Since it originated at Cafe 100 in Hilo a few years ago, "loco moco" has become a hot fast food item with many imitations and variations around the island. As for judging which drive-in has the best food, well you'll just have to try them all and decide for yourself.

BLANE'S DRIVE IN (935-8326) 150 Wiwoole St., Hilo, just off Kanoelehua Ave. (Volcano Hwy) in the industrial area

BLUE DOLPHIN RESTAURANT (882-7771) 61-3615 Kawaihae Harbor Road, Hwy. 270, 2 miles north of the Mauna Kea Beach Hotel, Kawaihae.

BOB'S DRIVE IN (935-8848) 217 Waianuenue Ave, Hilo, 1/2 block above the downtown post office

CAFE 100 (935-8683) 969 Kilauea Ave, Hilo, across from Kapiolani School

CAP'S DRIVE IN (323-3229) On Highway 11, Captain Cook, Kona

EARL'S DRIVE IN on Highway 19, in Paauilo, Hamakua Coast, open Mon-Fri 8:30am-7 pm, Sat 8:30 am-6 pm, Sun 8:30-noon

K'S DRIVE IN (935-5573) 194 Hualalai St., Hilo, 1/2 block below St. Joseph's School

KANDI'S SNACK SHOP (959-8461) 56 W. Kawailani St., Hilo, near the intersection of Kilauea Ave. and Kawailani Streets

KA'U DRIVE INN (929-9291) On Highway 11 near Hawaiian Ranchos Center in Hawaiian Ocean View Estates, Ka'u District; open daily 7AM - 7PM

OHANA DRIVE INN (929-7679) On Highway 11 at Hawaiian Ranchos Center in Hawaiian Ocean View Estates, Ka'u District; open daily 7AM - 7PM, Sunday 12 Noon - 7:30PM

SANDY'S DRIVE IN (322-2161) On Hwy 11, at Kainaliu, Kona, about 5 miles south of Kailua-Kona

TABBADA'S DRIVE INN (929-8022) In Naalehu, Ka'u, right on Highway 11

TEX DRIVE INN (775-0598) Just off Hwy 19 above Honoka'a, a must stop to try their fresh hot Portuguese malasadas (doughnuts)

VERNA'S DRIVE INN (966-9288) Just off Hwy 130, Kea'au, across from Kea'au School

VERNA'S III DRIVE INN (935-2776) Located at the intersection of Kamehameha and Kanoelehua Avenues, Hilo, where Banyan Drive and hotel row begins.

VERNA'S TOO DRIVE IN (968-8774) Located on Highway 11 in Mountain View Village

VOLCANO STORE DINER (967-7707) Located one block off Highway 11 in Volcano village, next door to the post office; part of the Volcano Store.

PLATE LUNCH SHOPS

Throughout the islands of Hawai'i, the plate lunch has become sort of a revered institution and an established regional cuisine. Everywhere you go, you're probably not far from a plate lunch shop or a lunch wagon. These generally offer a number of selections ranging from teriyaki beef, to fried fish, to noodles, potato salad, and the usual two scoops of rice plus a whole lot more. Plate lunch shops were the original Hawaiian fast food outlets. Many folks pop into one, get a plate and take it back to the office, or to the park, corner bench, or under the nearest shade tree to enjoy. And like comparing restaurants, no two are the same. Everybody has his/her own personal favorite.

You may see or hear the term "bento" being used for lunch also, and that is exactly what the Japanese term means. It generally refers to a box or picnic lunch to be taken out from an "okazu-ya" lunch shop. As with drive-ins, the quality of plate lunch shops varies from place to place and even day to day. Depending on where you are on the Big Island, you might want to drop into one of the following, pick up a plate lunch and judge for yourself.

ALOHA DELI - 1845 Waikoloa Road, Waikoloa Highlands Center, Waikoloa Village (883-8246)

BROKE THE MOUTH PLATE LUNCH SHOP - 55 Mamo Street (934-7670), downtown Hilo across from Hilo Farmers' Market, open Wed-Sat 7AM-2PM, Tue-Thu-Fri 9AM-2PM

CLYDE'S OKAZUYA - 74-5490 Kaiwi, Kailua-Kona (329-6476)

DAIZEN OKAZUYA - 67-974 Mamalahoa Highway, Waimea (885-8511)

EVA'S LUNCH SHOP - 321 Punahoa Street, Hilo (934-7899)

HILO LUNCH SHOP - 421 Kalanikoa, Hilo (935-8273)

KALEI'S KAMA'AINA KITCHEN - Holomua Center, Mamalahoa Hwy., Waimea (885-0344)

KAMUELA DELI - Two outlets: Waimea Center Mall, Highway 19 in Waimea (885-4147); Kona Coast Center, 74-5588 Palani Road, Kailua-Kona (334-0017)

KAREN'S LUNCH SHOP - 31 Haili Street, Hilo (935-0323)

KAWAMOTO LUNCH SHOP - 784 Kilauea Avenue, Hilo (935-8209)

KIMO'S ONO HAWAIIAN FOOD - 806 Kilauea Avenue, Hilo (935-3111)

KOJI'S BENTO KORNER - 52 Ponahawai St., Hilo (935-1417)

KONA MIXED PLATE - Kopiko Plaza, below Lanihau Center, Palani Road, Kailua-Kona (329-8104)

KUAKINI CAFE - 75-5629 Kuakini Highway, North Kona Shopping Center, Kailua-Kona (329-1166)

LISA'S KITCHEN - 333 Keawe St., Hilo (961-5656)

LUCI'S OKAZUYA - 421 Kalanikoa Street, Hilo (961-6364)

MIZOGUCHI SUSHI STORE - 856 Kilauea Avenue, Hilo (935-2051)

SATO LUNCH SHOP - 750 Kinoole St., Hilo (961-3000)

SHAKA'S GRILL - 270 Kamehameha Avenue, Hilo (935-5399)

SHIBATA LUNCH SHOP - 413 Kilauea Avenue, Hilo (961-2434)

Y'S LUNCH SHOP - 263 Keawe St., Hilo (935-3119)

LUAUS / HAWAIIAN DINNER SHOWS

There are several hotel luau-Hawaiian dinner show operations along a couple of dinner cruise boats in the Kona-Kohala areas. Most of the luau and Hawaiian dinner shows feature authentic Hawaiian luau food like roast pig cooked in an imu (underground oven), island fish, poi, and tropical fruits. Some of these allow for wide variations and adaptations of local-regional luau foods. Most of them also include performances of Hawaiian and Polynesian music and dance as part of the program. The following is a listing of luaus and dinner shows.

HILTON WAIKOLOA VILLAGE
Kohala Coast, Waikoloa (885-1234). The "Legends of Polynesia" dinner show takes place at Kamehameha Court each Friday at 6PM and includes a lavish and authentic Hawaiian luau complete with roast pork and all the traditional foods like poi, lomi salmon, chicken laulau, fish, crab, and fresh tropical fruits. Following dinner is a captivating show of Polynesian song and dance which is one of the most exciting and colorful productions on the Kohala Coast. Reservations required. Adults $50, children 5-12 years, $25, kids under 4 free.

KING KAMEHAMEHA KONA BEACH HOTEL ★

75-5660 Palani Road, Kailua-Kona (329-2911); Island Breeze reservations (808) 326-4969. This authentic Island Breeze luau is put on each Tue., Wed., Thurs., and Sun. evening at 6PM with showtime at 7:30PM. (You can watch the pig being placed in the underground oven, imu, at 10:15AM on Luau days.)

The luau begins with the arrival of torch bearers via canoe from Ahu'ea Heiau, King Kamehameha's temple fronting Kamakahonu Beach and the hotel grounds. Conch shells are sounded as the torch bearers land and light the pathway to the luau grounds. Visitors can then watch the ceremonial removal of the roast pig from the imu (underground oven). The luau that follows is a feast of authentic Hawaiian foods and specialties from Oceania. A Polynesian performance of song and dance follows the luau. It's all very colorful, touristy and good fun. Adults $49 children 6-12, $18, kids under 5 free. Reservations required and Aloha attire preferred.

KONA VILLAGE RESORT ★

Kaupulehu-Kona (325-5555). This luau held at the South Seas-style Kona Village Resort has an element of authenticity which the other hotels don't quite match. It has something to do with the beachside environment.

This luau is held each Friday evening at 6:15PM and begins with the traditional removal of the roast pig from the imu (underground oven). Following this are cocktails and the luau feast with an incredible buffet of Hawaiian and Polynesian foods, probably the grandest luau spread on the Big Island. A Polynesian performance of music and dance provides a stirring end to a memorable evening. Adults are $63, children 6-12 are $35, kids under 5 $21. Get there a little early to take part in the walking tour of this wonderful beach resort given by the general manager himself.

KONA VILLAGE RESORT

ROYAL KONA RESORT ★

75-5852 Alii Drive, Kailua-Kona (329-3111). This hotel luau is put on each Mon., Fri. and Sat. evening at 6PM. The luau includes an Aloha shell lei greeting and continuous island entertainment. Prior to the luau beginning, there is the traditional opening of the imu (underground oven) and removal of the roast pig. The lavish buffet with authentic Hawaiian foods includes an open bar. A Polynesian Review performance of song and dance follows. Adults are $49, children 6-12 are $18, kids under 5 free. Reservations are suggested and Aloha attire preferred.

ROYAL WAIKOLOAN HOTEL ★

Waikoloa (885-6789). The Royal Luau is held each Sunday evening at 6PM and begins with the traditional torch lighting ceremony and removal of the roast pig from the imu (underground oven). The music, dance, food, products and costumes are reflections of Hawai'i's history. The feast and entertainment are produced, prepared, and performed by the area's fastidious practitioners of authentic Hawaiiana. On Wednesdays, there is a traditional Hukilau feast where guests join in an help haul in the hukilau nets from the fish ponds. Then all enjoy a feast of fish, salads and barbecue steaks while enjoying Hawaiian entertainment. For either the Royal Luau or Hukilau Feast, adults are $42, children 6-12 are $22, kids 5 and under free.

DINNER CRUISES

CAPT. BEANS' DINNER CRUISE

P.O. Box 5199, Kailua-Kona, Hawai'i 96745-5199, (808) 329-2955. This sunset dinner cruise onboard Capt. Beans' Polynesian-style sailing canoe departs Kailua Pier daily at 5:15PM. The cruise along the famous Kona Coast includes island entertainment, an open bar and all you can eat for $45 per person; adults 21 and over only, no children. Call for reservations and transportation pick-up at area hotels and condos. Aloha attire is preferred.

LANAKILA VENTURES

Kailua Pier, Kailua-Kona, HI (326-6000). This twin-masted sailing yacht offers an Aloha Dinner Cruise with live entertainment as the boat cruises the coral reef waters along the Kona Coast at sunset. Rates are adults $38 and children $20. Reservations suggested.

SOUTH & NORTH KONA

INTRODUCTION

There is a real variety of cuisine available in Kailua-Kona. The fare ranges from the local plate lunch and drive-in to exotic Chinese and Thai dishes, to fine gourmet French and Continental-International food. In addition, there is lots of excellent fresh island seafood to choose from as many restaurants feature it on their daily menus. Dining out in Kailua-Kona can be a real adventure.

INEXPENSIVE

AC'S CHINESE RESTAURANT   *Chinese*
74-5596 Pawai Place, Kailua-Kona (326-2466). Cantonese cuisine is the mainstay of this Chinese restaurant. A variety of plate lunches and Chinese-style meals as well as take outs are available. It is located in the industrial park area of Kailua-Kona and caters to the working people. Open Mon-Thurs 9AM - 8PM, Fri 9AM -9PM, and Sat 9AM - 8PM.

AH DUNNO BAR & RESTAURANT   *American*
74-5552A Kaiwi St., Kailua-Kona (329-7113). The menu features all you can eat spaghetti or BBQ ribs plus broasted chicken, seafood platters, pasta, and some German dishes plus daily specials. Located on one of the main streets of the Kailua-Kona industrial area and are easily accessible. Open for lunch and dinner, Mon-Sat 11:30AM - 9PM.

AKI'S CAFE   *Sandwiches/Snacks*
75-5699 Alii Drive, (329-8956) just opposite Hulihee Palace in the Kailua Bay Shopping Plaza. The menu features a little bit of everything including a variety of lunch fare such as burgers, sandwiches, fish & chips, light meals, snacks, etc. and dinner selections like steak, chicken teriyaki, fish misoyaki, sushi and other Japanese specials. There is open-air dining with tables outside overlooking Kailua Bay. Open daily, 9AM - 9PM.

ALOHA CAFE   *Sandwiches & Burgers*
Kainaliu, Kona (322-3383) in the old Aloha Theater Building on Highway 11. The specialties here are fresh baked pastries and cookies, sandwiches, and charbroiled burgers. Meals are enjoyed on the open-air veranda along with fresh juices, Kona Espresso, beer & wine. Open Mon-Sat 8 - 8PM, Sun 9AM - 1PM.

A PIECE OF THE APPLE   *Sandwiches/snacks*
75-5799 Alii Drive, Sunset Alii Plaza, Kailua-Kona (329-9321). This New York-style deli features made-to-order sandwiches like reuben, New Yorker, Broadway, veggie, etc. with fresh sliced turkey, roast beef, corned beef, salami, salmon and more. Open daily except Sunday, 8AM - 4PM.

BAD ASS COFFEE CO.   *Coffee Shop/Espresso Bar*
This coffee bar has several Kona outlets: Kailua Bay Inn Shopping Plaza, 75-5699 Alii Drive, Kailua-Kona; Keauhou Shopping Village, 78-6831 Alii Drive, Kailua-Kona; Waterfront Row, 75-5770 Alii Drive, Kailua-Kona; on Highway 11 ten miles south of Kailua-Kona in Kainaliu. This small coffee bar features snacks, sandwiches and pastries along with a variety of freshly brewed Kona coffee. Open daily, 8AM - 5PM.

BASIL'S PIZZARIA & RISTORANTE ★   *Italian*
75-5707 Alii Drive, Kailua-Kona, right across from Hulihe'e Palace. The all Italian menu offers pizza, pasta, seafood, eggplant parmagiana, sausage and peppers, chicken cacciatore and more. Open daily, 11AM - 11PM.

BETTY'S CHINESE KITCHEN   *Chinese*
Palani Rd, Kailua-Kona (329-3770) in the Kona Coast Shopping Center. Specializes in a full range of Chinese dishes as well as manapua (steamed meat rolls). A good variety of food served in ample quantities. Take outs available. This is a popular spot with shopping center crowds. Open Mon-Sat 10AM to 9PM.

BUNS IN THE SUN BAKERY-DELI-COFFEE SHOP ★   *Sandwiches/snacks*
75-5595 Palani Road, Kailua-Kona (326-2774) in the Lanihau Shopping Center. This small shop is bright, clean, and very popular with residents and visitors alike. They serve up a full range of fresh baked pastries, breads, rolls, desserts, and gourmet sandwiches. Open Mon-Sat 5:30AM - 8PM, Sun to 7PM.

CANAAN DELI & RESTAURANT   *Sandwiches/snacks*
Kealakekua, Kona (323-2577) on the main street, Hwy 11. Specializing in fresh New York-style deli sandwiches, soups, and salads in addition to Italian pasta and pizza. Inside dining is limited but pleasant, and they do have an outside lanai table. Open for breakfast, lunch and dinner, Mon-Fri 7AM-8PM, Sat 7-2PM.

CAPTAIN COOK INN   *Family Dining*
Located on Highway 11 in Captain Cook, (323-2080). This is a family style operation featuring local specials and favorites including plate lunches, bentos, sandwiches and burgers, salads, seafood plates, Korean-style chicken by the bucket and more. They have drive-thru service, take outs or dine in service. Open daily for breakfast, lunch and dinner, 7AM - 8PM.

CRUISIN COFFEE KONA   *Coffee Shop/Espresso Bar*
75-5626 Kuakini Highway, Kamehameha Mall, Kailua-Kona (329-0992). This 24 hour coffee house features a variety of espresso, coffees, Italian sodas, milkshakes, pastries and snacks. They feature Kona coffee and "Seattle's Best" coffees.

CUZ'UNS *Sandwiches/snacks*
75-5744 Alii Drive, in the Kona Inn Shopping Village, Kailua-Kona. This small deli snack bar features fresh deli sandwiches, pizza, salads, snacks and beverages. Open daily 9AM - 9:30PM.

DAYLIGHT DONUTS & DELI *Sandwiches/snacks*
Located in the newly opened phase of Keauhou Shopping Village, Alii Drive, Keauhou, Kona (324-1833). This is the only donut and pastry shop in Keauhou and provides a variety of donuts, malasadas and specialty pastries. They also have freshmade deli items like breakfast rolls, deli sandwiches for lunch, salads and a selection of hot and cold beverages. Open daily 6AM - 4PM.

DON DRYSDALE'S CLUB 53 ★ *Sandwiches & Burgers*
Kailua-Kona (329-6651) in the Kona Inn Shopping Village. This pleasant open-air veranda dining room claims the "Best Hamburgers in Town." They are good, along with sandwiches and other specialty items. Baseball memorabilia of Don Drysdale, of Los Angeles Dodgers fame, decorates the walls. Cocktail lounge features TV sports events. This is a popular late night spot with residents and visitors alike. Lunch and dinner daily, 11AM till closing. Credit cards.

DRYSDALE'S TWO ★ *Steaks & Burgers*
78-6831 Alii Drive, Kailua-Kona (322-0070) in the Keauhou Shopping Village. This is an instant replay of Drysdale's Club 53 with large screen TV featuring cable sports. The menu features heavier fare however with prime rib, steaks, and fresh island fish leading off. Cocktail lounge. Lunch and dinner daily, 11AM till closing. Credit cards.

GOLDEN CHOPSTIX CHINESE RESTAURANT *Chinese*
74-5467 Kaiwi St., Kaahumanu Plaza, Kailua-Kona (329-4527). This Chinese eatery specializes in Mandarin, Szechwan, and Hunan cuisine. Many varied and interesting dishes using beef, pork, chicken, duck, and seafood, plus vegetarian staples. This is a bright, clean and well-kept restaurant in a shopping plaza adjacent to the industrial area. Open Mon-Sat for lunch 11AM - 2:30PM, dinner 4:30PM - 9:00PM; Sunday dinner only 4:30 - 9PM. Take out orders. Reservations accepted.

GOLDEN SUN RESTAURANT *Chinese*
75-5699F Alii Drive, Kailua-Kona (329-8836) in the Kailua Bay Shopping Plaza. This is a nondescript small eatery in the back of the shopping arcade. The menu features an extensive listing of Mandarin, Szechuan and Chinese cuisine specials. Open daily for lunch and dinner continuously, 11AM till late closing.

HARBOR HOUSE *American*
74-425 Kealakehe Parkway, located in Gentry Marina, Honokohau Harbor, Kailua-Kona, 326-4166. This open airy cafe offers harborside views great for watching gamefish weigh-ins and harbor traffic. The menu offers a variety of hot and cold sandwiches, burgers, seafood specials, and local favorites. Open daily for breakfast, lunch and dinner, 6AM - 8PM.

HOLUAKOA CAFE ESPRESSO BAR *Coffee Shop/Espresso Bar*
Located right in Holualoa Village on Highway 180, five miles above Kailua-Kona. This small snack bar offers fresh Kona coffee, local pastries, snacks and more. Open daily except Sunday, 6:30AM - 5PM.

HONG KONG CHOP SUEY ★ *Chinese*
Kealakekua, Kona (323-3373). On Highway 11 in the Kealakekua Ranch Center. This simple but clean Chinese kitchen serves up some delicious Cantonese food. Many daily plate lunch-dinner specials include chicken, pork, beef, and vegetarian dishes plus noodles. You'll find good Chinese food at reasonable prices here. Take outs are available. Open daily, 10AM - 8:30PM.

ISLAND LAVA JAVA ★ *Coffee Shop/Espresso Bar*
75-5799 Alii Drive, in the Sunset Alii Plaza, Kailua-Kona (327-2161). This bakery and bistro espresso bar features a range of fine coffees and teas, fresh baked croissants, muffins, scones, pastries, cakes, fresh sandwiches, snack items and more. Open daily from 6:30AM - 10PM, Friday-Saturday open until 11PM.

JENNIFER'S KOREAN BARBECUE *Korean*
75-5605 Luhia St., in Kailua-Kona's industrial area upstairs in Luhia Center next to Cablevision shop, 326-1155. This local style eatery features Korean and Yakiniku barbecue specials and lots of local favorites. Open daily for lunch and dinner continuously 10:30AM - 10:30PM.

JILL'S COUNTRY KITCHEN *Sandwiches/Snacks*
76-6246 Alii Drive, Kona Bali Kai Condo, Kailua-Kona (329-6010). This small operation serves up sandwiches, burritos, daily specials and a variety of snack items along with a range of bakery goods and products. Open Monday-Saturday 7AM - 7PM.

KAMINARI JAPANESE RESTAURANT ★ *Japanese*
Located in the Kopiko Plaza below the Lanihau Center, Palani Road, Kailua-Kona (326-7799). This dining spot features grilled Japanese cuisine specializing in chicken, yakitori, seafood and varied Japanese delicacies. Authentic Japanese atmosphere and cuisine. Open Mon-Sat for dinner only, 5 - 9PM.

KING YEE LAU *Chinese*
In Ali'i Sunset Plaza, 75-5799 Alii Drive, Kailua-Kona (329-7100). Their extensive menu lists 100 varied items including soups, chicken and duck, beef and pork, seafood, egg-veggie-tofu, noodles and rice dishes, Cantonese cuisine, served family-style. Their specialty is a "Peking Duck Dinner." They also feature an all-you-can-eat buffet lunch Mon-Sat, 11AM - 2 PM. Open Mon-Sat 11AM - 9PM, Sunday 4 - 9PM.

KONA GRILL *Sandwiches/snacks*
Located 75-5595 Palani Road, in the Lanihau Center, Kailua-Kona (329-3167). This small eatery serves up a variety of local-style favorites including bbq beef, grilled fish, loco moco, hamburger steak, chicken katsu, fried noodles, kal bi ribs, beef tomato, saimin plus bento take outs and plate lunches. Open daily, 10AM - 9PM.

KONA KAI COFFEE ESPRESSO BAR *Coffee/Espresso Bar*
Kona Inn Shopping Village (326-4684); the menu includes a variety of Kona coffees plus snacks and desserts. Open 7:30AM - 5PM daily.

MANAGO HOTEL ★ *Family Dining*
Highway 11, Kona (323-2642) ten miles south of Kailua-Kona at Captain Cook. The home cooking and Japanese-American specialties are popular with the local folks. Standard selections include teriyaki, tempura, noodle dishes, fried fish, and more. There's no menu, the day's selections are on a board on the wall. Good food in simple surroundings. Open Tuesday-Sunday for breakfast 7 - 9AM, lunch 11AM - 2PM, and dinner 5 - 7:30PM; closed Monday. Call ahead for box picnic lunches to pick up on the way to the Volcanoes National Park. Credit cards. This country hotel dining room earns recognition in this book's "**Best Bets - Top Local Style Restaurants**" ratings.

MONA'S BBQ *Sandwiches/snacks*
75-5799 Alii Drive, Alii Sunset Plaza, Kailua-Kona (326-2532). This small barbecue eatery features such items as kalbi ribs, spicy chicken-beef-pork, chicken katsu, hamburgers, varied sandwiches, mahimahi, fish & chips and daily plate lunch specials. Open Mon-Fri 11AM - 9PM, Sat 12 Noon - 9PM, closed Sun.

OCEAN VIEW INN ★ *Family Dining*
Located in the heart of Kailua-Kona on Alii Drive just down from Kailua Pier, (329-9998). This is a very popular family restaurant with local folks. The menu is extensive with varied Chinese, American, and Hawaiian food. The decor and ambience are simple and nothing fancy but the food is good and plentiful. Go early for dinner as it gets crowded rapidly. Breakfast 6:30 - 11AM, lunch 11AM -2:45PM, dinner 5:15 - 9PM. Also bar and take out food. Closed Mondays. This restaurant earns recognition in this book's "**Best Bets - Top Local Style Restaurants**" ratings.

PADDLERS BAR & GRILLE *Continental/International*
75-5660 Palani Road, King Kamehameha Kona Beach Hotel, Kailua-Kona (329-2911). This is the hotel's former coffee shop, converted into a bar-grill. The menu features lunch items and snacks including varied appetizers and salads, kalua pig quesadilla, fish taco, varied sandwiches like calamari steak, mahimahi, chicken, burgers and poi, poke, lomilomi salmon and daily specials. Open daily 11AM - 8PM.

PANDA HOUSE *Chinese*
75-5660 Kopiko Street, in the Kopiko Plaza, Kailua-Kona (329-1682). The menu offers varied Szechuan dishes and unusual selections from many different parts of China. Enjoy such exotics as gold ginger onion chicken, chicken Szechuan, Mongolian beef, orange beef, mapo tofu and many more. Open daily 10:30AM - 9:30PM. Takes outs available.

PEACOCK HOUSE RESTAURANT ★ *Chinese*
81-6587 Mamalahoa Highway #11 in Kealakekua, Kona, across from Kamigaki Market, (323-2366). The menu is Cantonese and Mandarin Chinese cuisine with dim sum, manapua, Chinese pastries, rice cake and a large selection of varied dishes featured. Lunch and dinner served Monday-Saturday, 10AM till closing. Dim sum served 10AM - 5 PM daily; lunch buffet 10AM - 5 PM daily. This restaurant earns recognition in this book's "**Best Bets - Top Local Style Restaurants**" ratings.

POQUITO MAS *Mexican*
Palani Road, in the Kona Coast Shopping Center, Kailua-Kona (329-3528). The menu features authentic Mexican selections of tacos, burritos, tostadas and quesadillas with choice of filling including carne asada, pollo, carnitas or vegetariano, plus nachos and more. Open daily, 10:30AM - 8PM.

POT BELLI DELI *Plate lunches, varied*
74-5543 Kaiwi Road, Kailua-Kona (329-9454). This full line deli serves sandwiches, salads, plate lunches, and other deli items. The booths and tables are jammed in tightly making for crowded conditions. It is located in the industrial area and caters to the working people there and is very busy during lunch. Take outs available. Open daily, 6AM - 4PM.

QUINN'S RESTAURANT *Seafood*
75-5655A Palani Road, Kailua-Kona (329-3822). This restaurant features a full menu of sandwiches and burgers, steaks, fresh island fish and seafood. They offer casual late night dining on the lanai, one of the few Kona dining spots serving late night dinner. Daily for lunch 11AM - 5:30PM, dinner 5:30 - 1AM.

REAL MEXICAN FOOD ★ *Mexican*
Highway 11, Kealakekua, Kona (323-3036) in the Kealakekua Ranch Center. Featured in this small cafe is excellent and varied Mexican food including tacos, burritos, enchiladas and more. Open Mon-Sat 9:30AM - 6PM, Sun 10AM - 2PM.

RICO'S MEXICAN RESTAURANT ★ *Mexican*
75-5799 Alii Drive, Alii Sunset Plaza, Kailua-Kona (326-7655). The menu features authentic Mexican fare like tacos, burritos, tamales, tostados, chimichangas, enchiladas, Mexican pizza and an extensive listing of veggie specials as well. Simple attractive decor provides atmosphere for a dozen tables. Open Mon-Fri for lunch 11:30AM - 2PM, dinner 5 - 9PM; dinner only Sat-Sun 4:30 - 9PM.

ROCKY'S PIZZA & DELI *Italian*
78-6831 Alii Dr, Kailua-Kona (322-3223) in the Keauhou Shopping Village, and 75-5595 Palani Rd, Kailua-Kona (326-2734) in the Lanihau Shopping Center. The menu features excellent pizza (whole or by the slice), sandwiches, and salads. Open daily, lunch and dinner, 10:30AM - 10PM.

ROYAL JADE GARDEN ★ *Chinese*
75-5595 Palani Road, Kailua-Kona (326-7288) in the Lanihau Shopping Center. This neat family-run restaurant offers a full line of delicious Chinese food. The varied cuisine features some regional hot and spicy dishes. The food is generally good quality and of ample quantity. The surroundings are clean, bright, and comfortable. Open daily, 10:30AM - 10PM. This restaurant earns recognition in this book's **"Best Bets - Top Local Style Restaurants" ratings.**

SAM CHOY'S RESTAURANT ★ *Hawai'i/Pacific Regional*
73-5576 Kauhola Bay 1, in the Kaloko Industrial Park near the airport, Kailua-Kona (326-1545). This is probably one of Kona's most popular "local style" eateries. Sam, chef-owner, is something of a local media celebrity and has opened a restaurant in Honolulu as well. The menu features excellent varied

local-style cuisine with a distinct Hawai'i/Pacific Regional accent. The menu features such things as tomato beef, teriyaki steak, chicken stir fry, fried fish, lau lau and lomi salmon and lots more. This dining spot is a little hard to locate but turn into the Kaloko Industrial Area just north of Kailua-Kona and south of the airport. Look for the Kauhola Street sign to locate the building. It's well worth the search. Open daily, except Sunday, from 5AM - 2PM for breakfast and lunch only. This restaurant earns recognition in this book's **"Best Bets - Top Local Style Restaurants" ratings.**

SANTANGELO'S PIZZARIA *Italian*
Located at Hawaiian Ocean View Estates center, Highway 11, South Kona (929-9677). This small country eatery's menu selections include pizza, pasta, chicken and Italian specials. Open daily for lunch and dinner, 11AM - 8PM.

SIBU CAFE *Indonesian*
75-5695E Alii Drive, Kailua-Kona (329-1112) in the Kona Banyan Court Shopping Arcade. Features Indonesian dishes such as chicken and beef sate', curry, and other special exotics. A variety of imported beers is featured. Inside and lanai-courtyard dining. If you like it hot, you'll like this hot spicy Southeast Asian cuisine. Open daily for lunch 11:30AM - 3PM, dinner 5-9PM. No reservations, no credit cards.

SIZZLER ★ *Steaks*
Palani Road, Kailua-Kona (329-3374) in the Kona Coast Shopping Center. This is the Big Island's only outlet for this national steakhouse chain and is popular with residents and visitors alike. The menu features reasonably priced steak, chicken, seafood and combination dinners. Good salad bar. Breakfast, lunch, dinner daily, Sun-Thurs 6AM - 10PM, Fri-Sat 6AM - 12 midnight. Credit cards.

STAN'S RESTAURANT *Family Dining*
On Alii Drive, back of Kona Seaside Hotel (329-2455). The restaurant has a beautiful open-air view of Kailua Bay right across the street. The menu features steak, seafood, chicken, scampi, lots of local favorites and many daily specials. Open daily for breakfast 7 - 9:30AM and dinner 6 - 8PM. Credit cards.

SU'S THAI KITCHEN *Thai*
74-5588A Pawai Place, Kailua-Kona (326-1222). The menu features many exotic offerings such as crab claw in pot, spicy ginger beef, garlic pork, Thai barbeque chicken, sweet-sour fish, seafood platter, Thai red curry, Mussamar yellow curry, green curry, noodle dishes and varied soups and appetizers. Hot chili pepper is used liberally! The restaurant is located in the middle of Kailua-Kona's industrial area which detracts somewhat from the exotic atmosphere. Open for lunch Monday-Friday 11:30AM - 2:30PM, dinner nightly 5-9PM.

TESHIMA'S RESTAURANT ★ *Japanese/American*
On Highway 11, Honalo, Kona (322-9140) seven miles south of Kailua-Kona. This neat clean family restaurant is popular and features friendly old-fashioned service by the Teshima family. Specialties are Japanese-American cuisine and local favorites and the menu has something for everyone. If you want to see what a country town Hawaiian cafe is like, this is the place. Open daily for

breakfast and lunch 6:30AM - 2PM, dinner 5 - 10PM. This family cafe earns recognition in this book's **"Best Bets - Top Local Style Restaurants" ratings.**

THAI RIN RESTAURANT ★ *Thai cuisine*
Located streetside in the Alii Sunset Plaza, 75-5799 Alii Drive, Kailua-Kona (329-2929). This restaurant turns out great versions of trendy hot and spicy Thai cuisine. The menu features over two dozen items including crispy and fried noodles, chicken satay, three kinds of curry, spicy soups, Thai garlic shrimp or squid and much more. Open Mon-Sat for lunch 11AM - 2:30PM, dinner 5 - 9:30PM, Sunday for dinner only.

THE ROYAL THAI CAFE *Thai cuisine*
75-5744 Alii Drive, Kailua-Kona, in the Kona Inn Shopping Village (329-1994). This upstairs airy dining room has lots of tropical decor combined with touches of Thailand. The extensive menu is authentic Thai with selections like red or yellow curry, Pahd Thai noodles, Thai dumpling soup, sweet & sour veggies, spicy fried rice and many more, with choice on several of mild, medium or Thai hot seasoning. Open Mon-Sat for lunch 11AM - 2:30PM, dinner 5 - 9:30PM; Sunday for dinner only.

TRES COMPADRE'S *Mexican*
74-5596Q Pawai Place, in the Kona industrial area (326-7422). This rather unpretentious place provides very informal dining featuring homemade Mexican and Spanish food at reasonable prices. If you're an aficionado of Mexican food, you might want to check it out. Open Mon-Sat for dinner only, 5-10PM.

TROPICS CAFE *Family Dining*
75-5852 Alii Dr. (329-3111) in the Royal Kona Resort. There are lovely views of Kailua Bay and the village from this edge-of-the-water location. The dinner menu features Euro-Asian specials while the lunch menu is light fare of sandwiches and burgers, varied seafood salads (a specialty), omelettes, and local favorites like saimin noodles, fish & chips, stir-fried beef and chicken, chow mein, fried noodles and more. Breakfast is served ala carte or buffet style. Open for breakfast 6:30 - 11AM, lunch and dinner 11AM - 9:30PM. Credit cards.

UNCLE GIL'S SAIMIN ★ *Japanese*
74-5563 Kaiwi Street, Kailua-Kona (326-2367). This small unpretentious diner is one of those "great discoveries in local-style cuisine" sort of places. It's got no decor or atmosphere, plywood booths/tables but lots of excellent saimin noodles. They serve it several ways including old fashion char siu pork, fish cake and green onion, or with won ton, shrimp or even fried saimin. Daily specials include BBQ beef, chicken and real local favorites like ox-tail soup. Eat in or take out. Uncle Gil himself cooks, waits tables and "talks story" with you. This diner's good local food and warm Aloha earn it a spot in this book's **"Best Bets -Top Local Style Restaurants" ratings.** Open daily except Sunday, 7AM - 9:30PM.

UNDER THE PALM   *Sandwiches/snacks*
75-5819 Alii Drive, Kailua-Kona (329-7366). This indoor/outdoor bar-cafe offers a breakfast menu of waffles, bagels, croissants, fresh pastries and other morning items.   For lunch and dinner, the menu features a variety of pizzas, salads, sandwiches and other specials plus bar beverages.   Open daily 7AM - 11PM.

WAKEFIELD GARDENS   *Family Dining*
On the road to Honaunau Bay, Kona (328-9930). This is an interesting little country house set amidst a macadamia nut orchard and botanical garden. They serve lunch daily from 11AM - 3PM and have a simple menu of salads, varied sandwiches, other light fare, and delicious homemade fresh fruit pies. After lunch or a snack, stroll the grounds and take in their self-guided botanical tour.

YU SUSHI ★   *Japanese*
75-5770 Alii Drive, Kailua-Kona, in the Waterfront Row shopping-dining complex across from St. Michael's Church (326-5653). This small eatery offers the best of authentic Japanese sushi, those artistically created rice rolls using fresh fish and seafood. For an unusual and intriguing experience in relaxing surroundings, give it a try. Open daily for lunch 11AM - 2:30PM, dinner 4:30 - 9:30PM.

YUNI'S SAIMIN & THINGS ★   *Korean*
Located in the Kopiko Plaza next door to and below the Lanihau Center on Palani Road, Kailua-Kona (329-1018). This small lunch counter's menu offers local-style plate lunches and many daily specials, plus all types of saimin like chicken, chai siu pork, seafood, mandoo, beef and a variety of Korean selections as well. Open for breakfast and lunch Mon-Sat 8AM - 5PM, Sun lunch only 10AM - 2PM.

ZAC'S ESPRESSO VERANDA   *Coffee Shop/Espresso Bar*
Palani Road, North Kona Town Center, Kailua-Kona (329-0006). This coffee house features espresso, cappuccino, cafe latte and other special brew and flavored coffees along with sandwiches, cheesecake, biscotti and other desserts and snacks. Open Mon-Sat 8AM - 7PM.

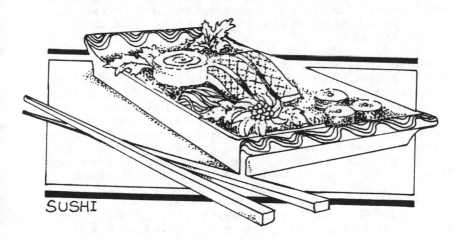

SUSHI

MODERATE

BANANA BAY CAFE ★ *Hawaii/Pacific Regional*
75-5739 Alii Drive (329-1393) in the Kona Bay Hotel. This open-air dining room sits just above busy Alii Drive in the heart of Kailua-Kona town. It has sort of a South Seas or early Hawaiian atmosphere and a buffet-only menu heavy in local-style Hawaii cuisine. The menu changes nightly but usually offers beef, chicken, seafood and other local favorite selections. There is often evening entertainment and a hula show included. Open daily for breakfast 7 - 11AM, dinner 5:30 - 9PM. Dinner reservations suggested. Credit cards.

BANGKOK HOUSES ★ *Thai Cuisine*
75-5626 Kuakini Highway, King Kamehameha Mall, Kailua-Kona (329-7764). This Thai cuisine restaurant offers a real variety of the popular spicy hot food of southeast Asia. The extensive menu features 100 selections including beef, chicken, seafood and vegetarian specials. Items like spring rolls, Pad Thai noodles, beef Panang curry, sizzling chicken Thai-style and fried rice are excellent. Open Monday-Saturday for lunch and dinner, 11AM - 9:30PM, Sunday dinner only 5 - 9PM. Take outs and delivery available.

CASSANDRA'S GREEK TAVERNA *Greek*
75-5719 Alii Drive, Kailua-Kona, in the Kona Plaza Arcade (334-1066). This inside/outside cafe is the Big Island's first Greek restaurant and presents a menu with some authentic Greek selections accented with local touches. Pizza, sandwiches, fish & chips and souvlaki highlight the lunch menu. For dinner, appetizers include dolmades, saganaki, octopus skaras, kalamari and loukaniko; entrees include souvlaki-kebobs, kota skaras, moussaka, prawns uvetsi, sountzoukia, fresh catch Greek-style, seafood platter and other mixed choices. Open daily for lunch 11AM - 4PM, dinner until 9PM.

EDWARD'S AT THE TERRACE *Continental/International*
78-261 Manukai (322-9625) in Kanaloa at the Kona Condominiums. There is a casual poolside-garden setting, in addition to being on the ocean's edge. The menu features Mediterranean specials along with beef, pork, lamb and seafood dishes. Open daily for breakfast 8 - 11AM, lunch 11AM - 2PM, and dinner 5-9PM. Credit cards.

FISHERMAN'S LANDING ★ *Seafood*
75-5744 Alii Drive, Kailua-Kona (329-2555) in the Kona Inn Shopping Village. This ocean front restaurant features the best in fresh island seafood. Located directly on Kailua Bay, the restaurant has five separate Hawaiian dining huts with nautical theme decor. Fresh island fish such as ono, opakapaka, ahi, etc. are mainstays along with lobster, shrimp, and a number of daily specials. Beef, veal, and chicken as well as local style specialties round out the menu. This is an especially nice location right on the water's edge, great for sunsets. Lunch 11:30AM - 2:30PM, dinner 5:30 - 10PM daily. Reservations suggested.

HAPPI YU JAPANESE STEAK HOUSE *Steaks*
75-5770 Alii Drive, Kailua-Kona (326-5653) in the Waterfront Row complex across from St. Michael's Church. This Japanese-style teppan-yaki steak house

is next door to Yu Sushi, a companion operation. The menu features varied grill selections including chicken, teriyaki steak, filet mignon, fresh island fish, lobster, shrimp, scallops and more. Place your order and be entertained by the chef as he slices, dices, chops, tosses and sizzles your meal at the table. Open daily for dinner, 5:30 - 9PM.

HUGGO'S *Steaks*
75-5828 Kahakai Road, Kailua-Kona (329-1493). This oceanside restaurant is just next door to the Royal Kona Resort and sits over the water's edge. There are beautiful views of Kailua Bay and romantic sunsets. The menu features steaks and prime rib. Cocktail piano bar and special free pupus daily 2:30 - 5:30 PM. Open for lunch Mon-Fri 11:30AM - 2:30PM, dinner 5:30 - 10PM, Sat-Sun, dinner only 5:30 - 10PM. Credit cards.

JAMESON'S BY THE SEA *Seafood*
77-6452 Alii Drive (329-3195) next to Magic Sands Beach. The beachside location lends a nice atmosphere with a menu featuring varied American-Continental selections such as pasta, beef, veal, lamb, chicken, and fresh island fish. Specialties include veal Marsala, veal piccata, filet mignon, lobster, calamari, and rack of lamb. Special silver platters include beef, seafood, and combo dinners. Pleasant Hawaiian background music, white table cloths, and cheerful bright surroundings add a nice touch. Beautiful sunsets complimentary with dinner. Open for lunch Mon-Fri 11:30AM - 2:30PM, dinner nightly from 6PM.

JOLLY ROGER *Continental/International*
75-5776 Alii Drive, Waterfront Row Complex, Kailua-Kona (329-1344). The menu at this open-air oceanside restaurant features steak, teriyaki beef or chicken, ribs, seafood, chicken Polynesian, pasta, sandwiches, salads, and more. The furnishings and decor are showing age and exposure to the salt air; the same could be said for the food as well. This place used to have a star rating denoting exceptional value, but it's been removed this time around. Both the place and the menu need work. Open daily for breakfast 6:30 - 12 noon, lunch 11AM - 4PM, and dinner 4 - 10PM. Credit cards.

KONA AMIGOS RESTAURANT *Mexican*
75-5669 Alii Drive, upstairs, across from Kailua Pier (326-2840). The menu here is obviously Mexican and features a variety of bontanos (appetizers), ensaladas (salads), soups and entradas (entrees). Dinner menu bontanos include nachos, calamari, and quesadilla; ensaladas include guacamole, taco, sea scallops/fish; soups-daily specials; entrees include burritos, fajitas fiesta, pescado Yucatan, crab enchiladas, chimichanga, pollo verde and pollo adoba, beef tenderloin and pork loin. There is a similar lunch menu with additional egg and sandwich items listed. Lovely open-air views of Kailua Bay. Open daily for lunch 11AM - 4PM, dinner 4-10PM, bar serves up fresh fruit margaritas and more till 11PM.

KONA BEACH RESTAURANT ★ *Continental/International*
75-5660 Palani Road (329-2911) in the Kona Beach King Kamehameha Hotel. This attractive dining room has a nautical-whaling decor theme. There are big picture window views of Kailua Wharf and Bay, Ahuena Heiau directly in front of the hotel and Kamakahonu Beach. The menu features specialties such as Pacific

Broiled Salmon, Kiawe-smoked Prime Rib, Herbal Breast of Chicken, Cajun Prawns with pasta and more. Delightful setting with live piano music, attractive wood paneling and fish tanks to amuse the kids. Good service and they take good care of youngsters, providing extra goodies. Open daily with breakfast buffet 6:30 - 10:30AM, lunch 11AM - 2PM and dinner 5:30 - 9PM. Reservations suggested. Credit cards. This restaurant's Sunday Brunch, 10AM - 2PM, earns recognition in this book's **"Best Bets - Best Buffets" ratings.**

KONA GALLEY ★ *Continental/International*
Across from King Kam Hotel and Kailua Pier on Alii Drive in the Seaside Shopping Mall (329-5550). There are open air harbor views of Kailua Bay and lovely sunsets from its upstairs location. The menu offers a Continental-International selection of fresh catch of the day, seafood, pasta, pizza, chicken, sandwiches and local favorites. Open daily for lunch 11AM - 5PM, and dinner 5 - 9:30PM. Reservations suggested. Credit cards.

KONA INN RESTAURANT *Seafood*
75-5744 Alii Drive (329-4455) in the heart of Kailua-Kona in the Kona Inn Shopping Village. There is a pleasant casualness in this open-air veranda restaurant which is the original dining room of the old Kona Inn Hotel. The ceiling fans add to the tropical ambiance and informality. There are lovely views of Kailua Bay and the waterfront. The menu features fresh island fish, seafood, prime rib, steaks, and local favorites. Open daily for lunch from 11:30AM with dinner served 5:30 - 10PM. Dinner reservations suggested. Credit cards.

KONA RANCH HOUSE ★ *Family Dining*
(329-7061) Near intersection of Kuakini Highway and Palani Road, just above the Shell Station. The restaurant has an attractive old ranch house decor with a casual, turn-of-the-century Hawaiian atmosphere. The menu features ranch fare including paniolo BBQ platters, roast beef, roast turkey, ribs, and chicken. Good food and friendly service in a very pleasant atmosphere. This is a good place for families. Open daily for breakfast and lunch 7AM - 2PM, dinner 5 - 9PM. Closed between 2 - 5 PM. Reservations for dinner suggested. Credit cards.

KUAKINI TERRACE ★ *Buffet*
78-6778 Alii Drive, Keauhou-Kona (322-3441) in the Keauhou Beach Hotel. Open daily from 6:30AM - 9PM serving breakfast, lunch and dinner. The dining room features a nightly buffet, 5 - 9PM. Monday through Thursday it's a Chinese Buffet with roast duck, dim sum, mandarin salad, and an array of Cantonese and Szechwan selections. Friday through Sunday it's a fabulous seafood buffet with Alaskan Crab, island fish, shrimp, Pacific clams, oysters, and even prime rib of beef. On Sunday, there is a Champagne Sunday Brunch from 9AM - 1:30PM featuring prime rib, special eggs, island fish, shrimp tempura, a variety of salads and tropical fruits and desserts. Reservations suggested. Credit cards. The nightly dinner buffet earns recognition in this book's **"Best Bets - Best Buffets" ratings.**

MICHAELANGELO'S ITALIAN & SEAFOOD RESTAURANT
Italian/Seafood
Waterfront Row, 75-5770 Alii Drive, across from St. Michael's Church, (329-4436). Located on the upper level of the complex, this room has a lovely open

veranda view of the ocean. The menu features varied Italian fare including soups, salads, appetizers, sandwiches, pasta, pizza and specials such as Chardonnay shrimp scampi, bell peppers & Italian sausage, pink penne regatoni, angel hair pasta & sun dried tomatoes, lava-fire calamari and fresh island fish plus much more. Open daily for lunch, 11AM - 4PM; dinner 4:30 - til closing. Special kids menu; dinner reservations suggested; credit cards.

OCEAN SEAFOOD CHINESE RESTAURANT   *Seafood*
King Kamehameha Mall, 75-5626 Kuakini Highway, Kailua-Kona (329-3055). The menu features lobster, crab, fresh scallops, shrimp, oysters and traditional Cantonese cuisine like beef, pork, chicken, duck and noodles. Open daily for lunch and dinner continuously, 11AM - 9:30PM.

PANCHO & LEFTY'S   *Mexican*
75-5719 Alii Drive across from Kona Inn Shopping Village in the Kona Plaza Condos (326-2171). The menu features the usual Mexican fare such as tacos, burritos, enchiladas, chimichangas, tamales, tostados and varied appetizers like buffalo wings, stuffed potatoes, calientitas (stuffed deep fried jalapeno peppers) and more. The decor is garage-sale junk with equally mediocre service and food, and unless you're absolutely desperate, Kona has other far better Mexican restaurants. Open Mon-Sat 11AM - 10PM, Sunday 12 Noon - 10PM. Upstairs open-air location in the heart of the village overlooks Alii Drive. Credit cards.

PELE'S COURT   *Continental/International*
78-128 Ehukai (322-3411) in the Kona Surf Resort Hotel. This is a lovely open-air dining room on the hotel's lower level with relaxing garden views. The lunch menu offers a variety of sandwiches, seafood, chicken and pasta dishes plus pizza. Dinner entrees featured include seafood, beef prime ribs, teriyaki steak, chicken, pasta, burritos, plus salad bar and sandwiches. A varied breakfast menu is also available. Daily for breakfast 6:30-11AM, lunch 11-2PM, dinner 5-9PM.

RESTAURANT YOKOHAMA ★   *Japanese*
Located in the Sunset Alii Plaza, 75-5799 Alii Drive, Kailua-Kona (329-9661). This Japanese style restaurant features teriyaki chicken and beef, tonkatsu, tempura, misoyaki pork, sukiyaki, shabushabu, sushi, sashimi, noodles and fresh island fish. Bento lunch takeouts are available. Open for lunch daily except Monday and Saturday, 11AM - 2PM, dinner nightly from 5:30 - 9PM.

THE CAPTAIN'S DECK   *Seafood*
75-5744 Alii Drive, Kailua-Kona, in the Kona Inn Shopping Village. This dining room is next to Fisherman's Landing and features a varied seafood menu. Specials include shrimp-teri beef combo, fish-shrimp combo, crab, poki (marinated raw fish) and other local favorites plus sandwiches, soups, salads and desserts. Open daily for lunch and dinner, 11:30AM - 9:30PM.

THE CHART HOUSE ★   *Steaks*
75-5770 Alii Drive, Kailua-Kona, in the Waterfront Row shopping-dining complex, across from St. Michael's Church (329-2451). This open-air verandah-style restaurant offers excellent steaks, prime rib and fresh fish and other seafood selections as well as an interesting appetizer and salad bar. Most dinner entrees are in the moderate range with some getting into the expensive bracket. Casual

relaxing atmosphere overlooking the ocean shoreline. Open for dinner daily 5-10PM. Reservations suggested. Credit cards.

THE MAKEE RESTAURANT   *Continental/International*
78-128 Ehukai (322-3411) in the Kona Surf Resort Hotel. This elegant dining room offers Continental/Pacific dining with menu selections such as fresh island fish, Big Island Parker Ranch beefsteak, veal chops, tiger prawns, Pacific lobster and other Hawaiian seafood specials. Open daily for dinner only, 6 - 9:30PM. Reservations suggested. Credit cards.

TOM BOMBADIL'S FOOD AND DRINK   *American*
75-5864 Walua Road (329-1292) at the intersection of Alii Drive and Walua Road, Kailua-Kona, across from the Royal Kona Resort. The menu features pizza, pasta, broasted chicken, and sandwiches like French dip, sausage and Reuben Burger plus some local specialties. Dinner specials include steak, chicken teriyaki, fresh island fish, soups and salads. Cocktail lounge. Open daily for lunch and dinner, 11AM - 10PM. Credit cards.

VISTA RESTAURANT   *Seafood*
78-7000 Alii Drive, Keauhou-Kona (322-3700) at the Kona Country Club. Open for breakfast and lunch only and features fresh island fish, burgers, sandwiches and many local favorites. Early morning golfers keep the place busy. Open daily, 6:30AM - 2:30PM.

YASU'S KONA SUSHI   *Japanese*
75-5799 Alii Drive, in the Sunset Alii Plaza, Kailua-Kona (326-1696). The menu here is authentic Japanese sushi including Nigiri, unagi eel, squid, fish, veggie California-style and many more. Daily lunch 11:30AM - 2PM, dinner 5 - 10PM.

EXPENSIVE

GOLF CLUB RESTAURANT & BAR   *American*
Kaupulehu-Kona (325-8000) at Four Seasons Resort Hawaii at Hualalai. This is the resort's golf club "19th. Hole" and serves up typical golf clubhouse fare such as sandwiches, light meals, salads, etc. *Exact hours of this restaurant opened in early fall, 1996, were unavailable at press time.*

HALE MOANA ★   *Continental/International*
Kaupulehu-Kona (325-5555) at the Kona Village Resort. This pleasant and airy dining room is the main restaurant for this South Seas hale-style (house) resort. It overlooks the beach for lovely sunset dining and has an adjacent garden area for daily open-air lunch. The menu changes nightly and the cuisine includes American, European and Hawaiian accented specialties. Among the entrees on a recent evening visit were stir-fry shrimp, lobster and chicken with veggie noodles, mixed grill of steak, lamb chop and sausage, veal loin, roast duck, prime rib, pasta special and fresh island fish. The daily buffet lunch is a magnificent spread of salads, hot and cold entrees, grills and delectable desserts. Reservations required. Open daily for breakfast, lunch, and dinner, 6:30AM - 10PM. Credit cards. This dining room earns recognition in this book's **"Best Bets - Top Restaurants with a Casual Atmosphere"** and **"Best Bets - Best Buffets"** ratings.

HALE SAMOA ★ *Continental/International*
Kaupulehu-Kona (325-5555) at the Kona Village Resort. This warm intimate dining room features a Samoan motif complete with an outrigger canoe hanging from the ceiling and decorative crafts. The menu is surprisingly international and changes nightly. On a recent visit, entrees included fresh island fish, broiled prime striploin steak, lamb loin roast, buffalo filet, fresh opakapaka snapper and salmon all done with an Asian-Pacific flair, plus a variety of creative appetizers, soups and salads. Attentive service in a romantic South Seas atmosphere is the tradition here. The sunsets are gorgeous. Reservations are a must. Open for dinner only, nightly 6 - 9PM. Credit cards. This restaurant earns recognition in this book's **"Best Bets - Top Restaurants"** ratings.

LA BOURGOGNE FRENCH RESTAURANT ★ *French*
Kuakini Highway #11, 4 miles south of Kailua-Kona, in the Kuakini Plaza South Center (329-6711). Specializing in fresh fish, shrimp, scallops, roast duck, chicken, pork tenderloin, lamb, steak, and veal all with a French accent. Luscious desserts like chocolate mousse, caramel creme, and cherries jubilee finish the menu. Dinner only, Mon-Sat 6 - 10PM. Reservations suggested. Credit cards.

OCEANFRONT RESTAURANT *Hawaii/Pacific Regional*
Kaupulehu-Kona (325-8000) at the Four Seasons Resort Hawaii at Hualalai. This is the resort's signature restaurant and features the finest international and Pacific Rim cuisine in a relaxed, elegant setting right on the beachfront. Terrace seating provides both indoor or open-air dining including sunset views over the ocean. Open for breakfast, lunch and dinner daily. *Exact hours of this restaurant opened in early fall, 1996, were unavailable at press time.*

PALM CAFE ★ *Hawaii/Pacific Regional Cuisine*
Located in the Coconut Grove Marketplace on Alii Drive (329-7765) adjacent to the Royal Kona Resort and across from the waterfront. This is an elegant open-air dining room with ceiling fans and nice views of Kailua Bay and boat traffic. Great for sunsets! The menu features Hawaii-Pacific cuisine with such items as mahi mahi Malia, island fish with cilantro crust, chicken with spicy bean sauce, fish and scallops, varied steaks, salads and appetizers prepared in creative ways. Open nightly for dinner only, 5:30 - 10PM. Reservations suggested. This restaurant earns recognition in this book's **"Best Bets - Top Restaurants with a Casual Atmosphere"** ratings.

POOLSIDE BAR & GRILL *Continental/International*
Kaupulehu-Kona (325-8000) at the Four Seasons Resort Hawaii at Hualalai. This poolside dining spot creates a relaxing and informal atmosphere for breakfast, lunch and cocktail hour as well as a casual evening dining option. The menu features lighter fare and continental/international selections. *Exact hours of this restaurant opened in early fall, 1996, were unavailable at press time.*

SOUTH KOHALA

INTRODUCTION

The accent in Kamuela is ranch country and that's what the restaurants offer, a country atmosphere and generally good hearty food. The fare ranges from local-style ranch fare, Oriental, Continental-International and Hawaii/Pacific Regional Cuisine at several inexpensive and moderate category restaurants. Down on the fashionable Kohala Coast where the world-class luxury resorts are, the accent is definitely upscale. Here dining is an indulgence in fine gourmet cuisine. With the large number of award-winning dining rooms from which to choose, the Kohala Coast is an epicurean's delight. However, due to the general visitor industry slowdown the past couple of years, be aware that some of the top resort dining rooms continue to change their hours, menus, etc. in trying to best meet the demand. Some dining rooms have even chosen to close for periods of time to meet fluctuating visitor demand. It's best to call ahead and check with any given restaurant before going.

INEXPENSIVE

ALOHA LUIGI *Italian*
This small eatery (885-1511) is in an old quonset hut building that doubles as the Waimea Express gas station and general store, next door to the more popular Edelweiss Restaurant on the Kawaihae Road on Waimea's west side. The kitchen at the back serves up varied Italian fare including spaghetti with a variety of sauces, five cheese lasagna, eggplant Parmigiana, pizza and a special gorgonzola white pie, sandwiches and salads. Eat here or take out. Open Mon-Sat 11AM - 8PM, Sun 1-7PM.

BAD ASS COFFEE CO. *Coffee Shop/Espresso Bar*
Kawaihae Center, Kawaihae (882-7019). This is another of the coffee company's espresso bar outlets; they have several in the Kona area. The menu features a variety of fresh brewed Kona coffees, smoothies, beverages, pastries and snacks. Open daily, 7AM - 7PM.

CAFE PESTO ★ *Italian*
Kawaihae Center, Kawaihae (882-1071). This small pizzeria offers a wide variety of excellent pizza, pasta & risottos, hot sandwiches, calzones, and specialties including fresh baked pastries. They even deliver to Kohala Coast resort area and Kamuela for an extra charge. Open daily 11AM - 10PM, Fri-Sat till 11PM.

DON'S PAKE KITCHEN *Chinese*
Highway 19 just east (Honoka'a side) of Waimea in the old Fukushima Store building (885-2025). This smallish Chinese kitchen serves up a varied menu of freshly prepared Cantonese and Szechwan specialties. House specials are char siu (pork) and roast duck. Look for the old-fashioned gas pump in front. Open daily 10AM - 9PM.

GREAT WALL CHOP SUEY ★ *Chinese*
This Chinese eatery is located in the Waimea Center Shopping Mall in the heart of Kamuela (885-7252). The variety of Cantonese food offered is excellent in quality and quantity. There is a full selection of beef, pork, chicken, seafood, and noodle dishes. Open daily for lunch and dinner except Monday, 11AM - 8PM.

HAWAIIAN CHILI BY MAX *Sandwiches/Snacks/Chili*
Located in the Kings' Shop Center at Waikoloa Beach Resort across from the Royal Waikoloan Hotel (886-1522). This small lunch-snack counter operation serves up several varieties of oven-baked chili, chili dogs, sandwiches, nachos and more. Open Monday-Saturday 10AM - 8PM, Sunday 11AM - 8PM.

HAWAIIAN STYLE CAFE *Sandwiches/Plate Lunches*
Kawaihae Road, Kamuela (885-4295); the menu features local-style favorites including teriyaki, fried fish, chicken, burgers, sandwiches and more. This is not a fancy place but they serve a good inexpensive meal if you're on a budget. Open Monday-Friday 4AM - 2PM, Saturday 7AM - 2PM, closed Sunday. Eat at the counter or take outs available.

JAVA JUNCTION *Coffee Shop/Espresso Bar*
On Highway 19, Waimea, in the Kamuela Business Center (885-9494). There is a wide selection of fresh espresso and coffees featuring their Hawaiian Angel Kona Coffee; also pastries, snacks and other beverages. Open daily, 7:30AM - 7:30PM.

KAWAIHAE HARBOR GRILL ★ *Seafood*
Across from the Kawaihae Wharf on Highway 270 in Kawaihae (882-1368). This small country-style restaurant is located in a renovated general store. It has bright simple decor with both tables and booth seating. The menu is heavy in seafood selections including local-style pupus (appetizers), salads, sandwiches and entrees like fresh island fish, laulau, Thai seafood curry, shrimp & farfalle, prawns or scallops & pasta, chicken and steaks plus daily specials and take outs. Open daily for lunch 11:30AM - 1:30PM, dinner 5:30 - 9:30PM.

LAVA TUBE *Sandwiches/Snacks*
Royal Waikoloan Hotel, Kohala Coast (885-6789). This is the hotel's poolside snackbar and has a menu of light fare, burgers, sandwiches, salads and snacks plus beverages.

MAHA'S CAFE ★ *Sandwiches/Snacks*
Located in Waimea at the Waimea Center on Highway 19 in the historic Spencer House, this small cafe shares space with *Cook's Discoveries*, a unique Hawaiiana giftshop (885-3633). The cafe specializes in a different Kona Coffee of the Month and light gourmet breakfasts, lunches and afternoon snacks. Breakfast items include fresh island fruit, juices, coffees, cereals and breads/pastries. Lunch features Waipi'o Ways combo of broiled island fish and steamed taro, sweet potato, garden greens; fresh made turkey, tuna, ahi, lamb or veggie sandwiches; and Kohala Harvest chef's salad, plus luscious desserts. Open daily 7AM - 5PM except Tuesdays.

MEAN CUISINE ★ *Sandwiches/Bentos*
Kawaihae Road, Kamuela (885-6354) in the Opelu Plaza Shopping Center. The menu here features local-style plate lunches, sandwiches, soups and special "Yuppie Bentos," sort of a blue-collar version of international dishes and the trendy Hawaii regional cuisine currently in vogue. A variety of daily special lunch entrees, fresh baked bread, criminal desserts and more are the mainstays of this gourmet deli. Definitely worth trying when passing through Kamuela. Open daily except Sunday for breakfast, lunch and dinner, 6AM - 8PM. This restaurant earns recognition in this book's **"Best Bets - Top Local Style Restaurants" ratings.**

NORI'S SAIMIN TOO ★ *Japanese*
64-1035 Mamalahoa Highway, Ululani Plaza, Waimea (885-9133). This country diner, like their original Hilo outlet, features a wide variety of saimin noodle dishes including won ton min, udon, soba and ramen with varied ingredients plus noodle salads and fried saimin. Plate lunch and take out items include loco moco, BBQ chicken sticks, teriyaki beef, burgers, sandwiches and daily specials. Open Mon-Sat 9AM - 9PM, Sun 10AM - 6PM. This restaurant earns recognition in this book's **"Best Bets - Top Local Style Restaurants" ratings.**

PANIOLO COUNTRY INN ★ *Family Dining*
Kawaihae Road in the heart of Kamuela (885-4377) next door to Parker Ranch Lodge. This family cafe has a real country ambience and ranch-style decor. The menu features a variety of burgers and sandwiches, BBQ ribs, chicken, pasta, Mexican food, and pizza. The food is excellent quality and service is courteous. There is an interesting collection of branding irons from Big Island ranches decorating the walls and a beautiful aquarium with Hawaiian reef fish that will interest youngsters. Open daily for breakfast, lunch, and dinner continuously from 6AM - 9PM, weekends till 10PM. This restaurant earns recognition in this book's **"Best Bets - Top Local Style Restaurants" ratings.**

WAIKOLOA VILLAGE RESTAURANT *American*
Waikoloa Village Golf Course, Waikoloa Village (883-9644). The menu features steaks, fresh island fish, chicken, local favorites, burgers, and special sandwiches. The dining room is bright, open, and airy with pretty golf course views. Open daily for breakfast 7 - 10:30AM, lunch 10:30AM - 5PM, and dinner 5 -9PM. Credit cards.

WAIMEA COFFEE & CO. *Sandwiches*
Located on Highway 19 at the Parker Square Center in Kamuela (885-4472). This small coffee shop offers light fare such as pastries, croissants, bagels, light lunches, sandwiches, soups, salads, desserts and daily specials. They specialize in over 20 varieties of arabica coffee from around the world. Daily beverages include a coffee of the day, espresso, cappuccino, chocolate drinks, fresh juices and more. Open Monday-Saturday 9AM til closing.

YONG'S KAL-BI ★ *Korean*
Located in the Waimea Center, Highway 19, Waimea (885-8440). This small family restaurant features local and Oriental foods with an emphasis on Korean cuisine. The menu lists kal-bi ribs, barbeque beef, Korean chicken, chicken katsu, mandoo (Korean won ton), fish and more. The food is very good with ample portions served plate-lunch style. Clean attractive location, simple decor; eat here or take out. Open daily for breakfast, lunch and dinner, 9:30AM - 9PM.

MODERATE

ARNIE'S *American*
Located at Mauna Kea Resort, Hapuna Golf Course opposite the Hapuna Beach Prince Hotel (882-1261). This is primarily a golf clubhouse restaurant operation serving a light menu of sandwiches, daily specials and snacks plus a standard daily buffet lunch. Open daily 11AM - 4:30PM.

BIG ISLAND STEAK HOUSE *Steaks*
Located in the Kings' Shops Center at Waikoloa Beach Resort across from The Royal Waikoloan Hotel (885-8805). This dining room has decor reflecting the romantic Polynesian image of 1950's movies and nostalgic travel posters from Hawai'i's early days. The menu features fresh Big Island produce, seafood and certified Angus beef. House specials include prime rib, filet mignon, New York steak, top sirloin, Porterhouse steak and bar-b-q Hawaiian-style ribs, plus appetizers like crab cakes, smoked marlin pate and much more. Open nightly for dinner from 5 - 10PM.

BRAVO PIZZA & PASTA *Italian*
68-1845 Waikoloa Road, Waikoloa Highlands Center, Waikoloa Village (883-8181). The extensive menu listing of gourmet pizzas and specialty toppings includes things like lemon-pepper chicken, BBQ chicken, Hawaiian style, Mexican style, fresh veggie-tomato and many others. The menu also features pasta dishes, salads, "Hot Hat" filled sandwiches and more. Open Mon-Sat 11AM - 10PM, Sun 12 Noon - 9PM.

BREE GARDEN *Italian*
Located just off Highway 19 on the east side of Waimea on Kinohou Street (885-8849). This restaurant recently reopened under the original owner-chef after being closed for a couple of years. Dinner selections include veal scallopini, chicken breast Florentina, chicken with risotto, scampi, island fish Adriatic-style, pasta, soups and salads. The dining room retains the same casual elegance and contemporary decor as before. Open daily except Tuesday for lunch 11AM - 2:30PM, dinner 4:30 - 9:30PM.

EDELWEISS ★ *Continental/International*
Highway 19, Kawaihae Road, Kamuela (885-6800). This delightful chalet-like village inn fits in with the cool upcountry ranch climate of Kamuela and features varied continental-international cuisine with European accents. Specialties include such items as weinerschnitzel, Black Forest chicken, venison ragu, veal, German sausage plates, several varieties of fresh island seafood and other creative dishes. Master Chef Hans-Peter Hager ensures a pleasant dining experience. The service is excellent as is the food. Open Tuesday through Saturday only for lunch 11:30AM - 2PM, and dinner from 5PM. No reservations. Credit cards. This restaurant earns recognition in this book's **The Big Island's Best and "Best Bets - Top Restaurants with a Casual Atmosphere" ratings.**

GRAND PALACE ★ *Chinese*
Located in King's Shops Center at Waikoloa Beach Resort across from the Royal Waikoloan Hotel (885-6668). This is a bright, clean Chinese dining room with formal table settings, fine Chinese artwork decor and white tablecloths. The menu is perhaps the Big Island's most extensive offering of Chinese cuisine, listing 151 separate items of primarily Cantonese selections. There are some varied Chinese exotics thrown in for good measure; things like drunken chicken and prawns, five spiced octopus, cold jelly fish, scalded shrimp, and traditionals like Peking duck, fish, crab, abalone, beef, pork and vegetable sihes. Open daily for lunch and dinner, 11AM-9:30PM.

HAMA YU JAPANESE RESTAURANT *Japanese*
Located in Kings' Shops Center at Waikoloa Beach Resort across from the Royal Waikoloan Hotel (885-6333). This small restaurant features bright contemporary Japanese decor. The menu includes such traditional Japanese favorites as teriyaki beef, pork tonkatsu, broiled fish, shrimp, donburi, noodles and more. Open daily for lunch 11:30AM - 2PM, dinner 5:30 - 9PM.

HANG TEN *Sandwiches*
Hilton Waikoloa Village, Kohala Coast (885-1234). This casual open-air deck eatery sits next to the famed dolphin lagoons where diners can watch the dolphins frolic and play. This restaurant offers lunch only and with a menu of sandwiches, burgers, hot dogs, chili, salads and desserts. The bar also serves up exotic drinks. Open daily for lunch continuously, 10:30AM - 5:30PM.

HIGHLANDS RESTAURANT *American*
68-1845 Waikoloa Road, in the Waikoloa Highlands Shopping Center, Waikoloa Village (883-8132). This grill-bar room is arranged semi-circle fashion with an open kitchen grill and dining area on one side and a bar/lounge and dance floor on the other. The bar features TV sports and live music for dancers. The lunch menu features varied sandwiches, burgers, chili, fresh island fish and more. Dinner items include New York steak, chicken breast, pork medallions, fresh catch, lime-tequila lamb chops, shrimp scampi and beef tenderloin. During the day, there are nice golf course views. Open daily for lunch 11AM - 2PM, dinner 5 - 9PM.

ISLAND BISTRO   *Continental/International*
Highway 19, Kawaihae Road, Waimea (885-1222). This small roadside restaurant is directly in front of the Kamuela Inn and across the road from the better known Edelweiss Restaurant. This is a small intimate room with a trendy-style open-kitchen. The dinner menu features a variety of appetizers, soups and salads and entrees such as pork tenderloin char siu, herb roasted lamb, Thai grilled chicken, wok-seared beef tenderloin, rib steak, fresh island fish, nori sautee salmon, scampi caribi, seafood linguine and pasta. The lunch menu features soups, salads, varied sandwiches, burgers and daily specials. Open Mon-Fri for lunch 11:30AM - 1:30PM, and dinner nightly 5:30 - 9:30PM

KAMUELA PROVISION COMPANY ★   *Continental/International*
Hilton Waikoloa Village, Kohala Coast (885-1234). This is a beautiful open air restaurant situated on a bluff overlooking the Kohala Coast surf and shoreline. The decor is provincial Thailand-Malaysian influenced with greenery, artwork, and
multi-leveled rooms much like a Thai-Malaysian house. Ceiling fans add a touch of relaxing ambiance. The menu is very creative featuring seafood, steaks, pasta, fresh island fish, exotic desserts and tropical ice creams and sherbets. Open nightly for dinner 5:30 - 10:30 PM. Credit cards.

MORELLI'S PIZZA ★   *Italian*
Parker Ranch Center Mall, Waimea (885-6100). This small pizza parlor serves up a variety of pizza including a Parker Ranch Special, Morelli's Deluxe or create your own. The menu also features oven-baked sandwiches and salads. Eat in or take out. Open daily Monday-Saturday 10AM - 8PM, Sunday 11AM - 7PM. Based on the judging of my two daughters, completely impartial when it comes to pizza, this restaurant earns special recognition for its best island pizza in this book's **"Best Bets - Top Local Style Restaurants" ratings.**

OCEAN BAR & GRILL   *American*
Located poolside at the Sheraton Orchid Mauna Lani Hotel (885-2000) at Mauna Lani Resort on the Kohala Coast. This open-air cafe offers daily breakfast, lunch and snacks from early morning until late afternoon. The menu features grilled American favorites, sandwiches, pasta, pizza, salads and a special childrens' menu. The daily breakfast buffet is especially pleasant if its not too windy.

OCEAN GRILL   *Continental/International*
Mauna Lani Bay Hotel, Kohala Coast (885-6622). This oceanside cafe provides a bright breezy location between the hotel pool and the beach. The menu offers snacks and light fare of sandwiches, seafood specials, salads and more. Open daily 10AM - 6PM.

ORCHID CAFE   *Family Dining*
Hilton Waikoloa Village, Kohala Coast (885-1234). This hotel coffee shop has a pleasant poolside setting surrounded by coconut trees. Colorful parrots squawk and talk while you enjoy a meal or snack under parasol-covered tables or under roof. The breakfast menu is quite traditional while lunch features specials like soups, salads, a variety of sandwiches, pasta and pizza. Open daily for breakfast and lunch continuously from 6:30AM - 3:30PM. Credit cards.

ROYAL TERRACE ★ *Continental/International*
Royal Waikoloan Hotel, Waikoloa (885-6789). This room has lovely views overlooking the gardens, the beach area and fishponds and glorious evening sunsets over Anaehoomalu Bay. The dinner menu features continental-international cuisine including a wide variety of appetizers, salads, soups and specials such as steaks, lamb, seafood, chicken, ribs, pasta and more. The daily morning buffet features a wide selection of breakfast entrees as well. Open daily for breakfast 6:30-11AM, lunch 11AM-2PM, dinner 5:30-10PM

SU'S THAI KITCHEN *Thai Cuisine*
Parker Ranch Shopping Center, Kamuela (885-8688). This small shopping center cafe features exotic spicy Thai cuisine but also has a wide selection of American, Japanese and Chinese items as well. Thai selections include seafood, chicken, beef and pork prepared in several ways plus daily specials and curry-of-the-day. There are also special Thai soups, salads, noodles and rice dishes. Open daily, for breakfast-lunch-dinner, 7AM - 9PM.

THE 19TH. HOLE *Sandwiches/light fare*
Located at the Mauna Kea Beach Golf Course Clubhouse, Mauna Kea Beach Hotel, Kohala Coast (882-7222). This restaurant provides relaxing country club privacy and a menu of light luncheon specials including sandwiches, salads, sushi, saimin and more. Open daily 11AM - 4:30PM.

TRES HOMBRES BEACH GRILL *Mexican*
Kawaihae Shopping Center, Kawaihae (882-1031). The menu is basically Mexican with selections such as tacos, enchiladas, quesadillas, fajitas, tostadas, burritos and other entrees like fresh island fish, chicken and more. Open for lunch and dinner continuously Sun-Thurs 11:30AM - 9PM, Fri-Sat 11:30AM - 10PM. Credit cards.

WAIKOLOA BEACH GRILL *Continental/International*
Located in the Waikoloa Beach Golf Course Clubhouse at Waikoloa Resort on the Kohala Coast (885-6131). The menu features a variety of appetizers, salads and sandwiches for lunch and steaks, chicken and seafood for dinner entrees. The menu also has a nice selection of wines. There is attractive contemporary decor and fairway views lend a nice accent. Golfers enjoy a continental breakfast from 7AM with lunch served daily 9:30AM - 4:30PM and dinner 5:30 - 10PM.

EXPENSIVE

BATIK ★ *Continental/International*
Mauna Kea Beach Hotel, Kohala Coast (882-7222). This is the hotel's signature fine dining room and is perhaps the best known of Mauna Kea's award-winning restaurants. The menu features European cuisine inspired by specialties from Provence with many classic selections. A full range of appetizers, soups, and salads is available as well as an extensive wine list. The ambiance, service, and dining experience are superb. Open daily for dinner, 7-10 PM. Credit cards. This restaurant earns recognition in this book's **"Best Bets - Top Restaurants"** **ratings.**

BAY TERRACE ★ *Continental/International*
Mauna Lani Bay Hotel, Kohala Coast (885-6622). This open-air garden terrace restaurant provides a delightful dining atmosphere. The a la carte dinner menu ranges from Continental to International selections of beef, fresh island fish, seafood, chicken, lamb, and many specialties. The daily lunch buffet is a lavish affair with a wide selection of salads, appetizers, hot and cold entrees, and desserts. The Sunday buffet is especially nice, and even more sumptuous, and includes many Japanese and Oriental specialties. The Friday and Saturday night seafood buffet is excellent with superb entrees, salads and dessert bar. Open daily for breakfast 6 - 11AM, lunch 11 - 2PM, dinner 6 - 9:30PM. Reservations recommended. Credit cards. This restaurant earns double recognition in this book's **"Best Bets - Top Restaurants"** and **"Best Bets - Best Buffets" ratings.**

BISTRO *Continental/International*
Hapuna Beach Prince Hotel, Kohala Coast (880-1111). This is the hotel's fine dining room with an elegant and relaxed setting. The menu features primarily Continental-International selections with an extensive wine list.

CANOE HOUSE ★ *Hawaii/Pacific Regional Cuisine*
Mauna Lani Bay Hotel, Kohala Coast, (885-6622). This pleasant dining room specializes in regional Pacific Rim cuisine in a beachside open air setting. The food is wonderfully diverse, the service is superb and the Hawaiian-contemporary music is relaxing. The dinner menu features exotic pupus (appetizers) such as sashimi and poke, baby back ribs, Chinese wontons, eand eggplant curry. Entrees include fresh seared mahimahi, hibachi salmon, pesto seared scallops, grilled marinated ono, New Zealand lamb chops, Thai seafood curry. Open for lunch daily, 11AM - 5PM; dinner nightly, 5 - 9PM. Reservations suggested; credit cards. This restaurant earns recognition in this book's **"Best Bets - Top Restaurants with a Casual Atmosphere" ratings.**

COAST GRILLE ★ *Hawaii/Pacific Regional Cuisine*
Hapuna Beach Prince Hotel, Kohala Coast (880-1111). This spacious dining room overlooks the north end of Hapuna Beach and the whale-shaped hotel pool and offers indoor-outdoor alfresco dining. The menu offers a wide selection of fresh island and imported seafood plus prime cuts of lamb, veal and beef. The emphasis is on Hawaii/Pacific Regional cookery. There is also an oyster bar with fresh oysters and assorted shellfish selections. All selections are exquisitely prepared and presented. There is an extensive wine list and sumptuous desserts as well. Open nightly for dinner only, 6:30-9:30PM. This restaurant earns recognition in this book's **"Best Bets - Top Restaurants with a Casual Atmosphere" ratings.**

DONATONI'S *Italian*
Hilton Waikoloa Village, Kohala Coast (885-1234). This Italian restaurant features fine northern Italian cuisine and offers an extensive menu of pastas, veal, seafood, chicken and more plus Italian desserts, cappuccino and international coffees. Open nightly for dinner only, 6 - 10PM with live music. Reservations suggested; credit cards.

HAKONE *Japanese*
Hapuna Beach Prince Hotel, Kohala Coast (880-1111). This fine dining restaurant features authentic Japanese cuisine in a tranquil and relaxed setting. The spacious dining room features contemporary furnishings with Japanese accents in decor and a pleasant ambiance. Specialty dishes include shabu shabu, sukiyaki and kaiseki dinners. There is also a sushi bar with an extensive selection. Dinner selections are served with miso soup, rice and various Japanese pickled vegetables. While the food is of an excellent nature, the portions are unduly small for the price paid. Open for dinner only, Friday-Tuesday, 6:30-9:30PM.

IMARI ★ *Japanese*
Hilton Waikoloa Village, Kohala Coast (885-1234). A visit to this distinctive Japanese restaurant allows you to step into the quiet serenity of old Japan. Reflecting ponds with koi carp swimming along, splashing waterfalls, and an accent of gentle Japanese music put you into a relaxing mood. The menu is traditional Japanese with sushi (rice rolls) and sashimi (raw fish) among a number of appetizers followed by varied specials of tempura, sukiyaki, shabushabu, teriyaki and several more creative Japanese dishes. For those wanting a little more flair, try the teppanyaki tables where gourmet chefs prepare your meal on cooking tables right in front of you. They do wonders with chicken, steak, shrimp, and all manner of traditional Japanese cuisine. Open nightly for dinner only 6 - 10PM. Reservations suggested, casual dress. Credit cards. This restaurant earns recognition in this book's **"Best Bets - Top Restaurants with a Casual Atmosphere"** ratings.

MERRIMAN'S ★ *Hawaii/Pacific Regional Cuisine*
Opelo Plaza, Route 19, Kamuela, 885-6822. Since its opening three years ago, this restaurant has won wide acclaim for fine dining specializing in fresh Big Island products expertly prepared. Chef Peter Merriman has established a reputation for excellence. The menu features Parker Ranch prime rib (house special), fresh island fish, cioppino, steaks, veal, Kahua Ranch lamb, chicken and daily specials. An interesting selection of appetizers, soups, salads and fancy desserts

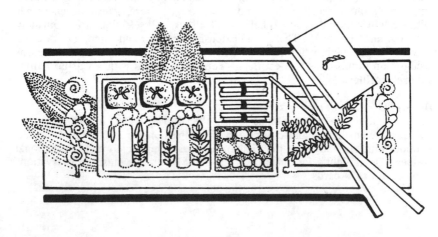

rounds out a fine menu. Merriman's is open for lunch Monday-Friday, 11:30AM -1:30PM; dinner nightly 5:30 - 9PM; Sunday brunch 10:30AM - 1:30PM. Reservations suggested; credit cards. This restaurant earns recognition in this book's **"Best Bets - Top Restaurants with a Casual Atmosphere" ratings.**

OCEAN TERRACE *Continental/International*
Hapuna Beach Prince Hotel, Kohala Coast (880-1111). This is the hotel's coffee shop and features a daily breakfast buffet and extensive a la carte Continental menu with many popular local specials plus a full Japanese-style breakfast. Open for breakfast daily 6:30-11AM.

PALM TERRACE *Buffet*
Hilton Waikoloa Village, Kohala Coast (885-1234). This dining room specializes in buffet dining for breakfast and dinner with the main attraction the varied international buffets for dinner. It is a lovely pastel peach-pink colored room with lots of greenery and lovely pool and waterfalls with swans floating about. The varied buffet menus change daily and feature Paniolo Barbeque, South of the Border, Chinese cuisine, Polynesian cuisine or an All American Prime Rib buffet. There is also an ala carte menu. Open daily for breakfast 6 - 11AM and dinner 5 - 9:30PM. Credit cards.

ROY'S WAIKOLOA BAR & GRILL *Hawaii/Pacific Regional*
Located at the Waikoloa Beach Resort, Kings' Shops Center (885-4321). This is the newest (opened summer, 1996) of Chef Roy Yamaguchi's Hawai'i restaurants and the first Big Island outlet. The cuisine is similar to the trendy local regional cuisine and culinary approach of his restaurants in Hawai'i and internationally. The emphasis is on combining fresh local products with equally fresh creative cookery methods. The menu features such items as mac nut crusted mahimahi, sesame seared opakapaka, lemongrass shutome & blackened ahi, Mongolian lamb, garlic herb chicken and many other creative dishes. Open for lunch and dinner daily. Check for specific hours.

THE CAFE *Hawaii/Pacific Regional Cuisine*
Located at the Sheraton Orchid Mauna Lani Hotel (885-2000) at Mauna Lani Resort on the Kohala Coast. This is a casual open-air terrace dining room offering indoor or outdoor seating. The menu features Pacific Rim specialties and American favorites including special fitness cuisine and childrens' selections. The Sunday Brunch is very special and features a wide variety of Hawaiian regional cuisine utilizing Big Island seafood and garden produce. Open from early morning until late.

THE DINING ROOM *Hawaii/Pacific Regional*
Located at the Sheraton Orchid Mauna Lani Hotel (885-2000) at Mauna Lani Resort on the Kohala Coast. This is the hotel's signature fine dining room and has lovely classical Continental decor. In contrast to its ambiance, the menu emphasis is on the trendy Hawaiian regional cuisine utilizing the best of Big Island fresh products. The menu changes monthly to take advantage of indigenous seasonal products. Selections include creative appetizers like ahi tartare, Ahualoa feta cheese and lamb carpaccio, kiawe smoked salmon; entrees include charbroiled onaga snapper, Lanai venison and other creative regional fare.

The restaurant features elegant indoor dining or optional casual open-air terrace dining. Open for dinner only, Tuesday-Saturday, 6:30-9:30PM. Jackets for gentlemen and reservations required; credit cards.

THE GALLERY ★ *Continental/International*
Located at the Golf Course Clubhouse, Mauna Lani Resort (885-7777). This award-winning dining room has relocated to the resort's golf course clubhouse. The menu features varied continental selections plus steaks, fresh island fish and seafood and pasta selections in elegant contemporary classic decor. The food is superb and service attentive. Open for lunch daily 11AM-3PM, dinner We-Sat only 5:30-9PM. Reservations recommended; credit cards. This restaurant earns recognition in this book's **"Best Bets - Top Restaurants' rating."**

THE GRILL ★ *Continental/Hawaii Regional*
Located at the Sheraton Orchid Mauna Lani Hotel (885-2000) at Mauna Lani Resort on the Kohala Coast. This room has the atmosphere of a plush manor house club room and offers varied Continental/Hawaiian regional cuisine. Menu selections include fresh pastas and appetizers, fresh island fish, steak, lamb, veal, Maine lobster, Hawaiian Fisherman's Stew and more. Service, presentation and quality are superb. Live dinner music featured. Open nightly for dinner 6 - 9PM. Reservations suggested. Credit cards.

THE PAVILION ★ *Continental/International*
Mauna Kea Beach Hotel, Kohala (882-7222). This award-winning hotel dining room offers a splendid varied menu each evening featuring an international array of gourmet Mediterranean cuisine with Italian accents. Menu selections include a wide range of creative dishes. A complete wine selection compliments the gourmet fare. Pleasant live dinner music with dancing lends a sophisticated yet relaxed manner to an evening's entertainment. Open daily for breakfast, 6:30 - 11AM, dinner 6:30 - 9:00PM. Credit cards. This restaurant earns recognition in this book's **"Best Bets - Top Restaurants"** ratings.

THE TERRACE ★ *Continental/International*
Mauna Kea Beach Hotel, Kohala Coast (882-7222). This is the home of the Mauna Kea's popular daily buffet luncheon, widely acclaimed as the finest throughout Hawai'i. It has a variety of salads, soups, fruits, hot and cold entrees, and a wide selection of incredible desserts. A la carte lunch sandwiches and other specialties are also available. It also has a very pleasant daily buffet breakfast. Open daily for breakfast 7 - 10AM, lunch 12 - 2:30PM. Credit cards. This buffet dining room earns recognition in this book's **"Best Bets - Best Buffets"** ratings.

TIARE ROOM ★ *Continental/International*
Royal Waikoloan Hotel, Waikoloa (885-6789). The contemporary elegant decor of this lovely dining room make for a most pleasant ambiance. The menu features a full offering of creative appetizers, soups and salads. Entrees are offered with continental/international accents and include fresh island fish, Pacific salmon, lobster, beef tenderloin, New York steak, veal, lamb, venison, chicken and several types of pasta. The service is attentive and pleasant. There is an extensive wine list. Open for dinner only, 6 - 9:30PM, closed Sun. and Wed. evenings. Casual evening attire; reservations suggested; credit cards. This restaurant earns recognition in this book's **"Best Bets - Top Restaurants"** ratings.

HILO

INTRODUCTION

Dining out in Hilo has always been something of an adventure. For a long time, Hilo had few worthy dining out options, diners having to choose from a handful of local ethnic restaurants such as a chop suey house, saimin noodle shop or two, a coffee shop, a plate lunch shop or a simple drive-in. Luckily, for both Hilo residents and visitors alike, the dining out options have diversified and improved considerably of late. The Hilo area now offers a wide selection of ethnic cuisines in a variety of local-style and trendy contemporary-style cafes and restaurants for every budget. There is something of a renaissance going on in downtown Hilo what with old buildings being renovated and restored and many of the new businesses relocating in the once decrepit spaces are, fortunately, restaurants. It's all part of the new image being created in downtown Hilo. While there is much variety in quality, price and service, the genuinely good restaurants are marked with a ★ indicating good value, good food and good service.

While Hilo may not yet be quite ready to proclaim itself the gourmet cuisine capital of the Pacific, it has made some positive strides in providing residents and visitors some enjoyable dining experiences.

INEXPENSIVE

ARIRANG LUNCH KOREAN BAR-B-Q   *Korean*
165 E. Kawili Street, across from Hawai'i Community College campus (969-7151). The menu features Korean bar-b-q, plate lunches, spicy soups and special burgers. The best items are bulgogi (charbroiled lean beef), kal-bi ribs, yukejang spicy soup, and bulgogi kimchee burger (hot!). The menu has many more items plus daily steam table buffet selections. Open Monday-Friday 9AM - 8PM, Saturday 10:30AM - 8PM, closed Sunday.

BEAR'S COFFEE   *Sandwiches*
106 Keawe St., downtown Hilo (935-0708). This small deli shop and espresso cafe features a variety of salads, sandwiches, individual pizza, and other light lunch specials. A full range of international coffees, espresso and pastries are also mainstays. Sidewalk tables are nice, however, a real negative is the restroom which is accessible only by walking through the middle of the kitchen where food is prepared. A recent visit revealed that patrons and others will stop in mid-kitchen and "chat" with cooks preparing food while leaning against counters and over food-preparation areas. In spite of these undesirable characteristics, it remains a popular place with locals. You be the judge. Open Mon-Fri 7AM - 5PM, Sat 8AM - 5PM. Closed Sunday.

CAFE ICHIBAN & DELI   *Japanese/American*
413 Kilauea Avenue (969-1454). The deli counter features local-style hot plate lunches and bentos to go while the restaurant side features local-style Japanese and American menu selections. Open Tuesday-Saturday 7AM - 2PM for breakfast and lunch, 5 - 8:30PM for dinner. Closed Sunday and Monday.

CAFE PARADISE   *Sandwiches/Snacks*
1438 Kilauea Avenue (935-6667), next to Tyke's Laundromat, shares the same facility as Scruffles Restaurant. This is the snack shop/bakery operation of the restaurant. They feature a day-long menu of breakfast selections, sandwiches, soups and salads and pastries from the bakery. Take-outs available. Open 6AM -7:30PM.

CANOES CAFE ★   *Sandwiches/Snacks*
308 Kamehameha Avenue, in the S. Hata Building, downtown Hilo (961-0301). This deli occupies the ground floor Atrium Court area of this restored Hilo landmark building and features gourmet fresh-made sandwiches, soups, salads, pastries, desserts, espresso coffees and local specials like somen salad, daily stew, Chinese chicken salad and others. The Atrium Court provides a pleasant atmosphere with tables for a relaxing coffee break or lunch. Open Mon-Sat 8:30am-4:30pm, Sun. 9AM-8PM.

CHENG'S CHOP SUEY HOUSE ★   *Chinese*
777 Kilauea Ave. in the Kaiko'o Mall (935-3404). An extensive Cantonese menu with a full selection of soups, chop suey, noodles, seafood, pork, beef, chicken, duck, and egg dishes. Specialties include egg flower soup, cake noodles, abalone, lup chong sausage, chicken with ginger, pineapple duck, and combination plates. The won ton min (noodle soup) is excellent. There are only 10 tables and it can get busy at peak lunch and dinner hours. Decor is simple with generally clean surroundings. They provide good food at very reasonable cost. Open daily 10AM - 12PM, Fri. 10AM - 2AM, Sun. 10AM - 3PM.

DICK'S COFFEE HOUSE   *Coffee Shop*
In the Prince Kuhio Shopping Plaza (959-4401). A family restaurant featuring beef, chicken, and fish in a variety of complete coffee shop meals. Soup and sandwich items, light meals also. Both food and service are below average. Popular with local folks. Open daily for breakfast, lunch and dinner. Mon-Fri 7AM - 9PM, Sat-Sun 7AM - 5PM.

DON'S GRILL ★   *Family Dining*
485 Hinano Street, Hilo (935-9099). Since its opening a few years ago, this pleasant family restaurant has proven to be one of Hilo's consistently best inexpensive dining out options. The menu features beef, chicken, pork chops, fish, sandwiches, burgers, soups and salads, daily specials and many local favorites. The house specialty is an excellent rotisseried chicken.   And should you have to wait in line awhile, its well worth it. Open daily for lunch and dinner Tues-Thurs 10:30AM - 9PM, Fri-Sun 10AM - 10PM, closed Mon. Credit cards. The clean facilities, fast courteous service, generally great food and very reasonable prices have continuously earned this restaurant a spot in this book's **THE BIG ISLAND'S BEST** for family restaurants and "Best Bets - Top Local Style Restaurants" ratings.

DOTTY'S COFFEE SHOP ★   *Filipino*
2100 Kanoelehua Avenue, in the Puainako Town Center (959-6477). The daily dinner menu offers several specials including one or two Filipino dishes. Homemade cornbread, banana muffins and fruit cream pies are delicious! Generally

good food at reasonable prices. The dining room expanded into an empty space and there is now more room for smoking/non-smoking areas. Open Mon-Sat for breakfast-lunch 7AM - 2PM, dinner 5 - 8PM, Sun 7AM - 1:30PM and 5 - 9PM. Credit cards.

FREDDY'S RESTAURANT   *Family Dining*
Corner of Manono and Piilani Streets, opposite the Civic Auditorium in Hilo, (935-1108). The menu features such items as teriyaki beef and chicken, beef and noodles, beef stew, island fish, plate lunches, burgers, sandwiches plus daily specials. Their general store-deli next door offers a variety of fresh made deli-style sandwiches and other goodies. There is sit down ala carte dining on one side of the restaurant and plate lunch/fast food dining on the other side with a buffet hot table of varied selections for take outs. The fast-food/take-out room is open Mon-Sat 6:30AM - 9:30PM, Sun 7AM - 9PM; dining room is open Mon-Sat 10AM - 9PM, Sun 7AM - 9PM.

HIRO'S PLACE   *Japanese*
50 E. Puainako (959-6665) in the KTA Supermarket Center. This is a local fast-food operation serving up Oriental-American specialties including teriyaki beef, chicken, fish, plate lunches, sandwiches, sushi rice, noodles, bentos and more. Tables on walkway; eat here or take out. Open daily for breakfast and lunch, 6AM - 5PM.

HUKILAU RESTAURANT ★   *Seafood*
136 Banyan Way, in the Hilo Seaside Hotel off Banyan Drive (935-4222). This local style family restaurant specializes in a complete line of seafood entrees for lunch and dinner. They usually have three or four fresh island fish entrees, along with crab, lobster, scallops, calamari steak, salmon, prawns and more. It's also about the only restaurant on the Big Island with frog legs on its menu. In addition, the menu lists traditionals like prime rib roast, steaks, fried chicken, pork chops, lamb and more. The place is especially popular at lunchtime with local folks. The decor is simple but there is lots of good food and friendly service at reasonable prices. All dinners include soup, salad bar and dessert. Open for breakfast, lunch, and dinner, Mon-Sat 7AM - 8:30PM, Sunday 7AM - 1PM. This restaurants earns recognition in this book's **"Best Bets - Top Local Style Restaurants ratings.**

JIMMY'S DRIVE INN ★   *Family Dining*
362 Kinoole St. (935-5571). Despite its name, this popular restaurant features sit-down dining service and does not have traditional drive-in service. Specializing in Hawaiian cuisine but also offering Japanese, Korean, and American dishes as well. Open breakfast, lunch, dinner Mon-Sat 8 AM - 9:30 PM.

JOY'S PLACE   *Sandwiches/snacks*
1261 Kilauea Avenue in the Hilo Shopping Center (961-6852). This small cafe is next door to Lanky's Bakery. The cafe specializes in local fast food favorites including a special "Joy Burger," sandwiches and burgers, loco moco, stew, plate lunches and more. Open daily 6AM until closing.

KAY'S LUNCH CENTER ★ *Korean*
684 Kilauea Avenue, across from Kaiko'o Mall (968-1776). This sit-down dining spot also provides plate/box lunches to take out. This is a real local-style restaurant featuring Korean cuisine including BBQ beef, short ribs, and the original crispy Korean chicken. Homemade cream cheese pies for dessert are wonderful. The decor and ambiance here are simple, nothing fancy, nothing glitzy. Despite its name, Kay's is open for breakfast, lunch, and dinner Tues-Fri 6 AM -2PM and 5 PM - til closing, Sat-Sun 5AM - 2PM and 5PM - til closing. Closed Mon. The generous servings of well-prepared food and equally reasonable prices have continuously earned this restaurant a spot in this book's **BEST OF THE BIG ISLAND and "Best Bets - Top Local Style Restaurants ratings.**

KEN'S HOUSE OF PANCAKES ★ *American*
1730 Kamehameha Avenue (935-8711) at the intersection of Kam Avenue and Banyan Drives near Hilo's hotel row. The menu features all types of pancakes and breakfast items in addition to a full range of American foods, sandwiches, and some local-style dishes. Popular with visitors as well as locals because it is open 24 hours a day, every day of the year, the only 24-hour restaurant in Hilo.

KIMO'S ONO HAWAIIAN FOOD ★ *Hawaii/Pacific Regional Cuisine*
806 Kilauea Avenue, across from Kaiko'o Mall (935-3111). This tiny shop features, just as their name says, "ono" (Hawaiian for delicious!) authentic Hawaiian food. The menu features fresh made daily specials and a regular menu of plate lunches with laulau, kalua pig, lomi salmon, chicken luau, haupia (coconut) pudding and more. You could spend the usual $45-50 or so per person for a fancy hotel luau and not get anywhere near the quality of this Hawaiian food. It's without a doubt the best Hawaiian food anywhere on the island of Hawai'i. The shop is so small inside there are no tables only a couple of counters with stools. They will provide everything for your own take out luau. Excellent! Open Monday-Saturday for lunch 10AM -2PM, dinner 5 - 8PM, Sunday lunch only 11AM - 3PM. This small diner earns recognition in this book's **"Best Bets - Top Local Style Restaurants"** ratings.

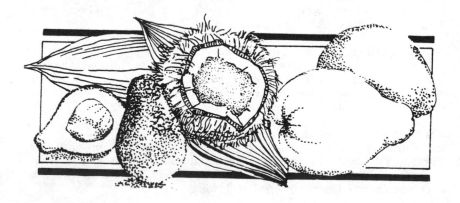

KK TEI RESTAURANT   *Japanese*
1150 Kamehameha Avenue (961-3791) across from Naniloa Golf Course. This is a Japanese-American theme restaurant with private dining rooms for Japanese style dining, low tables and cushions on the floor rather than chairs. General dining room also. The menu features steaks, shrimp tempura, ahi (tuna), and oxtail soup plus many Japanese specialties. The restaurant has a Karaoke sing-along bar now. Reservations recommended. Open Mon-Sat for lunch 11AM - 2PM and dinner 5 - 9PM. Credit cards.

KOREANA RESTAURANT   *Korean*
200 Kanoelehua Avenue (961-4983) in the Waiakea Square Shopping Center. This small restaurant offers a full menu of Korean cuisine including kal-bi ribs, Korean spicy chicken, BBQ beef, and more. Korean food tends toward the hot spicy side and those with that preference will enjoy trying these dishes. Open daily for lunch 10:30AM - 2:30PM, dinner 5 - 10PM. Credit cards.

KOW'S DELI & CHINESE RESTAURANT ★   *Chinese*
87 W. Kawailani St. (959-3766) open Mon.-Sat. 10AM - 10PM, Sunday 10AM - 9PM, credit cards. Featuring Cantonese style food, Kow's serves up a wide range of delectable items such as beef broccoli, chicken and Chinese peas, sweet and sour shrimp, won ton, cake noodles, and more. Everything is good. Order from the menu board or select from the buffet counter. This restaurant earns recognition in this book's **"Best Bets - Top Local Style Restaurants" ratings.**

KUHIO GRILLE *Family Dining*
Located at the back of the Prince Kuhio Shopping Plaza on Kanoelehua Avenue (959-2336). This small eatery features a local-style menu of short orders, plate lunch items and light meals. Menu items include corned beef hash, teriyaki beef, chili, homemade biscuits, burgers, sandwiches and daily plate lunch specials and bento takeouts. Open Mon-Fri 5AM - 8PM, Sat-Sun 5AM - 2PM.

LEUNG'S CHOP SUEY HOUSE ★   *Chinese*
530 E. Lanikaula St. (935-4066) at the intersection of Kanoelehua Avenue. This small eat-in/take out Chinese kitchen is popular with folks working in the nearby industrial area of Hilo. A range of Cantonese a la carte dishes and a buffet counter to select your own plate lunch-dinner are available. Cake noodles are a must! Good quality food at good prices in a not too fancy place. Open daily except Tuesday, 9AM - 8:30PM. This restaurant earns recognition in this book's **"Best Bets - Top Local Style Restaurants" ratings.**

LOW INTERNATIONAL FOOD   *Continental/International*
Corner of Kilauea and Ponohawai Streets (969-6652). This place is operated by the Low family which runs Sun Sun Lau Chop Sui House, one of Hilo's better known Chinese restaurants. This is basically a fast-food counter operation with a varied menu of Chinese, Korean, and local-style favorite plate lunches, sandwiches, and specials. Chicken tonkatsu, teriyaki beef, and burgers are popular items here. You can eat here - several tables are available on the lanai area - or take out. They also bake a line of unusual breads such as sweet potato, taro, pumpkin, passion fruit, mango, coconut, banana, guava and others. Open daily 9AM - 8PM, except closed Wednesday.

MIYO'S ★ *Japanese*
400 Hualani Street (935-2273) in the Waiakea Villas shops complex. This inexpensive family-style restaurant features excellent Japanese cuisine. Sample selections include sesame chicken, tonkatsu, tempura, teriyaki beef, fish, noodles, and donburi soups. The upstairs location (makes for nice views) overlooks lovely Waiakea Fish Pond and Wailoa Park. Open daily except Sunday, lunch 11AM - 2PM, dinner 5:30 - 8:30PM. No credit cards.

MR. RAHMEN *Filipino*
714 Kilauea Avenue, Kaiko'o Mall, Hilo, (934-0428). This small lunch counter dining room features a self-proclaimed "The Best Noodle in Town." The menu selections are mostly Filipino specials like pork & peas, penakbet, pork adobo, pork blood (isn't there a better name for this dish?) and others plus a variety of noodle dishes like yakisoba, gyoza, shumai, saimin and donburi soup bowls. Open for lunch and dinner, Mon-Thurs 10AM - 8PM, Fri-Sat 10AM - 12 midnight.

MUN CHEONG LAU *Chinese*
172 Kilauea Avenue (935-3040) in downtown Hilo. This Chinese eatery provides basic Cantonese-style food in something less than sparkling surroundings. But if less than elegant decor is no problem, you'll find good reasonably priced food here. The menu offers a variety of beef, chicken, duck, pork, and seafood dishes or one can order combination plates. Open daily 10:30AM - 9:30PM.

NANI MAU GARDEN RESTAURANT ★ *American*
421 Makalika Street (959-3541) just south of town off Volcano Highway #11. This eatery is part of the Nani Mau Gardens floral/botanical gardens attraction. The dinner menu features various appetizers and local-style regional specials such as hibachi steak and chicken, paniolo pork chops and fresh island fish and several garden special entree plates. Lunch is buffet style local specials and ala carte dinner is served in the Orchid Pavilion. The Sunday brunch features a variety of breakfast and luncheon specials including Hawaiian, Chinese, Japanese and other regional dishes. Open daily for lunch only, 11AM-2PM, dinner Friday-Saturday only 5-10PM, Sunday brunch 10AM -2PM.

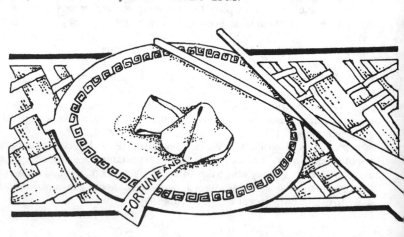

NEW CHINA RESTAURANT ★ *Chinese*
510 Kilauea Avenue (961-5677) next to Hawai'i Hardware Company. The menu features Cantonese and Hong Kong-style cuisine with a wide selection of beef, pork, chicken, duck, seafood, and noodle dishes. They feature some interesting special platters like oyster with ginger and onion, pork chop Hong Kong style, stuffed clams, fresh scallop and chicken along with unusuals like abalone soup, lemon chicken, squid with green pepper and black beans, and lots more to tempt your exotic palate. Try the pot stickers (small appetizer-like fried cakes stuffed with meat filling). You'll find good food at reasonable prices here. This is a very clean, bright restaurant with simple pleasant decor. Open daily 10AM - 10PM.

NORI'S SAIMIN ★ *Japanese*
688 Kinoole St. (935-9133) across from the Hilo Lanes bowling alley. This Japanese-American noodle shop promotes itself as having "the best saimin in town." Granted they do have great saimin noodle dishes and other oriental specialties, but *the* best?, you'll have to decide for yourself. They also have Bento box lunches as well as rare chocolate mochi, a rice cake dessert. The varied hours are a little confusing however: Sun 5 - 12PM, Mon-Thu 10:30AM - 2PM and 4 -12PM, Fri 10:30AM - 2PM and 4PM - 1AM, Sat 5PM - 1AM. This restaurant earns recognition in this book's **"Best Bets - Top Local Style Restaurants" ratings.**

PANDA EXPRESS *Chinese*
Kanoelehua Avenue, in Prince Kuhio Plaza (959-1277). This national chain outlet features Mandarin-style Chinese cuisine with a menu of varied buffet selections. Specials include such exotic selections as lemon chicken, Szechwan tofu, Szechwan shredded pork, beef and green peppers, spicy chicken and more. Open Mon-Fri 9AM - 9PM, Sat 9AM - 5:30PM, Sun 10AM - 5PM.

PARAMOUNT GRILL ★ *Family Dining*
777 Kilauea Avenue, Kaiko'o Mall (935-7756). This local-style eatery, after several relocations the past few years, has finally found a home for its self-acclaimed "Hilo's Best Fried Rice." The rest of the menu features a variety of favorites like teriyaki beef and chicken, island fish, daily specials and plate lunch take-outs. Open daily for breakfast and lunch, 5AM - 2PM.

PICKLE BARREL *Sandwiches/Snacks*
Located in the Hilo Shopping Center, corner of Kekuanaoa and Kilauea Avenues, Hilo (935-1077). This small island-style eatery features sandwiches and lots of local specials like saimin, Japanese bento (box) lunches, chili and rice and more. They also have a nice selection of that famous local favorite, "cracked seed." Open Mon-Thurs. 9AM-5PM, Fri. 9AM-7PM, Sat. 9AM-4PM. Closed Sunday.

RESTAURANT OSAKA *Japanese*
762 Kanoelehua Avenue (961-6699). This restaurant-lounge combination has a good variety of Japanese-American food. Complete meals Japanese or American style include beef, pork, chicken, and seafood as well as sandwiches. The floor and general condition of the restaurant are somewhat unkempt but the quality of food is generally good. Open Mon-Wed 5:30AM - 9PM, Tues 11AM - 9PM, Thurs-Fri 5:30AM - 10PM, Sat 7AM - 10PM., Sun 7AM - 9PM. Credit cards.

RESTAURANT SATSUKI ★ *Japanese*
168 Keawe St. (935-7880) in old downtown Hilo. This small restaurant features Japanese style lunches and dinners. Menu items include tempura, yakitori, beef teriyaki, butterfish, tonkatsu, donburi, sukiyaki, noodles, tofu dishes, a unique local style salad bar, and more. This is a generally neat, clean, and well-kept restaurant with simple decor. Open for lunch 11AM - 1:45PM, dinner 5-8:45PM; closed all day Tuesday and Wednesday evening. Credit cards.

REUBEN'S MEXICAN FOOD *Mexican*
336 Kamehameha Avenue (961-2552) on the bayfront in old downtown Hilo. Featuring crab enchiladas, chicken flautas, La Canasta, chile rellenos. Mexican food lovers will appreciate this fare which is good in quality, variety, and quantity. Margaritas too. Open Mon-Sat 11AM - 9PM. Take outs available.

REYCHEL'S RESTAURANT ★ *Thai Cuisine*
1261 Kilauea Avenue in the Hilo Shopping Center (934-SIAM/934-7426). This is a bright cheery contemporary decor dining room. The menu features hot spicy Thai and Filipino cuisine. Items include green, yellow or red curry, stuffed chicken wings, spicy shrimp salad, beef or chicken satay, pinacbet, pork & peas, pork adobo and more. Take-outs available. There is a special lunch buffet Mon-Fri 10:30AM - 2:30PM; dinner Mon-Sat 6 - 9PM. Closed Sunday.

ROYAL SIAM ★ *Thai Cuisine*
68 Mamo St., downtown Hilo (961-6100). This is a popular eatery, recently expanded and renovated, but still serving up spicy hot Thai food. The menu features over 50 items including chicken, seafood, beef, pork and veggie dishes. There are also wonderful Thai curries, appetizers and daily specials. Food can be ordered either mild, medium or spicy hot. Take-outs available. Open Monday through Saturday for lunch 11AM - 2PM, dinner 5 - 9PM; closed Sunday.

SACHI'S GOURMET ★ *Japanese*
250 Keawe St. (935-6255) in old downtown Hilo. This small Japanese-style eatery features good quality Tokyo-style Japanese food. Take outs and bentos available. Good selection and variety of beef, pork, chicken, and fish dishes on the menu. Open for breakfast, lunch, and dinner daily except Sunday, 8AM - 2PM, evenings 5 - 9 PM.

SCRUFFLES RESTAURANT *Continental/International*
1438 Kilauea Avenue (935-6664) next to Tyke's Laundromat. This is a family coffee shop-style restaurant with a menu featuring a variety of cuisines and special dishes. The menu lists burgers and sandwiches, curries, Mexican specials, varied pasta dishes, Korean, Japanese, and American specials like smoked chicken and bbq ribs, plus varied soups and salads. Bright attractive contemporary decor in booth-style tables. Open Sun-Thurs 10:30AM - 9PM, Fri-Sat 10:30AM - 11:30PM.

SUM LEUNG CHINESE KITCHEN *Chinese*
50 E. Puainako St. (959-6025) in the KTA Supermarket Center. Offers a full range of Chinese plate lunches, noodles, and varied Chinese specialties. Take outs available. Open daily except Sun. 8:30AM - 6:45PM, Fri. till 7:45PM.

SUN SUN LAU CHOP SUI HOUSE ★   *Chinese*
1055 Kinoole St. (935-2808). This large and attractive dining room is one of Hilo's oldest Chinese restaurants. They have an extensive menu of Cantonese dishes in beef, pork, chicken, duck, and seafood. Cocktail lounge and banquet room available. Good food in a bright clean dining room cooled by ceiling fans. Open daily except Wed 10:30AM - 8PM, weekends till 9PM. Credit cards.

THE COFFEE HOUSE   *Coffee Shop*
1261 Kilauea Avenue, Hilo Shopping Center (969-7479). This very plain cafe features a standard coffee shop menu of daily specials, sandwiches, oriental specials, several types of noodles and more. However, it's a pretty unexciting place as the food and service are both mediocre. Open for breakfast, lunch and dinner Monday-Saturday 6:30AM - 8:30PM, Sunday breakfast only 7-11AM.

THE FIREHOUSE RESTAURANT   *Family Dining*
Kilauea Avenue, in the Kaiko'o Mall (935-1016). This is a very small place with dining booths jammed into a long narrow space. If you don't mind cramped quarters and aren't subject to claustrophobia, you can enjoy a meal from their selection of Filipino and Oriental local favorites, American dishes, sandwiches, etc. They serve an unusual fried rice omelette at breakfast. Open Mon.-Sat. for breakfast and lunch, 6AM - 2PM, Sunday for breakfast only 6-11AM.

THE GOURMET ROOM   *Continental/International*
1175 Manono Street, Hawai'i Community College cafeteria (933-3431). This room, open to the public, is operated by the college's Food Services Program. Lunch is served weekdays during the academic year from September-May from 12 Noon - 1PM by students. The menu changes daily and usually offers a choice of entrees. A complete lunch usually costs less than $5 per person. The food and service are a great value for the money. It's probably one of the least known best lunch deals in Hilo. Reservations suggested; call before going.

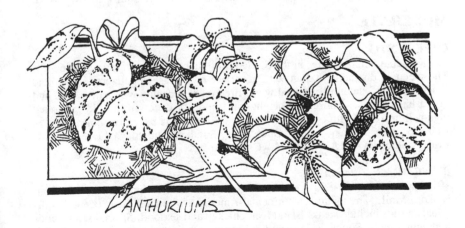

ANTHURIUMS

TING HAO MANDARIN RESTAURANT ★ *Chinese*
Kanoelehua Avenue (959-6288) in the Puainako Town Center. This Chinese restaurant offers authentic Mandarin cuisine. The menu is similar to their other outlet at the Hawai'i Naniloa Hotel. It features exotic spicy meals from Szechwan and Hunan, delicious non-spicy gourmet dishes from Taiwan, Beijing, and other parts of China, as well as healthy vegetarian delights. Cocktails too. Excellent food at reasonable prices. A real dining adventure to sample some of its menu offerings. Open daily for lunch 10:30AM - 2:30PM, dinner 4 - 9PM, Sunday 4:30 - 9PM only. This restaurant earns recognition in this book's "**Best Bets - Top Local Style Restaurants**" ratings.

WHAT'S SHAKIN' *Sandwiches/snacks*
27-999 Old Mamalahoa Highway, 4-mile scenic route, Pepeekeo, HI 96743 (964-3080). This new country style snack bar is located near Hilo, two miles north of the famous Hawaii Tropical Botanical Gardens on old Highway 19. The menu features fresh tropical fruit smoothies, island juices, fruit snacks, sandwiches, daily specials and desserts. There is a restroom plus tables on the lanai or picnic tables under the shade of the banana patch. Open daily 10AM-5:30PM.

WOOLWORTH'S RESTAURANT ★ *Family Dining*
Kanoelehua Ave. (959-3591) in the Prince Kuhio Plaza. This bright colorful coffee shop is popular with the shopping center crowds. The menu provides typical American coffee shop meals as well as a few local style dishes. Very popular with local folks who spend time strolling the center after dinner. Open Mon-Wed-Sat 7:30AM - 5PM, Tues-Thurs-Fri 7:30AM - 8:30PM, closed Sun. Credit cards.

YAMMY KOREAN BBQ *Korean*
Located in the Prince Kuhio Shopping Plaza on Kanoelehua Avenue (959-9977). This small diner serves up a variety of Korean specials like kal-bi ribs, spicy Korean chicken, BBQ beef and several daily specials. Open daily 10AM - 9PM.

MODERATE

CAFE PESTO *Italian*
130 Kamehameha Avenue, in the S. Hata Building, downtown Hilo (969-6640). The menu is distinctly Italian with a variety of pastas, appetizers, salads and sandwiches and the house special wood-fired pizzas scented with native ohia and guava hardwoods. There is a bright contemporary decor in the old-fashioned high-ceiling room with open kitchen area. But there is excessive noise level as well especially at busy times. Open daily, Sundays-Thursdays 11AM - 9PM, Fridays-Saturdays 11AM - 10PM. Credit cards.

d'ANGORAS *Italian*
101 Aupuni St. (935-8501) in the Hilo Lagoon Center building across from Kaiko'o Mall. The menu is Continental-American with an Italian accent. Traditional entrees include steak, island fish, chicken and seafood. Special sandwiches highlight lunch. Soups, salads and appetizers round out the offerings. Lunch served Mon-Fri 11AM - 2:30PM and dinner served daily from 5:30PM. Credit cards.

FIASCO'S ★ *Family Dining*
200 Kanoelehua Avenue (935-7666) in the Waiakea Kai Shopping Plaza. This popular eatery offers American and some local-style selections of beef, chicken, and seafood. Also Mexican, pasta, and sandwich plate selections from a varied menu. Salad bar and cocktail lounge. Individual booths decorated with old photographs and posters of early Hawai'i. Good food served in a festive atmosphere. Daily for breakfast 6:30 - 9AM, lunch and dinner, 11:30AM -10PM, Sat. till 11PM. Credit cards.

HENRI'S ON KAPIOLANI *Steaks*
139 Kapiolani St. (961-9272) in residential building of Urawatandai Hawaii College, a Japanese-English language training school. This small restaurant features prime rib on its dinner menu as well as other beef selections. Lunch is mainly sandwiches but with a varied selection including pastrami, turkey, corned beef, French dip, etc. The decor and atmosphere are simple. Daily except Mon, lunch 11AM - 2PM, dinner 6 - 9PM. Credit cards.

LEHUA'S BAY CITY BAR & GRILL *Continental/International*
Corner of Waianuenue and Kamehameha Avenues (935-8055). This is one of downtown Hilo's trendy dining spots. The menu features varied sandwiches, salads and light entrees for lunch while dinner features fresh island fish, seafood, steaks, charbroiled chicken, combo platters, pasta dishes, burgers and sandwiches. Try the fruit juice iced tea-delightful! There is an "old Hilo" atmosphere created with old shop signs, logos, early era photos, etc. However, don't take groups of more than four because they have difficulties in serving larger groups at the same time. A recent visit with a party of fifteen resulted in mixed up orders, inedible food and the worst of service. In the past, smaller group visits have usually fared better. Open for breakfast 7-9AM, lunch and dinner daily 11AM - 9PM.

NIHON RESTAURANT ★ *Japanese*
123 Lihiwai St., just opposite the Liliuokalani Gardens and Banyan Drive hotels, on Hilo Bayfront. The building is Japanese style with private dining rooms, lots of Japanese art and decor, and Japanese music as a background. Waitresses are dressed in kimonos. The menu offers a full range of Japanese cuisine including beef, pork, chicken, and seafood, plus noodle dishes and a sushi bar serving a wide variety of excellent sushi. Good Japanese food in authentic surroundings. Open daily except Sunday, lunch 11AM - 2PM, dinner 5 - 8:30PM. Credit cards.

PESCATORE ★ *Italian*
Corner of Keawe and Haili Streets in old downtown Hilo (969-9090). The restaurant features genuine Italian cuisine. Tasty soups, salads and appetizers compliment a wonderful variety of creative seafood, chicken, veal, vegetarian and pasta dishes. Melt-in-your-mouth bread and scrumptious desserts begin and end a filling lunch or dinner. Warm woodwork decor, great food and pleasant service make this small eatery a real dining-out discovery. Open for lunch Monday-Saturday 11AM - 2PM, dinner Sunday-Thursday 5:30 - 9PM and Friday-Saturday 5:30 - 10PM. Reservations suggested; credit cards.

QUEEN'S COURT ★ *Continental/International*
71 Banyan Drive (935-9361) in the Hilo Hawaiian Hotel. This is one of Hilo's nicest dining rooms with lovely views of Hilo Bay and Coconut Island. The menu features varied Continental, American, and local-style items. Try the fresh Big Island rainbow trout, raised right in Hilo. Weekend buffets Fri-Sat feature seafood and Hawaiian cuisine and are very popular with local folks and visitors. Live relaxing dinner music. Reservations suggested. Open daily, lunch 11AM - 1:15PM, dinner 6 - 8PM. Credit cards. This dining room earns recognition in this book's **"Best Bets - Best Buffets" ratings.**

RESTAURANT MIWA ★ *Japanese*
At Kekuanaoa and Kilauea Avenues (961-4454) in the Hilo Shopping Center. This dining spot offers high quality Japanese cuisine in an exceptionally clean well-kept environment, right down to the white tablecloths. The menu listings are extensive and varied featuring beef teriyaki, tonkatsu, seafood selections, and noodle dishes; the combination plates are excellent. The sushi bar turns out a full range of interesting and delightful varieties for those who like that form of rice. Service is attentive. This is a fine choice for Japanese food and should delight and excite anyone from first-timers to veterans. Lunch and dinner, Mon-Sat 11AM - 10PM. Reservations suggested. Credit cards.

SEASIDE ★ *Seafood*
1790 Kalanianaole St. (935-8825) Keaukaha area of Hilo. This small local family run restaurant is located in the middle of Keaukaha's fish ponds area where seafood for the table can't get any fresher. Local mullet, trout, and other fresh fish selections make up the menu. Reservations accepted for groups of four or more only. Open daily except Monday 11AM - 2PM, 5 - 8PM. Credit cards. This restaurant earns recognition in this book's **"Best Bets - Top Local Style Restaurants" ratings.**

TING HAO SEAFOOD RESTAURANT *Chinese*
97 Banyan Drive, Hawai'i Naniloa Hotel lower lobby (969-6660). This small attractive dining room has neat modern decor with hotel courtyard views and Hilo Bay. The menu is somewhat similar to their other location at Puainako Town Center but with more emphasis on seafood dishes. Selections include soups, appetizers, pork, beef, chicken, duck, seafood and vegetarian dishes plus noodles, fried rice, spring rolls and pot stickers. Menu items include scallops and veggies, oyster with tofu, lobster with black bean sauce, seafood treasure and many more Szechwan-inspired dishes. Open daily except Monday for lunch 11AM - 2PM, dinner 5-10PM.

UNCLE BILLY'S *Seafood*
87 Banyan Dr. (935-0861) in the Hilo Bay Hotel. The attraction here is casual dining in a Polynesian atmosphere with island decor. An extensive menu features steak and fresh island seafood. Nightly Hawaiian hula show from 6PM and Hawaiian dinner music 7:30 - 9PM. Breakfast, lunch, dinner daily. Credit cards.

EXPENSIVE

HARRINGTON'S ★ *American*
135 Kalanianaole Avenue, Hilo (961-4966) right on the Ice Pond, Reed's Bay, opposite Banyan Drive. The restaurant features relaxed dining overlooking the pond and bay. Menu highlights include fresh island fish and seafood, slavic steak, filet mignon, prime rib, and calamari. Dessert selections are simply rich and wonderful! Lunch daily 11AM-2PM, dinner from 5:30 PM nightly. Reservations suggested. Credit cards.

SANDALWOOD ROOM *Continental/International*
93 Banyan Drive (969-3333) in the Hawai'i Naniloa Hotel. The menu features Continental selections, specialties include seafood, steaks, local favorites and a Hawaiian plate. Dining is in a tropical garden setting overlooking Hilo Bay. Breakfast 6:30 - 11AM, lunch 11AM - 2PM, dinner 5:30 - 9PM daily. Reservations recommended for dinner. Credit cards.

SOUTH HILO &
THE HAMAKUA DISTRICT

INTRODUCTION

The South Hilo and Hamakua Districts are basically rural small village and small town areas with few restaurant options. The available fare tends to be local-style Oriental and pretty ordinary otherwise. Some of the eateries are interesting since they are located in old buildings or facilities that reflect Hawai'i's old sugar plantation days when these small coastal towns were booming places. History can be quaint.

INEXPENSIVE

CC JON'S SNACK IN SHOPPE *Sandwiches*
Honoka'a, Hamakua Coast (775-0414). There is a wide range of local and international foods, short order items, and snacks available in this small deli-cafe. Open Mon-Sat 6:30AM - 5PM.

EARL'S DRIVE IN *Drive In*
Paauilo Store on Highway 19 in the small village of Paauilo, on the Hamakua Coast. The menu features local-style fast foods and snacks including sandwiches, teri beef and chicken plates, saimin, chili and rice, and more. There are a couple of tables on the veranda of this old plantation store where you can relax and enjoy the genuine country atmosphere of the place. Open Monday-Friday 8:30AM - 7PM, Saturday 8:30AM - 6PM, Sunday 8:30AM - 12:30PM.

HERB'S PLACE   *Family Dining*
Main Street, Honoka'a, Hamakua Coast (775-7236). The menu features prime rib, chicken, and other local favorites with a salad bar. Located in heart of Honoka'a town in a non-descript building on the main street. Open daily except Sunday, 5AM - 9PM. Credit cards.

HOTEL HONOKA'A CLUB ★   *Family Dining*
Main Street, Honoka'a, Hamakua Coast (775-0533/775-0678). The dining room in Honoka'a's only hotel is a popular local spot for lunch and dinner. The room is wide and rambling with plenty of tables and chairs and a 1940's era plantation house decor, very plain, very simple. The menu features steaks, chicken, and some local-style dishes served up in an old fashioned country atmosphere. The cocktail lounge adjacent gets lively on the weekends with local folks partying. Open daily for breakfast 6 - 11AM, lunch 11AM - 2PM, dinner 5:30 - 8PM. Credit cards.

ISHIGO'S STORE ★   *Family Dining*
Main Street, Honomu Village (963-6128). This is a country general store and bakery featuring fresh rolls, pastries and Kona coffee. Other snacks and light meal 'selections are available. A pleasant stop right on the main road through Honomu Village on the way to Akaka Falls State Park. Open Mon-Fri 7AM - 6PM, Sat-Sun 7AM - 5:30PM.

JOLENE'S KAU KAU KORNER   *Continental/International*
Located in Honoka'a at the intersection of Lehua and Mamane Streets (775-9498). This nicely renovated old shop space was made clean and bright with attractive simple decor and curtains on the windows. They have a varied menu of mahi mahi, shrimp tempura, seafood platter, beef teriyaki, New York steak, captain's plate, chicken katsu, plus burgers, sandwiches, salads and desserts. Open Monday-Saturday 10AM - 8PM, closed Sunday.

KONA COFFEE   JBAYOT

NORTH KOHALA DISTRICT

INTRODUCTION

The top end of the Big Island, the North Kohala District, is rural, quiet and sparsely populated. Even with its handful of historic attractions, most visitors don't linger too long here. There are also just a handful of eateries worth noting here.

INEXPENSIVE-MODERATE

BAMBOO RESTAURANT & BAR *Hawaiian Regional*
Main street, just near intersection of Highways 250-270, Hawi (889-5555). This restaurant is located in the old Takata Store building which for nearly 70 years served as a family-run general store. The restaurant keeps a "Hawaii-1950's" theme in decor and ambiance with colorful artwork and old Matson ocean liner menus on the wall as conversation pieces. It's sort of a funky old place with Kohala Koa Gallery gift shop sharing the same space on one side. It's real localized with occasional live music, etc. While the dinner menu is not really the trendy "Hawaiian Regional cuisine" that is all the rage, they emphasize fresh island products and their cuisine has various Pacific accents. Menu selections include fresh island fish, Thai-broiled prawns, New York steak/pepper steak, kalbi ribs, teriyaki chicken and saimin plus soups and salads. The lunch menu offers sandwiches and lighter fare and there is also a Sunday brunch. Open Mon-Sat for lunch 11:30AM - 2PM, dinner 6PM - until closing. Sunday brunch 10:30AM - 2PM.

DON'S FAMILY DELI *Family Dining*
Main street, Highway 270, Kapa'au (889-5822) right across from the King Kamehameha Statue and the courthouse. This is an ice cream parlor-cafe featuring sandwiches, salads, international foods and desserts. Open daily 10AM - 6PM.

KOHALA COFFEE MILL *Coffee Shop/Espresso Bar*
1 block W. of intersection of Hwys 250-270 in the heart of Hawi town (889-5577). This coffee shop serves up fresh brewed Kona coffee, espressos, cappucinos and other coffees and beverages along with special snacks. They also have gift bags of various Kona plantation coffees, whole beans or fresh-ground. Open Mon-Fri 6:30AM - 4PM, Sat 8AM - 4PM, Sun 8AM - 3PM.

KOHALA VILLAGE RESTAURANT *Continental/International*
At intersection of Hwys 250-270 in Hawi town (889-0105). The menu at this country coffee shop features varied sandwiches, salads, and entrees such as chicken stirfry, red pesto pasta, Honolulu fried noodles, fried rice, Oriental chicken salad and daily specials. Open daily for breakfast, lunch and dinner, 7:30AM - 2PM, 6 - 9PM.

MATTHEW'S PLACE *Sandwiches*
1 block W. of intersection of Hwys 250-270 in the heart of Hawi town (889-5500). This tiny hole-in-the-wall place features Italian food, pizza, sandwiches, snacks, etc. Varied hours. Strictly for the budget conscious traveler.

PUNA DISTRICT

INTRODUCTION

Puna's population is spread among several country subdivisions in the sprawling district southeast of Hilo. While it has a handful of small towns and villages, it doesn't have any real district center unless Pahoa qualifies, since it has a high school, police and fire station, and a main street. The restaurants are located in or near the village shopping centers and offer fairly ordinary food with a little Mexican and Italian for spice. The one exception is the Kilauea Lodge Restaurant near Hawai'i Volcanoes National Park, which is surprising many folks with its Continental-International menu in a relaxing country lodge atmosphere.

INEXPENSIVE

HUNA OHANA *Coffee shop/espresso bar*
On the main street in Pahoa, Hwy 130 (965-9661). This simple eatery located in the old town row of buildings combines a metaphysical bookstore with its espresso cafe. The menu is extensive and features organic natural foods for breakfast, lunch and snacks. Selections include tofu scramble, croissants, varied sandwiches, pastries, miso soup, salads and more. There is a wide selection of special teas, coffees, espresso, cappuccino, chocolate, etc. Open Mon-Sat 8AM - 5PM, Sun 8AM - 1PM.

KEAAU CAFE *Korean*
Keaau Town Center, Keaau (966-6758). This dine-in or take out eatery features Korean cuisine including kalbi, bbq chicken, meat jun, bbq pork ribs, oxtail soup, fried mandoo, spicy beef, several Japanese dishes, seafood, sandwiches and daily specials. Open Mon-Sat 9:30AM - 9PM, closed Sunday.

KEA'AU CHOP SUEY HOUSE *Chinese*
Keaau Town Center, Keaau (966-7573). This Chinese restaurant specializes in Cantonese cuisine and the menu features 60 items. Among the selections are things like saimin noodles, seaweed soup, beef chow mein, Mongolian beef, lemon chicken, roast duck, hot & spicy chicken, egg fu young, mu shu pork, pork chop suey, and a variety of appetizers. Take outs available. Open Mon-Sat 9AM -7:30PM.

KEAAU JUNCTION ★ *Mexican*
Keaau Town Center, Keaau (966-6885). This restaurant was recently restored after a fire and has a railroad-train decor theme with a menu featuring broiler selections, rotisseried chicken and South-of-the-Border selections like tacos, burritos, tostadas, chimichangas and quesadillas, plus pizza and sandwiches. Open daily for lunch and dinner 11AM - 9PM. Credit cards.

LUQUIN'S MEXICAN RESTAURANT   *Mexican*

On the main street in Pahoa, Hwy 130 (965-9990). The menu features a variety of Mexican dishes like tacos, burritos, enchiladas, botanas (appetizers), soups, salads and other specialties. The decor is Mexican and tempers the rough exterior of the old wooden building in which it's located. The bar serves tropical fruit margaritas by the pitcher. This place will appeal to the adventurous diner who likes Mexican food. Open daily, 11AM - 9PM.

NAUNG MAI THAI KITCHEN   *Thai cuisine*

In Pahoa on the main street (965-8186). This small eatery is located in Pahoa's old town row of early-era buildings. The menu is authentic Thai cuisine with such things as red, green or yellow curry, seafood, chicken, evil jungle beef, pork specials and vegetarian dishes, also rice and noodles. They offer a different special each evening. The small room has just five tables. Good Thai food at reasonable prices. Open daily for lunch 12-2PM, dinner 4:30-8:30PM.

PAHOA CHOP SUEY HOUSE   *Chinese*

Just off the main highway in Pahoa town, across from the 7/11 Store (965-9533). This Chinese eatery offers a full menu of Cantonese-style cuisine. The menu features seafood, pork, beef, chicken and duck dishes, a variety of chop sueys and noodles. Set dinners for 2-4 people are also available. Open daily, 10AM - 8PM.

PARADISE CAFE   *Family Dining*

On the highway in the middle of Pahoa town (965-9733). This small local-style cafe offers a varied menu featuring breakfast and lunch local favorites like eggs, pancakes, fresh island fish and seafood, steaks, homemade soups, sandwiches, burgers, vegetarian specials and more. Open daily, 7:30AM - 9PM.

MODERATE

KILAUEA LODGE RESTAURANT ★   *Continental/International*

On Highway 11 in Volcano Village (967-7366). This cozy dining room is part of the Kilauea Lodge Bed & Breakfast operation (see "Bed & Breakfast" in the ACCOMMODATIONS section). It offers a mixed Continental-International cuisine menu featuring fine seafood, beef, veal, and chicken selections, along with a variety of appetizers and salads. Fine service in an attractive setting with dining room fireplace and relaxed country lodge atmosphere. Open nightly for dinner 5:30-9:00PM. Credit cards. This restaurant earns recognition in this book's **"Best Bets - Top Restaurants with a Casual Atmosphere" ratings.**

PAOLO'S BISTRO   *Italian*

In Pahoa on the main street row of old town buildings (965-7033). This small restaurant has just a dozen tables and bright simple decor, nothing elegant. The dinner menu changes daily and features authentic Italian cuisine. Menu features are soups, salads, antipasto and entrees like seared Mediterranean ahi, chicken marsala, cioppino, seafood pasta, rack of lamb and several types of pasta, with a daily fresh-made pasta special. There is also espresso, cappuccino, special coffees and desserts. Open Tuesday-Sunday for dinner only, 5:30-9:30PM.

THE GODMOTHER   *Italian*
In Pahoa on the main street at the south end of the old town row of buildings. This is a new building with a bright clean simple decor. The menu is Italian and features selections like meatballs and pasta, ravioli, parmigiana, lasagna, fettuccine, piccata, marsala, scampi and special Godmother pork chops. There are also appetizers and special daily desserts. Breakfast is traditional and the lunch menu offers pasta and sandwiches. Open daily 8AM - 11PM.

KA'U DISTRICT

INTRODUCTION

Like the top end at North Kohala, the lower end of the Big Island is rural, quiet, and sparsely populated. Its few small villages are remote and far from the district's main attraction of Hawai'i Volcanoes National Park. There are few restaurants, but those that follow do serve some interesting, local-style and Continental-International cuisine.

INEXPENSIVE

FABRICS 'N FASHIONS COFFEE HOUSE   *Coffee shop/deli*
Highway 11 in Na'alehu, Ka'u District (929-7404. This is a small country store combining handmade clothing and handicrafts with a coffee/deli bar serving coffee, beverages, fresh-made sandwiches, pastries, ice cream and other goodies. Open Sun-Fri 8AM - 5PM.

MARK TWAIN SQUARE   *Sandwiches/Snacks*
Highway 11 in Waiohinu, Ka'u District (929-7550). This is one of the southern Big Island's newer dining spots. The attractive early-Hawaiian style building is a family-owned and operated cafe and gift shop. It stands next to the Mark Twain monkey-pod tree planted by the famous author during his 1860's visit to Hawai'i. The cafe serves up good local-style plate lunch specials, sandwiches, burgers, snacks, coffee, beverages, etc. Open Mon-Sat 7AM - 6PM.

NA'ALEHU FRUIT STAND   *Sandwiches/Snacks*
Main street, Highway 11, in Naalehu, the self-proclaimed "Southernmost Community in the USA." This snack shop features a variety of sandwiches, pizza, fresh baked pastries, macadamia nut treats, and fresh squeezed juices. Open Mon-Thurs 9AM - 6:30PM, Fri-Sat 9AM - 7PM, and Sunday 9AM - 5PM.

SANTANGELO'S PIZZARIA   *Italian*
Ocean View Town Center, Highway 11, Hawaiian Ocean View Estates (929-9677). This small eatery features pizza, chicken, sub sandwiches, soup, salads, breads, desserts and more. Open daily 11AM - 8PM.

VOLCANO COUNTRY CLUB RESTAURANT ★ *Family Dining*
Near Hawai'i Volcanoes National Park, just off Highway 11 at the 30 mile
marker from Hilo, across from Kilauea Military Camp (967-7721). This rustic
dining room is located in the golf course clubhouse and features a variety of
sandwiches, beef, chicken, fish, and local style favorites. Open daily for breakfast 7AM - 11AM, lunch 11AM - 3PM, cocktails only 11AM till closing.

MODERATE

KA OHELO ROOM ★ *Continental/International*
Volcano House Hotel, Hawai'i Volcanoes National Park (967-7321). The menu
features prime rib, steaks, Cornish hen, pork medallions, fresh island fish,
several types of pasta and a variety of soups, salads and appetizers. The daily
buffet lunch is popular with visitors and features a variety of hot entrees, salads
and more. The dining room overlooks majestic Kilauea Caldera and it's steaming
vents. The rustic country lodge atmosphere makes for a nice ambiance. It is
nice to see the Ka Ohelo Room making a strong comeback as a quality restaurant.
A recent visit proved very satisfactory and gained the dining room a star-ranking
from this book. Dining on the edge of the volcano adds a special charm to the
generally good cuisine and pleasant service. Open daily for breakfast 7 - 10AM,
lunch 11AM - 1:30PM, dinner 5:30 - 9PM. Credit cards.

NAALEHU COFFEE SHOP ★ *American*
Across the street from the Naalehu Shopping Center in the middle of the "Southernmost Community in the USA" (929-7238). This delightful country coffee shop
serves up American-style food including steaks, seafood, fresh island fish,
chicken and salads. Sandwiches are featured for lunch. Open Mon. through Sat.
for breakfast, lunch and dinner continuously 8AM - 8PM; closed Sunday. Some
days they may close for short periods in mid-afternoon but re-open for dinner
hour. This restaurant earns recognition in this book's **"Best Bets - Top Local
Style Restaurants" ratings.**

SOUTH POINT RESTAURANT *Continental*
This isolated eatery is located in the desolate lavalands of the Ka'u district in the
Hawaiian Oceanview Estates subdivision area (929-9343). It's located right on
Highway 11 between South Point and Milolii right out in the middle of nowhere.
The menu features sandwiches and burgers for lunch. For dinner, entrees include
honey and lemon chicken, teriyaki chicken, kalua pig, veal, New York steak,
calamari steak, prime rib, ahi, shrimp, several pastas, plus soups and salads.
They also have a cocktail lounge. Open Monday-Saturday for lunch and dinner,
11AM -9PM, dinner only on Sunday, 5 - 9PM.

ACTIVITIES AND TOURS

INTRODUCTION

The Big Island's diversity in climate, terrain, and geophysical features, not to mention its sheer size in comparison to the other islands of Hawai'i, provides a wide range and scope of activities. There is something to please everyone from the sedentary toes-in-the-water set to the adventure-seeking backpacker bent on exploring the island's most remote areas. This chapter details the more popular activities available to visitors.

BEST BETS

A glassbottom boat cruise along the famed Kona Coast and over its famous coral reefs; or better yet, a submarine or semi-submersible cruise through Kona's fabulous underwater world.

A golf outing at either the Mauna Kea Beach Hotel Golf Course or the Mauna Lani Resort Golf Course, both named among "America's Top 12 Resort Courses."

An air tour over Hawai'i Volcanoes National Park and/or current/recent eruption sites or along the scenic Hamakua Coast.

A snorkeling adventure at Kahalu'u Bay at Keauhou-Kona, Kealakekua Bay Underwater Marine Preserve in Kona, Anaeho'omalu Bay on the Kohala Coast, or Leleiwi Beach Park in Hilo.

If conditions permit, a ski run down Mauna Kea's fabulous snow-covered slopes.

A 4-wheel drive tour to the summit of 13,796 ft. Mauna Kea or into the lush Waipio Valley.

For adventurous anglers, a fishing boat charter to pursue the mighty marlin in the fabled waters of the Kona Coast.

A hike through any of Hawai'i Volcanoes National Park trails to take in the awesome natural beauty and wonders of the volcanoes.

OCEAN ACTIVITIES

BEACHES - SNORKELING

Contrary to popular belief among many visitors, the Big Island of Hawai'i does have many beaches. In fact, it has more than 100 of them. Some are black sand, some white sand, some golden and some even have green sand. At the same time, many are very rugged rocky shorelines that have not yet fully eroded to a fine sand consistency. This is due to the geologic fact that the Big Island is still young and has not fully developed its beaches like Hawai'i's other islands. It is still a growing island and its volcanic eruptions still create new beaches while transforming old coastline.

The problem is that many of these beaches are not easily accessible for the average visitor or resident. This is due to poor or non-existent access roads, access via private roads and lands only, access through difficult and remote country, or access only from the ocean and often through treacherous waters. And even if a remote isolated beach is accessible via a road, it is usually via four-wheel drive off-road vehicle due to the difficult terrain. For these reasons, this section contains a listing only of those beaches, parks, and recreation areas that are easily accessible to the average visitor or resident. Most of the beaches listed in this section are directly accessible from main roads or well-marked and designated trails. Others are available via marked public beach access over private lands. The listings note the location of the beach area and any facilities and activities available at that site. For more detailed information on the Big Island's beaches, readers are referred to *Beaches of the Big Island*, by John R. K. Clark, published by the University of Hawai'i Press (1985).

Beach and park users should also be aware that some of the areas listed in this section have, over the last few years, become long-term residential locations for local homeless and transient folks. Some beaches and parks have significant clusters of tents and other temporary shelters of those who have set up residence at these locations.

Snorkelers will find lots of good areas to explore near some of the more popular beaches around the island. However, much of the better snorkeling is done over lava rock outcroppings and rocky coves and small bays where the water is usually fairly calm. There are lots of good coral patches and beds growing around these areas which attracts varied marine life. However, because the Big Island is so young geologically, there are no extensive fringing coral reefs that encircle the island or extend out from the shoreline. The best snorkeling is at Napo'opo'o Beach Park and the adjacent Kealakekua Bay State Marine & Historic Underwater Preserve with its teeming marine life, Kahalu'u Beach Park in Keauhou-Kona with myriad schools of colorful reef fish, Anaeho'omalu Beach at Waikoloa, Kohala Coast, Leleiwi Beach Park in Hilo with its tide pools and rock formations, and Kapoho Bay in Kapoho with its calm tide pools, clear water, and abundant marine life. As in all ocean areas, snorkelers need to be aware of their direction, distance from the shore, and keep alert to currents, surges and surf action especially near rock outcroppings.

WATER SAFETY

Whether you are experienced or inexperienced with the ocean, it is advisable to use caution and think safety when you are going into it. There are a few rules to follow:

1. An old Hawaiian saying states: "Never turn your back to the sea." Don't be caught off guard, waves come in sets with spells of calm in between.

2. Use the buddy system, never swim or snorkel alone.

3. If you are unsure of your abilities, use flotation devices attached to your body, such as a life vest or inflatable vest. Never rely on an air mattress or similar device from which you may become separated.

4. Study the ocean before you enter; look for rocky areas and breakers or currents.

5. Duck or dive beneath breaking waves before they reach you.

6. Never swim against a strong current which will tire you rapidly. Swim across it.

7. Know your limits.

8. Small children should be allowed to play near or in the surf ONLY with close supervision and should wear flotation devices.

9. When exploring tidal pools or reefs, always wear protective footwear and keep an eye on the ocean for high surf. Also, protect your hands from sharp rocks and coral. When swimming or snorkeling around coral, be careful where you put your hands and feet. Sea urchin stings can be painful and coral cuts can be dangerous.

BEST BETS:

Most Beautiful Beaches
Anaeho'omalu Beach - Waikoloa, Kohala Coast
Hapuna Beach State Park - Kohala Coast
Kauna'oa Beach (Mauna Kea Beach) - Kohala Coast

Safest Playing - Swimming Beaches for Youngsters
Spencer Beach Park - Kawaihae Bay, Kohala Coast
Onekahakaha Beach Park - Keaukaha area, Hilo
Kamakahonu Beach - next to the pier, Kailua-Kona
Kahalu'u Beach Park - Keauhou-Kona

Shelling-Tidepooling Beaches
Onekahakaha Beach Park - Keaukaha area, Hilo
Holoholokai Beach Park - South Kohala at Mauna Lani Resort

Snorkeling Beaches
Napo'opo'o Beach Park - Kealakekua Bay, Kona
Pu'uhonua O Honaunau National Historic Park - Honaunau, Kona
Kahalu'u Beach Park - Keauhou-Kona
Anaeho'omalu Beach - Waikoloa, Kohala Coast
Spencer Beach Park - Kawaihae Bay, Kohala Coast
James Kealoha Park - Keaukaha area, Hilo
Leleiwi Beach Park - Keaukaha area, Hilo
Kapoho Bay - Kapoho area, Puna District

Sunbathing Beaches
White Sands Beach Park - Kailua-Kona
Anaeho'omalu Beach - Waikoloa, Kohala Coast
Hapuna Beach State Park - Kohala Coast
Kauna'oa Beach (Mauna Kea Beach) - Kohala Coast

BEACH INDEX

SOUTH KONA AREA

The beaches of South Kona are mostly used by local residents. None of these listed are near any resorts. The Pu'uhonua O Honaunau Park and marine reserve at Kealakekua Bay-Napo'opo'o Park do get some visitor use due to other attractions of the sites. These beaches are fairly isolated and not near any major town or commercial areas.

HO'OKENA BEACH PARK

Three miles south of Pu'uhonua O Honaunau National Historic Park at the end of a narrow, winding and bumpy paved spur road off Highway 11. Ho'okena has a small coconut grove, a handful of old Hawaiian homes and beach houses, restrooms and picnic tables, and some shade trees. The beach is a combination of black and white sand and mixed lava debris giving the sand a gray cast. The bay is generally calm and swimming, snorkeling, and diving are generally good but caution is advised during high surf times.

PU'UHONUA O HONAUNAU NATIONAL HISTORIC PARK ★

Honaunau Bay is one of the Big Island's most popular attractions. In addition to the visitor's center displays and the old Hawaiian heiau (temple) structures, the park has restrooms, a picnic area, and some of the best near shore snorkeling and scuba diving on the island. The generally rocky shoreline has pockets of sandy beach here and there and the shoreline waters teem with marine life. For further information, call the Visitor Center at 808 328-2288.

NAPO'OPO'O BEACH PARK ★

Adjoins the village of Napo'opo'o at Kealakekua Bay. The beach consists of pebbles, cobblestones, and boulders with only a very narrow strip of sand at the water's edge. The beach attracts many sunbathers and swimmers and the limited wave action attracts some surfers and boogie boarders. The adjacent Napo'opo'o Beach Park has very limited parking, restrooms, and a couple of picnic tables. Also next to the park are the ruins of Hikiau Heiau, an old Hawaiian temple. Snorkelers will revel in the offshore Kealakekua Bay State Historical & Underwater Parks Marine Preserve. The area teems with fascinating and colorful marine life and offers excellent snorkeling and scuba diving. Many of the commercial boat tours from Kailua-Kona include Kealakekua Bay as part of their route. At the north end of the bay beyond the towering cliffs and on a flat point of land jutting into the bay is the Captain James Cook Monument which marks the spot where the famous explorer met his fate.

NORTH KONA AREA

The beaches listed for North Kona will have a considerable number of visitors as well as local residents using the facilities. These beaches are generally quite nice and popular for all sorts of outings and activities. Their proximity to the hotels and resorts of Kailua-Kona make them busy places on most good beach days.

KAHALU'U BEACH PARK ★

This one of the most popular swimming and snorkeling sites in the Kona area. Located next to the Keauhou Beach Hotel at Keauhou-Kona, just south of Kailua-Kona. The beach is composed of white sand speckled with black lava pebbles, cobblestones, and fragments. The bay waters provide excellent snorkeling and near shore scuba diving in waters protected by a fringing reef and the area is generally free of strong currents. Outside the reef, surfers can find good waves to ride but the rip currents along the reef edge are extremely strong. Caution is advised. Park facilities include picnic pavilions, restrooms, showers, water, lifeguard, parking, and concession stands.

WHITE SANDS BEACH PARK ★

Located on Alii Drive four miles south of Kailua-Kona town. Facilities include restrooms, showers, lifeguard, and small parking lot. A grove of coconut trees provides some shade and lends a touch of beauty to this small beach park. The lovely white sand and small wave action make this a popular swimming and boogie boarding beach for both residents and visitors. Winter storms often wash the white sand into deeper water only to carry it back later, hence the park's other names of "Disappearing Sands" and "Magic Sands."

KAMAKAHONU BEACH ★

This is a small cove of sandy beach immediately next to the Kailua Pier and fronting the King Kamehameha Kona Beach Hotel. Extending onto a peninsula in front of the beach is Ahuena Heiau, the temple of King Kamehameha the Great. Kamehameha resided here at Kamakahonu during the last years of his life. The beach is very protected and is excellent for sunbathing and swimming. The beach is especially good for young children. No public facilities exist on the beach itself but there are public restrooms on the adjacent pier.

OLD KONA AIRPORT STATE RECREATION AREA

The area consists of a long beach composed of storm and reef debris, pebbles, and rocks with a few pockets of white sand with safe sand channels for entering the water. However the coast here tends to be rocky overall. The swimming and snorkeling are generally fair to good here, but best on calmer days. Facilities include picnic pavilions, restrooms, showers, water, and plenty of parking.

'ALULA BEACH

The beach is located in a small protected cove just to the south of Honokohau Harbor near Kailua-Kona, and is a lovely crescent of white sand speckled with lack lava fragments. It is a secluded spot for sunbathing, swimming, snorkeling, and near shore scuba diving. The boat traffic of Honokohau Harbor can be viewed easily from the beach. The shallow sandy bottom makes this a pleasant calm beach especially for youngsters. Public facilities at adjacent boat harbor.

KALOKO-HONOKOHAU NATIONAL HISTORIC PARK

This park is still under development. It was established as a national park in 1978, but was mostly inaccessible until 1995. The 1160-acre park spans a two mile stretch of the Kona coast adjacent to and north of Honokohau Small Boat Harbor, north of Kailua-Kona. The park was founded to preserve, protect, interpret and demonstrate native Hawaiian activities and culture and to demonstrate historic land use. Archaeological resources include ancient Hawaiian house platforms, fishing shrines, canoe landings, petroglyph rock carvings, religious temples and fishponds. The tidal wetlands are home to many waterbirds including the Hawaiian black-necked stilt and Hawaiian coot, both endemic to Hawai'i. The park landscape also includes scenic coastlines, sandy beaches, marine tidal pools and native plants. Located three miles north of Kailua-Kona, three miles south of Keahole airport. There is an unimproved access road just opposite Kaloko Industrial Park open daily 8AM - 3:30PM. There is also access to a hiking trail into the park from Honokohau Harbor. This is a hot, dry windy area of open rough lava flows. Hikers and visitors should come prepared with sunscreen, hats, hiking shoes and water. No water or services available other than restrooms at the fishpond and beach. No camping or fires are allowed. For further information, contact Kaloko-Honokohau NHP, 73-4786 Kanalani St., #14, Kailua-Kona, HI 96740; 808 329-6881.

KA'UPULEHU BEACH
Fronts the Kona Village Resort north of Kailua-Kona. The white sand beach is speckled with black lava fragments and pebbles. The waters of Kahuwai Bay here are good for swimming and snorkeling. There is convenient public access and some parking is provided by the privately-operated Kona Village Resort. There are no public facilities at the beach.

KONA COAST STATE PARK ★
This beach park is located just a couple of miles north of Kona's Keahole Airport. It is reached off Highway 19 by a narrow somewhat bumpy road that winds across the lava fields for 1.5 miles. A regular car can make it but drive slowly. The beach is a high sand dune beach with good tidal pools for snorkeling and swimming but don't go out too far. The park is still being developed and there are only temporary restroom facilities and a few picnic tables plus an unimproved parking lot area. Bring your own water.

SOUTH KOHALA AREA

South Kohala probably has the best sandy beaches on the island. Some like Hapuna and Spencer Parks are used by both local residents and visitors alike. Others like 'Anaeho'omalu and Kauna'oa Beaches front major hotels, and while public access is provided, the majority of beach-goers are hotel guests. Still, the public has access and full use of the beaches.

'ANAEHO'OMALU BEACH ★
This is a long curving white sand beach speckled with grains of black lava. It is a lovely crescent accented with graceful coconut palms and backed by two old fishponds, Ku'uali'i and Kahapapa, which were reserved for Hawaiian royalty in the old days. The beach park fronts the Royal Waikoloan Hotel. Swimming, snorkeling, scuba diving, windsurfing, and board surfing are enjoyed in the bay. A water sports-activities concession on the beach provides equipment rentals and instruction for hotel guests and other visitors. The beach park facilities include restrooms, showers, and picnic tables plus parking.

KALAHUIPUA'A BEACH
Located at the Mauna Lani Resort. The beach is adjacent to a series of well maintained old Hawaiian fishponds which are still used for aquaculture purposes. The beach access is through a historic preserve and public park maintained by the Mauna Lani Resort. The best swimming area of the beach is Nanuku Inlet, a wide, shallow, sandy-bottomed cove enclosed by natural lava rock barriers. This part of the lovely white and black sand speckled beach immediately fronts the Mauna Lani Bay Hotel.

HOLOHOLOKAI BEACH PARK ★
This public access beach park is located just north of the Sheraton Orchid Mauna Lani Hotel. The park was developed by the Mauna Lani Resort Company and provides restrooms and showers, parking stalls for over 30 cars and barbeque grills on the beach. The beach is not sandy but composed of white coral rocks and some black lava and debris. There are small pockets of sand here and there. It's a good beach for sunning, tidepool exploring, shelling and snorkeling in the larger tidal pools. Great views of the Kohala Coast. A trail from the parking lot leads to the **Puako Petroglyph Fields** which provide an interesting view of old Hawaiian rock carvings and drawings. The trail is a 1.4 mile round trip (about 40 minutes) through kiawe and haole koa trees and brushland. Wear good hiking shoes and take sunscreen and water as it can be a warm dry hike.

PUAKO BEACH
The beach extends the entire length of shoreline along Puako Road in North Kohala below Hapuna Beach State Park. The beach is mostly rocks and pebbles indented by inlets, coves, and tidal pools but sunbathers, swimmers, and snorkelers can find some white sand beach stretches to enter the water. Public access is via the boat ramp at Puako Bay or any of several points along Puako Road which follows the shoreline homes.

HAPUNA BEACH STATE PARK ★
This is undoubtedly one of the Big Island's largest expanses of fine white sand beach. It stretches for over a half mile. The beach provides shallow waters that slope gently to deeper offshore waters. Swimming, snorkeling, bodysurfing, windsurfing, and near shore scuba diving are excellent. Shallow, protected coves at the beach's north end provide sandy-bottomed pools that are ideal for little children to splash and play. Beach facilities include picnic pavilions, restrooms, showers, food concession and parking.

KAUNA'OA BEACH ★
This is better known as Mauna Kea Beach and fronts the Mauna Kea Beach Hotel. It is a long, wide crescent of fine white sand which slopes gently into the deeper offshore waters and offers excellent swimming, snorkeling, and windsurfing. Surf conditions often permit good bodysurfing and boardsurfing also. The hotel provides some public parking and maintains a public access right-of-way and there are restrooms and showers on the beach.

SPENCER BEACH PARK ★
The park is located near the port village of Kawaihae and immediately below Pu'ukohola Heiau National Historic Park, a famous temple built by Kamehameha

the Great. The beach here is a fine white sand expanse with a very gentle slope to deeper water. The conditions are excellent for swimming, snorkeling, and near shore scuba diving. The protected nature of the bay affords very calm waters with usually gentle surf. It is an excellent swimming beach for little children.

KAWAIHAE BEACH
This is a coral rubble and landfill beach next to the boat harbor which resulted when the harbor was dredged years ago. Many local folks use the area for varied activities such as fishing, canoe paddling, sailing, windsurfing, swimming, and picnicking. From the south end of the landfill area is a great view of the nearby Pu'ukohola Heiau.

NORTH KOHALA AREA

The beaches of North Kohala tend to be of a more rugged variety, often composed of small pockets of coral pebbles and small rocks with an isolated pocket of sand. Often the beach area is rugged lava rock outcropping.

LAPAKAHI STATE HISTORICAL PARK ★
The park is north of Kawaihae Harbor and has no good sandy beaches. There are small pockets of coral pebbles and rocky beaches where swimmers and snorkelers can enter the water. At the point where the park trail follows the shoreline and meets a small peninsula of land, there is a small cove with remarkably clear water which slopes gradually before dropping off sharply. Swimmers and snorkelers should not venture out more than fifty yards into the cove however due to strong alongshore currents in the area. There are no facilities right on the shore but restrooms are located near the parking lot area and entrance.

MAHUKONA BEACH PARK
Between Kawaihae and Hawi on Highway 270 is the site of an old port of the Hawai'i Consolidated Railway Company, which transported sugar from the Kohala Mill to boats for trans-ocean shipment. Remnants of the old railway port still exist and old train wheels, parts, and related rubble attract snorkelers and divers in the bay's clear waters. There is no real sand beach here, only coral rubble and pebbles. Facilities include picnic tables, a pavilion, restrooms, showers, camping area, and parking lot but all facilities are rough and in need of some maintenance work.

POLOLU VALLEY BEACH
At the end of Highway 270, past the village of Kapa'au, the beach is reached by a difficult trail down to the valley at the end of the highway. The trail is often treacherous if wet and caution is advised. The beach is a wide expanse of fine black sand with high dunes at the back shore. While swimmers, bodysurfers, and surfers use the beach, there are dangerous rip currents that are real hazards. This is a remote, isolated beach, and extreme caution is advised. The flatlands of the valley were once extensively planted in taro farms but are now abandoned. There are no facilities of any kind on the beach.

HAMAKUA AREA

The eastern side of the Big Island, the Hamakua Coast, is marked by a high pali (cliff) which is often a sheer vertical drop of more than 200 feet. The coastline here is very rough and rugged with very few places where sandy beaches have had a chance to form. The fact that there is no coral reef extending outwards from the coast accounts for the lack of coral sand here. Waipio Valley Beach, the one exception listed, is composed of black lava sand eroded from the surrounding lava rock.

WAIPIO VALLEY BEACH

At the end of Highway 240, at the Waipio Valley State Park lookout, the beach fronting the valley is reached via a hazardous and very steep single lane road carved along the valley wall. A four-wheel drive vehicle is required to gain access to the beach. The beach is a long black sand crescent bisected in the middle by the Waipio River. There are many large smooth boulders and rubble at the south end. While some swimmers, bodysurfers, and surfers ride the often good waves here, the presence of strong rip currents make the beach extremely dangerous to even advanced swimmers. Caution is advised. There are no facilities of any kind on the beach.

NORTH HILO AREA

Like the Hamakua Coast, the North Hilo area has formed few sandy beaches. There are small pockets of black lava rock sand in some areas, but coral sand beaches are non-existent. The generally high coastline pali (cliff) also accounts for a lack of good beaches in the area. But the area has a special rugged beauty that is captured in places like Laupahoehoe Park listed here.

LAUPAHOEHOE POINT PARK ★

The park is a lava rock peninsula jutting into the ocean at Laupahoehoe. The area is typical of the Hamakua Coast in that there are steep rugged cliffs throughout the area and hardly any safe sandy beaches. The beach on this sea-level peninsula is mostly coral pebbles and rocks. Strong surf and rip currents prevent most water activities although some do swim and surf. The rocky shoreline requires extreme caution. Park facilities include picnic pavilions, restrooms, showers, water, parking, and camping sites. A new small boat launching facility was recently completed. It is a pleasant park to picnic and enjoy the scenic beauty of the Hamakua Coast. On a warm day, lots of ironwood trees provide cool shade to enjoy the pastoral Hawaiian scenery.

SOUTH HILO AREA

The South Hilo area is marked by a few lovely beach parks. Most of these facilities are frequented by local residents enjoying a pleasant day at the beach usually with youngsters. The Keaukaha area beaches in Hilo have generally calm tide pools that are good for children. Onekahakaha Park has a protected pool with a sandy bottom which is especially good for youngsters.

KOLEKOLE BEACH PARK ★
Despite not having a sandy beach this is one of the Big Island's loveliest parks. It is fronted by a shoreline of smooth waterworn lava rocks with an adjacent coldwater stream and waterfall. The park grounds and surrounding valley walls are lush and full of tropical vegetation. The stream flows from the beautiful Akaka Falls Park located upstream some four miles. While water activities are somewhat limited, the park is an excellent place for a day outing to picnic, explore, and enjoy Hawaii's tropical outdoors. Park facilities include restrooms, pavilions, water, showers, and camping areas.

HONOLII BEACH PARK
Located just north of Hilo off Highway 19, on the old scenic route, Mamalahoa Highway. This is a favorite with local teenagers as it is one of the best surfing beaches in the Hilo area. Restrooms and very limited parking along the roadside are available. It's a good spot for just watching local kids catch the waves on a nice day.

REED'S BAY BOAT HARBOR AND ICE POND
These are just off Kalanianaole Avenue on Banyan Drive and across from the Hilo Seaside Hotel. Though not exactly a beach area, the Ice Pond is a spring-fed stream which flows into Hilo Bay via Reed's Bay small boat harbor. It's a popular swimming hole for local kids.

Spread out along Kalanianaole Avenue in the Keaukaha area of Hilo town and past the airport and harbor piers are Hilo's beach parks.

ONEKAHAKAHA BEACH PARK ★
The park features a protected sandy bottom swimming area for youngsters, pavilions, picnic tables, camp sites and restrooms.

JAMES KEALOHA PARK
The park has a smooth lava rock beach and picnic areas and restrooms. Good swimming, surfing and snorkeling are available here.

LELEIWI BEACH PARK
This park also has smooth lava rock beach and pavilions, picnic areas, and restrooms. Swimming, snorkeling and surfing are good here. This is the site of the Richardson Ocean Center, a marine education and aquatic display center open to the public. See the GENERAL INFORMATION chapter, "Traveling With Children/Entertainment" section for details on the Richardson Ocean Center. There is no charge.

PUNA AREA

The Puna beaches tend to be in fairly isolated areas several miles from the nearest town or commercial areas. The black sand beaches of Puna have long been among the Big Island's more notable features and attractions for their contrasting beauty.

CAUTION!: The beaches of the Puna area have had extremely heavy use by area residents since the lava flows of 1990-93 have destroyed the Kalapana area and its famed black sand beaches. Area residents who used to frequent the Kalapana beaches have now moved on to the other beaches in the area, causing serious problems of overcrowding, heavy facilities use, etc. These beaches for the most part were undeveloped and had virtually no restroom, water-showers, parking and other park facilities. One new beach park was established at Puala'a but serious overcrowding of park facilities and heavy use continue. Visitors should keep in mind that the following beaches may be very crowded and facilities non-existent or seriously overloaded.

KAPOHO BAY
The bay is the back shore area fronting Kapoho Beach Lots and Vacationland Estates subdivisions in the Kapoho area. While there is not a sandy beach here, it is a beautiful tidal pond and pool area which is great for snorkeling and swimming. The tidal pools have a variety of marine life and small fish to view. There are no facilities.

ISAAC HALE BEACH PARK
The park is on Cape Kumikahi, along the Puna Coast, and is the site of a busy boat launching ramp used by commercial fishermen. Other activities of the bay include surfing, bodyboarding, and swimming. The beach here is mostly smooth pebbles and cobblestones and not fine sand. There are restrooms and showers available. Behind the beach area in a natural lava rock pool are the Pohoiki Warm Springs, a natural warm water bath heated by underground geothermal action that are used for bathing and soaking.

KEHENA BEACH
Located on Pohoiki Road between Cape Kumikahi and Kaimu-Kalapana. The beach is a broad expanse of fine black sand below the Kehena Lookout and parking area. Access is via a steep trail down the cliff face. Kehena Beach is popular with swimmers and bodysurfers. No facilities available.

PUALA'A PARK
This is recently developed beach park was established with a federal grant to replace parks lost at Kalapana to recent volcanic lava flows. The park is located two and a half miles south of the junction of Highways 132 and 137 on the Kapoho coast southeast of Pahoa town. The three-acre park features a half-acre pond fed by thermal freshwater springs mixed with seawater. There are limited facilities such as portable restrooms and no drinking water. Government officials hope that additional improvements can be made to make the new park fully functional for recreation.

KA'U AREA

The Ka'u area is most famous for its Green Sand Beach which is quite remote, but accessible with some effort and a 4-wheel drive vehicle, or a long hot hike. Ka'u is very dry and warm with long stretches of empty countryside. The South Point area from which Green Sand Beach can be reached is an interesting historical site with old Hawaiian canoe landings and ruins in place.

PUNALU'U BEACH PARK
Located near Pahala. This is a moderately long black sand beach backed by low dunes. The bay has a small boat launching ramp. Swimmers and snorkelers will find conditions here only fair and should be cautious about venturing beyond the boat ramp due to a powerful rip current which constantly runs out to the boat channel. The current converges with an even stronger shore current outside the bay which makes it even more hazardous for swimmers. Hawaiian green sea turtles are quite numerous in this bay and easily spotted as they surface and feed close in to shore where they graze sea weed on the rocks and coral. Showers, restrooms and picnic pavilion are available.

GREEN SAND BEACH
The beach at Mahana Bay is reached via the end of South Point Road and a very rough four mile (round trip) coastal road, negotiable only by 4-wheel drive vehicle. The really adventurous can opt to hike the four miles. If you hike, just be sure you take enough water and other necessities. The beach is accessed by a steep and hazardous trail down the cliff side which has loose rocks and cinders making for slippery footing. Caution is advised. The tinted sand is loaded with green olivine crystals, a component of Hawai'i's lava. Big grains of olivine give the sand a distinctly green color and glassy luster. The beach, at the base of a huge eroding volcanic cinder cone, is exposed to the sea directly and heavy surf and storms create dangerous surf conditions. Swimming and snorkeling are advised on only the calmest of days and extreme caution is in order.

BOOKING AGENTS
AND REPRESENTATIVES

Check with your hotel or resort activity desk, or any of the following agencies to make reservations and arrangements for a full range of ocean or water sports activities on the Kona and Kohala Coasts. They can help you arrange everything from whale watching cruises, to diving and snorkeling cruises, fishing charters, sailboat rentals, surfboard and windsurfing rentals, etc. They represent many of the individual cruise, snorkel, and dive operators and fishing charters that are listed in the following sections. Reservations can be made directly with the operators or charter boats or through any of these agencies. You will notice that the bulk of the listings in this and other ocean activities sections are in the Kona-Kohala area of the island. The Hilo area does have a couple of charter fishing boats listed but most visitor activities take place along the Kona and Kohala Coasts.

The following are sample approximate prices for some of the various cruises and sailings available. Check the individual listings for details and call the tour operators for the most current rates or specials and children's rates. As in the rest of this book regarding costs, prices shown are the latest at publication time and are subject to change without notice.

One hour glassbottom boat cruise	- $15-20 per person
One hour submarine dive	- $80 per person
One hour semi-submersible cruise	- $35 per person
1 or 2 tank scuba dive cruise	- $65-85 and up per person
1/2 day whale watch/snorkeling cruise	- $35-55 and up per person
1/2 day raft trip	- $65 per person
Sunset dinner boat cruise	- $45-55 per person
Sunset cocktail cruise	- $25 per person
Charter yacht sunset sail	- $175 for the boat
One week comprehensive scuba diving cruise aboard an exclusive yacht	- $2,000 per person.

Aloha Kai Sailing - Waikoloa, HI 96743; (808) 883-9696. This booking service can arrange customized sailing adventures on several different sailing vessels in the Kona and Kohala areas. Customized sailing adventures range from 2 hours to 2 weeks, from around the Big Island to inter-island cruises in Hawai'i. Sailings are recreational and educational focusing on oceanography, marine science, sailing, fishing and more.

Kona Charter Skippers Association, Inc. - 75-5663 Palani Road, Kailua-Kona, HI 96740; 1-800-367-8047 ext. 360, Hawai'i (808) 329-3600. This operation provides complete booking service for Kona's charter fishing fleet, recreational, snorkel-diving cruises and related water sports and activities.

Kona Coast Activities - 75-5744 Alii Drive, Kona Inn Shopping Center, Kailua-Kona, HI 96740; 1-800-367-5105, or 808 329-2971. This service specializes in deep-sea fishing charters, snorkel and dive cruises, pleasure cruises, dinner cruises, jet-skiing, parasailing and other water sports activities.

Kona Marlin Center - 74-381 Kealakehe Parkway, Honokohau Harbor, Kailua-Kona, HI 96740; 1-800-648-7529, Hawai'i (808) 326-1177. This booking service offers charter deep-sea fishing from a fleet of over 35 boats. Watch the daily fish weigh-ins at 11:30AM and 3:30PM on the Honokohau Harbor docks from free public viewing area. Deli, gas station and general store also available.

Kona Marina Sports Activities - 74-425 Kealakehe Parkway, #6A, Honokohau Harbor, Kailua-Kona, HI 96740; (808) 329-1115, FAX (808) 329-9104. This service can arrange a variety of ocean sports activities and specialize in deep-sea fishing and dive charters. They can arrange full or half day as well as share-parties.

Kona Pier Activity Shack - at the Kona Pier on Alii Drive in front of the King Kamehameha Kona Beach Hotel, Kailua-Kona (808) 329-7494). This service can arrange a variety of water sports activities, fishing, boating, cruises, etc.

Kona Water Sports Inc. - 75-5695G Alii Drive, Kailua-Kona, HI 96740; (808) 329-1593. This agent provides bookings for jet boats and jet skis as well as parasailing reservations. They also carry a complete line of rental and sales water sports equipment including snorkel gear, boogie boards, underwater cameras, air mattresses, inflatable kayaks and boats, and glass bottom boats.

Ocean Sports-Waikoloa - located on Anaehoomalu Beach in front of the Royal Waikoloan Hotel, 69-275 Waikoloa Beach Drive, Kohala Coast, HI 96743; U.S. 1-800-367-8088, Hawai'i (808) 885-5555. Specializing in champagne sunset sails, whale watching, scuba dives, deep-sea fishing charters, and glass bottom boat cruises. Water sports equipment rentals.

Red Sail Sports - One Waikoloa Beach, Hilton Waikoloa Village, Kohala Coast, HI 96743, (808) 885-2876; and One North Kaniku, Sheraton Orchid Mauna Lani, Kohala Coast, HI 96743, (808) 885-2000; and Hapuna Beach Prince Hotel, Mauna Kea Resort (808) 880-1111. This general booking agency handles everything from catamaran cruises for lunch snorkel sails, sunset cocktail sails and scuba dives, to bicycle adventures and a complete line of water sports equipment and lagoon toys.

The Charter Locker - Kealakehe Parkway, Honokohau Harbor, Kailua-Kona, III 96740; 1-800-247-1484, Hawai'i (808) 326-2553. This service specializes in fishing and boat charters, private or shared basis, full or half day.

HUMUHUMUNUKUNUKUAPUAA

SEA EXCURSIONS AND
GLASSBOTTOM BOAT CRUISES

The following cruises generally sail along the Kona Coast taking in historic sites, fascinating reefs for glassbottom viewing or snorkeling, historic Kealakekua Bay marine reserve and Captain Cook Monument, and the Pu'uhonua O Honaunau National Historic Park at Honaunau, the best preserved ancient Hawaiian heiau (temple) site in the islands. The cruises generally last from 2 hours to half-day and vary in cost depending on length and what is included. Check the following listings for details.

BEST BETS:

Nautilus II Semi-submersible - underwater dive/cruise over Kona Coast coral reefs for close-up look at marine life and fish

Royal Hawaiian Cruises - half-day swim-snorkel cruise to Kealakekua Bay marine reserve

Adventure Sailing - (1-800-726-7245, or 808 326-5174) P.O.Box 44335, Kamuela, HI 96743. This operator offers a variety of special cruises aboard the 50' Gulfstar "Maile" including overnight and interisland outings, whale encounters, snorkeling explorations, ecology tours, sunset sails and more.

Atlantis Submarine ★- (329-6626, FAX 808 329-3177) 75-5660 Palani Road, Hotel King Kamehameha, Kailua-Kona, HI 96740. These unique underwater cruises operate with a $2.5 million submarine designed to take guests down to depths of 150 ft. through Kona's fabulous underwater world. The cruises take you along Kona's colorful reefs where you get a fish's-eye view of marine life. Morning and afternoon hourly departures Monday-Friday only, 9AM-3PM, are from Kailua Pier. Adults $79, children under 12, $39.

Captain Bob's Kona Reef Tours ★- (322-3102) P.O. Box 2016, Kailua-Kona, HI 96745. This service offers glassbottom boat cruises over two miles of Kona Coast reefs. This is Kona's original glassbottom cruise since 1968. Departures are daily except Saturday and Monday from Kailua Pier at 10:30AM, 11AM, 1:30PM, and 3PM. Adults are $18, children $9.

Captain Zodiac - (1-800-247-1484, or 808 329-3199, FAX 329-7590) P.O.Box 5612, Honokohau Harbor, Kealakehe Parkway, Kailua-Kona, HI 96740. Daily expeditions in motorized inflatable rubber white-water rafts along the Kona Coast which take in sea caves, old Hawaiian village sites, and snorkeling in Kealakekua Bay marine reserve on a 4 hour cruise. Snorkel equipment and tropical lunch included. Departures at 8AM and 1PM. Adults $65, children under-12 $55.

Hawaii Sailing Company Inc. - (326-1986) 76-6268B Alii Drive, Kailua-Kona, HI 96740. This operator offers a variety of sailings and cruises including half-day and weekly cruises, picnic sails, whale watching and snorkeling. Check for rates.

Kona Whale Watching - (325-5556) P.O.Box 1522, Kailua-Kona, HI 96745. This operator uses a 28' vessel that is limited to just six whalewatchers. The standard cruise is a three-hour quest to site humpbacks, sperm, false killer, melon-headed, and pilot whales plus four-species of dolphins along the Kona Coast. Daily departures at 8:30AM and 12:30PM Cruise cost is $47.50 adults, $32 kids under 12. Exclusive three-hour charters available.

Moana Pua - (885-5555) Ocean Sports Waikoloa, 69-275 Waikoloa Beach Drive, Kohala Coast, HI 96743; this is a 58' deluxe catamaran which is available for exclusive charters for up to 25 people. Based at Anaehoomalu Bay in front of the Royal Waikoloan Hotel. Customized cruises along the Kohala Coast including premium bar beverages and gourmet fare. Call for rates.

Nautilus II ★- (1-800-821-2210, 808/326-2003) 75-5663 Palani Road, Kailua-Kona, HI 96740. Office located under The Gallery Restaurant directly across from the pier. This undersea adventure uses a 58-foot 49-passenger semi-submersible craft which cruises Kona's coral reefs for spectacular views of fish and reeflife. The spacious air-conditioned cabin has large windows for underwater viewing so everybody gets to see and there is topside deck viewing too. One-hour narrated tour cruises depart daily beginning at 9:30AM from Kailua Pier. If you've never seen the underwater world of the coral reef first-hand and have always wanted to, then this is the adventure for you. This is an excellent educational tour for youngsters of all ages. Tour rates are $40 for adults, $25 for children under 12. aged 3 and under are free.

Royal Hawaiian Cruises ★ - (326-2999) 74-5606 Pawai Place #101, Kailua-Kona, HI 96740. Captain Cook VIII glassbottom boat cruise has twice daily departures from Kailua Pier, 9AM - 1PM, 1:30 - 5:30PM. Half-day cruise along the Kona Coast includes swimming and snorkeling at the Kealakekua Bay marine reserve, glassbottom viewing of reefs and fish, live Hawaiian entertainment, and continental breakfast/lunch or afternoon snack/dinner. Adults $75, children under 12 $55.

Whale Watch - (322-0028) P.O.Box 139, Holualoa, HI 96725. Operated by long-time Kona marine biologist and whale researcher, Captain Dan McSweeney, Whale Watch guarantees a whale sighting. The cruises use 36' and 32' U.S. Coast Guard approved vessels, fully equipped with underwater window for viewing the whales. Three hour cruises depart daily at 9AM and 1PM from Honokohau Harbor just north of Kailua-Kona. Adults $42. children under 12 $32.

SNORKELING AND DIVING CRUISES

Several of the cruise operators listed in the previous section are briefly cross-listed here as they also offer snorkeling and/or diving cruises often combined with their general sight-seeing pleasure cruises. Specific information is listed in the previous section for each operator and further information and reservations can be obtained by calling the numbers listed. Other cruise operators cater to snorkelers or scuba divers exclusively and these are detailed here.

BEST BETS: **Fair Wind** - daily scuba and snorkeling cruises depart from Keauhou Bay pier, **Jack's Diving Locker** - operates special scuba charters, **Dive Makai Charters** - offers scuba dives at the Kona Coast's best dive locations.

Body Glove Cruises - (326-7122) P.O.Box 4523, Kailua-Kona, HI 96745. This 55' trimaran offers a 4 1/2 hour daily morning sail and snorkel, snuba, scuba cruise along the Kona Coast departing from Kailua Pier at 9AM. Continental breakfast and deli lunch included. Snorkel-diving adventure includes rich marine life, caves, arches and dolphins, manta rays and turtles. Rates start at adults $58, children $25.

Dive Makai Charters - (329-2025) 74-5590I Alapa, Kailua-Kona, HI 96740. This charter shop offers a full range of snorkel-dive tours and charters.

Fair Wind ★ - (322-2788) 78-7130 Kaleopapa Road, Keauhou Bay, Kona, HI 96740. This sailing catamaran offers two daily snorkel and scuba diving cruises with instruction and snorkeling gear included. The luncheon cruise departs at 9AM and returns at 1:30PM. Cruise includes continental breakfast and burgers for lunch. The cruise visits Kealakekua Bay for 2 1/2 hrs. Adults are $59, children 5-12 yrs are $33, toddlers free. The afternoon cruise departs at 1:45PM returning at 4:45PM and includes all gear and snacks. There is a charge for scuba diving tanks and gear. Cruises depart from Keauhou Bay pier. Rates start at adults $40, children 5-12 yrs $26.

Jack's Diving Locker ★ - (329-7585 or 1-800-345-4807) 75-5819 Alii Drive, Coconut Grove Marketplace, Kailua-Kona, HI 96740. This dive operator offers special scuba diving charters, night dives, instruction and certification, and complete diving equipment sales and rentals. Dive rates begin at $78 per person.

Kamanu - (329-2021) 74-425 Kealakehe Parkway, #16, Kailua-Kona, HI 96740. This is a 36 ft. catamaran offering daily snorkeling cruises along the Kona Coast. Each 3 1/4 hour cruise includes 1 1/2 hours of snorkeling time plus all gear, instruction, drinks and tropical lunch. Good for beginning snorkelers, novices or experts. Hand feed colorful fish at Pawai Bay. Cruises depart daily from Honokohau Harbor at 9AM and 1:30PM. Adults $40, children under 12 - $22.

Kona Aggressor II - (1-800-344-5662 or 808 329-8182, FAX 808 329-2628) Live/Dive Pacific Inc., 74-5588 Pawai Place, Bldg.F, Kailua-Kona, HI 96740. This dive operation features one week trips with unlimited diving. Guests live aboard a 110 ft. luxurious full service diving yacht. There are private staterooms with bath, a 24-hour open galley, an onboard photo processing lab, and a sundeck. This is the ultimate in diving luxury. The boat can accommodate up to 20 people. Rates start at about $2000 per person for a week of cruising and diving. The cost includes all meals and bar beverages. Four and five day charters are available at special rates. Cruises depart Kailua Pier each Saturday.

Kona Water Sports Inc. - (329-1593) 75-5695G Alii Drive, Kailua-Kona, HI 96740. Offers a complete line of water sports equipment rentals and sales including snorkeling gear, boogie boards, underwater cameras, kayaks and boats, and glass bottom boats.

Lanakila Ventures - (326-6000) Kailua Pier, Kailua-Kona; this twin-masted sailing yacht cruises the coral reef waters along the Kona Coast on morning and afternoon snorkel cruises, tropical brunch cruise and an Aloha Dinner Cruise in the evenings. Cruise rates start at adults $55, children $23; dinner cruise is adults $38, children $20.

Miller's Snorkeling - (326-1771) 76-6246 Alii Drive, 3 miles south of Kailua-Kona at the Kona Bali Kai Condo. This outfitter rents all types of watersports and beach equipment including masks, snorkels, fins, flotation vests, beach chairs, boogie boards, viewing boards, picnic coolers, umbrellas and more. Open daily 8AM - 5PM.

Party Boat - (334-0444) P.O.Box 3540, Kailua-Kona, HI 96745. This 46' sailing catamaran offers snorkeling cruises along the Kona Coast. Cruise includes narration of Kona Coast, continental breakfast, full BBQ lunch, full bar service, complete snorkeling gear and instruction, snorkeling at Kealakekua Bay Marine Reserve. Daily cruises depart at 8AM and return at 1:30PM; adults $46, children (4-12) $22. Departs from Kailua Pier.

Second Wind Sail/Snorkel Charters - (334-0577) P.O.Box 4516, Kailua-Kona, HI 96745. This operator offers a variety of sailing and snorkeling cruises along the Kona Coast area. Rates start at $58 for a half day cruise, $37 for a 2.5 hour sail.

Sea Quest - (329-7238) P.O.Box 390292, Kailua-Kona, HI 96739. This operator offers snorkeling cruises with inflatable boats taking in the remote areas between Keauhou Bay and Honaunau. The cruises take in sea caves, lava tubes, Captain Cook's Monument at Kealakekua Bay and the Pu'uhonua O Honaunau National Historic Park at Honaunau with diving time allowed. $55 per person for a four hour morning adventure or $45 per person for a three-hour afternoon outing; includes snacks, beverages and snorkel gear.

Snuba - (326-7446) 74-5660 Palani Road, Kailua-Kona, HI 96740. This operator offers various snuba diving adventures and can book snorkel dives with other cruise boats in Kona. Snuba dives begin at $55 per person.

The Exploration Co. - (1-800-238-1008, 808/327-9409) 75-5669 Alii Drive, Kailua-Kona, HI 96740, across from Kailua Pier. This outfitter offers a variety of half-day and longer snorkel-dive and kayaking paddle tours along the Kona Coast and to the marine reserve at historic Kealakekua Bay.

DIVE SHOPS

Aqua Nuts Hawaii - (969-6887) 70 Keaa St., Hilo, HI 96720. This outfitter provides island-wide shore dives, equipment, rentals and dive tours specializing in East Hawaii coastal areas.

Big Island Divers - (329-6068) 75-5467 Kaiwi St., Kailua-Kona, HI 96740. Complete charter packages, introductory lessons, sales and rentals of equipment and certifications available. Open daily 8AM - 6PM.

Dive Makai Charters - (329-2025) 74-5590 I Alapa Road, Kailua-Kona, HI 96740. Personalized diving cruises and personal service are the emphasis of this dive shop. Complete dive packages and equipment rentals are available.

East Hawaii Divers - (965-7840) P.O.Box 2001, Pahoa, HI 96778. This outfitter offers a range of dives and full scuba equipment rentals.

Eco-Adventures - (329-7116) Kailua-Kona. This operator has daily boat dives and special night dives and manta ray dives available.

Jack's Diving Locker - (1-800-345-4807, 329-7585), 75-5819 Alii Drive, Coconut Grove Marketplace, Kailua-Kona, HI 96740. This operator offers a variety of scuba charters and cruise dives, certification lessons, introductory dives and equipment sales and rentals.

King Kamehameha Divers - (329-5662) 75-5660 Palani Drive, King Kamehameha Kona Beach Hotel, Kailua-Kona, HI 96740. This shop offers scuba and snorkel charters, instruction, sales and rentals of equipment, underwater video and camera services, etc. Open Monday - Saturday 7AM - 7PM, Sunday 7AM - 5PM.

Kohala Divers Ltd. ★ - (882-7774) Kawaihae Shopping Center, Kawaihae, Kohala Coast, HI 96743. This shop offers a full range of professional diving services, equipment sales and rentals, and dive charters along the Kohala Coast. Open daily 8AM - 5PM.

Kona Coast Divers ★- (329-8802) 75-5614 Palani Road, Kailua-Kona, HI 96740. They offer diving charters and a full range of sales-service-rentals on professional diving equipment. Open daily 7AM - 6PM.

Live Dive Pacific Inc. - (1-800-344-5662, or 808 329-8182, FAX 808 329-2628) 74-5588 Pawai Place, Bldg. F, Kailua-Kona, HI 96740. This operator offers varied diving/snorkeling cruises along the Kona Coast and they operate the Kona Aggressor II luxury diving yacht (see previous section for details).

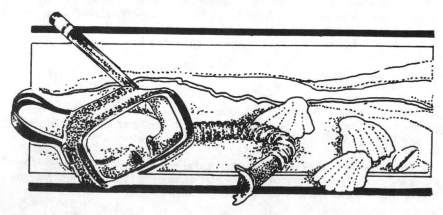

Mauna Kea Divers - (882-7730) located at the Mauna Kea Beach Hotel, Kohala Coast, HI 96743. Complete diving packages, underwater tours, charters and equipment rentals are available.

Nautilus Dive Center Inc. - (935-6939) 382 Kamehameha Ave., Hilo, HI 96720. This shop features complete sales-service-rentals of professional diving equipment. They also provide instruction and have a five day certification program. Scuba charters along the East Hawai'i coast are available. Open daily 9AM - 4PM.

Ocean Sports Waikoloa - (885-5555) 69-275 Waikoloa Beach Drive, Waikoloa Resort, HI 96743. Located at Anaeho'omalu Beach in front of the Royal Waikoloan Hotel, Kohala Coast. This outfitter can arrange scuba and snorkeling dives and a whole range of water sports activities.

Red Sail Sports - (885-2876) Hilton Waikoloa Village, Waikoloa Resort; (885-2000) Sheraton Orchid Mauna Lani, Mauna Lani Resort; (880-1111) Hapuna Beach Prince Resort, Mauna Kea Resort. This water sports outfitter provides a full range of diving equipment rentals, cruises and dive tours on the Kohala Coast.

Sandwich Isle Divers - (329-9188) 75-5729I Alii Drive, Kailua-Kona, HI 96740, in the Kona Marketplace. This shop provides small charters with a personal touch offering daily trips along the Kona Coast. Open daily 8AM - 8PM.

Sea Dreams Hawai'i - (329-8744) P.O. Box 4886, Kailua-Kona, HI 96745. This shop can arrange complete scuba dive charters for the Kona Coast area.

Sea Paradise Scuba - (1-800-322-5662, in Hawai'i 322-2500) 78-7128 Kaleopapa Road, Kailua-Kona, HI 96740. This shop offers a full range of morning, afternoon and night dives as well as beginner "Try Scuba" dives and snorkeling outings on dive cruises. A complete line of equipment rentals is available. Cruises depart from Keauhou Bay dock.

Snorkel Bob's - (329-0770) 75-5831 Kahakai Road, Kailua-Kona, HI 96740. This outfitter will rent a complete snorkel set for $15 a week or by the day. Complete snorkeling equipment available, including mask, fins, sterilized snorkel, underwater cameras and boogie boards.

Snorkel Surf & Dive Hawaii - (329-0046) 75-5744 Alii Drive, Kona Village Inn Shopping Center, Kailua-Kona, HI 96740. This outfitter provides a range of boat charters, dive tours and complete dive equipment rentals.

DEEP SEA FISHING

There are few places in the world that can match the renown or reputation of the Kona Coast for the thrill and excitement of big game fishing. Kona is the site for the annual Hawaiian International Billfish Tournament which for the past 30 years or so has attracted participants from around the world. In addition, there are numerous other fishing tournaments held throughout the year.

273

Kona and its harbors homeport a large fleet of charter fishing boats that offer a complete range of full and half-day arrangements. Prices vary depending upon the size of the boat and how it is equipped (showers, beds, fully-stocked galley, etc.). Full day charters can range from $275-300 and up while half-day charters can range from $175-200 and up. These prices are for the entire boat, not a per person rate. You can private charter the entire boat or share charter with other anglers. Half-day share rates start at about $50 per person. Most boats take no more than 6 anglers at a time and provide all fishing equipment. No license is required in Hawai'i. Generally you must bring your own food and beverages as these are not included in charter rates.

Because of Hawai'i's generally low charter boat rates in comparison to other areas, the general policy among charter boat associations is that any fish caught belong to the boat rather than the fisherman. Boat captains and owners use fish caught to sell on the market to augment their low charter fares. This is the reason for the policy. However, if a fisherman really wants his catch, or part of it, he must request it from the captain. In the case of good table fish such as mahimahi or ahi tuna, most captains will be more than happy to share the catch with the fishing party to enjoy a fresh fish dinner. However, it is always best to inquire beforehand and put in a request to keep some of the catch.

And so what can you expect to catch, with a little traditional fishing luck? Kona's waters teem with a variety of Hawaiian game fish. Perhaps most popular is the Pacific Blue Marlin with an average size of 300-400 lbs., but with fish up to 1000 lbs. entirely possible. Striped marlin average 50-100 lbs. and black marlin average 200 lbs. Sailfish are also common in Kona's waters and average 50 lbs. or less. Swordfish are generally more difficult to catch but average 250 lbs. when they are landed. The popular yellow fin tuna ranges up to 300 lbs. while the dolphin (mahimahi) averages 25 lbs.

CHARTERING A BOAT: If you're familiar with deep sea fishing and boat chartering, you may contact any of the following boats directly. However, if you are unsure of just what chartering a boat entails, you would be best advised to contact one of the Booking Agencies/Representatives listed earlier in this section. Some of these agencies represent several boats and can give you complete information on booking a charter. These agencies include:

Kona Activities Center - (1-800-367-5288 or 808/329-3171) P.O.Box 1035, Kailua-Kona, HI 96745

Kona Marlin Center - (1-800-648-7529 or 808/326-1177) 74-381 Kealakehe Parkway, Honokohau Harbor, Kailua-Kona, HI 96740

Kona Charter Skippers Association - (329-3600) 75-5663 Palani Road, Kailua-Kona, HI 96740

Kona Marina Sports Activities - (329-1115) Kealakehe Parkway, Honokohau Harbor, Kailua-Kona, HI 96740

The Charter Locker Activities - (326-2553) Kealakehe Parkway, Honokohau Harbor, Kailua-Kona, HI 96740

Note!: All charter fishing boats are completely certified and licensed. In addition to being licensing as commercial fishing boats, the captain(s) and boat must be fully certified and licensed by the United States Coast Guard.

Adobie - 30' Topaz, Ron Platt, P.O. Box Y, Kailua-Kona, HI 96745 (808) 329-5669

Aerial - 38' Bertram, Capt. Rick Rose, 74-425 Kealakehu Parkway #16, Kailua-Kona, HI 96745, (808) 329-5603

Anxious - 31' Bertram, Capt. Ed Issacs, 75-217 Nani Kailua Dr. #189, Kailua-Kona, HI 96745, (808) 326-1229.

Bill Buster - 36' Trojan Sportfisher, Capt. Butch Lo Sasso, P.O.Box 4235, Kailua-Kona, HI 96745; (808) 329-2657, 326-8272 or FAX (808) 329-2657.

Blue Hawai'i - 53' Hatteras, Capt. Del Cannon, 78-6645 Alii Drive, Kailua-Kona, HI 96740, (808) 322-3210

Catchem One - 30' Force, Capt. Chuck Haupert, 77 6451 Leilani, Kailua-Kona, HI 96740, (808) 329-2670

Cheers - 30' Glas-Ply, Capt. Gary Travis, 75-6509 Sea View Circle, Kailua-Kona, HI 96740, (808) 329-6484 or 322-9777

Cherry Pit II - 26' Blackman, Capt. Jim Cherry, P.O.Box 278, Holualoa, HI 96725, (808) 326-7781

Foolish Pleasures - Kaloko Mauka, Kailua-Kona (325-7637)

Foxy Lady - 42' Uniflite, Capt. Bobby Erickson, P.O. Box 762 Kalaoa, Kailua-Kona, HI 96745, (808) 325-5552

Hapa Laka - 21' Custom, Capt. Alan Borowski, P.O. Box 2051 Kailua-Kona, HI 96745, (808) 322-2229

Holiday - 44' Custom, Capt. Doug Pattengill, P.O. Box 1964, Kailua-Kona, HI 96745, (808) 325-5230 or boat (808) 329-3050

Hua Pala - 35' Uniflite, Capt. Larry Pries, 73-1089 Ahulani Street, Kailua-Kona, HI 96740, (808) 325-3277 or 325-7595

Humdinger - 37' Rybovich, Capt. Jeff Fay, P.O.Box 1995, Kailua-Kona, HI 96745
(808) 325-3449 or boat phone 936-3034

Hustler - 34' Blackfin, Capt. Glen Hodson, P.O. Box 4976, Kailua-Kona, HI 96745, (808) 329-6303

Illusion - 39' Topaz, Capt. Juan Waroquiers, P.O. Box 1816, Kamuela, HI 96743 1-800-482-FISH or (808) 883-0180, or boat (808) 936-4557

Intrepid - 38' Bertram, Capt. Richard Keith, P.O. Box 3168, Kailua-Kona, HI 96745, (808) 322-8012

Island Girl - 44' SeaRay, Capt. John Llanes, P.O. Box 732, Kailua-Kona, HI 96745, (808) 322-6605

Janet B - 35' Luger, Capt. Phil Bell, P.O.Box 5432, Kailua-Kona, HI 96745, 1-800-658-8624, or (808) 325-6374, FAX (602) 894-2993

Jun Ken Po - P.O. Box 4841, Kailua-Kona, HI 96745 (808) 325-7710

Lady Dee - 47' Bertram, 78-6626 Alii Drive, Kailua-Kona, HI 96740 (808) 322-8026

Layla- 31' Innovator, Capt. Bruce Evans, 75-411 Hoene St., Kailua-Kona, HI 96740 (808) 329-6899, or boat (808) 936-3232

Lei Aloha - 40' Jersey, Capt. Mike Holtz, Kailua-Kona, (808) 329-4262

Lil' Hooker - 26' Blackman, Capt. Jeff Parish, 75-327 Aloha Kona Drive, Kailua-Kona, HI 96740, (808) 326-1666

Long Ranger - 50' Hatteras, Capt. Bob Russell, 74-5603 Alapa, Kailua-Kona, HI 96740, (808) 329-4549

Lucky Lil - 73-1078 Ahikawa, Kailua-Kona, HI 96740, (808) 325-5438

Marlin Magic - 43' Custom, Capt. Marlin Parker, Kaloko, Kona, HI, (808) 325-7138

Medusa - 38' Ocean Yacht, Capt. Steve Kaiser, P.O. Box 857, Holualoa, HI 96725, 1-800-367-8047 ext. 458 or (808) 329-1328

No Mercy - 28' Tollycraft, Capt. Todd Stemer, Kailua-Kona, HI, (808) 325-5200

Northern Lights - 37' Merritt, Capt. Kelley Everette, P.O. Box 2098, Kailua-Kona, HI 96745, (808) 325-6522

Omega - 28' Smartfisher, Capt. Klaus Kropp, P.O. Box 5323, Kailua-Kona, HI 96745, (808) 325-7859 or 325-7593

Pacific Blue - 41' Hatteras, Capt. Bill Casey, 74-5071 Kumakani, Kailua-Kona, HI 96740, (808) 329-9468 or boat (808) 936-3055

Pamela - 38' Bertram, Capt. Peter Hoogs, P.O. Box 345, Kailua-Kona, HI 96745, (808) 329-1525

Reel Pleasure - 36' Topaz, Capt. Ed Gordy, Kawaihae Harbor, Kohala Coast (808) 882-1413

Sea Baby III - 35' Sportfisher, Capt. W. Kobayashi, Kalaoa, Kona, HI, (808) 325-7727

Sea Genie II - 39' Rybovich, Capt. Gene Vander Hoek, P.O.Box 4126, Kailua-Kona, HI 96745, (808) 325-5355 or FAX (808) 325-5366

Sea Genie - 36' Harris, Capt. Guy Terwilliger, P.O. Box 4126, Kailua-Kona, HI 96745, (808) 324-0341 or FAX (808) 325-5366

Sea Wife - 38' Delta, Capt. Tim Cox, P.O. Box 2645, Kailua-Kona, HI 96745, (808) 329-1806

Show Time - 44' Ocean Yacht, Capt. K.Y. Rogers, P.O. Box 5382, Kailua-Kona, HI 96745, (808) 326-SHOW or FAX (808) 326-2561.

Stars & Strikes - 34' Bayliner, Capt. Dan Harrigan, 73-4342 Pahee Place, Kailua-Kona, HI 96740, (808) 325-6357 or 325-3277

Sundowner - 35' Bertram, Capt. Norm Isaacs, P.O. Box 5198, Kailua-Kona, HI 96745, (808) 329-7253

White Roc - 38' Pacemaker, 78-505 Puuiki Road, Kailua-Kona, HI 96740, (808) 322-3832

Wild West - 39' Kris Kraft, Capt. Robert West, 78-6918 Kia Aina, Kailua-Kona, HI 96740, (808) 322-4700

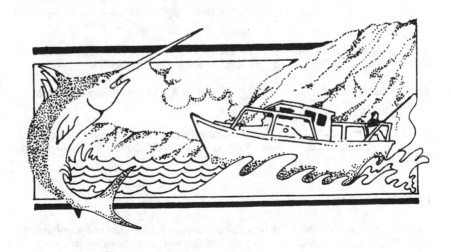

WINDSURFING/JETSKIIS
PARASAILING/KAYAKS-HOBIE CATS

WINDSURFING

Windsurfing conditions and locations are best on the west side of the Big Island. The Kona and Kohala beaches generally have the most favorable wind and surf conditions for windsurfing over other areas of the Big Island. Check with the following water sports concessions for equipment rental.

BEST BETS: **Anaeho'omalu Beach** - Waikoloa, Kohala Coast, **Hapuna Beach** - Kohala Coast, **Kauna'oa Beach** - Kohala Coast

Activity Information Center - (329-7700 or Fax 326-9150) 76-5828 Alii Drive, Kailua-Kona, HI 96740; (885-0000) Kings Shops, Waikoloa Resort, Kohala Coast.

Kona Water Sports Inc. - (329-1593) 75-5695G Alii Drive, Banyan Court Mall, Kailua-Kona, HI 96740.

Ocean Sports - (885-5555) 69-275 Waikoloa Beach Drive, Royal Waikoloan Hotel, Kohala Coast, HI 96743.

Red Sail Sports - (880-1111) Hapuna Beach Prince Hotel, Kohala Coast; (885-2876) Hilton Waikoloa Village, Kohala Coast; (885-2000) Sheraton Orchid Mauna Lani, Kohala Coast.

JET SKIING

Jet skiing is centered in Kona on Kailua Bay and up and down nearby areas of the Kona Coast. Rates vary and restrictions apply; consult booking agencies below for details.

Activity Information Center - (329-7700 or Fax 326-9150) 76-5828 Alii Drive, Kailua-Kona, HI 96740; Waikoloa Resort, Kings Shops (885-0000)

Kona Water Sports Inc. - (329-1593) 75-5695G Alii Drive, Banyan Court Mall, Kailua-Kona, HI 96740

Red Sail Sports - (880-1111) Hapuna Beach Prince Hotel, Kohala Coast; (885-2876) Hilton Waikoloa Village, Kohala Coast; (885-2000) Sheraton Orchid Mauna Lani, Kohala Coast

PARASAILING

Parasailing is done on the relatively calm waters of Kailua Bay and along nearby areas of the Kona Coast. Contact any of the following booking agencies for details.

Activity Information Center - (329-7700 or FAX 326-9150) 76-5828 Alii Drive, Kailua-Kona, HI 96740; (885-0000) Kings Shops, Waikoloa Resort, Kohala Coast

Kona Charter Skippers - (329-3600) 75-5663 Palani Road, Kailua-Kona, HI 96740

Kona Water Sports Inc. - (329-1593) 76-5695G Alii Drive, Banyan Court Mall, Kailua-Kona. HI 96740

UFO Parasail of Kailua-Kona - (325-5836) P.O.Box 5438, Kailua-Kona, HI 96745

KAYAKS - HOBIE CATS

Kayaking and Hobie Cat sailing are popular resort activities. The best places are the Kohala Coast resorts and beaches. The hotel activity desks and beach concessions can help make arrangements. Individual raft-floats with glass viewing panels can also be used to float over areas where fish and marine life can be observed. Check with the following water sports concessions for equipment rentals.

Activity Information Center - (329-7700 or FAX 326-9150) 76-5828 Alii Drive, Kailua-Kona, HI 96740; (885-0000) Kings Shops, Waikoloa Resort

Kayak Historical Discovery Tours - (328-8911) 87-3187 Holomoku Road H, Captain Cook, HI 96704; this operator provides kayak tours along the Kona Coast and customized 2-5 day kayak outings around the Big Island.

Kona Kai-Yaks - (326-2922) Kona Marina, Honokohau Small Boat Harbor, Kailua-Kona

Kona Water Sports Inc. - (329-1593) 76-5695G Alii Drive, Banyan Court Mall, Kailua-Kona, HI 96740

Ocean Safari's Kayaks - (326-4699) Kailua-Kona

Ocean Sports - (885-5555) Royal Waikoloan Hotel, Waikoloa Resort, Kohala Coast, HI 96743.

Red Sail Sports - (880-1111) Hapuna Beach Prince Hotel, Kohala Coast; (885-2876) Hilton Waikoloa Village, Kohala Coast; (885-2000) Sheraton Orchid Mauna Lani, Kohala Coast.

LAND ACTIVITIES

LAND TOURS

The tour operators in this section offer a range of tours through some of the Big Island's most spectacular, historic and culturally unique attractions. The itineraries vary as do the costs.

If you are considering a circle island tour such as that offered by Polynesian Adventure Tours, you should compare the cost of $50-60 per person with the cost of renting your own car which would be considerably less. Having your own car would mean greater mobility and independence and perhaps even more comfort in addition to the savings realized. A circle island tour can be somewhat tiring since it is a distance of about 260 miles and would require a full-day (8-10 hours) allowing time for scenic stops and lunch along the way. A mini-van or bus coach tour is a comfortable way to see the Big Island since you "leave the driving to us." Generally, such tours include narration on the scenic and historic attractions taken in on the tour. A rental car on the other hand can be equally comfortable since you don't have others around and you are on your own. And with a good tour map of the major attractions, you can get by without the narration and find your own way around.

My personal recommendation is to rent a car and experience the Big Island at your own pace. You can't get lost as there is essentially only one road all the way around the island. And there is lots to explore and experience at your leisure.

In addition to regular land tours, this section lists some unique tours to places like Waipio Valley and the summit of Mauna Kea. You'll find that these operators provide special insight on their respective attractions and areas of the Big Island.

Gerhard's Big Island Adventures - (Tel 895-9999, Fax 329-7970) *Wir sprechen Deutsch*. Tour the Big Island with German-speaking guides. Full day excursions to Volcanoes National Park and other Big Island attractions; rates $69 per person; hotel pick up/return.

Hawai'i Resorts Transportation Company - (775-7291) P.O.Box 183, Honoka'a, HI 96727. They run a variety of tours around the Big Island including Waipi'o Valley on horseback, Waipi'o Valley Van tours, and Mauna Kea Summit tours.

Jack's Tours ★ - (961-6666) 226 Kanoelehua, Hilo, HI 96720 and (329-2555) 73-4770 Kanalani, Kailua-Kona, HI 96740. They provide a variety of Hilo, Kona, Kohala and circle-island bus-coach tours.

Oceans Apart Vacations - 75-5799B Alii Drive, Kailua-Kona, HI 96740, 808/334-1888. This operator offers a variety of personally escorted and narrated tours around the Big Island to all the major attractions and sites. Different tours are offered daily and range from 5 to 12 hours duration; most tours include picnic box lunch or restaurant meal plus hotel pickup/return. Rates $75 and up.

Paradise Safaris - (322-2366) P.O.Box A-D, Kailua-Kona, HI 96745. This operator specializes in evening-sunset 4-wheel drive vehicle tours to the summit of 13,796 ft. Mauna Kea and the telescope observatory complex. Hotel pick-ups in Kona and Kohala are provided for the daily tour departure at 3PM, returning about 10:30PM. Tour rates are $105-110 per person, depending on hotel pickup location.

Polynesian Adventure Tours - (329-8008) 74-5596 Pawai Place, Kailua-Kona, HI 96740. This operator specializes in deluxe "Grand Circle Island Tour", a complete 260 mile ten hour drive around the island. All the major sites and attractions are included. Daily departures in spacious, deluxe "big window" mini-coaches are 8-8:30AM from Kona with return at 6-6:30PM.

Tour price from Kailua-Kona area, adults $47, children under 12, $44; from Waikoloa Resort area, adults $53, children under 12, $48; from Mauna Lani and Mauna Kea Resorts, adults $58, children under 12, $55. They also offer a special "Volcano Tour" which includes the national park, blacksand beach and coffee plantation.

Robert's Hawai'i Inc. ★- (935-2858) Hilo International Airport, Hilo, HI 96720 and (329-1688) Kailua-Kona, HI 96740. They offer a variety of Hilo and Kona-Kohala area and circle-island bus-coach tours.

Russ Apple Tour Tapes - (967-7375) P.O. Box 47, Hawai'i Volcanoes National Park, Volcano, HI 96718. This is not a tour company as such but rather a service providing narrated cassette tapes for touring some of the Big Island's more noted areas and attractions.

Russ Apple, Ph.D., is a retired national park service employee and noted historian, lecturer, and columnist for the local newspaper who has produced a set of cassette tapes detailing Hawai'i's unique natural history, flora and fauna, geology, geography, culture and color. The tapes can be used as a self-drive narration to highlight one's own tour. The tapes include coverage of the Hilo to Volcano route, the national park Crater Rim Drive and other areas. The tapes are available in Hilo at the Lyman House Museum, the Hilo Hawaiian and Hawai'i Naniloa Hotels and in the national park at the Volcano Art Center and Kilauea Military Camp on a rental or sale basis. Tape players can be rented at $7, tapes are rented at $3 each or purchased for $10 each or $25 per set. Mail orders are accepted.

Waipi'o Valley Shuttle - (775-7121) P.O.Box 5128, Kukuihaele, HI 96727. They specialize in comprehensive 4-wheel drive tours of the lush Waipi'o Valley and its history, culture, and use, adults $31, children under 12, $15. Also a tour to the summit of Mauna Kea and the telescope complex, flat rate of $75 per person.

BOOKING AGENTS/REPRESENTATIVES

The following agents and representatives can book various land tours and activities as well as ocean-related activities, cruises, and the like. They would be a good source of additional information on tours or activities in a given area of the Big Island.

Activity Information Center - 76-5828 Alii Drive, Kailua-Kona, HI 96740 (808) 329-7700, Fax (808) 326-9150; Kings Shops at Waikoloa Beach Resort, (808) 885-0000

Island Resort Activity Desk - 75-5663A Palani Road, Kailua-Kona, HI 96740 (808) 329-1187

Kohala Coast Activities & Tours Center - Waikoloa Resort, Kohala Coast, HI 96743, (808) 885-5532

Kona Coast Activities - 75-5744 Alii Drive, Kona Inn Shopping Center, Kailua-Kona, HI 96740, (808) 329-2971

BICYCLE TOURS

The Big Island offers some of the most varied scenery anywhere in the Hawaiian Islands. It also has some of the largest expanses and stretches of wide-open uninhabited country in the islands. The geography ranges from desert beaches, to tropical rain forests, to dry lava deserts. An excellent way to see and experience the changing scenes is by bicycle touring.

Many visitors to the Big Island bring their own bicycles and camping equipment with them and make up their own itinerary. The Big Island's highway system is generally good to excellent in most areas but often the shoulders are unimproved. Bikers need to exercise caution on the open road especially in narrow winding sections of highway. If you are an adventurous bicyclist, you may want to plan your own tour of the island. Just keep in mind the long distances between towns in some areas like the Ka'u, South Kona, and Kohala Coast areas and plan accordingly for water, food, lodging, etc.

If you're interested in general information on biking the Big Island, contact the following: The Mayor's Bicycle-Pedestrian Advisory Committee, c/o County of Hawai'i Finance Dept., 25 Aupuni St., Hilo, HI 96720. If you want to opt for an organized commercial bicycle tour you might try the following operators.

Adventure Tours - P.O.Box 182, Pahoa, HI 96778, 808 966-4968. This operator offers various biking, hiking, camping and shorefishing tours.

Chris's Bike Adventures - P.O. Box 657, Kula, HI 96790, 808 326-4600. This operator offers two basic Big Island biking tours: Kohala Mountain Adventure, a leisurely bike tour for all ability levels and The Mauna Loa Challenge, a day-long 54-mile adventure for expert riders through rugged picturesque country.

Hawaiian Pedals Bicycle Rentals - 75-5744 Alii Drive, Kona Inn Shopping Village, Kailua-Kona, HI 96740 (808) 329-2294 or 325-6416. This operation offers a full range of bike rentals including standard road bikes, performance bikes, mountain bikes and tandem touring bikes. Free pickup and delivery in the Kailua-Keauhou area. They also provide full-service bike tours including the Downhill Tour and Mauna Kea Tour for beginners to advanced riders featuring the history, culture and hidden beauty of the Big Island.

Mauna Kea Mountain Bikes Inc. - P.O. Box 44672, Kamuela, HI 96743 (885-2091). This operator offers private varied guided tours of rain forest trails, scenic highways, backcountry mountain and ranch areas, mountain slope runs and Volcanoes National Park tours. They provide a full range of mountain and off road touring bikes and equipment.

BICYCLE RENTALS

Dave's Bike & Triathlon Shop - (329-4522) On Alii Drive across from Hulihee Palace, Kailua-Kona. This shop has a variety of mountain bikes and road bikes to rent by the hour, day or week. They also provide service, repairs, accessories and supplies.

Mid Pacific Wheels - (935-6211) 1133C Manono St., Hilo, HI 96720

Red Sail Sports - (885-2876) Hilton Waikoloa Village, (885-2000) Sheraton Orchid Mauna Lani

Bikers and backpackers looking for overnight lodging in the South Point area of the Big Island may want to try **Margo's Corner**, P.O.Box 447, Na'alehu, HI 96772, 808 929-9614. This bicyclist camping retreat is in the Discovery Harbor subdivision two miles from Waiohinu village off Highway 11. The facility has several campground tent sites as well as guesthouse lodging, hot showers, sweat lodge and offers family-style meals.

GOLF

Golfers will find some extremely challenging, exciting and incredibly beautiful golf courses on the Big Island. Courses range from Hilo's fine, though somewhat damp, Municipal course, to the lovely Volcano Country Club near Volcanoes National Park, and the stunning Kohala Coast resort courses including Waikoloa Beach Resort courses, the Mauna Lani Resort and Mauna Kea Resort links which are widely acclaimed and recognized. Greens fees vary widely from around $20-25 at Hilo, Hamakua and Ka'u courses to well over $100 a round at the Kona and Kohala Coast resort courses (resort guests get a discount). Cart fees are extra. Call the course clubhouse for current greens and cart fees.

Discovery Harbour Golf and Country Club - Located in the small town of Waiohinu, Ka'u District (929-7353). This is a very nice 18-hole course in the middle of a country residential sub-division in a remote southern coast area of the Big Island.

Hamakua Country Club - P.O.Box 751, Honoka'a, HI 96727, no phone, is located on Highway 19 in Honoka'a on the Hamakua Coast about 40 miles north of Hilo. It's a nine hole course laid out on very sloping terrain. Lovely views of Honoka'a and the ocean. Entrance is easy to miss, just off the highway and next to the Union 76 gas station.

Hapuna Golf Course - at the Hapuna Beach Prince Hotel, Mauna Kea Resort, (880-3000). This is an 18-hole championship Arnold Palmer designed course. It is nestled on the natural contours of the hilly coastlands about 700 ft. above sea level. There are stunning views of coastline, ocean and surrounding volcanic mountains. Arnie's Restaurant on premises.

Hilo Municipal Golf Course - 340 Haihai Street, Hilo (959-7711). This is a very nicely maintained 18-hole course operated by the County of Hawai'i. It gets a lot of use from local golfing cadres especially on weekends. During Hilo's rainy periods the fairways can get pretty water-logged. There is a driving range lighted for night use.

Kona Country Club - 78-7000 Alii Drive, 6 miles south of Kailua-Kona in the Keauhou resort area (322-2595). Open daily, starting times required. This is actually two golf courses in one. The 18-hole Ocean Front championship course runs oceanside and in the heart of the Keauhou resort condo area. The Alii Country Club 18-hole layout runs upslope providing spectacular ocean and coastline views. Complete pro shop with rental clubs, carts, and instruction available. The Vista Restaurant & Lounge are on premises.

Makalei Hawai'i Country Club - 1-800-606-9606 or 808/325-6625; located on Highway 190, 72-3890 Mamalahoa Highway, Kailua-Kona, HI 96740, about five miles above Kailua-Kona town on the cool, breezy forested slopes of Mount Hualalai with a pristine pastoral setting and spectacular views at 2000-ft. elevation. The 18-hole layout is a par-72 championship length of 7,100 yards. Most of the holes play downslope with undulating fairways and challenging greens.

Mauna Kea Beach Hotel Golf Course - located at the Mauna Kea Beach Hotel, Kohala Coast (882-7222). This championship golf course has won wide acclaim for its consistent golfing excitement and challenge. *Golf Magazine* ranks it as one of "America's Top 12 Resort Courses" while *Golf Digest* ranks it among "America's 100 Greatest," "Hawai'i's Finest," and as one of "America's Top 10 in Aesthetics." Call one day in advance for tee time.

Mauna Lani Resort Golf Course - Located at the Mauna Lani Resort, Kohala Coast (885-6655). This is a gorgeous and challenging 36-hole layout with two separate North and South championship courses. There are several breath-taking holes and fairways carved out of raw lava rock and next to the pounding ocean surf. The links surround the Mauna Lani Bay Hotel, Sheraton Orchid Mauna Lani and condo complexes. It's the home of the PGA Senior Skins Tournament held each January and provides an incredibly beautiful golfing experience. *Golf Magazine* ranks it as one of "America's Top 12 Resort Courses." Call for tee time.

Naniloa Country Club - 120 Banyan Drive, Hilo, on hotel row along Hilo Bay, (935-3000). This is a short 9-hole, par 36 course. There is a pro shop with club and cart rentals available. Given the facilities, it's really not worth playing golf here. If you really want to play, you'd be better off at the Hilo Muny or one of the Volcano, Kona, or Kohala courses.

Sea Mountain Golf Course - At Punalu'u, in the Ka'u District (928-6222). This is a superb 18-hole championship course located in the peaceful southern coast area of the Big Island. The fairways are nicely landscaped with lots of greenery and flowering plants. The biggest factor are the strong coastal breezes.

Volcano Golf and Country Club - Located in Hawai'i Volcanoes National Park (967-7331). This is a lovely and lush 18-hole course set amidst the grandeur of the national park country. There is a pro shop with club and cart rental available and the Volcano Country Club Restaurant is on premises. Call for tee time.

Waikoloa Beach Resort Golf Club - Located between the Royal Waikoloan Hotel and the Hilton Waikoloa Village at Waikoloa Resort, Kohala Coast (885-6060). This is an 18-hole course designed by Robert Trent Jones Jr. and set amidst the dramatic contrast of black lava flows and the blue Pacific Ocean. Beach Grill Restaurant is located at the clubhouse. Call for tee time.

Waikoloa Resort King's Course - Located adjacent to the Hilton Waikoloa Village, Kohala Coast (885-4647), this par 72 championship layout was created out of barren lava desert by Tom Weiskopf and Jay Morrish and was influenced by the famous open, windswept links of Scotland. The course features some of the most intimidating bunkers and sand traps of any Big Island course. We are talking about major chasms and gorges here. The challenges to golfers are natural: the strong Waikoloa winds, lava rock formations, sand traps, bunkers and an occasional water hazard. Masochists and those doing penance for past wrongs will take special delight in this course.

Waikoloa Village Golf Club - Located at Waikoloa Village in the cool and breezy uplands between Highways 19 and 190, and above the Waikoloa resorts (883-9621). Robert Trent Jones Jr. artfully designed this fine golf course to challenge the serious golfer and please the beginner as well. Call for tee time.

Waimea Country Club - Located about two miles east of Kamuela on the Mamalahoa Highway #19 in the heart of Parker Ranch country (885-8777). The 6,661-yard par-72 layout is spread through former ranch pasturelands and takes in the natural undulating and rolling hill terrain. Stands of forest and pastures border the fairways along with strategic water hazards and sand traps. It can get breezy and foggy out in the fairways at times when low cloud fronts move through.

TENNIS

PUBLIC COURTS

The County of Hawai'i maintains a number of tennis courts at county parks and locations around the island. Some are lighted for evening use and are basically on a first-come first-served basis. For a map detailing public tennis court locations around the island contact the Department of Parks and Recreation, County of Hawai'i, 25 Aupuni St., Hilo, HI 96720 or call (808) 935-1842. The following is a listing of tennis court facilities around the island.

Hilo
Hoolulu Park Tennis Stadium - (935-8213) 3 indoor lighted courts and 5 outdoor courts. Operated by County of Hawai'i. Fees for indoor courts are $2 per hour 9AM-4PM, $4 per hour 4-10PM. Reservations suggested.

South Hilo District
Ainaola Park, *Hakalau Park*, *Lincoln Park*, *Lokahi Park*, *Malama Park*, *Mohouli Park*, *Panaewa Park* (most of these are right in the Hilo town area)

North Hilo District
Papaaloa Park - in Papaaloa Village.

Hamakua District
Honokaa Park - in Honokaa town.

North Kohala District
Kamehameha Park - in Kapaau town.

South Kohala District
Waimea Park - in Waimea-Kamuela town.

North Kona District
Greenwell Park - in Captain Cook
Higashihara Park - in Keauhou
Kailua Park - at Old Kona Airport
Kailua Playground - on Kuakini Hwy. near town

Ka'u District
Naalehu Park - on the highway through Naalehu town
Pahala School Grounds - at the school in Pahala Village

Puna District
Kurtistown Park - on the hwy. in Kurtistown
Shipman Park - at junction of Volcano and Pahoa Highways in Keaau town

PRIVATE TENNIS COURTS OPEN TO THE PUBLIC

King Kamehameha Kona Beach Resort - Kailua-Kona (329-2911), has four hard-surface courts with two lighted for night play; pro shop available. Hotel guests fee is $5 for all day, non-guests $7.

Hilton Waikoloa Village - Kohala Coast (885-1234), Tennis Garden features eight hard surface courts, two clay courts and a tournament stadium; pro shop available. Fee is $20 per hour for hotel guests and non-guests.

Holua Tennis Center - Holua at Mauna Loa Village, Keauhou-Kona (322-0091), features 14 hard surface courts, seven lighted for night play and a stadium court; pro shop available. Fee is $10 for all day.

Keauhou Beach Hotel - Keauhou-Kona (322-3441), has six hard surface courts, two lighted for night play; pro shop available. Fee is $3 an hour for hotel guests, $6 an hour for non-guests.

Mauna Kea Beach Hotel - Kohala Coast (882-7222), features 13 hard surface courts, none lighted; pro shop available. For hotel guests the fee is $18 per hour 7-11AM and 3-7PM, and $9 per hour 11AM - 3PM. Non-guests fees are $20 and $10 respectively.

Mauna Lani Bay Hotel & Bungalows - Kohala Coast (885-6622), features 10 hard surface courts; pro shop available. Fee is $7 per hour for resort guests only; juniors under 18 are half-price.

Mauna Lani Racquet Club - Kohala Coast (885-7755), has six hard surface courts, two grass courts and a stadium court, three courts are lighted for night play; pro shop available. For resort guests, fee is $7 per hour for hard courts, $10 per hour for grass courts; memberships available.

Sheraton Orchid Mauna Lani - Kohala Coast (885-2000), the Tennis Pavilion has 11 hard surface courts, seven lighted for night play, a stadium court, and pro shop. Fee is $10 per hour for hotel guests, $12 per hour for others.

Royal Kona Resort - Kailua-Kona (329-3111), has four hard surface courts, three lighted for night play; pro shop available. $5 per hour/$7 all day for hotel guests, $6 hour/$8 day for others.

Royal Waikoloan Hotel - Kohala Coast (885-6789), the Tennis Club has six hard surface courts for day play only; pro shop available. Fees are $4 per hour or $5 for all day, for both hotel guests and non-guests.

BOWLING

For those who want to enjoy a workout on the local bowling lanes, the Big Island has locations on both sides of the island in Hilo and Kona. Both are full-service bowling lanes with a full line of equipment rentals from shoes to balls. They're open daily, except major holidays, but check for specific hours as they may vary from time to time.

Hilo Lanes, 777 Kinoole Street, Hilo (935-0646)

Kona Bowl, 75-5586 Ololi Road, in the Lanihau Center, Kailua-Kona (326-2695)

PUBLIC SWIMMING POOLS

The County of Hawai'i maintains seven free public swimming pools around the island. These facilities are generally excellent and include full programs of swimming and aquatics instruction, adult lap swimming, and open recreational swimming hours daily and weekly. For specific daily and weekly schedules of activities contact the individual pools listed.

Honokaa Swimming Pool - in Honokaa, Hamakua (775-0650)

Kawamoto Swim Stadium - in Hilo (935-8907)

Kohala Swimming Pool - in Kapaau, North Kohala (889-6933)

Kona Swimming Pool - at Konawaena High School (323-3252)

Laupahoehoe Swimming Pool - at Laupahoehoe (962-6993)

NAS Swimming Pool - which stands for Naval Air Station, is a remnant of Hilo's World War II military airfield, at the old Hilo Airport (935-4401).

Pahala Swimming Pool - in Pahala, Ka'u District (928-8177)

HIKING

Hawai'i Volcanoes National Park has an excellent system of hiking trails for everyone from novice casual strollers to adventurous independent backpackers. There are easy hikes of less than an hour to several hours in length to full-scale 2-3 day remote country treks. The national park is by far the best place on the island to hike and backpack over some startling, stunning and desolate country. It has the best marked and well laid-out trail system on the island.

Some of the easiest and most popular hikes in Hawai'i Volcanoes National Park are Kilauea Iki Trail and Kipuka Puaulu (Bird Park). The Kilauea Iki Trail hike is a 2 1/2 hour loop trip of 2.5 miles from Crater Rim Drive in the park down into and across the floor of the still steaming Kilauea Iki crater. One gets an incredible closeup view of Hawai'i's volcanism with lava rubble and cinder cones and the ominous steaming cracks in the crater floor.

The Kipuka Puaulu (Bird Park) hike is a 1 hour loop trip of 1.1 miles. The trail courses through a virtually unspoiled native Hawaiian forest at the cool elevation of 4100'. There are numerous examples of native Hawaiian plants and glimpses of rare and endangered Hawaiian birds. The park service maintains a nature trail with many of the plants marked and booklets available at the trailhead which explain the unique ecosystem of this plant and bird sanctuary. This is a hike well worth taking. A word of caution is in order here. When hiking the national park or anywhere on the Big Island for that matter, be sure to check first with rangers or let someone know where you are going. Some national park trails require you to sign in and sign out. Also, *do not* venture out onto lava flows and fields by yourself. Old lava flows are marked by deep holes and crevasses which are extremely hazardous to hikers. The hardened crust of lava can be deceiving. What looks like a firm rigid shell can be a thin weak cover to a large hole or crevasse and there are many instances of people falling in and being lost. You could be badly injured or even lost in a remote area with little chance of rescue. Over the years, several people have died as a result of such incidents.

The *Akaka Falls State Park* (near Honomu Village) nature trail is a 30 minute 0.4 mile loop trip. It is a very popular and easily accessible hike. The trail winds down into the canyon where Akaka and Kahuna Falls plunge some 400+ feet. The trail meanders through lush tropical rain forest of hapu ferns, red and white ginger, banana trees, bird-of-paradise, plumeria, and giant philodendrons. Handrails aid in areas where the paved trail is quite steep and tends to be slippery when wet.

There are some commercial hiking tour operators who run various hikes and outings into Big Island wilderness areas. Hikers might want to try any of the following:

Arnott's Hiking Adventures - 98 Apapane Road, Hilo, HI 96720, (808) 969-7097. These are the same folks who operate Arnott's Lodge, a budget lodging for backpacker types. They operate a number of varied hiking tours and excursions around the island including Mauna Kea Summit, Volcano Hike and Nite Lava, South Point-Green Sand Beach, Waipio Valley, Hilo Discovery and others. Rates range from $50-75 per person depending on destination. Free pickup/dropoff at Hilo area hotels.

Hawai'i Forest & Trail Ltd. - P.O.Box 2975, Kailua-Kona, HI 96745, (808) 329-1993. This tour operator offers soft-adventure hiking tours to the Big Island's unique forest ecosystems. Hikers are led to remote locales by a naturalist-guide and enjoy moderately difficult hikes through the primeval forest complete with geologic wonders, incredible views and native Hawaiian flora and fauna. Hikes are fully equipped and serviced with morning coffee, snacks, lunch, beverages/water and daypacks, sweatshirts, ponchos, binoculars, etc.; hiking time varies from 2-4 hrs over moderate terrain; small groups of up to 8 hikers accommodated; hikers provide their own hiking/walking footwear; hotel pick-ups included.

Hiking

Hiking costs are adults $135, children under 12 yrs $100. Customized hikes available. Reservations are essential.

Hawaiian Walkways - P.O.Box 2193, Kamuela, HI 96743, (808) 885-7759. This hiking tour operator offers a variety of half-day and full day hikes over the Big Island's mountains and valleys and along its shorelines. Spectacular mountain and coastline vistas, secluded beaches, upland meadows, lush tropical rain forest, hidden pools and streams, fishponds and ancient Hawaiian petroglyphs or rock carvings are some of the features of these hiking tours. Costs range from $45 for half-day to $80 for full day, per person. There are also special 3 day/2 night camping hikes at $425 per person and a heavy-duty 14-day cross-island trek with backpacking, mountain biking and sea kayaking combined on a 150 mile journey. The 14-day trek cost varies and is custom planned.

Visitors are invited to join the local *Moku Loa Group* of the *Hawai'i Sierra Club* on the Big Island for its monthly hikes on island trails. It's a great way to see some of the Big Island and meet a group of local folks who enjoy Hawai'i's great outdoors and are knowledgeable about its history and culture. You can write to the Moku Loa Group-Hawai'i Sierra Club, P.O. Box 1137, Hilo, HI 96721-1137 for information on its hiking schedule. Or you can contact the Hawai'i Sierra Club office in Honolulu for information at 1100 Ala Kea Street, Room 330, Honolulu, HI 96813, (808) 538-6166. They have a listing of all the scheduled hikes and activities on all the islands.

Another active hiking group is the *Kona Hiking Club*, an informal group which takes monthly day hikes to the Big Island's less accessible and private beaches, forests and backcountry areas. Most of these hikes are not difficult or long and require minimal gear or hiking experience. The group encourages family hiking outings. The club generally takes hikes on the first Saturday and third Thursday of each month. Membership is open to everyone. There are no dues or fees and visitors are welcome to participate. This is a good way to get to know some local folks and enjoy a Hawaiian outdoors experience. Watch the local Big Island newspapers community news files for hike announcements.

For maps and information on hiking the national park, write to: Superintendent, Hawai'i Volcanoes National Park, Volcano, HI 96718.

For information and maps relating to state forest reserve lands, write to: Division of Forestry, Department of Land and Natural Resources, Island of Hawai'i, 75 Aupuni St., Hilo, HI 96720.

For information on state parks write to: Division of State Parks, Hawai'i District Office, Dept. of Land and Natural Resources, P.O. Box 936, Hilo, HI 96720.

For information on county beach parks write to: Department of Parks and Recreation, County of Hawai'i, 25 Aupuni St., Hilo, HI 96720.

Other good sources of hiking information are *Hawaii Trails*, by Kathy Morey, Wilderness Press (1992), *Hiking Hawaii-The Big Island* by Robert Smith, HOA Publications (1990) and *Hawaiian Hiking Trails* by Craig Chisholm, Fernglen Press (1994).

CAMPING

See the section on Camping in WHERE TO STAY - WHAT TO SEE.

SNOW SKIING

To the surprise of many, visitors can enjoy some fabulous seasonal snow skiing on the Big Island, the only place in Hawai'i where it is possible. Granted, snow skiing is a strictly seasonal activity and at best is sporadic and unpredictable given the erratic nature of snowfall on Mauna Kea the past few winters. However, from approximately November through March and sometimes into April and May, the nearly 14,000 ft. summit of Mauna Kea can be covered with snow. When conditions are just right, skiers can enjoy some incredible downhill runs on the treeless slopes. There are no ski lifts, no lodge, and no facilities whatsoever on the summit and most skiers transport themselves via a four-wheel drive vehicle rental.

However, there is one ski tour operator specializing in Mauna Kea ski tours. Contact *Ski Guides Hawai'i*, P.O. Box 1954, Kamuela, HI 96743, (808) 885-4188. They offer complete package tours to Mauna Kea on snow days including four-wheel drive transportation, ski rental, equipment, and lunch. Contact them for the current season schedule and rates.

HORSEBACK RIDING-TRAIL RIDES

For the would-be "paniolos" (Hawaiian cowboys and cowgirls) there are a few stables and trail ride operators with a variety of trail rides and horseback outings available in different island locations. Horseback rides provide an opportunity to see and experience some of the Big Island's fascinating landscapes, scenery, ranch and mountain backcountry areas. Prices vary but start at about $50 per person for a basic 1 1/2-2 hour trail ride but are varied for other excursions. Some age restrictions (no very young children) also apply. Check the following operators for the latest rates.

Chalon International of Hawaii - (889-6257) This operator takes trailrides through the sloping Kohala ranch country to the ocean shoreline and varied scenery including tropical gulches, rolling hill country and mountains. Novice to experience riders welcome.

Dahana Ranch Roughriders - (885-0057) This operator specializes in open-range rides in the uplands of Waimea ranch country. They take first timers to experienced riders and children as young as three. Guided rides are 1 1/2 hours four times daily.

E-Z Riders Trail Rides - (928-8410) P.O. Box 524, Pahala, HI 96777. This operater is located five minutes from the small town of Pahala in the southern Ka'u District. E-Z Riders offers various trail riding tours through some of the most beautiful parts of the rolling Ka'u countryside.

Fallbrook Trail Rides - (322-1818) Kealakekua, Kona, HI 96750. This operator provides backcountry horseback rides on the cool slopes of Mount Hualalai above Kailua-Kona village. Rides follow a grass bridle path through tropical rain forest to see native birdlife, wild fruits and beautiful ocean views.

King's Trail Rides O' Kona - (323-2388) Kealakekua, Kona, HI 96750. They offer horseback trail rides exploring the backcountry lands of 20,000 acre Kealakekua Ranch and Kona Coast trail rides to beaches for a picnic lunch and snorkeling.

Kohala Na'alapa Trail Rides - (775-0330) Honoka'a, HI 96727. This operator offers trail rides at scenic Kohala Ranch in the Kohala Mountains; ride through a working cattle ranch with panoramic vies of Mauna Kea, Hualalai and the Kohala Coast.

Mauna Kea Beach Hotel Stables - (885-4288), P.O. Box 218, Kamuela, HI 96743. This outfitter arranges trail rides, picnics and sunset rides for Mauna Kea Beach Hotel guests and others interested in seeing back country areas of Waimea's famous Parker Ranch country.

Paniolo Riding Adventures - (889-5354) P.O. Box 1400, Kamuela, HI 96743. This operator offers trail rides on an 11,000 acre working ranch in the scenic Kohala Mountain country. Skilled knowledgeable guides lead riders on trained horses through lush pasturelands with scenic vistas of the Kona and Kohala coastlines. They also offer mule rides using special Australian stock saddles. There is a standard 2 1/2 hr. trail ride or a 4 hr. picnic adventure ride with gourmet lunch included.

Rain Forest Trailrides - (322-7126) This outfitter takes trail rides on the beautiful slopes of Hualalai Mountain, through majestic lush 400 acres of rolling upcountry grasslands and rain forest areas. There are 1 hr. and 2 1/2 hr. rides. The 2 1/2 hr. ride includes lunch. Rides daily 9AM - 5PM.

Waipi'o Na'alapa Trail Rides - (775-0419) P.O.Box 992, Honoka'a, HI 96727. This operator offers a standard 2 1/2 hour trail ride through the lush beauty of the famous Waipi'o Valley on the Hamakua Coast taking in waterfalls, taro patches and the beach. Riders should be agile and in good health; no children under 8 years of age.

Waipi'o on Horseback - (775-7291) P.O. Box 183, Honokaa, HI 96727. This outfitter takes riders down into the beautiful scenic Waipi'o Valley on the Hamakua Coast. Explore trails through the lush rain forest jungles, see Hawaiian taro patches, waterfalls, streams and black sand beach.

Waipi'o Valley Wagon Tours - (775-9518) P.O. Box 1340, Honokaa, HI 96727. This operator takes guests on tours in a horse-drawn wagon along the roadways and across streams of the beautiful Waipi'o Valley on the Hamakua Coast. Take in lush tropical valley scenery, rain forest, waterfalls and taro patches.

HEALTH AND FITNESS CENTERS

In recent years, the newer resorts and hotels and even some of the older ones, have added health and fitness centers, exercise rooms, and work-out equipment to meet the growing demand for such services among visitors. And with Hawai'i's emphasis on outdoor activities, it is easy to see why there is a lot of interest in keeping healthy and fit. If your hotel or condo doesn't have such a facility and you want to workout with the weights and other exercise equipment, you might try any of the following health and fitness centers. They welcome the public on a walk-in basis. They generally charge an hourly use fee for the equipment, spa, pool, etc.

Big Island Gym - 74-5603B Alapa Street, Kailua-Kona, HI 96740 (329-9432)

Keauhou Massage & Spa - 78-6740 Alii Drive, #227, Kailua-Kona, HI (322-0048)

Leisure Time - 1133 Manono St., Hilo, HI (934-7868)

Orchid Isle Fitness - 29 Shipman, Suite 104, Hilo, HI (961-0003)

Pacific Coast Fitness - 65-1298A Kawaihae Road, next to Kamuela Inn, Waimea, HI 96743 (885-6270)

Pahoa Ironworks - P.O. Box 1453, Pahoa, HI 96778 (965-6644)

Paradise Spa - 93 Banyan Dr., Hawai'i Naniloa Hotel, Hilo, HI 96720 (969-3333)

Spencer Health & Fitness Center - 197 Keawe St., Hilo, HI 96720 (969-1511)

The Club in Kona - Kona Center, Kailua-Kona, HI 96740 (326-2582)

Too the Max Gym & Fitness - 81-951 Halekii, Kealakekua, HI (322-7766)

HUNTING

Outdoors and hunting enthusiasts will enjoy the challenge of an outing to the fields and slopes of Mauna Kea or other island hunting grounds. Whether it would be for Hawaiian big game like wild boar, Mouflon sheep, or mountain goat or wild game birds like turkey, quail, pheasant, chukar or francolin partridge, hunting the Big Island will provide special thrills, action, and unique outdoor experiences. The following hunting guide services and outfitters can make all the arrangements.

Ginger Flower Charters - 78-7049 Mamalahoa Highway, Holualoa, Kona, HI 96725, (808) 324-1444. Fishing and hunting guide, Kenny Llanes, specializes in deepsea fishing charters and wild boar hunting on the Big Island's remote mountain and forest slopes. In addition, bird hunting for wild turkey, pheasant, quail, chukar and francolin is available November through January. Archery hunts are available for sheep and goat in season.

Hawai'i Hunting Tours - P.O. Box 58, Paauilo, Hamakua, HI 96776, (808) 776-1666. Guide Eugene Ramos specializes in custom hunts for sheep, wild boar, goat, and game birds on private hunting grounds on the slopes of Mauna Kea. Scenic 4-wheel drive tours through majestic backcountry are also available.

AIR TOURS
SMALL PLANE FLIGHTSEEING

Scenic flights in a small plane are a good way to see the Big Island from a bird's-eye view. Scenic flight operators fly from Hilo or Kona airports and generally include the island's most outstanding features and attractions, volcano activity and lava flows, waterfalls and valleys, lava deserts and rainforests, and rugged coastlines, on their fixed routes and standard air tours.

Big Island Air - Kailua-Kona, 1-800-367-8047 ext.207, Hawai'i Inter-island 1-800-533-3417, Big Island (808) 329-4868. This small airline offers complete 2 hour circle-island, island scenic and volcano flights, and historic Kona-Kohala Coasts flights plus custom charter flights are arranged. Tours begin at $100 per person; circle island tours at $170 per person.

Classic Aviation Corporation - Keahole Airport, P.O.Box 1899, Kailua-Kona, HI 96745; in Hawai'i 1-800-695-8100, Big Island 329-8687. This flying service offers a unique experience flying in a reproduction of an open-cockpit 1935 WACO bi-plane. The plane carries two passengers and the pilot. You get the special thrill of open-air flight while enjoying the incredible aerial views only possible on the Big Island. Most tours last 30-40 minutes but there are short hop rides of 15-25 minutes. Prices range from $50-100 and up per person. Departures available from Hilo International Airport also; call for details.

Hawai'i AirVentures - Keahole Airport, P.O. Box 5259, Kailua-Kona, HI 96745 (329-0014). This small airline offers charters, scenic flightseeing tours, and photographic air tours including a Circle Island-Volcano Tour.

Hawai'i Island Hoppers - Old Air Terminal, Hilo International Airport, Hilo, HI 96720 (969-2000). This airline provides personalized volcano and scenic coastal flights, twilight flights and circle-island tours. Rates begin at $75 per person.

'Io Aviation - Hilo International Airport, Hilo 935-3031, Keahole Airport, Kona 329-3031; toll free 1-800-942-3031. Charter flights and tours are offered. A basic Volcano Tour of 45-60 minutes takes in recent eruption and lava flow sites and the Island Tour takes in coastal Hamakua, agricultural areas, waterfalls/gulches in a 45-60 minute flight. Special Waipio Valley photo flights are also offered. Call for current rates.

Koa Air Service Hawai'i - Keahole Airport, Kailua-Kona, HI 96740 (326-2288). This air tour operation has Cessna airplanes equipped with intercom for personalized narrated airtours of the Big Island. They specialize in air photo safaris covering volcanoes, waterfalls, rainforests, seacliffs, beaches, blue lagoons, tropical gardens and wildlife.

HELICOPTER TOURS

Helicopter tours are a thrilling way to see the island's scenery up close. They are a wonderful way to get some fantastic video or photography of your Big Island experience. The standard tours offered by most helicopter lines take in all the attractions of Hawai'i Volcanoes National Park including eruption sites, recent or current lava flows, the site where lava enters the ocean, and more. Other tours highlight the town of Hilo, the beautiful Hamakua Coast with its tropical rain forest and countless waterfalls, the grand Waipio Valley, Parker Ranch, mountain meadows, and rugged coastline vistas. The costs are generally expensive, as one might expect. One hour Volcanoes National Park tours range from about $150-175 per person. Tours along the Kohala or Hamakua Coasts are about $135 and up per person for a 1-1 1/2 hour tour. Some of the lines offer deluxe circle island tours from about $275 per person for a two hour tour. Most lines require a minimum number of people for their various tours. Check with the helicopter lines for specifics.

Blue Hawaiian Helicopters - Hilo International Airport, Hilo, 961-5600. This tour service offers a full range of island air tours to the volcano areas and Big Island attractions.

Chopper Shop - Hilo International Airport, Hilo, 969-4900. This operator provides a wide range of standard and custom tours to Big Island attractions and the volcano area.

Hawaii Helicopters Inc. - USA toll free 1-800-346-2403, Hawaii 1-800-994-9099, Kona's Keahole Airport 329-4700; this operator offers daily scenic flights to Hawaii Volcanoes National Park eruption sites.

'Io Aviation - Hilo International Airport, Hilo, 935-3031; Keahole Airport, Kona, 329-3031; toll free 1-800-942-3031. They offer personalized volcano area and general island air tours in helicopters. One hour volcano and island tours are $99 per person, two person minimum.

COMMON 'AMAKIHI

Island Helicopter Hawaii - Hilo International Airport, Hilo 969-1172, or 1-800-829-5999. This operator provides a full range of island air tours to the volcano area and all scenic attractions.

Kenai Helicopters - P.O.Box 4118, Kailua-Kona, HI 96745; U.S. 1-800-622-3144, Waikoloa Kings' Shops 885-5833, Hilo International Airport 969-3131. They offer a full range of varied air tours to the Big Island's most spectacular coastal, mountain, volcano, and forest scenery. The Circle Island Deluxe Tour is $265 per person, three person minimum. A Hamakua Coast and Waipio Valley Tour is $149 per person, three minimum.

Kona Coast Aviation - P.O. Box 2565, Kailua-Kona, HI 96745, 325-5943, Kona's Keahole Airport.

Lacy Helicopters - Kohala Airport, Kamuela, HI 96743; 885-7272 or Fax 885-6998. They offer complete helicopter service including charters, custom tours, and aerial photography.

Mauna Kea Helicopters - P.O. Box 1713, Kamuela, HI 96743; Waimea/Kohala Airport, 885-6400. This line provides complete island sightseeing tours, charters, aerial photography and video expertise. The Waipio Valley tour using an exclusive Waipio helipad takes in the beauty of the valley and the North Kohala Coast ($80 per person).

Volcano Heli-Tours - Volcano Golf Course Heliport, P.O. Box 626, Volcano, HI 96785, 967-7578. They offer a full range of sightseeing tours into Hawai'i Volcanoes National Park and surrounding countryside.

Safari Helicopters - Hilo International Airport, Hilo, 969-1259. This operator specializes in airtours of volcano country with a special 3-video camera system that captures all the scenery of your flight along with the pilot's narration and your conversation as well.

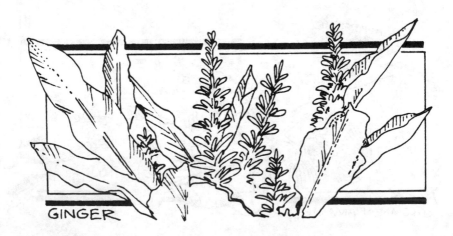

GINGER

HAWAIIANA READING FOR CHILDREN

Adair, Dick. *The Story of Aloha Bear*. Honolulu: Island Heritage. 1986.

Adair, Dick. *Aloha Bear and the Meaning of Aloha*. Honolulu: Island Heritage. 1987.

Carpenter, Allan. *Hawaii*. Chicago: Childrens Press. 1979.

Day, A. Grove. *Kamehameha, First King of Hawaii*. Honolulu: Hogarth. 1974.

Feeney, Stephanie. *Hawaii is a Rainbow*. Honolulu: University of Hawaii Press. 1980.

Feeney, Stephanie and Fielding, Ann. *Sand to Sea: Marine Life of Hawaii*. Honolulu: University of Hawaii Press. 1989.

Fradin, Dennis. *Hawaii: In Words & Pictures*. Chicago: Childrens Press. 1980.

Hale, Bruce. *The Legend of the Laughing Gecko*. Honolulu: Geckostufs. 1989.

Hazama, Dorothy. *The Ancient Hawaiians. Who Were They? How Did They Live?* Honolulu: Hogarth. 1974.

Kahalewai, Marilyn. *Maui Mouse's Supper*. Honolulu: Bess Press. 1988.

Kahalewai, Marilyn. *Whose Slippers are Those?* Honolulu: Besss Press. 1988.

Knudsen, Eric A. *Spooky Stuffs*. Aiea, Hawaii: Island Heritage Publishing. 1989.

Laird, Donivee Martin. *The Three Little Hawaiian Pigs and the Magic Shark*. Honolulu: Barnaby Books. 1988.

Laird, Donivee Martin. *'Ula Li'i and the Magic Shark*. Honolulu: Barnaby Books. 1985.

Laird, Donivee Martin. *Wili Wai Kula and the Three Mongooses*. Honolulu: Barnaby Books. 1983.

Laird, Donivee Martin. *Keaka and the Lilikoi Vine*. Honolulu: Barnaby Books. 1982.

Land-Nellist, Cassandra. *A Child's First Book About Hawaii*. Hawaii: Press Pacifica. 1987.

Lyons, Barbara. *Maui, Mischievous Hero*. Hilo: Petroglyph Press. 1969.

McBarnet, Gill. *A Whale's Tale*. Hawaii: Ruwanga Trading. 1988.

HAWAIIANA READING FOR CHILDREN

McBarnet, Gill. *Fountain of Fire*. Hawaii: Ruwanga Trading. 1987.

McBarnet, Gill. *The Wonderful Journey*. Hawaii: Ruwanga Trading. 1986.

McBarnet, Gill. *The Whale Who Wanted to be Small*. Hawaii: Ruwanga Trading. 1985.

McBride, Leslie R. *About Hawaii's Volcanoes*. Hilo: Petroglyph Press. 1986.

Missler, Dux. *Hawaii Fun Activity Book*. Hilo: Petroglyph Press. 1986.

Pape, Donna L. *Hawaii Puzzle Book*. Honolulu: Bess Press. 1984.

Radlauer, Ruth. *Hawaii Volcanoes National Park*. Chicago: Childrens Press. 1979.

Thompson, Vivian. *Hawaiian Tales of Heroes and Champions*. Honolulu: University of Hawaii Press. 1986.

Tune, Suelyn Ching. *How Maui Slowed the Sun*. Honolulu: University of Hawaii Press. 1988.

Wagenman, Mark A. *The Adventures of Aloha Bear and Maui the Whale*. Honolulu: Island Heritage. 1989.

Warren, Bonnie. *Aloha from Hawaii!* Honolulu: Warren Associates. 1987.

Williams, Julie Stewart. *And the Birds Appeared*. Honolulu: University of Hawaii Press. 1988.

NIGHTBLOOMING CEREUS

HAWAIIANA READING FOR ADULTS

Bailey, Paul. *Those Kings and Queens of Old Hawaii.* Tucson, Arizona: Westernlore Press. 1988.

Ball, Stuart M. *The Backpackers Guide to Hawai'i.* Honolulu: University of Hawaii Press. 1996.

Boylan, Dan. *Hawaii Aloha.* Kailua, Hawaii: Press Pacifica. 1987.

Berger, Andrew J. *Hawaiian Birdlife.* Honolulu: University of Hawaii Press. 1981.

Brennan, Joseph. *The Parker Ranch of Hawaii.* New York: Harper & Row. 1974.

Brown, DeSoto. *Hawaii Recalls: Nostalgic Images of the Hawaiian Islands, 1910-1950.* New York: Methuen Inc. 1986.

Cahill, Emmett. *The Shipmans of East Hawai'i.* Honolulu: University of Hawaii Press. 1995.

Chisolm, Craig. *Hawaiian Hiking Trails.* Oregon: Fernglen Press. 1994.

Clark, John R. K. *Beaches of the Big Island.* Honolulu: University of Hawaii Press. 1985

Clay, Horace F. and Hubbard, James C. *The Hawaii Garden Tropical Exotics.* Honolulu: University of Hawaii Press. 1987.

Day, A.G., Editor. *Mark Twain's Letters from Hawaii.* Honolulu: University of Hawaii Press. 1975.

Day, A.G. and Stroven, Carl. *Hawaiian Reader.* Honolulu: Mutual Publishing Co. 1985.

Daws, Gavan. *Shoal of Time: A History of the Hawaiian Islands.* Honolulu: University of Hawaii Press. 1974.

Fielding, Ann and Robinson, Ed. *An Underwater Guide to Hawaii.* Honolulu: University of Hawaii Press. 1989.

Greenberg, Idaz. *Hawaiian Fishwatcher's Field Guide.* Miami: Seahawk Press. 1983.

Hobson, E. and Chave, E.H. *Hawaiian Reef Animals.* Honolulu: University of Hawaii Press. 1979.

Hoffman, Phil. *Comprehensive Guide to Scuba Diving in Hawaii.* Kailua, Hawaii: Press Pacifica. 1984.

HAWAIIANA READING FOR ADULTS

Hosaka, Edward. *Shore Fishing in Hawaii.* Hilo, Hawaii: Petroglyph Press. 1987.

Laudan, Rachel. *The Food of Paradise - Exploring Hawaii's Culinary Heritage.* Honolulu: University of Hawaii Press. 1996.

Martin, Lynn, Editor. *Na Paniolo O Hawaii.* Honolulu: Honolulu Academy of Arts. 1987.

McMahon, Richard. *Camping Hawai'i - A Complete Guide.* Honolulu: University of Hawaii Press. 1994.

Merlin, Mark. *Hawaiian Forest Plants.* Honolulu: University of Hawaii Press. 1996.

Morey, Kathy. *Hawaii Trails: Walks, Strolls and Treks on the Big Island.* Berkeley, CA: Wilderness Press. 1992.

Pratt, H. Douglas, Bruner, P.L., and Berrett, D.G. *The Birds of Hawaii and the Tropical Pacific.* Princeton, N.J.: Princeton University Press. 1987.

Rayson, Ann. *Modern Hawaiian History.* Honolulu: The Bess Press. 1984.

Soehren, Rick. *The Birdwatcher's Guide to Hawai'i.* Honolulu: University of Hawai'i Press. 1996.

Sohmer, S. H. and Gustafson, R. *Plants and Flowers of Hawaii.* Honolulu: University of Hawaii Press. 1987.

Smith, Robert. *Hiking Hawaii.* Maui: HOA Publications. 1990.

Tinker, Spencer Wilkie. *Fishes of Hawaii.* Honolulu: Hawaiian Service. 1982.

Westervelt, W. *Hawaiian Legends of Volcanoes.* Vermont: C.E.Tuttle. 1963.

Zurick, David. *Hawaii, Naturally.* Berkeley, CA: Wilderness Press. 1990.

INDEX

ORDERING INFORMATION : Available from Paradise

Publications are books and videos to enhance your travel library and assist with your travel plans, or provide a special gift for someone who is planning a trip! Prices are subject to change without notice.

ENJOY PARADISE GUIDES & NEWSLETTERS FOR OTHER ISLANDS!

MAUI AND LANA'I: Making the Most of Your Family Vacation by Christie Stilson & Dona Early. This completely revised guide is packed with information on over 150 condos & hotels, 200 restaurants, 50 great beaches, sights to see and travel tips for the valley island. The island of Lana'i, as a part of the County of Maui, is included in this popular guide. Here the visitor will enjoy fine dining, local eateries, remote beaches, wonderful hikes and peaceful enchantment. *"A down-to-earth, nuts-and-bolts companion with answers to most any question."* L.A.Times. Nearly 400 pgs, multi-indexed, maps, illustrations, $15.00, 7th ed. Copyright 1997.

KAUA'I, A PARADISE FAMILY GUIDE: Making the Most of Your Family Vacation. by Dona Early & Christie Stilson. Completely revised and rewritten since Hurricane Iniki, this information packed guide describes island accommodations, restaurants, secluded beaches, plus recreation and tour options. "If you need a 'how to do it' book to guide your next to Kaua'i, here's the one." 300 pages, multi-indexed, maps, illustrations, $15.00. Fourth edition. Copyright 1996.

HAWAI'I: THE BIG ISLAND, A PARADISE FAMILY GUIDE by John Penisten. Outstanding for its completeness, this well-organized guide provides useful information for people of every budget and lifestyle. Each chapter features the author's personal recommendations and "best bets." In addition to comprehensive information island accommodations, you will find a full range of water, land and activities and tours from which to choose. Then enjoy dining at one of the more than 250 restaurants which range from local style drive-ins to fine dining establishments. Sights to see, beaches, and helpful travel tips. 300 pages. $15.00. 5th edition. Copyright 1997.

UPDATE NEWSLETTERS! *THE MAUI UPDATE, THE KAUA'I UPDATE,* and *HAWAI'I: THE BIG ISLAND UPDATE* are quarterly newsletters published by Paradise Publications that highlight the most current island events. Each features late breaking tips on the newest restaurants, island activities or special, not-to-be missed events. Each newsletter available at the single issue price of $2.50 or a yearly subscription (four issues) rate of $10. Canada $12 per year.

FREE! A complimentary copy of Paradise Publication's quarterly newsletter, **THE BIG ISLAND UPDATE**, is available (at no charge) by writing Paradise Publications (Attention: Newsletter Dept.) 8110 S.W. Wareham, Suite 306, Portland, OR 97223, and enclosing a self-addressed, stamped, #10 envelope.

MAPS! A great addition to your travels is a full-color topographical maps by cartographer James A. Bier. Maps are available for $3.95 each for the islands of O'ahu, Maui, Kaua'i, Lana'i & Moloka'i and the Big Island of Hawai'i.

MORE MAPS! The Hawaii Volcanoes National Park, Earthwalk Press Topographical Map is a must-purchase if you are planning to enjoy this park in-depth. Water resistant, too! $3.95.

KAUA'I, THE UNCONQUERABLE, HALEAKALA and *HAWAII VOLCA-NOES*. Each of these fascinating and informatives book is filled with vivid full color photographs depicting these natural volcanic wonders. A great gift or memento. 9 x 12, $6.95 each.

VIEWBOOKS Doug Peebles is quite possibly Hawai'i's best photographer, and his finest photography has been showcased in these full-color paperback books. Ideal for the armchair traveler or trip planner, these affordable pictorial guides are wonderful souveniers and great gifts. Choose from these five: HAWAII (Big Island), MAUI, KAUA'I, O'AHU, VOLCANOES. Each is 10 x 13. 32 pages, $7.95.

THE NEW CUISINE OF HAWAII. This 150 page hardcover cookbook is subtitled "Recipes from the Twelve Celebrated Chefs of Hawaii Regional Cuisine" and that about sums it up. The culinary wizardry of Sam Choy, Roger Dikon, Mark Ellman, Beverly Cannon and others are shared in this fascinating cookbook. Color photographs highlight each chef's magic touch. 1994. $30.00.

COOKING WITH ALOHA. Discover the flavors and smells of the Hawaiian islands in your own kitchen with this easy-to-follow cookbook. Appetizers to desserts are covered. A great and inexpensive guide to cooking your favorite Hawaiian foods. 9 x 12, paperback, 184 pages, $9.95.

A TASTE OF ALOHA and *ANOTHER TASTE OF ALOHA*. Each of these cookbooks have already becoming classics. A Taste of Aloha premiered in 1983 and is nearly 400 pages of island favorites, reflecting the influence that each new of the many ethnic groups introduced to the island. Another Taste of Aloha has all new recipes reflects the trend toward a low-fat lifestyle. Both cookbooks are hardbound. Price is $21.95 each.

MAJESTIC MOLOKAI. Explore Hawaii's "Friendly Isle" with this attractive and information-filled book. Through the pages you'll discover the beauty and splendor of this island. 144 pages, plus hundreds of color photographs. $14.95

HAWAIIAN HIKING TRAILS by Craig Chisholm. This very attractive and accurate guide details 49 of Hawaii's best hiking trails. Hikes for every level of ability. Includes photography, topographical maps, and detailed directions. An excellent book for discovering Hawai'i's great outdoors! 152 pgs., $15.95. 1994.

KAUAI HIKING TRAILS by Craig Chisholm. Also from Fernglen Press this 160 page book features color photographs, topographical maps and detailed directions to Kaua'i's best hiking trails. A quality publication. $12.95. 1991.

HIKING MAUI by Robert Smith. Discover 27 hiking areas all around Maui. 5 x 8 paperback, 160 pages. $10.95. Also by Robert Smith. *HIKING KAUA'I*, over 40 hiking trails throughout Kaua'i. 116 pages, $10.95. *HIKING HAWAII (The Big Island)*, 157 pages, $10.95. Black & white photographs and maps. Compact and easy-to-use.

NEW POCKET HAWAIIAN DICTIONARY. This concise dictionary will help resolve just what those Hawaiian words mean and how to pronounce them! $4.95.

DIVING HAWAII This book features nearly 50 dives on all of the islands. Good photography. Maps. 128 pages. $19.95.

NEW POCKET HAWAIIAN DICTIONARY. This concise dictionary will help resolve just what those Hawaiian words mean and how to pronounce them! $4.95.

DIVING HAWAII This book features nearly 50 dives on all of the islands. Good photography. Maps. 128 pages. $21.95

COMPUTER/VIDEO *(All Videos are VHS format)*

HAWAIIAN POSTCARDS This is a screen saver program for you computer. Enjoy a little piece of Hawai'i everyday. Postcards of Hawai'i's most famous vistas flash past. Fun! $8.95 MacIntosh or PC.

HAWAIIAN PARADISE -- by International Video Network. More than a travel log, this is one of the best of many, many videos we have reviewed. The journey covers all six of the major Hawaiian islands, Kaua'i, Hawai'i, Lana'i, Moloka'i, Maui and O'ahu. The narrative begins with the formation of the Hawaiian islands and deviates from the average video by exploring the culture, legend, lore and history of the island. The lover of Hawai'i will learn new and interesting island facts and points of history and the new-comer to Hawaii will be thrilled with this visual taste of the islands. The next best thing to being there. $29.95. 90 minutes.

FOREVER HAWAII -- This 60 minute, video portrait features all six major Hawaiian islands. It includes breathtaking views from the snowcapped peaks of Mauna Kea to the bustling city of Waikiki, from the magnificent Waimea Canyon to the spectacular Halakeala Crater. A lasting memento. 1992. $24.95

FOREVER MAUI -- An in-depth visit to Maui with scenic shots and interesting stories about the Valley Isle. An excellent video for the first time, or even the returning Maui visitor. $19.95. **FLIGHT OF THE CANYON BIRD** -- An inspired view of the Garden Island of Kaua'i from a bird's eye perspective; an outstanding 30 minute piece of cinematography. This short feature presentation explores the lush tropical rainforests surrounding Waialeale (the wettest spot on earth), the awesome Waimea Canyon and the Napili Coastline. The narration explores the geologic and historic beginnings of the island. A lasting memento or gift! Each tape is 30 minutes. Cost $19.95 per tape.

KUMU HULA: KEEPERS OF A CULTURE -- This 85-minute tape was funded by the Hawaii State Foundation on Culture and Arts. This beautifully filmed work includes hulas from various troupes on various islands, attired in their brilliantly colored costumes and explores the unique qualities of hula as well as explaining the history. $29.95. **HULA - LESSONS ONE AND TWO** -- "Lovely Hula Hands" and "Little Brown Gal" are the two featured hulas taught by Carol "Kalola" Lorenzo who explains the basic steps of the hula. A fun and interesting video for the whole family. 30 minutes. $29.95.

SHIPPING: In the Continental U.S.-- Please add $4 for 1 to 2 items (books or videos). Each additional item over 2, please add $.50. Orders shipped promptly by US First class mail If you'd prefer items shipped bookrate mail, we'll be happy to quote you shipping costs. Canadian Orders -- Please add $4 for the first book and $1 each additional book/tape. Orders shipped U.S. small parcel airmail. Federal Express or overnight mail services are available. Include your check or money order/Visa or Mastercard information and send to:

PARADISE PUBLICATIONS, 8110 S.W. Wareham, Portland, OR 97223
        Phone or FAX (503) 246-1555

MAUI AND LANA'I, 7th Edition

Dona Early and Christie Stilson

In the seventh edition of this comprehensive guide to the islands of Maui and Lana'i, authors Christie Stilson and Dona Early give families the information they need to make the most of their next Hawaiian vacation. As long-time visitors and part-time residents of the island, Stilson and Early offer readers up-to-date listings of restaurants children will love, hotels that let kids stay free, and other tips to help families make the most of their travel dollars.

**Available now
from Prima**

$15.00

KAUA'I, 4th Edition

Dona Early and Christie Stilson

Here is the complete traveler's reference and guide to the tropical paradise of Kaua'i. It has been completely revised and updated to reflect changes in accommodations, scenery, roads, and more following the hurricane that ravaged Kaua'i in 1992. With an emphasis on family travel (and an eye on the family budget!), this book provides travelers with all they need to know about this sun-drenched getaway, including more than 125 restaurants and recommendations, Hawaiian language and history, accommodations for all budgets, and recreational opportunities.

Available now from Prima

$14.95

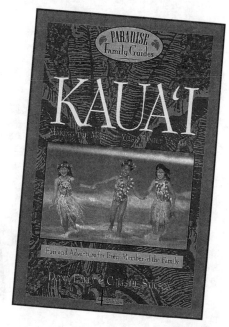

WALT DISNEY WORLD WITH KIDS, 1997 Edition

Kim Wright Wiley

Millions of families travel to Walt Disney World every year, but even "the happiest place on earth" can be exhausting and expensive without a knowledgeable guide. Author Kim Wright Wiley to the rescue! The nation's leading expert on traveling to Walt Disney World with kids in tow tells parents how to plan a wonderful, carefree vacation the kids will never forget. Included are tips on the best hotels and restaurants for families, smart ways to beat the crowds, and ratings for the most kid-pleasing rides.

**Available now
from Prima**

$13.00

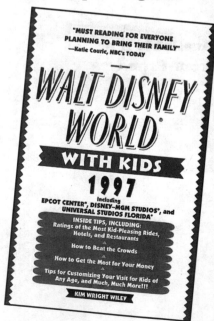

DISNEYLAND AND SOUTHERN CALIFORNIA WITH KIDS, 1996–1997 Edition

Kim Wright Wiley

Disneyland and Southern California with Kids is an essential guide to "kid-proofing" a visit to Southern California's many attractions. Not simply a guide to Disneyland, this book offers advice for parents and children headed to Knott's Berry Farm, Universal Studios, Magic Mountain, the San Diego Zoo, and many other Southland attractions. Also included are tips on restaurants and hotels in the Anaheim area with "kid appeal," ways to save money on the Disneyland trip, plus parades, fireworks, and special shows that first-timers frequently miss.

Available now from Prima

$9.95

CRUISE VACATIONS WITH KIDS

Candyce H. Stapen

Cruise lines all over the world now include activities for people young and old, adventurous and tame, active and leisurely—something for every member of any family. On today's cruises, members of every generation can enjoy their vacation fun. Candyce Stapen includes information on the world's best cruises for you and your family, ships with single parent pricing, comprehensive kids programs, and reunion packages.

**Available now
from Prima**

$14.95

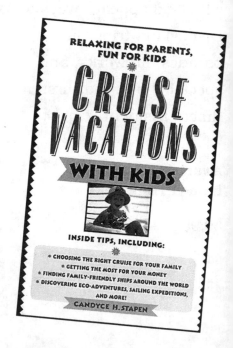

CAMPING WITH KIDS IN CALIFORNIA

Bill McMillon

In *Camping with Kids in California*, family camping expert Bill McMillon has compiled a comprehensive resource of classic sites and off-the-beaten path delights that are ideal for both avid campers and first-timers. This book covers campgrounds throughout the state and focuses on family-oriented adventures. Bill McMillon is the author of *Best Hikes with Children in the San Francisco Bay Area* and *Best Hikes with Children in the Sacramento Area*.

Available now from Prima

$15.00

LAS VEGAS WITH KIDS

Barbara Land

Las Vegas is no longer just a playground for adults! With its new focus on families, the town is teeming with family-oriented attractions. Now, kids and parents alike can enjoy the glitter and excitement of this popular city. In *Las Vegas with Kids*, parents will find information for hours (and days!) of fun family activities. Inside are helpful tips on everything parents need to know!

Available now from Prima

$12.95

BRANSON WITH KIDS

Toni Eugene

Country Music lovers from around the world are flocking to the tiny town of Branson, Missouri, and many of those fans are including their kids. But how can a parent decide which of the many music shows are best for children, choose a restaurant with a menu designed for kid's tastes, or find a hotel where kids stay free? Toni Eugene has the answers to all of these questions and more. With the help of *Branson with Kids*, parents can design a headache-free family vacation in and around the Branson area.

**Available now
from Prima**

$14.95

WHERE THE TRAINS ARE!

Heather Taylor

Since the pioneer days when steam engines first
chugged their way across the frontier plains, the
imaginations of young and old alike have been captured by the awesome magic of trains. From the
Orient Express to the *Little Engine That Could*,
trains have always fascinated travelers, armchair
and otherwise. In this unique and comprehensive
guide, train lovers will find a state-by-state listing of
all the great kid-friendly train attractions.

**Available now
from Prima**

$16.95

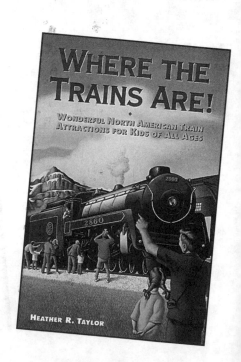

ALL ABOARD!

Jim Loomis

Few can deny the romance of traveling by train—the thrill of gazing out windows at passing towns, meadows, and mountains as you chug along in comfort. But in a territory as vast as North America, many of the best routes are easily overlooked—even by the most avid train travelers. From lifelong devotees to novice admirers, everyone will discover new ways to enjoy riding the rails in *All Aboard!*

**Available now
from Prima**

$15.95

To Order Books

Please send me the following items:

Quantity	Title	Unit Price	Total
_____	_____	$ _____	$ _____
_____	_____	$ _____	$ _____
_____	_____	$ _____	$ _____
_____	_____	$ _____	$ _____
_____	_____	$ _____	$ _____

Shipping and Handling depend on Subtotal.

Subtotal	Shipping/Handling
$0.00–$14.99	$3.00
$15.00–$29.99	$4.00
$30.00–$49.99	$6.00
$50.00–$99.99	$10.00
$100.00–$199.99	$13.50
$200.00+	Call for Quote

Foreign and all Priority Request orders:
Call Order Entry department
for price quote at 916-632-4400

This chart represents the total retail price of books only
(before applicable discounts are taken).

Subtotal **$** _____

Deduct 10% when ordering 3–5 books $ _____

7.25% Sales Tax (CA only) **$** _____

8.25% Sales Tax (TN only) **$** _____

5% Sales Tax (MD and IN only) **$** _____

Shipping and Handling* **$** _____

Total Order **$** _____

By Telephone: With MC or Visa, call 800-632-8676 or 916-632-4400. Mon–Fri, 8:30–4:30
WWW {http://www.primapublishing.com}

Orders Placed Via Internet E-mail {sales@primapub.com}

By Mail: Just fill out the information below and send with your remittance to:

Prima Publishing
P.O. Box 1260BK
Rocklin, CA 95677

My name is _____

I live at _____

City_____ State_____ Zip_____

MC/Visa#_____ Exp. _____

Check/Money Order enclosed for $_____ Payable to Prima Publishing

Daytime Telephone_____

Signature_____